GOTHA TERROR

Dedicated to the memory of all those who lost their lives,
both on the ground and in the air,
during Germany's First World War air offensive against Britain
1914–1918.

GOTHA TERROR

The Forgotten Blitz 1917-1918

IAN CASTLE

FRONTLINE BOOKS

First published in Great Britain in 2024 by
Frontline Books
An imprint of
Pen & Sword Books Ltd
Yorkshire - Philadelphia

Copyright © Ian Castle, 2024

ISBN 978 1 39904 935 1

The right of Ian Castle to be identified as the Author of this work has been asserted by him in accordance with the Copyright, Designs and Patents Act 1988.

A CIP catalogue record for this book is available from the British Library.

All rights reserved. No part of this book may be reproduced or transmitted in any form or by any means, electronic or mechanical, including photocopying, recording or by any information storage and retrieval system, without permission from the Publisher in writing.

Typeset in INDIA by IMPEC eSolutions
Printed and bound in England by CPI (UK) Ltd.

Pen & Sword Books Limited incorporates the imprints of Archaeology, Atlas, Aviation, Battleground, Digital, Discovery, Family History, Fiction, History, Local, Local History, Maritime, Military, Military Classics, Politics, Select, Transport, True Crime, After the Battle, Air World, Claymore Press, Frontline Publishing, Leo Cooper, Remember When, Seaforth Publishing, The Praetorian Press, Wharncliffe Books, Wharncliffe Local History, Wharncliffe Transport, Wharncliffe True Crime and White Owl.

For a complete list of Pen & Sword titles please contact

PEN & SWORD BOOKS LIMITED
George House, Units 12 & 13, Beevor Street,
Off Pontefract Road, Barnsley, S71 1HN, UK
E-mail: enquiries@pen-and-sword.co.uk
Website: www.pen-and-sword.co.uk

or

PEN AND SWORD BOOKS
1950 Lawrence Rd, Havertown, PA 19083, USA
E-mail: uspen-and-sword@casematepublishers.com
Website: www.penandswordbooks.com

Contents

Introduction		vii
Acknowledgements		x
Chapter 1	1917 – They Think It's All Over	1
Chapter 2	'The scene was too awful'	11
Chapter 3	Gothas Over London	25
Chapter 4	'The lights of death'	39
Chapter 5	'The damned impudence'	55
Chapter 6	'A senior officer of first-rate ability'	71
Chapter 7	'I shall never forget that night'	87
Chapter 8	'Am I dead or alive?'	99
Chapter 9	'If only we had had a warning'	116
Chapter 10	'A growing confidence'	131
Chapter 11	The Silent Raid	144
Chapter 12	'Got it!'	160
Chapter 13	'I'll shoot the first man to light a match'	175
Chapter 14	'A desperate struggle for life'	189
Chapter 15	Giants in the Sky	204
Chapter 16	The Zeppelins Return	220

| Chapter 17 | 'Dawn of a fine spring morning' | 235 |
| Chapter 18 | 'This giant flame of sacrifice' | 249 |

Appendix I: Air Raids 1917–1918	266
Appendix II: Summary of Air Raid Statistics 1914–1918	269
Appendix III: Individuals Killed in Air Raids 1917–1918	271
Bibliography	308
Notes	312
Index	325

LIST OF MAPS

Map 1	25 May 1917 – The First Gotha Raid	xiii
Map 2	13 June 1917 – The First Gotha Raid on London	xiv
Map 3	17 June 1917 – The Last Raid of Zeppelin L 48	xv
Map 4	South east England's airfields	xvi
Map 5	19/20 October 1917 – The Silent Raid	xvii
Map 6	12/13 April 1918 – The Last Zeppelin Raid	xviii
Map 7	The London Air Defence Area (LADA) 1918	xix
Map 8	LADA Control	xx

Introduction

Back in the late 1990s I became aware of a building in Farringdon Road, London, bearing a plaque at pavement level. The plaque describes how the building was destroyed in a Zeppelin raid in September 1915, and subsequently rebuilt. It is now known as the 'Zeppelin Building'. This plaque fascinated me. I was born a Londoner and had been writing about aspects of military history since the late 1980s, but here was an aspect of the capital's history – Germany's First World War air raids on Britain – that I knew virtually nothing about. I began reading the available books on the subject but quickly became disappointed with their lack of depth and detail. This pushed me on to dig deeper, to unearth more on this largely unnoticed period in the nation's history. In more recent times this German air campaign has become popularly dubbed the 'First Blitz', but if anyone asked about my work and I told them I was researching the 'First Blitz', the response was almost universal: 'There was more than one?' This first overseas bombing campaign in history has become overlooked, dwarfed by the enormity of the Blitz of the Second World War. For me, the 'First Blitz' had become the 'Forgotten Blitz'.

In pursuit of a comprehensive understanding of the campaign, I turned my attention to The National Archives in London. There my quest struck gold, for within the records of the Air Ministry are folders bringing together all documents relating to each individual German air raid on Britain during the Great War, and within the War Office records are summary reports, encapsulating the information contained in the Air Ministry documents, along with maps tracing the routes of raiding German airships and aeroplanes. Over the coming years, I consulted every document available there. I now had the foundations for a detailed history of this campaign. But I wanted more; I wanted to give voice to Britain's civilian population, those individuals who had been the first to experience the horrors of attack from the air, those long-forgotten victims.

The government of the time produced statistics at the end of the war, revealing that 1,414 people in Britain had died as a result of air raids. This, however, may be a little under-reported as those who died of injuries after the figures for individual raids were compiled were missed, and there is an inconsistency in the way deaths due to 'shock' during raids were recorded in different regions. Whatever the actual final figure, the government of the time made no attempt to compile an official list of the victim's names. I determined to do what I could to redress this oversight. It was not easy.

In more recent years some local historians have looked at raids in their own areas, revealing the names of victims there, which has proved extremely helpful, but in places, particularly in London, where almost half of all the deaths occurred, no work of this nature has ever been published.

The early air raids received in-depth coverage in local newspapers, giving details of streets where bombs fell and the names of the dead and injured. That all changed after the first Zeppelin raid on London in May 1915; from then on, no specific details were allowed to be reported. Newspapers now told of attacks on an 'east coast town' or 'a midlands town', without naming the place. Likewise, victim's names were excluded but, thankfully, reporting of coroner's inquests often did include names, just not places.

Uncovering the names of these long-forgotten victims required focused detective work, comparing newspaper, police and military reports, inquests and the General Register Office Death Indexes, and the occasional shot in the dark following up a hunch and ordering death certificates with fingers crossed, hoping to discover another victim. Sometimes I hit the bullseye, other times I did not. With the completion of this third book, the lists I have compiled give names to 1,285 of the 1,414 victims, who still remain officially unidentified – 91 per cent of the total. I hope that readers may be able to help trace the final missing 129, allowing them to emerge from the shadows and be united with the others who shared their fate.

A similar amount of detective work involved tying anonymous newspaper reports to specific incidents. Comparing these reports with damage and casualties listed in police reports has allowed me to attribute some accounts to exact addresses, which in turn has given voice to individuals who experienced all the horrors of aerial bombing:

the destruction of their homes, the death or mutilation of loved ones and their own injuries.

I set out at the beginning of this project to present a detailed and balanced account of the campaign, bringing it to life with the stories of those who played a part in it. Beyond the civilians' experiences, I have enhanced the narrative by weaving in accounts from those who took to the skies to defend Britain from attack, and welcomed the views of German airmen too. Each experienced the campaign in a different way, but those experiences all form part of the same story.

Through the three books in the Forgotten Blitz series – *Zeppelin Onslaught, Zeppelin Inferno,* and now *Gotha Terror* – I have completed the story that began in December 1914, when an unopposed German aeroplane dropped a single bomb on Dover, blasting an unsuspecting gardener from a tree. It ended three and a half years later, in May 1918, when the final raid saw forty bombers target London and south-east England. Between those raids, the populations of cities, towns and villages, from the Highlands of Scotland to Portsmouth on the south coast of England, had also found themselves on the front line in this new age of aerial warfare.

Technological advances across all areas of the military during the years of the First World War were remarkable, but the progress in military aviation was simply astonishing. At the beginning of the war aeroplanes were limited to a reconnaissance role, were unarmed, and had a very limited lifting ability, but by 1917, Germany was sending bombers across the North Sea capable of carrying a bombload of 1,000kg and that had a greater wingspan than any aircraft that flew operationally in the Second World War, until the development of the B-29 Superfortress by the United States in 1944 (and then only by 3ft). The management of aerial defence, virtually non-existent at the beginning of 1914, progressed too, slowly at first but gaining pace as the war progressed, ultimately laying the foundations for future air defence systems.

The focus of this book is 1917-1918, the final two years of the war. This period marked the decline of the Zeppelin threat and the emergence of a new deadly scourge: the bomber aeroplane. Having won the battle against the Zeppelins, Britain, taken by surprise by this unexpected development, returned to the drawing board to create a new plan of defence.

This first sustained strategic bombing campaign in history deserves to be more widely known. Its lessons, impact and experiences were still widely felt when Britain went to war with Germany again in September 1939. Yet it remains the Forgotten Blitz. The time has come to change that.

Acknowledgements

Writing a book is a lonely experience. For me it revolves around a laptop, untidy piles of books strewn across the floor, and reams of documents filed away on the aforementioned computer, or accessed online – and tea, steaming hot mugs of tea. It is also a silent experience, I need quiet to focus and follow my train of thought, and to remember where I once saw that obscure fact or in which folder I filed that document. Sometimes not even quiet helps in the search.

But a book cannot be written without the help of others. I always include the address of my website in my books to allow people to contact me and this often provides information from relatives of those who had first-hand experience of the air raids. Richard Willcocks was one who contacted me and I have included in the book the story of the death of his uncle in Folkestone in May 1917. On a similar vein, John Henderson showed me extracts from his great-uncle's log book; he served on the minesweeper *London Belle,* whose guns came into action at Sheerness on 7 July 1917. From Sheerness I also received much excellent information from local historian Janys Thornton, while contact with David Jones resulted in him kindly granting permission to quote from a letter written by his grandfather relating to the Gotha raid on the town in December 1917. And from Southend-on-Sea I received help from local historian Chris Langdon in my pursuit of the names of air raid victims in the town.

In London, Keith Foster, generously allowed me access to copies of coroner's reports pertaining to the Gotha raid of 13 June 1917 – this following a chance meeting at an archive a few years back. An email exchange with Karen Freeberne brought information about her great-grandfather, Philip Frantzmann, killed in the Gotha raid of 7 July

1917, and contact with Thomas Genth, the grandson of *Kagohl 3* officer, *Leutnant* Adolf Genth, was useful regarding his role in that July raid. The July raid also led to interesting exchanges with Paul Bessemer, a liveryman of the Worshipful Company of Ironmongers, whose hall was bombed that same day. Conversations with John Rochester, the archivist at the Royal Hospital Chelsea, also revealed useful information about the impact of the bomb dropped there in February 1918. I have also found documents relating to *Kagohl 3/Bogohl 3*, provided by John Penny, to be extremely helpful.

I would also like to express my admiration for the work of the late Doug Robinson, which I have referenced throughout this series of books. In the 1950s and 1960s, Dr Robinson, an American historian, met many German airship veterans and included translated material from the German archives in his work. I also would like to acknowledge the work of Ray Rimell whose books on Zeppelins are at the forefront of research.

And then I must express my gratitude to two good friends, David Marks and Ian Campbell. David shares my great interest in the air raids of the First World War and owns a unique collection of illustrative material from the period which he is ever-generous in making available for my use in whatever projects I am working on, whether books, magazine articles or lectures. They would all be much duller without his input. Ian is a friend on the other side of the world, residing 'Down Under' in Australia, and an aviation historian himself. Ian has a family connection with the Zeppelin raids and has subsequently become bitten by the air raid bug. He has been in the background while I have written each of the three 'Forgotten Blitz' books, reading the manuscripts, commenting on clarity, suggesting changes and correcting my typos – and offering encouragement when needed. Thanks, David and Ian, your support is greatly appreciated.

Finally, I must express my gratitude to my partner, Nicola. I began working on this series in 2015, now, eight years later it is finished (having squeezed another book in along the way). During that time, I have spent many hours shut away each day, obsessing over the comings and goings of German airships and aeroplanes in my silent, high-altitude world, only returning to earth when food miraculously appears each evening! Nicola accompanies me when I give talks – she could probably give some of those herself now – we have shared a Zeppelin-based holiday in Germany and have visited a few too many empty muddy fields together, places where something monumental (well, to me anyway) once happened many, many moons ago. Without her understanding and support, I would never have been able to achieve what I have.

And, lastly, many thanks to you for reading this book.

Ian Castle FRHistS
January 2024
www.IanCastleZeppelin.co.uk

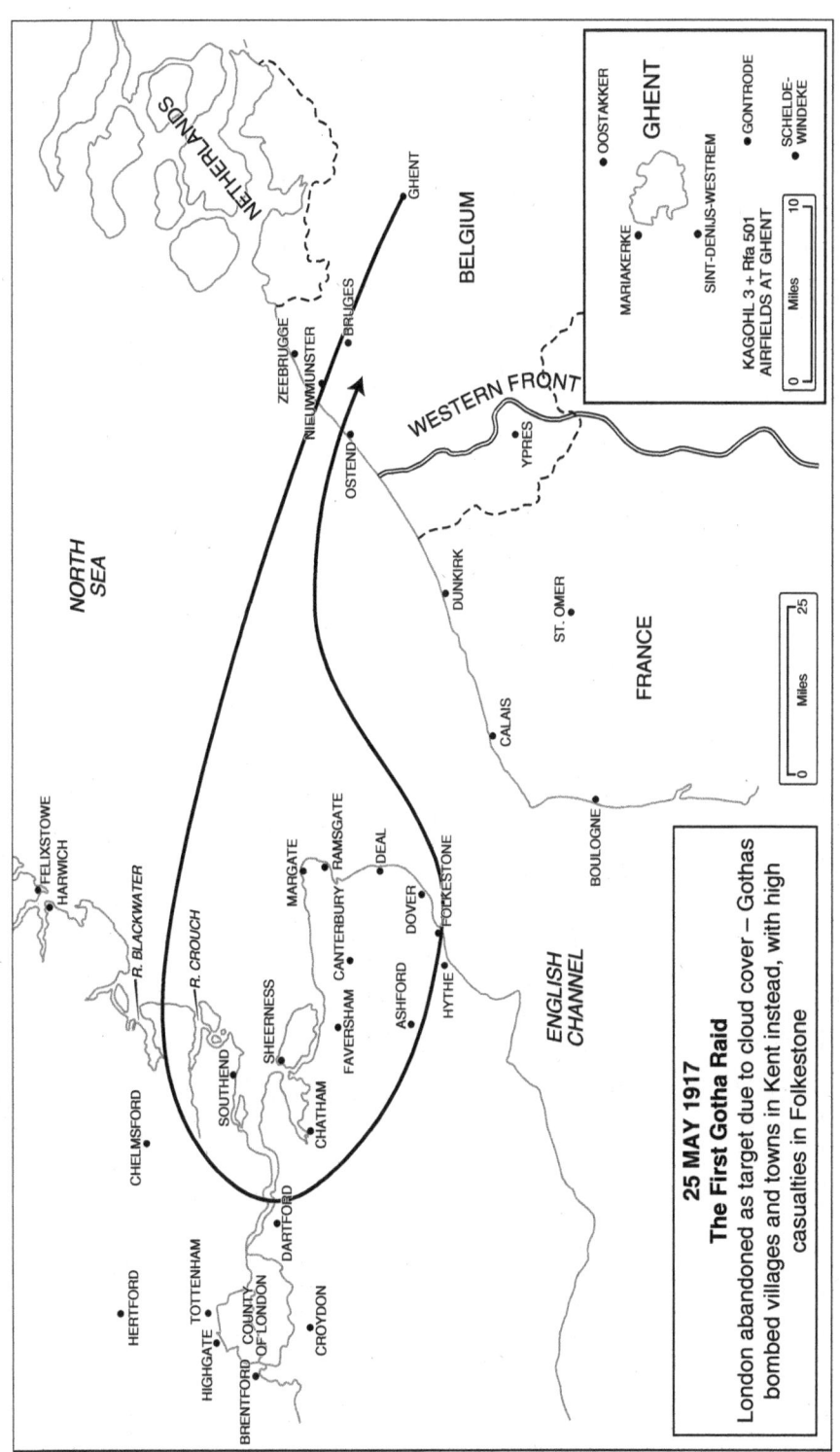

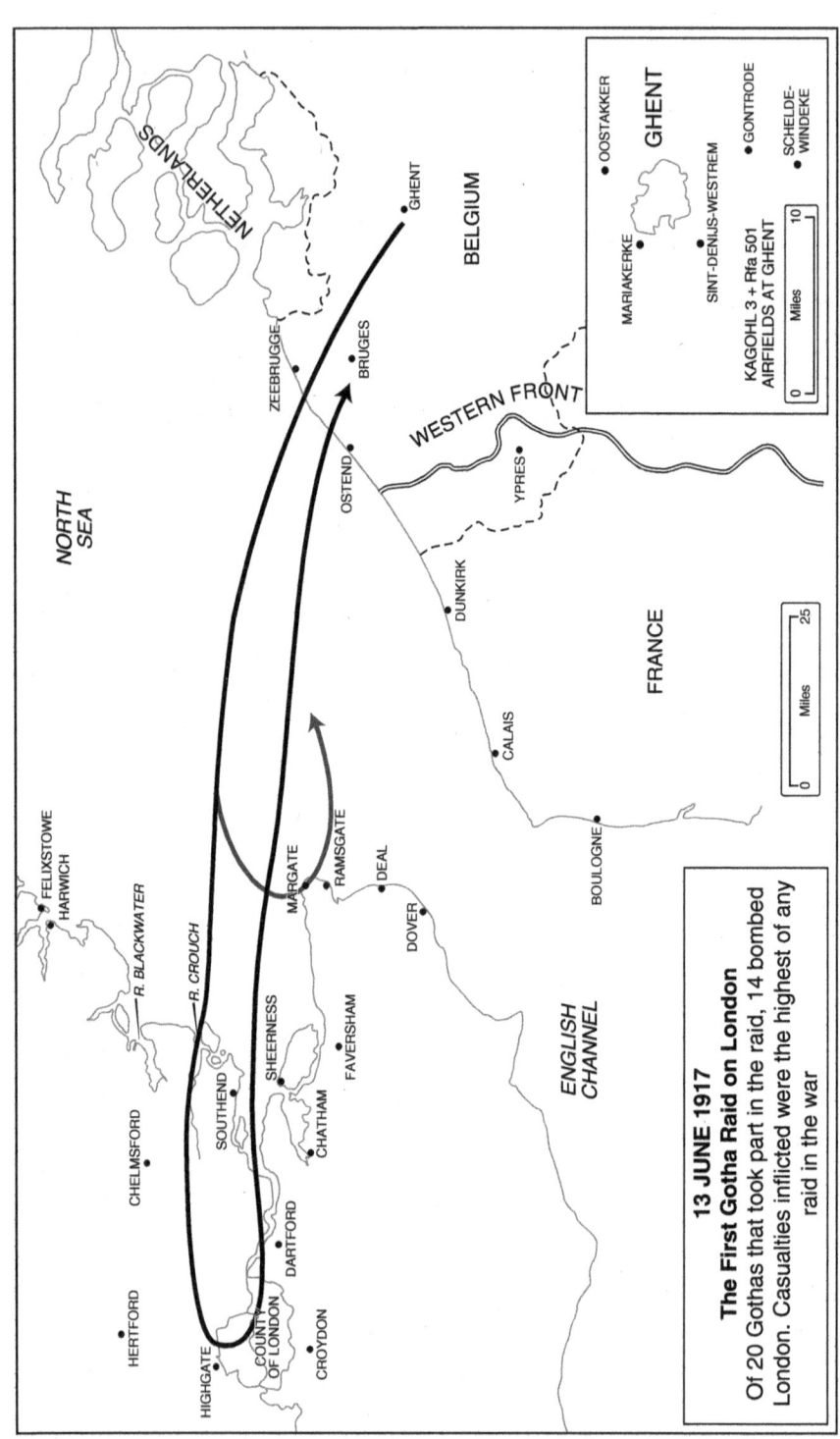

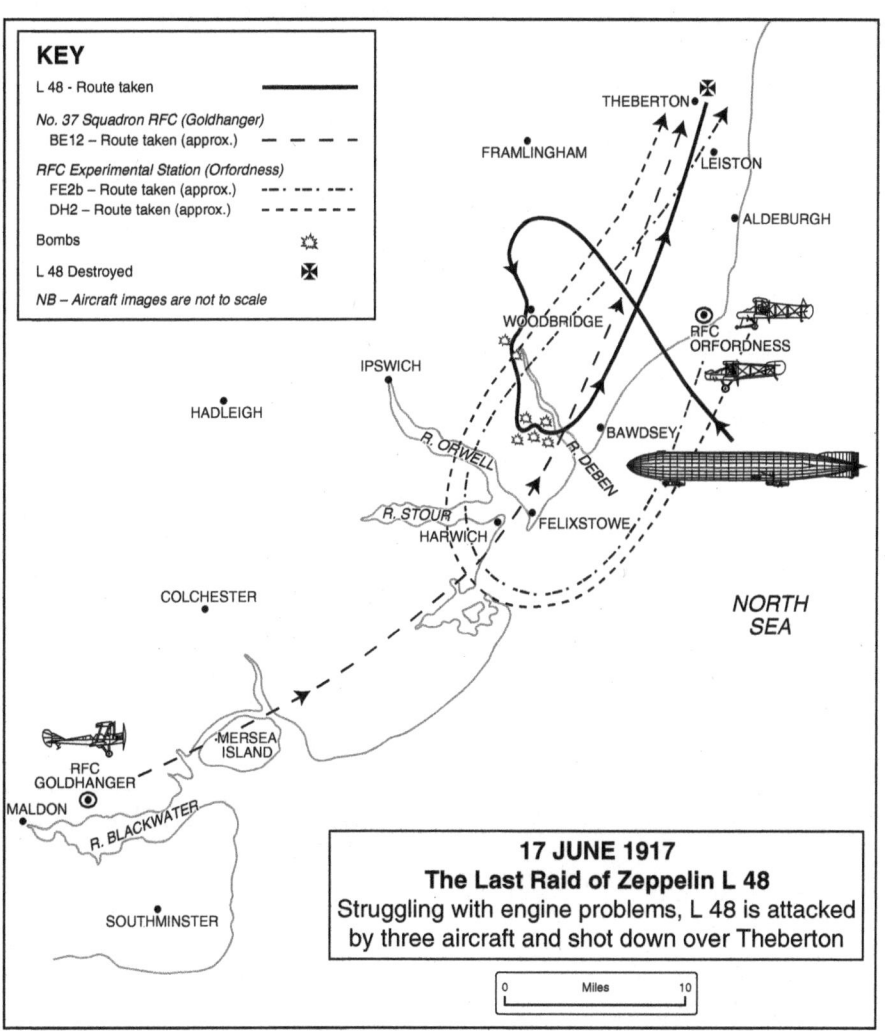

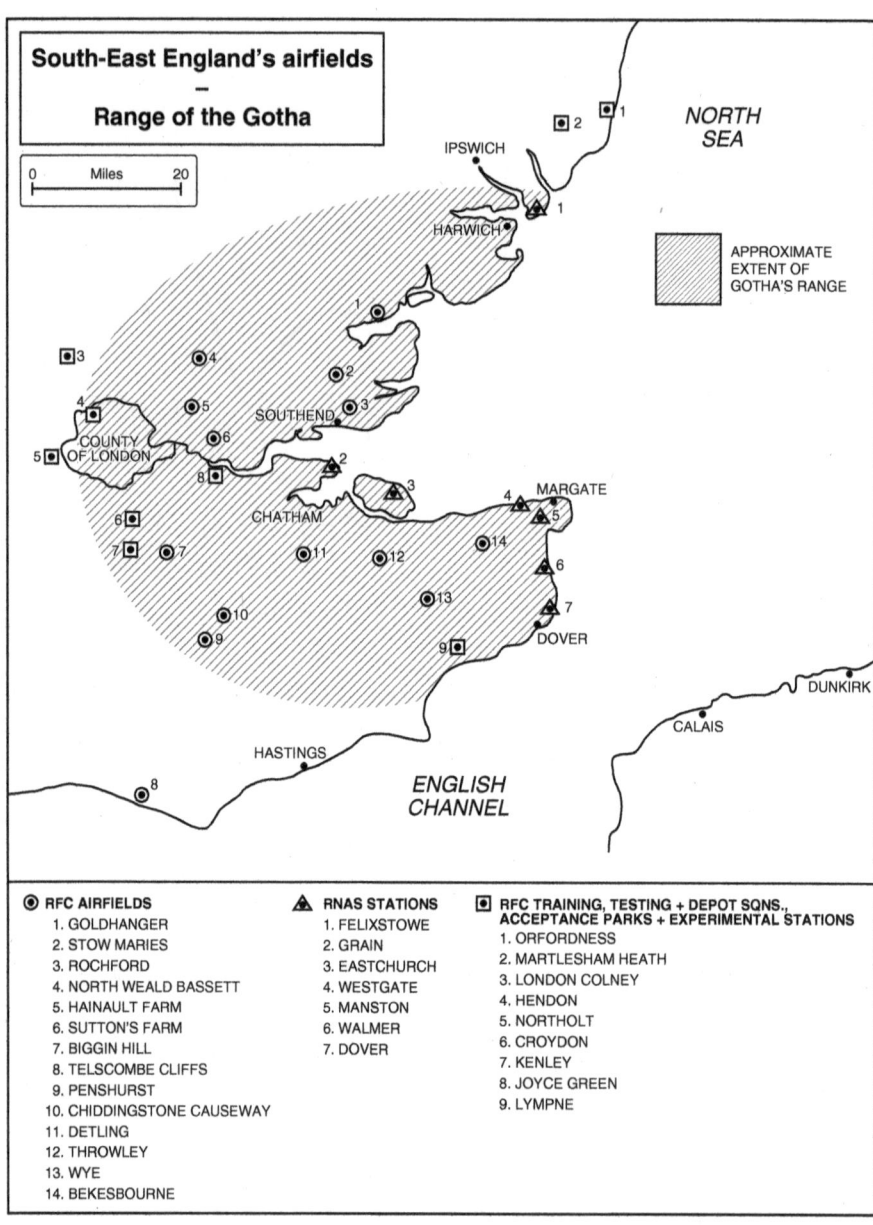

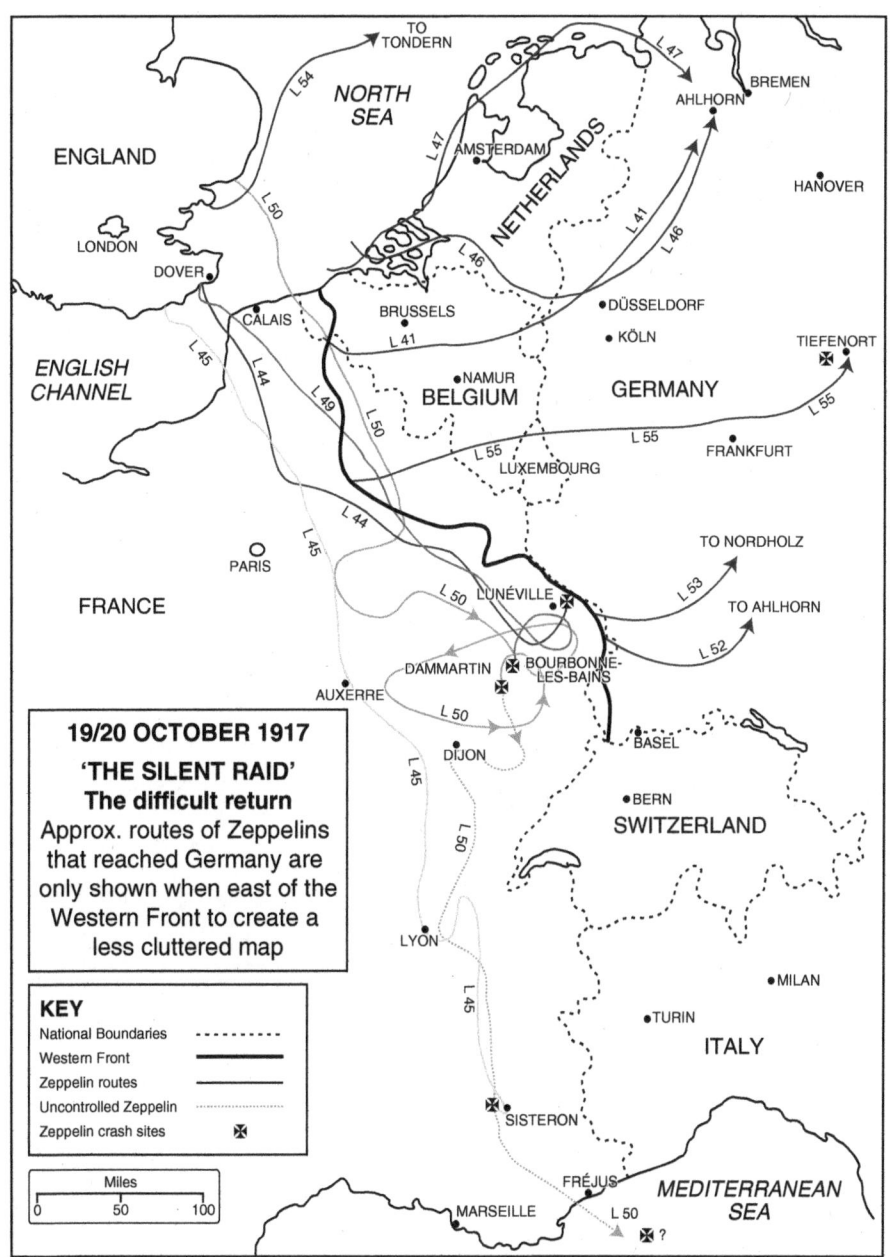

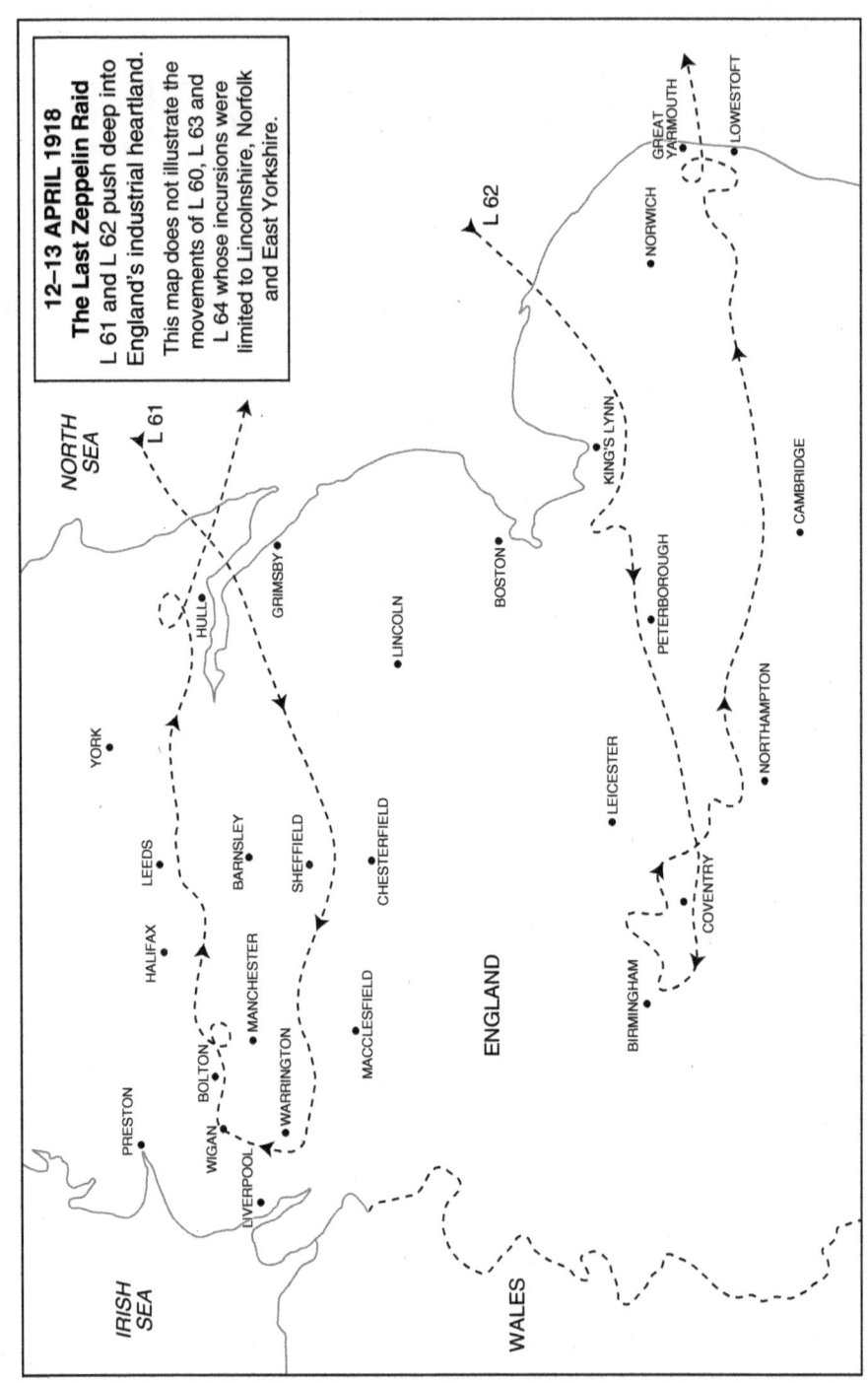

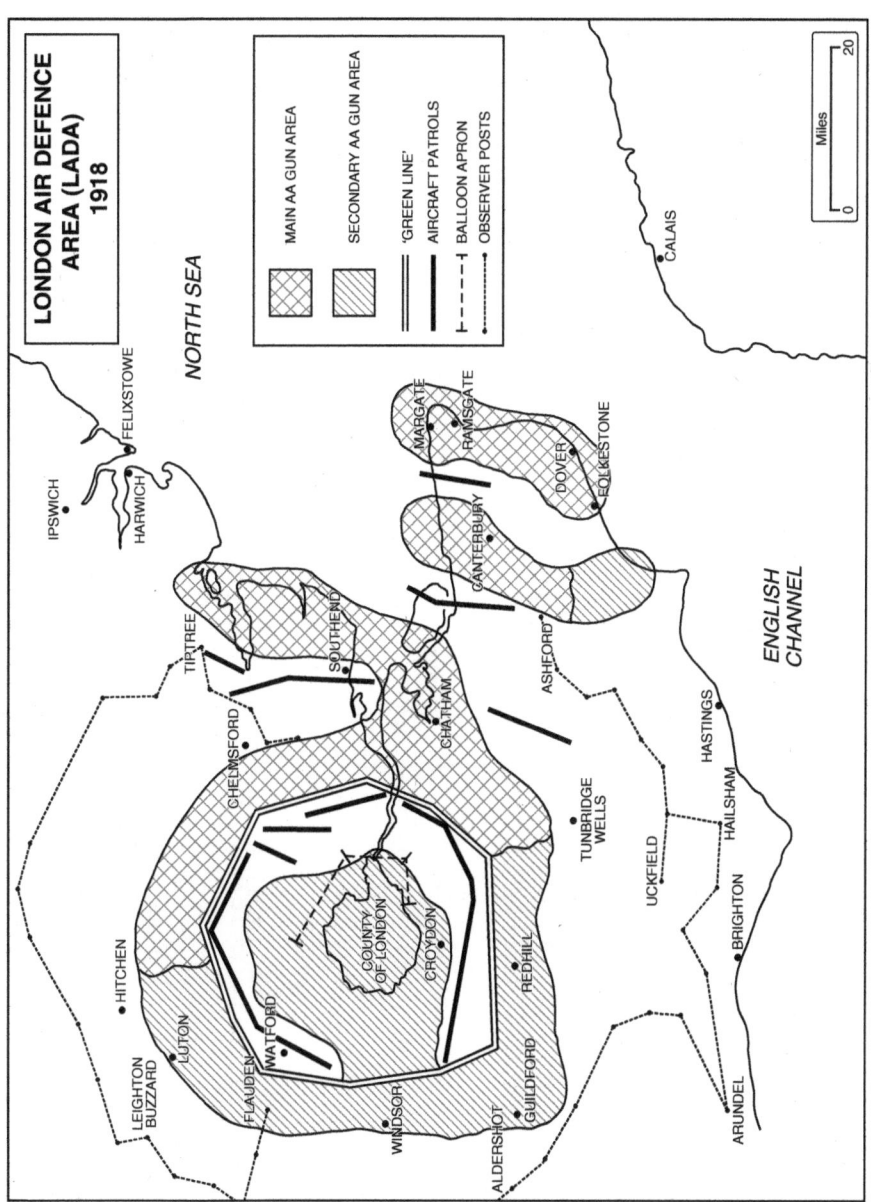

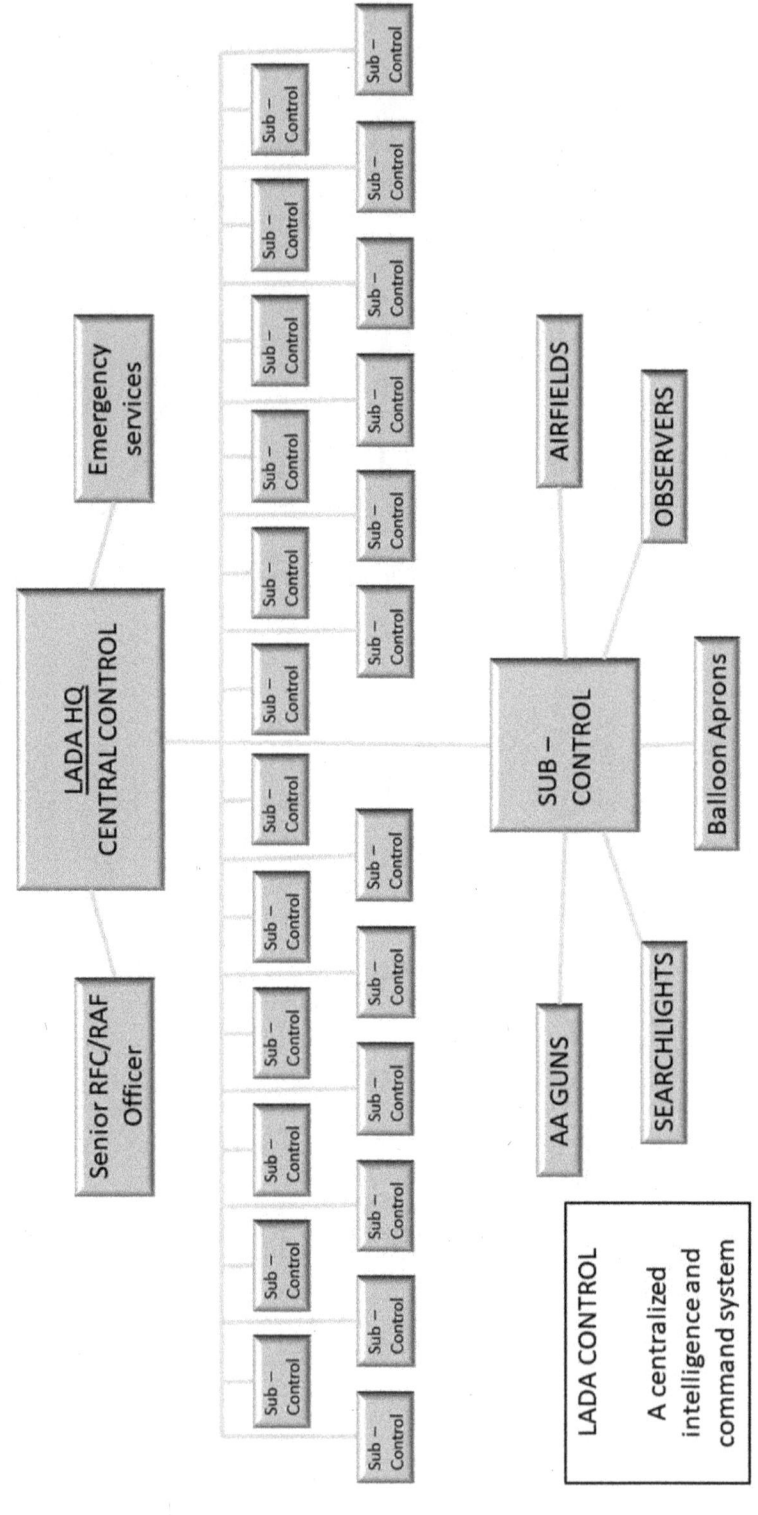

Chapter 1

1917 – They Think It's All Over

In London the final hours of 1916 were defined by a drizzling rain. Restaurants closed at 11.00pm and while a few people lingered in the streets awaiting the arrival of the New Year, there would be no peal of church bells to usher it in. A few thousand rather damp people gathered in good spirits around St Paul's Cathedral and in the surrounding streets, where vast crowds had gathered before the war, and by 11.30pm the sound of noisily sung patriotic songs filled the air, but it did not last long. A strong force of City Police enforced the order to 'move on', and by midnight most of the crowd began to return homeward. Before 12.30am the streets were comparatively quiet.

After almost two and a half years of war there was no end in sight, no suggestion of a return to normality in the immediately foreseeable future. Yet there were positives for those who had ventured out into the gloom of the blackout and the drizzle to celebrate the New Year. Since January 1915 German airships had raided Britain 41 times, claiming the lives of over 500 people, inflicting injuries to over 1,200 more, while smashing and burning homes and businesses to the value of £1.4 million. But in the autumn of 1916 the issue of new bullets, both explosive and incendiary types, to the defending aircraft finally solved the surprisingly difficult task of igniting the hydrogen gas contained inside the great framework of every airship. In the 20 months between January 1915 and August 1916, Britain's anti-aircraft guns had only managed to damage two raiding Zeppelins, both coming down in the sea, but the introduction of the new bullets heralded a seismic change. In just one month from 2 September 1916 Germany lost four airships, followed by two more on one night in November. The British population no longer felt defenceless in the face of the Zeppelin menace that had haunted the nation for so long, and there appeared a growing sense of optimism that the aerial threat to the country was over.

Beyond airships, those in the capital paid little attention to the threat from aeroplanes. The very first German raids on Britain had been made by seaplanes (more correctly, floatplanes) over Christmas 1914 and had continued irregularly ever since. These mainly consisted of hit-and-run attacks on south-eastern coastal towns, their effect generally limited. The 20 aeroplane raids since December 1914 had resulted in the deaths of 20 people and injuries to 67, while causing damage estimated at £11,500. At the end of November 1916, however, a single German aeroplane reached London and dropped a string of small bombs across the Knightsbridge/ Belgravia area, largely unnoticed except by those close to the detonations. The raid caused little concern but there were those who raised a note of caution, including the editor of *The Times* newspaper.

> ... like all fresh portents of the kind, this isolated visit is by no means to be ignored. It may have been largely an act of bravado, or it may have had some definite object of reconnoitring or destruction. In any case it is wise to regard it as the prelude to further visits of the kind on an extensive scale, and to lay our plans accordingly. We have always believed that the method of raiding by aeroplanes, which are relatively cheap and elusive, has far more dangerous possibilities than the large and costly Zeppelins.[1]

Not everyone, however, shared *The Times'* opinion.

January – February 1917: the Home Front

Of great concern to the government at the beginning of 1917 was the impact of German U-boat attacks on merchant ships bringing essential foodstuffs and materiel into Britain. If the attacks increased there remained a possibility that Britain would be forced to seek peace on unfavourable terms. With the Zeppelin threat apparently in decline, the Admiralty requested the transfer of seemingly superfluous guns intended for Home Defence to arm more of the merchant fleet. At the beginning of the year, Britain's anti-aircraft defence plan required 403 fixed guns, 78 mobile types and 12 for training. At this point, however, only 217 were in place and, following the government's decision, the outstanding 186 guns, as well as 11 of those already in position, were reassigned to the Admiralty.

At a stroke London's allocation of 84 guns reduced to 64. Previously guns defending London were deployed in pairs but now, to cover as wide an area as possible, they were redistributed singly.

Until the end of 1916, the London gun and searchlight defences had been under seven sub-commanders each responsible for their own area and answerable to Lieutenant General Sir Francis Lloyd, General Officer Commanding, London District, for training matters, and to Field Marshal Lord French, Commander-in-Chief, Home Forces, for operations. Outside London, anti-aircraft commanders had responsibility for both aspects. In December 1916, however, London aligned with the rest of the country following the appointment of Lieutenant Colonel Maximilian St Leger Simon, an engineer officer, as Anti-Aircraft Defence Commander, London. Since early in 1916 he had been supervising the construction of gun and searchlight positions around the capital. Shortly after taking on his new role, however, Simon found his command seriously reduced.

With a general belief that the threat of Zeppelin raids had now greatly diminished, the Home Defence squadrons of the Royal Flying Corps (RFC) also came under scrutiny. On 6 February 1917, Sir David Henderson, Director-General of Military Aeronautics, informed the Chief of the Imperial General Staff, Sir William Robertson, that the RFC urgently needed 36 night-flying trained pilots for two new night-bomber squadrons destined for France, as well as nine replacement pilots per month. These he felt, in the current situation, could be released from Home Defence squadrons. The proposal received approval three days later.

Already well under-strength, a snapshot of the RFC's 11 Home Defence squadrons on 7 March 1917 shows their establishment set at 222 aircraft, of which the squadrons could muster just 147, with only 125 of those serviceable. It was a similar story with the pilots. Of 113 pilots that rostered, of an establishment set at 198, only 82 were fit to fly.[2]

Despite these shortages within the RFC, plans were also under discussion to further reduce the role of the anti-aircraft guns in Britain to allow the redeployment of manpower elsewhere, and a surprising proposal put forward by Lord French received swift approval, leaving London Anti-Aircraft Defence Commander, Lieutenant Colonel Simon, dumbfounded. The order read,

> No aeroplanes or seaplanes, even if recognized as hostile, will be fired at, either by day or night, except by those anti-aircraft guns situated near the Restricted Coast Area which are specially detailed for this purpose.[3]

The 'Restricted Coast Area' included Dover, Newhaven, Shoeburyness, Harwich, the Medway and the mouth of the Thames. An explanatory note rationalised the decision, explaining that aeroplanes flying at great height were difficult to identify as friend or foe, resulting in a great deal of ammunition being expended for little or no return, while falling shells inflicted damage on property and injuries to civilians in populous areas. It meant anti-aircraft gunners inland or defending London could no longer engage enemy aeroplanes. Zeppelins were still a legitimate target, but as they only attacked at night it seemed unnecessary to man the guns during daylight hours, enabling the surplus men to be transferred to the Western Front.

Lieutenant Colonel Simon took stock of the situation. He had lost almost a quarter of his guns and now his command received orders not to fire at enemy aeroplanes. He could engage Zeppelins but all these high-level decisions were made in the belief that the Zeppelin threat was all but over. Simon, however, uncomfortable with the non-engagement order, diligently prepared a detailed new plan for defence against aeroplanes which he filed away, ready for retrieval should Lord French's order be rescinded.

During this time there had been little in the way of German raids. Lone seaplanes attempted to bomb shipping close to the Kent coast on 14 February and again two days later, while a Zeppelin appeared in the same area on 17 February but did not venture inland. All of which no doubt reinforced the decisions to reduce Britain's air defences.

On 1 March, the first German bombs of 1917 fell on British soil, putting all these confident assumptions to the test.

1 March 1917, 9.45am: Broadstairs

At 9.45am, a man in Broadstairs, on the Kent coast, standing in his garden noticed a dark cloud in the sky then, suddenly, an unidentified German aeroplane emerged and began to drop bombs. This type of raid always proved difficult for the pilots of the RFC and Royal Naval Air Service (RNAS) to oppose because it was almost impossible to spot a single high-flying aircraft until it reached the coast. They rarely lingered more than a few minutes before turning for home, having dropped a handful of bombs. This occasion was no different.

The first three bombs all fell in the sea as the raider approached Victoria Gardens where the next bomb exploded, showering a rather surprised Chairman of the Council, Dr Brightman, with clods of earth.

Heading inland on a straight course, the raider dropped bombs in King Edward's Avenue, Cinder Path by the railway, two in Grosvenor Road and one in Gladstone Road. In Grosvenor Road, one exploded in the playground of the County Council School (now St Mildred's Primary) just a few feet from a classroom full of children. The teacher, Miss Webb and five of her class were cut by flying glass. The other bomb in Grosvenor Road, exploding in the garden of No. 15, also narrowly avoided causing a tragic incident.

> In an upstairs room, a little girl three and a half years of age, was looking out of the window. Her mother had just placed her arms around the child's face when the bomb exploded and shattered the window. The mother's hand was very slightly cut and the child, though her head was covered with powdered glass, escaped injury.[4]

A family in Gladstone Road were fortunate too. The final bomb destroyed the upper storey of their villa, Fern Cottage. Moments before the explosion, Mrs Catt, wife of the town's Registrar of Births and Deaths, had just returned to the house from the garden where, 'The lawn ... was studded with slates shot from the roof and embedded in the ground like arrows from a bow'. Those inside emerged from the house shaken but, miraculously, uninjured.

The pilot, well on his way back to Zeebrugge by the time any RFC or RNAS aircraft were airborne, escaped unmolested. It was a similar story to many of the seaplane raids that had gone before.

16 March 1917, 5.20am: Westgate

Two weeks later another unidentified single German seaplane appeared over Kent. The pilot intended to bomb shipping in the Downs, a favoured anchorage off the Kent coast near Deal, but he lost his way in low cloud. At 5.20am, having descended to about 1,300ft, somewhat surprised he found himself overland between Margate and Westgate, and heading north towards the coast.

Six bombs fell in fields, four of them on Mutrix Farm where the RNAS had a seaplane station, resulting in a few broken windows in nearby cottages. Turning back towards Westgate, the ten small 5kg bombs he dropped only smashed windows in Belmont Road. The final five bombs fell on the lawn of the Streete Court Preparatory School, on a greenhouse in Rowena Road, and 20 yards from the bandstand on the seafront, with the last two swallowed up by the waves. Again, the raider departed before any defence pilots could effectively react. The police gave a top estimate of £45 for the damage caused by the raid and, despite the rude early awakening, the town's residents escaped injury.

***

In Germany, the New Year heralded a period of re-evaluation. The Naval Airship Division, under the command of the *Führer der Luftschiffe*, *Fregattenkapitän* Peter Strasser, had suffered considerable losses in the last four months of 1916. The introduction of new bullets, both explosive and incendiary types, meant that any airship venturing over Britain faced likely destruction if located by aircraft of the RFC and RNAS. After these losses, Strasser now faced questions as to the value of continuing the raiding programme. But he remained convinced that his Zeppelins offered a chance to unsettle Britain. His argument won over those who doubted the value of the raids.

> It was not on the direct material damage that the value of the airship attacks depended, but rather on the general result of the German onslaught upon England's insularity, otherwise undisturbed by war. The disturbance of transportation, the dread of airships prevailing in wide strata of society, and above all the occupation of very considerable material and military personnel were considered outstanding reasons for continuing the attacks.[5]

Strasser had a point. In Britain the RFC had 11 squadrons allocated to Home Defence, as well of those of the RNAS, and in total, over 17,000 personnel were committed to the nation's aerial defence.

Approval to continue raiding was one thing, but the unanticipated vulnerability of the current model of Zeppelin, the 'r-class', meant changes were necessary. Introduced in the summer of 1916 with Zeppelin L 30, Strasser and the men of the Naval Airship Division had great hopes for its impact on the air war over Britain, but its arrival coincided with the development of the new bullets, and the latter held the upper hand. Suggestions that an increase in speed might be the answer were rejected by Strasser and, on 17 January 1917, he advocated a reduction in weight to allow Zeppelins to attain greater heights – to 16,500ft when fully loaded

– thus taking them beyond the ceiling of any of the aircraft currently allocated to Britain's Home Defence. A meeting followed and eventually a series of changes met with approval, including the removal of one of the three engines in the rear gondola, fuel load reduced to be sufficient for a 30-hour mission, a reduced bombload of between 1,500 and 1,800kg (approx. 1.5 to 1.8 tons),[6] as well as a lightened frame structure and a more compact control gondola.

While engineers set to work on the new plans, Strasser returned to his headquarters at Nordholz and, unwilling to wait idly by for the new designs to be completed, ordered an immediate weight reduction for five of the latest 'r-class' Zeppelins: L 35, L 36, L 39, L 40 and L 41. All changes were made by 5 February. He achieved this by the removal of one engine from the rear gondola and some of the bomb release mechanisms. This work resulted in an average weight reduction of about 2,000kg or 2 tons. Altitude trial flights saw the ships attaining heights between 16,100 and 17,100ft while carrying slightly varying loads. The changes added an additional 3,000+ft over the original 'r-class'. That, however, was as far as it went for Zeppelin L 36. On 7 February she crashed on a frozen river in fog when a loss of hydrogen caused handling problems. While the crew survived, L 36 did not.

Later that month, on 28 February, the first of the new design Zeppelins, L 42, entered service under the command of *Kapitänleutnant* Martin Dietrich, although it did not yet feature all the planned changes. Designated the 's-class', these Zeppelins, designed to fly beyond the reach of the British defences, were later nicknamed the 'Height Climbers' by the British authorities. While the general appearance remained similar to the 'r-class', one obvious difference struck all who saw them – the vast envelope of the airship now painted with black dope, except the upper portion, making it harder for searchlights to find the target in the night sky.

Away from the race to complete the conversion of 'r-class' Zeppelins and the development of the new 's-class', sad news emerged for Germany. Count Ferdinand von Zeppelin, the father of the rigid airship, died on 8 March 1917. Although no longer directly involved with airship development, he attended an aeronautical exhibition in Berlin. Struck down with appendicitis while there, he died from post-operative pneumonia.

On 10 March, Strasser joined Martin Dietrich onboard L 42 for a test flight during which she ascended to 19,700ft. Although delighted with the performance, Strasser struggled when moving around the airship in the rarified air at this unprecedented altitude. When he returned slowly down the ladder into the control gondola he gasped breathlessly to Dietrich, 'One-has-to-talk-slowly-up-here!'[7] Containers of compressed oxygen were issued to the crews for use over 16,000ft, but many of the men were initially reluctant to do so, the oxygen having an unpleasant taste and using it could lead to terrible headaches that lasted for days.

Strasser's plan to take his Zeppelins to new heights had come to fruition, but the practical limitations operating at such unprecedented heights would impose on his airships and crews had yet to be fully understood.

Just six days after L 42's altitude test, she joined a force of four other converted Zeppelins (L 35, L 39, L 40 and L 41) in an attack aimed at London, the first in over four months. It did not go well.

16-17 March 1917, 10.20pm: Kent and Sussex

On the same day that the single seaplane had bombed Westgate on the Kent coast, Strasser's Zeppelins ascended between 12.30 and 1.30pm. The weather seemed perfect but unknown in Germany a storm was rumbling towards Britain from the north-west. At sunset, as they climbed above 10,000ft, the Zeppelin commanders found solid cloud and at 12,500ft encountered fierce winds running at an estimated at 45mph. Attempts to ascertain their position by wireless bearings were thwarted by British blocking attempts, while the wind pushed all five airships further south than they estimated based on dead reckoning. Instead of crossing the coast north of the River Thames as intended, they made landfall over Kent and Sussex. And matters were further compounded by thick cloud overland lying between 3,000 and 9,000ft. In short, the Zeppelin commanders had no idea where they were and could see little or nothing of the ground. One, L 42, never even reached the British coast, engine failure leading to a long battle with the wind which forced it, with Strasser on board, ever deeper back into Germany, finally landing 26 hours after take-off. While the Zeppelin crews held an unswerving devotion to Strasser, they had always regarded him as a 'Jonah' figure when he flew on missions as technical problems often occurred with him onboard. This mission reinforced that perception. Even so, as difficult as L 42 found the conditions, she fared infinitely better than L 39.

Kapitänleutnant Robert Koch, the 35-year-old commander of L 39, crossed the Kent coast at 10.20pm.[8] Koch's first command had been Schütte-Lanz 3 from October 1915, before taking over Zeppelin L 24 in May 1916, then transferring to the new L 39 in December of that year. Over Kent, Koch dropped a bomb at Bekesbourne from where flares burning at the RFC airfield were visible; a BE2e had taken off from there

10 minutes earlier. The bomb exploded on farmland. Three other RFC pilots were in the air as were two from the RNAS but the low cloud ceiling made the already difficult task impossible. Heading south-west across Kent, L 39 dropped five explosive bombs and an incendiary near Wye, where there was another airfield, but all fell harmlessly between the villages of Sole Street and Waltham. Koch left the coast of Sussex at 11.40pm. Continuing to struggle against the elements, the wind carried L 39 over France where anti-aircraft gunners found her and shot her down near Compiègne: 'The crew were all burned to death. A few of the bodies were seen to drop from the falling airship. The rest were found in a charred condition in the wreckage.'[9] The brief three-month existence of L 39 ended in disaster. Strasser had lost another experienced captain in Robert Koch, along with his crew.

The other crews had little to show for their night's work.

Kapitänleutnant Herbert Ehrlich, commanding L 35, came inland over Kent about 20 minutes after L 39. At 10.55pm, Ehrlich dropped three bombs on farmland close to villages around Canterbury. He reported that he had bombed London. Another six bombs fell close to those dropped by L 39 near Sole Street and Waltham, bringing down a cottage ceiling near Crundale. Now heading towards the Dover area, L 35 aimed five more explosive bombs (two of them big 300kg types) at the RFC's Swingfield Emergency Landing Ground (ELG), but they only damaged nearby farms. One of the Zeppelin's crew left a personal message for those below, dropping 'facetious postcards' overboard.[10]

Ehrlich dropped six more bombs, doing little damage, before L 35 went out to sea west of Dover at 12.15am. The wind took her towards Calais then Belgium before pushing her south of her home base at Ahlhorn. Running low on fuel, Ehrlich found apparent sanctuary at Dresden, but things did not go well. As L 35 entered the shed, a strong gust of wind lifted her tail, smashing it down hard and breaking her back. Repairs took three months.

Like Ehrlich in L 35, *Kapitänleutnant* Erich Sommerfeldt commanding L 40, also claimed to have bombed London. Heading a second wave, L 40 crossed the north Kent coast at 1.00am. A few miles east of Ashford, his first bomb smashed a few roof tiles at Nackholt, before something inexplicably drew Sommerfeldt south towards the vast flat expanse of Romney Marsh where, at about 2.00am, five large explosive bombs and three incendiaries dropped close to Newchurch. Continuing south towards Ivychurch, 14 incendiary bombs fell around Appledore Farm but all were quenched by the sodden ground, but an explosive bomb killed four sheep. Another seven explosive bombs blasted fields around the villages of Old and New Romney. Sommerfeldt reported this concentration of 30 bombs within an area of about 4 miles as his attack on 'London'. L 40 battled against the wind to get back to Ahlhorn, finally arriving there after a 26-hour flight.

The last of the raiders, L 41, commanded by the former army airship officer *Hauptmann* Kuno Manger, came inland at Pett Level between Hastings and Winchelsea at 1.20am, making a rare Zeppelin appearance over the county of Sussex. Manger immediately released eight explosive and two incendiary bombs. Two fell in the sea while the concussion from the others shattered windows and doors in two unoccupied bungalows and at a pair of farmhouses. Manger now appears to have spotted flares burning along the coast at East Guldeford, about 6 miles to the northeast, the site of another RFC ELG. The historic town of Rye, from where the River Rother flows to the sea, stood just in advance of the airfield, with Rye Harbour about a mile and a half downstream from the town. Ignoring, or not noticing the town, Manger dropped seven explosive and six incendiary bombs on the Camber Marshes, either side of the Rother, only inflicting minor damage and no bomb landed within 400 yards of the airfield. L 41 passed out to sea near Dungeness at about 2.05am, about 10 minutes ahead of L 40. Manger also battled to get back to Ahlhorn, eventually landing with only two working engines.

Because of the cloud cover, none of anti-aircraft guns in the threatened area opened fire and by the end of raid the RFC and RNAS had flown 17 sorties. Amongst these the first operational sortie flown by the RFC's No. 78 Squadron ended in tragedy when Second Lieutenant David Fowler, aged 19 and characterised as 'fearless as a lion, and as playful as a kitten', crashed his BE2e and died just 9 minutes after taking off from Telscombe Cliffs airfield.[11]

For Germany this raid presented the first experience of operational high-altitude flying. New challenges presented themselves in the form of unexpected high winds in the sub-stratosphere as they edged up to 20,000ft and with multiple cloud layers obscuring the ground. The results were far from what Strasser had anticipated. Of the five latest Zeppelins, one abandoned the mission, one was shot down and the crew killed, one suffered serious damage when landing and the other two limped back to Germany. The British recorded a weight of bombs amounting to 4.3 tons (4,360kg), with others dropped out at sea, achieving material damage estimated at just £163. The Zeppelins appeared safe from attack but their offensive capabilities were compromised.

Chapter 2

'The scene was too awful'

While Peter Strasser maintained the belief that his naval Zeppelins still offered a serious threat to Britain, the same could not be said for the new man commanding German Army aviation. Acknowledging its growing importance, an Imperial decree issued in October 1916 announced the creation of a new air force body and the appointment of a senior officer with authority over all aspects of the army's commitment to aerial warfare, from anti-aircraft guns and aircraft to the meteorological service – and, of course, airships. This new man, 56-year-old General Ernst von Hoeppner, was charged with 'securing unity and method in the construction, concentration and use of all aerial means of waging war'.[1] Von Hoeppner, the commander of this new army air force – the *Luftstreitkräfte* – received a new title: *Kommandierender General der Luftstreitkräfte*, conveniently abbreviated to *Kogenluft*. But events in England in the autumn of 1916 meant airships did not feature significantly in his plans. In a book written after the war he explained his view.

> Successful attacks were only possible when especially favourable conditions prevailed and these were seldom present and we had to reckon on the chance that in each large attack a ship would be shot down and fall into enemy hands as a trophy. This knowledge influenced [me] to decide to limit the use of army dirigibles after January 1917.[2]

The army would continue to operate airships in the East where the aerial defences were less effective but, by summer 1917, von Hoeppner dismantled his airship fleet completely, offering them to the Navy who took two 'r-class' Zeppelins but rejected the earlier types and the army's wooden-framed Schütte-Lanz airships.

Although von Hoeppner dismissed the use of airships, he had not abandoned the idea of bombing Britain; for that he intended using aeroplanes. This was not a new idea. It had previously been championed as early as 1914 by Major Wilhelm Siegert and a special squadron had been formed under the innocuous codename, *Brieftauben-Abteilung Ostende* – the Ostend Carrier Pigeon detachment. But when the army failed to capture Calais, the plan collapsed as the aircraft available at that time needed the shortest possible Channel crossing to make it viable. Siegert's plan was shelved, but not forgotten.

In the intervening period aircraft design advanced significantly and the development of the G-type bomber, the *Grosskampfflugzeug* or 'large battle aeroplane', better known as the Gotha, offered an opportunity for squadron strength attacks against London.[3] It was the G.IV version that was earmarked to take the war to England. Von Hoeppner understood he would have 30 available by 1 February 1917, but production difficulties ensured they would be late. He could also anticipate the arrival of a new class of bomber later in the year, the massive R-type, the *Riesenflugzeug* (literally, Giant aeroplane). By September the first of these would be ready to add their enormous bomb-carrying ability to the assault on London.

In 1916, the army's *Kampfgeschwader 1 der Obersten Heeresleitung (Kagohl 1)*, or 1st Battle Squadron of the Army High Command, had seen action over the Verdun and Somme sectors of the Western Front. In August, however, the six *Kampfstaffeln* (flights) – abbreviated to *Kasta* – split into two separate *Halbgeschwader* (half-squadrons); *Halbgeschwader 1* remained on the Western Front while *Halbgeschwader 2* redeployed to the Balkans. With plans for the bombing campaign against Britain progressing, von Hoeppner selected *Halbgeschwader 1* as the nucleus for a new squadron, *Kampfgeschwader 3 der Obersten Heeresleitung (Kagohl 3)*. The first Gotha IVs arrived in March 1917 and the squadron established itself at two new airfields constructed on the outskirts of Ghent – at Sint-Denijs-Westrem and Gontrode – with a third airfield, Mariakerke, awaiting completion. However, under its new commander, *Hauptmann* Ernst Brandenburg, the squadron would not be ready for action until May.[4]

A professional soldier, Brandenburg, now 33, had attended an aviation training course in 1911. Severely wounded while serving in the trenches in 1915 and having completed his recovery, he transferred to the air service. His abilities as an organiser and administrator soon brought him to the notice of von Hoeppner, who, in March 1917, gave him the task of creating *Kagohl 3* and leading it against England. Brandenburg worked his crews hard, but he had the choice of the best men available and under his leadership they soon developed a strong *esprit de corps*. The men were not officially informed of their mission at this stage but intense training on long-distance flights over the sea and formation flying seemed to suggest what lay ahead. In a short time, the men of *Kagohl 3* began to refer to the unit as *Der Englandgeschwader* – The England Squadron.[5]

Back in Britain this new threat building on the horizon went unnoticed. Unaware of *Kagohl 3* and its mission, Britain continued to reduce and restrict its air defences. But Lord French strongly expressed his concerns on the transfer of night-flying trained pilots to the Western Front. After the Zeppelin raid of 16/17 March, he had reported having only 71 pilots available for service, stating to the Army Council,

> ... in view of my responsibility for Home Defence it is necessary for me to say that in my opinion the Home Defence Wing, Royal Flying Corps, has been reduced to a dangerously low point, and one which does not enable the general scheme of defence on which the present disposition of the squadrons is based to be carried out effectively.[6]

Frustratingly, Lord French received notification that his shortage of pilots was shared across all fronts and no minimum allocation could be set.

After the futile Zeppelin raid in March, all remained quiet in the night skies for the next 19 days, but when the short-lived peace broke on 5 April the results again were negligible.

5 April 1917, 10.30pm: North Kent

A single floatplane from *Seeflieger Abteilung 1 (SFA 1)*, based at Zeebrugge, arrived off the north-east corner of Kent on a beautifully clear night. At 10.30pm it came inland between Broadstairs and Ramsgate, where a gentleman taking an evening stroll noted an ominous sound.

> Walking along the sea front I could hear the whirr of an aeroplane engine, but could not discern the machine, presumably owing to the great altitude at which it was flying. There were two heavy double explosions, from bombs evidently dropped in pairs, but these fell in soft, open ground causing no damage of note and no casualties.[7]

Those four bombs broke a few windows to the value of £4.

Of the remaining four bombs, one damaged fruit trees in the grounds of Eastcliff Lodge on the outskirts of Ramsgate, and the other three landed in marshy ground just north of Sandwich, between a Royal Engineers' camp at Stonar and the Shingle End Coastguard Station. And then it was gone. With no chance of interception, all RFC and RNAS aircraft remained on the ground. But the threat remained the same, with nothing new to concern those in command of Britain's aerial defence.

A month passed before any German aircraft returned. This time, surprisingly, a single army aeroplane reached London, dropping the first bombs on the capital for over five months.[8]

7 May 1917, 12.40am: North London

At *Feldflieger Abteilung 19's* Handzame airfield, about 15 miles south of Ostend, *Oberleutnant* Walter Leon and his pilot, *Offizierstellvertreter* Rudolf Klimke, clambered into their *Albatros* C.VII. Their squadron commander knew of their plan to bomb London but it had passed no higher up the chain of command. They carried just six 12kg explosive bombs, really little more than a show of bravado. Flying across Essex at 14,000ft, the lone raider remained undetected all the way to North London. At 12.40am those manning an AA gun at Wanstead heard an aeroplane passing to their south and almost immediately afterwards a bomb exploded near the White House Inn on Hackney Marshes. The next bomb exploded in the garden of a house at 130 Stoke Newington Road, smashing nearby windows, but caused no casualties. The explosion startled a woman from her sleep: 'I jumped out of bed and almost immediately there followed three other reports. It was a brilliant moonlight night, but I could see no sign of the aeroplane. Everything was over in a few moments.'[9]

At home on the top floor of Newington Green Mansions, a three-storey block of flats on Green Lanes, Frederick Dawson, a pianoforte maker, his wife Annie and their 15-year-old niece were asleep. A bomb that exploded in the Dawson's bedroom blasted a water cistern in the roof out into the garden leaving water cascading down through the flats. It left the niece bewildered and confused.

> I went to my aunt's bedroom door, and tried to open it, but could not. The water stopped me for one thing. There was a great deal of damage, and the walls were knocked down.[10]

Help arrived quickly. Hearing shouts, a policeman forced the bedroom door to find Frederick Dawson lying on his back and covered by debris. Still in the bed, his distraught and injured wife cried out, 'Oh, where is my husband!' Frederick was already dead. '[He had] very severe injuries all over the body,' a doctor reported. 'His skull was crushed, there were five big wounds over the left shoulder at the back, one on the knee, and others on the back.'[11]

Moments later a bomb just missed a house at 19 Aberdeen Park, exploding on a path in the garden. The blast broke a few windows and smashed a chicken house, killing one of the fowls. Another exploded on the recreation ground at Highbury Fields, smashing a water main. The crew of an anti-aircraft gun about 300 yards away recorded the time of the explosion as 12.48am. A final bomb struck the rear of 65 Eden Grove, Holloway. It wrecked a bathroom but failed to explode. Leon and Klimke flew back across Essex, undetected by four defence aircraft that were searching for the intruder. News of their exploits, however, did not go down well in Germany. Von Hoeppner had not wanted to alert the British defences to the imminent commencement of aeroplane raids against London. Both Leon and Klimke were reprimanded for their actions, however, they earned a grudging respect for their achievement and their audacity. Shortly afterwards the pair were transferred to *Kagohl* 3 for the coming campaign.

Von Hoeppner need not have worried. The negligible achievements of the raid, following others in the first four months of 1917, had done nothing to spark a re-think of Britain's revised aerial defence policy. Now, Ernst Brandenburg finally had everything in place, ready to launch *Kagohl* 3 against London, he now just needed the weather to be in his favour.

While Brandenburg awaited his opportunity, Peter Strasser, following his own course, prepared to unleash his new 'height-climber' Zeppelins for the second time that year, unaware of a new danger about to threaten his airships. The first four H-12 'Large America' seaplanes, part of a larger order for the RNAS, were ready for service at Great Yarmouth and Felixstowe on the east coast.

Developed by the Curtiss company in America, the H-12, classed as a flying boat rather than a floatplane, meaning that the fuselage acted like the hull of a boat on the water, whereas the fuselage of a floatplane remained above the surface, supported by floats. With a wingspan of about 93ft and a length of 46.5ft, the H-12 'Large America' carried a crew of four with an armament of four 100lb bombs and four Lewis guns. It boasted a maximum speed of 85mph and an endurance of 6 hours.

This meant it could patrol far out over the North Sea, searching for U-boats and Zeppelins. It did have its problems but undoubtedly offered a significant step up for the RNAS, for it carried wireless equipment that could receive and transmit messages, something no other British aeroplanes at that time were able to do.

14 May 1917, 4.48am: North Sea

On 14 May, Zeppelin L 22 undertook a scouting patrol off the Netherlands coast. On previous missions the Admiralty had picked up wireless transmissions from L 22 which enabled her position to be tracked. Hoping for more of the same, H-12 No. 8666 took off when the Admiralty picked up L 22's departure transmissions from Wittmundhafen in East Frisia, and continued to send developing information directly to No. 8666.[12] The four-man crew, Flight Lieutenant Christopher Galpin, Flight sub-Lieutenant Robert Leckie, Chief Petty Officer Vernon Whatling and Air Mechanic John Laycock, spotted L 22 at 4.48am and, after giving chase, opened fire with incendiary and explosive bullets, setting L 22's envelope 'thoroughly alight', and by the time she crashed into the sea only the bare framework remained, sending up a 'column of brown smoke about 1,500ft high'.[13] With no survivors, no word of the cause of the loss reached Strasser; he believed she had been shot down by a British warship.[14]

On 23 May, Strasser ordered the next attack, intending to target London. Six Zeppelins were detailed to take part: L 40, L 42, L 43, L 44, L 45 and L 47. Both L 44 and L 47 failed to cross the British coast; with the 'Jonah', Peter Strasser, on board, L 44 suffered serious engine failure and limped home, initially on only one engine.

24 May 1917, 12.19am: East Anglia

The first to cross the coast, Erich Sommerfeldt's L 40, came inland at Kessingland on the Suffolk coast at 12.19am, but strong south and south-west winds hindered all the raiders and prevented any attempt on London. Carried over Norfolk by the wind, and blinded by low-lying heavy cloud, Sommerfeldt dropped only two bombs; at 12.45am a huge 300kg bomb exploded 500 yards from the village of Little Plumstead, a few miles east of Norwich, smashing cottage windows and a greenhouse, then, 15 minutes later, another detonated at the village of Knapton, bringing down telegraph wires. Crossing back out to sea at 1.05am, local people reported 14 further explosions out to sea, each one gradually growing fainter as L 40 headed home.

The H-12 flying boat that had shot down L 22 ten days earlier, picked up the returning L 40 near the Dutch island of Terschelling at 5.38am. When the flying boat failed to respond to the Zeppelin's recognition signals, Sommerfeldt climbed steeply. The H-12 closed to 200 yards and opened fire, but L 40 found refuge in the clouds.[15]

Sommerfeldt reported the encounter, but made one crucial omission. He had not recognised his adversary as something new and reported it as a floatplane which he presumed had been brought out to the area by a seaplane carrier. Clearly no one onboard L 40 had time to study the rapidly approaching aircraft in any detail.

L 42 came inland further to the south, crossing the coast at Walton-on-the-Naze in Essex. Commanded by *Kapitänleutnant* Martin Dietrich, L 42 flew over Essex and Suffolk at 18,700ft, finding navigation extremely difficult above the clouds. For the first two hours L 42 dropped only individual bombs, at Halstead, Radwinter, on West Row Fen near Mildenhall, and another near Lakenheath, hoping to provoke a response which might indicate a target. They failed.

At 2.40am, when north-west of Thetford, something caught Dietrich's eye and over the next seven minutes he released nine explosive and three incendiary bombs over the agricultural landscape of Norfolk. Dietrich claimed to have attacked the dockyard town of Sheerness in Kent, about 70 miles to the south. Five of these bombs fell around the village of Hockwold-cum-Wilton breaking windows and roof tiles of farm buildings and damaging crops. Others fell at Weeting Heath, Cranwich, Ickburgh and Hillborough, without inflicting any damage. L 42 went back out to sea between Weybourne and Sheringham at 3.25am.

At 1.00am the third Zeppelin, L 45, crossed the coast at Hollesley Bay in Suffolk; the first raid undertaken by *Kapitänleutnant* Waldemar Kölle and his crew. The weather conditions made it a miserable debut and she appears to have dropped only three bombs. An incendiary (only discovered 16 days later) fell in a field at Banham, between Thetford and Norwich, and an explosive bomb and an incendiary were released over Docking where they broke windows as a thunderstorm raged. L 45 passed back out to sea at 2.30am.

The final Zeppelin, L 43, commanded by *Kapitänleutnant* Hermann Kraushaar, came inland on the same stretch of Suffolk coast as L 45, but over an hour later. The wind carried him across Norfolk where he dropped 38 bombs (20 explosive and 18 incendiary) on a string of small villages. Between 3.05 and 3.25am eight incendiaries fell at Wretham, Tottington and Little Cressingham, with no damage recorded, while explosive bombs at Houghton-on-the-Hill and North Pickenham damaged crops, roof tiles and windows. At 3.35am six bombs landed near the village of Little Dunham smashing a few windows, and three incendiary bombs at West Lexham and Weasenham St Peter were completely ineffective. Ten minutes later three bombs dropped at Wellingham causing minor damage to a farmhouse, farm buildings, five cottages and a chapel. However, there was a tragic outcome. On hearing the approaching explosions, Frederick Pile, a 45-year-old farm labourer, died when he ventured out to warn his employer.

The last bombs wrecked the interior of a cottage at South Raynham and smashed many windows in the village, including at St Martin's Church. At East Raynham there were more smashed windows and damaged roof tiles, and many greenhouses were shattered at Raynham Hall, where the bombs also killed two horses. When L 43 reached the north Norfolk coast at 4.05am the sky had already begun to lighten and an anti-aircraft gun at Holkham managed to fire a few parting shots.

Despite the bad weather conditions, the RNAS and the RFC flew 76 sorties (RNAS 37 and RFC 39) searching for the raiders throughout the night. However, only one pilot, of No. 37 (Home Defence) Squadron, claimed a sighting. In the first operational sortie flown from the squadron's Stow Maries airfield in Essex, Lieutenant George Keddie saw a Zeppelin off the coast at Harwich but could not urge his BE12a up to a height from where he could attack. His target, the engine-troubled L 44 with Peter Strasser on board, escaped. A superior aircraft may have resulted in the critical loss of the commander of the Naval Airship Division.

The weather conditions forced some pilots to terminate their patrols early, and one lost his life. Flight sub-Lieutenant Harold Smith, aged 21, took off in a BE2c from the RNAS air station at Holt in Norfolk. He never returned. Flight Lieutenant Egbert Cadbury noted the loss in a letter.

> He was seen chasing a Zeppelin and gave his life. The coast at Holt runs practically east and west. Thus, a strong south-west wind would blow him right out to sea. At 7,000 feet I could hardly make any headway against it. Thus, he evidently chased it right out to sea and was unable to get back.[16]

The first two Zeppelin raids of 1917 were over. Eight Zeppelins had reached Britain, dropping bombs which had caused damage estimated at just £762 and killed one man. It appeared that the decision to cut back Britain's aerial defences was valid. But any complacency would be dispelled within 24 hours. The day of the Gotha had dawned.

***

Ernst Brandenburg avidly studied the weather reports each day, while the crews of *Kagohl 3* continued practising take-offs and landings; the latter appeared to be a problem. Powered by two 260hp Mercedes D.IVa engines, the Gotha G.IV produced a speed of 80mph in favourable conditions, with a ceiling of 18,000ft. The overall length of 40ft and wingspan reaching 78ft, accommodated a crew of three. The commander, an officer, occupied the front nose position, acting as navigator, observer, bomb-aimer and front gunner. The pilot could be either an officer or senior NCO, with the third member of the crew, the rear gunner, generally a junior NCO. The Gotha carried two or three machine guns, the rear one having the option to fire down through a 'tunnel' in the open lower fuselage to attack any aircraft in the traditional blind spot below the tail. If carrying a third machine gun it could be fixed to the floor of the fuselage giving a wider field of fire below. A general bomb load on the daylight raids amounted to 300kg, typically made up of four 50kg and eight 12kg explosive bombs. These were designed by the *Prüfanstalt und Werft der Fliegertruppen* (PuW) (Test Establishment and Works for the Air Service) and were much more streamlined than the bombs used by Zeppelins. They became known as 'aerial torpedoes' in Britain. There remained one significant problem. When a Gotha returned to base without the ballast provided by bombs and fuel, it became unstable, requiring a tired and exhausted pilot to be fully alert when landing or disaster could strike in a moment. Three Gothas crashed at the end of training flights between 23 April and 10 May.

By May 1917 the HQ flight of three Gothas and four of the six planned *Kasta* were ready, giving a strength of 27 bombers. The standard fuel tanks could hold only enough for the most direct return flight to London, leaving no contingency for deviation caused by the effects of weather or enemy action. Until additional fuel tanks could be fitted, aircraft would top-up with fuel at Nieuwmunster, near the coast, before continuing their journey towards London.

By targeting the capital, Germany hoped to undermine the morale of the population and shake the resolve of the government. In addition, attacks were to be made on munitions factories, military depots, lines of communication to the coast ports and shipping crossing the English Channel. While London remained the prime goal, the coastal area from Felixstowe/Harwich right around to Folkestone, including the Thames Estuary and Dover, were all potential targets. On 24 May, the day the Zeppelins returned from their ineffective foray over East Anglia, Brandenburg received advice of potential good weather for the next day. Keen to put *Kagohl 3* to the test, he issued the long-awaited order: the *Englandgeschwader* would attack London. Under the codename *Türkenkreuz* (Turk's Cross), the latest German attempt to strike at Britain, and London in particular, began.

25 May 1917, 5.10pm: Essex Coast

At 2.00pm (British time) on 25 May, with Brandenburg leading, *Kagohl 3* despatched 23 Gothas from the Ghent airfields. One dropped out almost immediately, while the rest landed at Nieuwmunster to refuel, taking off again at 3.30pm (see map, p.xiii).

At 4.45pm a lightship moored 8 miles north of Margate telephoned news that a large squadron of aircraft had passed, the formation now down to 21 as another Gotha dropped out with engine trouble. Between 4.45 and 4.55pm, the RNAS station at Manston in Kent launched five aeroplanes and RNAS Westgate also got two airborne at 4.55pm, with others following. A delay in transmitting the information to the RFC meant their first aircraft only took off at 5.10pm. By then *Kagohl 3* had crossed the Essex coast between the estuaries of the Crouch and the Blackwater, and had split into two groups about 3 miles apart. The RFC Home Defence squadron nearest the coast, No. 37, mainly equipped with slow-climbing BE12s, had no chance to intercept the high-flying Gothas before they were long gone. The unusual sound created by the large number of aeroplanes resulted in reports of a Zeppelin raid and some even 'saw' Zeppelins in cloud formations. And clouds were now becoming a problem. Far ahead, over London, a threatening build-up of heavy dark clouds, extending down to a low level, left Brandenburg with no choice but to abort the mission and seek alternative targets. Turning away from the capital, *Kagohl 3* crossed the Thames to Kent, towards a clear sky and, heading on a south-east course, made for the coast at Folkestone.[17]

The first bombs dropped on Britain by *Kagohl 3* fell at 5.42pm, with 28 released between Luddesdown, south of Gravesend, and Ashford, a distance of 28 miles. Most fell on farmland. They killed a sheep at Marden, but only at the village of Snarden did any damage occur, albeit trifling.

At 6.10pm part of the squadron passed over Ashford dropping six bombs (2 x 50kg and 4 x 12kg). One exploded in the air above Providence Street, killing 18-year-old Gladys Sparkes and injuring three others, and another injured a woman in Bond Street. South of Ashford, 15 bombs fell on farmland between Shadoxhurst and Bilsington, resulting in two dead sheep at Mersham.

25 May 1917, 6.15pm: Hythe and Shorncliffe, Kent

The two formations drew together again as they approached Lympne where 22 bombs (3 x 50kg and 19 x 12kg) were released over the RFC's No. 8 Aircraft Acceptance Park, but caused little damage. Beyond Lympne a single bomb near the eastern end of the Sandling railway tunnel failed to detonate as *Kagohl 3* approached Hythe, passing over the town at about 6.15pm and taking local people completely by surprise. Of the 15 bombs (7 x 50kg and 8 x 12kg) released, one burst over the Metropole Steam Laundry where a fragment of the bomb pierced the roof of the busy ironing room but surprisingly hurt no one. Another exploded over Ormonde Road, sending jagged metal fragments flying in all directions. One struck 42-year-old Mrs Amy Parker, cutting into her left breast and severing the main artery to her heart. She died instantly. Another, exploding in St Leonard's churchyard, cut the vicar's wife about the head and the verger, Daniel Lyth, died from a deep thigh wound. The other bombs exploded with no loss of life, the last falling on a golf course at the eastern end of Hythe. Directly ahead now lay the sprawling military camp at Shorncliffe.

The bustling camp, largely populated by Canadians, suddenly erupted as 18 bombs (4 x 50kg and 14 x 12kg) tumbled from the sky. One of the 50kg bombs exploded on the howitzer lines. A group of soldiers were formed up, about to set off on a route march, when bomb fragments scythed through the men, leaving 11 dead and many others injured. Another 50kg bomb exploded on the tailors' shop situated in the 8th Infantry Battalion's camp lines, injuring at least 25 men. At Risborough Barracks a group of artillerymen were erecting a tent when one of the smaller bombs exploded and killed five of them. On the Cavalry Drill Ground another Canadian died, as did a British soldier in a quarantine camp. Over 90 soldiers were injured.

There were civilian casualties too, at the village of Cheriton on the northern edge of the camp: 54-year-old Alfred Down died in his garden in Royal Military Avenue and two others, Dorothy Burgin, 16, and

Francis Considine, 5, were killed in Oaks Road. Damage also occurred at Sandgate, to the south of the camp, but no casualties. Ahead, the crews of *Kagohl* 3 could now see the streets of Folkestone laid out below like a map. They had about 40 bombs left to drop.

25 May 1917, 6.20pm: Folkestone, Kent

People in Folkestone had heard booming explosions from the west but presumed there were firing exercises underway at Shorncliffe. And when the 'silver specks' appeared in the sky they believed they were British aeroplanes. At about 6.20pm, 16-year-old Doris Walton was playing tennis in school grounds on Shorncliffe Road when a bomb exploded about 200 yards away, shattering the peaceful sunny evening. Cut down by razor-sharp flying fragments she died the following day. A gardener, Albert Castle, died at another school in Shorncliffe Road. A bomb at the corner of Jointon and Trinity Roads fatally injured Maggie Bartleet as she crossed the road, while a cluster of nine fell around the Central railway station although most were duds. One that did explode killed 45-year-old Edward Horn, butler to Sir Thomas Devitt, who had driven a carriage to the station to collect Sir Thomas from the London train. On the north side of the railway, George Butcher, delivering coal at the corner of Radnor Park Road suffered bad injuries. Doctors amputated his leg but he died in hospital some days later. There were no more deaths north of the railway, but between the tracks and the sea the killing now began in earnest.

Eight bombs fell between Christchurch Road and the end of Bouverie Road East causing significant damage. At 21 Manor Road a large part of West Lodge collapsed: 'The entire staircase was cut in half, and nothing remained but a heap of dust, bricks, and broken furniture.'[18] It took a day to recover the lifeless body of the cook, Jane Marshment, from the rubble. Moments later a bomb exploded outside 19 and 21 Bouverie Road East, killing David John Burke, a boot and shoe repairer. The blast also fatally injured Kathleen Chapman and soldier George Bloodworth who were on their way to collect a pair of shoes, and killed May Arnold who ran the café at No. 19 as well as Harold Banks who died while waiting in the street to meet a friend. Then matters went from bad to worse.

Tontine Street led down to the harbour, a popular shopping street with 'the poorer classes'. A long queue had formed outside Stokes Greengrocers after word spread that there had been a delivery of potatoes. Only about 50 seconds had elapsed since the first bomb fell on

Folkestone and there had been no time to realise what was happening or react before a bomb fell on the street.

> At one moment it was crowded with a gay throng of busy shoppers... the next it was a shambles. Shops which had been packed with customers had collapsed like houses of cards, burying all within under the wreckage. Out in the street women and children were dotting the highways and paths, some dead, some dying, some screaming horribly in the agony of terrible injuries.[19]

A little girl and her mother were inside one of the shops when chaos descended.

> Suddenly came loud explosions – and darkness. Screams filled the air as I struggled to the door. Then I missed my mother's hand, and turned to find her pinned down by fallen rolls of linoleum. Glass was falling on us as I helped her to get free; then we crawled over a counter and across blackened bodies.

> We helped a little child, whose white dress was turning crimson with her own blood... Then a mother who had left her baby outside started frantically struggling to get out, punching my mother in her frenzy.[20]

When the dust settled, Stokes Greengrocers had ceased to exist, other premises were shattered and the true extent of the horrors inflicted on Tontine Street were revealed; there were 44 shattered and bleeding bodies lying in the street or buried in the wreckage of the buildings, while 17 more suffered the agony of their fatal wounds. A single bomb had claimed 61 lives.

For 14-year-old John Pannett it all proved too much. He had heard the explosion and ran towards it.

> [W]hen I got to the point of impact I saw... people lying everywhere, a terrible sight... Hardly anyone seemed to be moving... I looked and looked but the damage was too much, I don't think I took it all in. There must have been blood and lots of it, but I can't recall seeing any, it was too much to take in. I can't even remember screaming, it was shock, shock,

shock, that I must have been in. There were horses there with all their insides running out. The scene was too awful and I ran back the way I had come as fast as I could.[21]

There are numerous stories of how chance played a part in claiming or saving the lives of many of those in the street. In one, a shopping trip took 6-year-old Ernest McGuire to Tontine Street with his mother and sister that Friday evening to look for a new school satchel. Ernest saw one he liked but they decided to check out shops in other streets first. Ernest preferred the one in Tontine Street so they returned to buy it just as the bomb exploded. Ernest's mother, Charlotte, shocked by injuries to her legs and pregnant at the time, suffered a miscarriage. His little sister Irene's clothes were holed and torn but she escaped harm, however, Ernest, so terribly injured, bled to death in the street.[22]

Making their way up the English Channel, the Gothas came under anti-aircraft gunfire from the Capel-le-Ferne and Dover areas. Due to the gun restrictions no weapon had opened fire since a mobile anti-aircraft gun had fired a single round in Essex when *Kagohl 3* first came inland. British pilots flew 77 sorties (RFC 37 and RNAS 40) in opposition to the raid, which seems impressive at first glance, but 34 of those flown by the RFC were made by BE-type aircraft, which were slow to climb and lacked the ability to reach the heights flown by the Gothas. In addition, 21 of the sorties were made after the raid had ended. The RNAS had acquired improved aircraft types and had nine Sopwith Pups, a Sopwith Camel and two Sopwith Triplanes in action during the raid, but without wireless communications it proved difficult to find the enemy once they were airborne, even in daylight. Over in France, however, five Sopwith Pups of No. 4 (Naval) Squadron pounced on the returning Gothas out at sea, shooting down one and possibly damaging another as one later exploded in mid-air south-east of Bruges and crashed with the loss of the crew.

Britain's decision to scale back its aerial defences had been exposed. While the anti-aircraft guns fired just 359 rounds, the majority stood impotent, muzzled by standing orders, and the RFC and RNAS searched the skies over south-east England in vain; 96 people were dead and 194 injured. A new chapter in the air war over Britain had begun.

Chapter 3

Gothas Over London

The immediate reaction to the raid on Folkestone, Hythe and Shorncliffe was one of words not deeds. Understandably the residents of Folkestone were outraged by the loss of life and damage to property, while the calm confidence that had permeated to all corners of Britain after the success against the Zeppelins in autumn 1916 had evaporated in an instant. The fact that the Gothas had been over Britain for about 75 minutes before they bombed Folkestone, yet the town received no warning caused angry debate at a public meeting in the town. On 30 May, a delegation had an audience in London with Lord French to deliver a resolution that bemoaned the lack of warning. It ended by urging the government to 'take such steps as will prevent further attacks of a similar nature and the wholesale murder of the women and children of the town'.

Lord French offered calming words and assured the delegation that, 'measures being taken would make any future raid a very risky operation with heavy losses to the enemy'.[1] Yet at that moment this was an empty promise. Nothing had been done, the ban on anti-aircraft guns firing except in certain locations remained in place and French's own concerns over a lack of home defence pilots had not been addressed. But a conference planned for the next day, 31 May, had as its purpose: '... to consider and report upon the question of the defence of the United Kingdom against attack by aeroplanes.'[2] The conference did not discuss the anti-aircraft guns, but did resolve to transfer 24 trained aircraft spotters from the Western Front to lightships at the mouth of the Thames Estuary and elsewhere, to take up this now vital role from the untrained lightship crews. There was no progress on airborne communications. Sir David Henderson, Director-General of Military Aeronautics, put forward a proposal that aircraft should be fitted with wireless equipment to allow information to be passed to pilots from the ground, but the Admiralty blocked it, believing this traffic could potentially interfere with fleet communications, relegating this important step to further discussion. The conference also considered the shortage of aircraft and pilots for the RFC Home Defence squadrons. Although no new squadrons were authorised, plans were approved for pilots based at training squadrons, experimental stations and aircraft parks to fly daytime patrols when needed.

Concerns were expressed outside the conference too. On the following day, Colonel Thomas C.R. Higgins, commanding Home Defence Group, wrote to Lord French of his unease over the creation of two night-flying squadrons destined for the Western Front. Since February, he asserted, 77 trained pilots had been transferred from Home Defence squadrons, with the loss of 420 trained mechanics and engineers about to follow. He wanted both squadrons delayed to give him time to replace his losses. Lord French backed Higgins and forwarded his letter to the War Office, adding his own comments. He pointed out that the previously unsatisfactory reliance on training squadrons filling the gaps in Home Defence had been one of the reasons that led to the creation of Home Defence Wing the previous year, and with the drain on its manpower, 'the object with which the Home Defence Wing was originally constituted appears in danger of being lost sight of'. French concluded: 'I cannot too strongly impress on the Army Council my opinion that the means placed at my disposal for aeroplane defence are now inadequate and that a continuance of the present policy may have disastrous results.'[3]

Lord French's comments were written on 5 June, but before anyone had the opportunity to digest them, Brandenburg's *Englandgeschwader* returned.

***

In Ghent, Brandenburg had kept the pressure on his meteorological officer, *Leutnant* Cloessner; those above Brandenburg were demanding to know when he would make his first strike against London. On 5 June the weather offered a chance for a raid, not London but a closer target might be possible. As he had already shown his hand, Brandenburg reasoned he had nothing to lose and advised his crews to prepare for a raid that afternoon. This time he would target Shoeburyness and Sheerness, about 6 miles apart on opposite banks of the Thames Estuary. Both were military targets, Shoeburyness with its artillery testing and instructional facilities, and Sheerness, a dockyard town with an army garrison.

5 June 1917, 6.20pm: Shoeburyness, Essex, and Sheerness, Kent

Brandenburg mustered 22 Gothas for the raid, all fitted with auxiliary fuel tanks so refuelling on route became unnecessary. Having been alerted to the threat from the RNAS aircraft at Dunkirk, he initially followed a more northerly course, keeping away from the coast, but even so a routine patrol from No. 4 (Naval) Squadron spotted *Kagohl 3* and gave chase but without any success. At 5.55pm, observers on the Kentish Knock lightship telephoned news of the appearance of the German bombers, with the alert received at GHQ, Home Forces within five minutes. At 6.15pm *Kagohl 3* crossed the coast between the estuaries of the rivers Blackwater and Crouch, fired at by a mobile anti-aircraft gun positioned near Southminster. Directly in the path of the raiders, pilots from No. 37 (Home Defence) Squadron, rushed to get airborne. From airfields at Goldhanger, Stow Maries and Rochford, five Sopwith 1½ Strutters and two BE12as took off between 6.15 and 6.19pm, with more following, but they had no time to reach the Gothas' height. The other Home Defence squadrons protecting the London area, No. 39, No. 50 and No. 78, also had pilots climbing as rapidly as they could. Training squadrons and aircraft parks offered limited assistance too. The RNAS were quick to respond, however, with two Bristol Scouts and a Sopwith Pup taking off from Manston at 6.05pm. Defence aircraft flew 62 sorties, but 20 of those were not in the air until after the last bombs fell. While the first aircraft from No. 37 Squadron were rumbling across their airfields, Brandenburg, in the nose position of the leading Gotha, fired a pre-arranged signal flare and the formation banked to port, towards the Thames and Shoeburyness.

The first two bombs fell in fields at Great Wakering at about 6.20pm, followed by one at North Shoebury. Directly ahead lay South Shoebury and the Shoeburyness artillery complex. Only two of the 20 bombs landed within the military area. One, on the gun park, killed Gunner William Staines and Driver Thomas Toone of the Royal Field Artillery.

A handful of bombs landed in the town within 150 yards of the artillery barracks but had no more serious impact than breaking a few windows. At 6.23pm, two 3-inch, 20cwt guns at the Artillery School of Instruction and one from the Experimental Ranges opened fire; they were in the permitted fire zone. The Gotha formation broke up as the guns fired 172 rounds at the receding target.

Startled by the explosions, local people had emerged from their homes.

> From doorways and windows hundreds of excited inhabitants watched the wonderful air battle. 'The silver sprats,' as someone aptly called the German aircraft, dived and rose, twisted and turned, as though thoroughly surprised.[4]

As *Kagohl 3* crossed the Thames, two Gothas left the formation and turned back east, leaving 20 bombers with Sheerness in their sights. As they approached the town six guns opened fire from the south side of the river. Although not mentioned in the official report of the raid, at least one of the paddle minesweepers anchored nearby, the *London Belle*, also engaged.[5]

The Gothas made a quick and confusing attack on Sheerness, approaching from two directions. Five bombs hit the dockyard where one caused a huge fire which burnt out the top floor of the Grand Store, and another exploded on the quay of No. 3 Dry Dock, narrowly missing a ship but killing dockyard worker, George Frier, and injuring others. Another man also died; Joseph Davies, an officer's steward serving on the battleship HMS *Dominion*. Beyond the dockyard more bombs fell.

In Blue Town High Street an eyewitness saw the next one.

> I was standing outside my place of business, when a huge bomb dropped within 50 yards of me. There was a terrific explosion, and the air was filled with dust and flying pieces of road metal. The bomb had fallen in an open space, which was paved. It made a great hole in the ground.[6]

The explosion, outside Messrs Gieves, Military and Naval Outfitters, destroyed the premises. The manager of the shop, Edward Perry, had been away in Plymouth visiting his sick wife and only returned the previous day. Rescuers worked overnight sifting through the rubble to finally recover his body at 9.00am the following morning. Two days later, with the inquest underway, rescuers discovered another body in the ruins, that of a customer, Herbert Gandy, a gunner serving on HM *Torpedo Boat No.7*.

Beyond Blue Town another bomb killed three soldiers of 5th Battalion King's Royal Rifle Regiment at Well Marsh Camp, besides injuring six others and an officer of the 6th Battalion. Bombs also fell among the tents at the Botany Road camp, killing two more soldiers and injuring 11.

The civilian population did not escape unscathed either, as more bombs fell across the streets in the Mile Town and Marine Town districts of Sheerness. Samuel Hawes, Chief Armourer at the Royal Navy's shore establishment, HMS *Actaeon*, left a meeting at his Masonic lodge when the guns began firing, worried about the safety of his wife and daughter at home. As he emerged from an alley into Cavour Road, a bomb exploded in the street. Samuel Hawes' family were fine but he died instantly. Many houses were damaged by the bombs, which caused further injuries and another man, Herbert Lucas, a launchman employed at the docks, met a gruesome end at the corner of Clyde Street and Richmond Street: '... a man standing on the kerb had his head blown off, and his body was hurled some yards across the road.'[7]

The Gothas were only over Sheerness for five minutes but throughout that time anti-aircraft guns on the Isle of Sheppey and across the Medway on the Hoo Peninsula bombarded the sky, the six guns firing 330 rounds at the swirling, confusing mass of aircraft. One of the shells, fired by the 3-inch, 20cwt gun positioned at Barton's Point, just to the east of Sheerness, claimed success.

Gotha G.IV 660/16, out over the Thames, had descended to about 9,000ft, apparently to attack the gun, when hit: 'The machine fell in spirals into the sea, taking 4½ minutes to fall.' Rescue boats picked up two of the crew, but the pilot, *Vizefeldwebel* Erich Kluck, could not be found. His lifeless body washed ashore two days later. The commander, *Leutnant der Reserve* Hans Francke, barely alive when picked up, died soon after. Miraculously the gunner, *Unteroffizier* Georg Schumacher, survived, with just a broken leg to show for the Gotha's fall from a height of 1.7 miles.

Various attempts were made by pilots of the RFC and RNAS to close and engage the raiders as they headed away, but most struggled to approach the heights of 17,000 to 18,000ft that the now lightened Gothas were flying at, although one, Squadron Commander Charles Butler, RNAS, flying a Sopwith Triplane from Manston made a spirited effort, attacking two of the Gothas. As the formation neared the coast of Belgium, pilots of the RNAS patrolling from Dunkirk also attacked, but this time Brandenburg had the foresight to arrange for fighter cover as he neared home and a confusing dogfight broke out with the RNAS claiming a couple of victories, but they were never confirmed in German records.

After two damaging bomber raids in less than two weeks it became clear to the War Office and the Admiralty that the air war over Britain had taken a new direction and, inevitably, London would soon be targeted. On 7 June, two days after the raid on Shoeburyness and Sheerness, and three months after its introduction, the order banning most anti-aircraft guns from engaging enemy aeroplanes was scraped. As a mark of urgency, GHQ, Home Forces issued the order verbally rather than wait for written orders to circulate. Lieutenant Colonel Simon retrieved his plan to deal with enemy bombers, shelved in March, and immediately issued it to all gun commanders. They did not have long to wait to put it into practice.

On 12 June, German weather experts unanimously predicted ideal conditions for the following day, but *Leutnant* Cloessner added a note of caution; he advised of a possibility of thunderstorms in Belgium after 3.00pm. *Kagohl* 3 would need to be back before then, which demanded an earlier start than on the two previous missions.

13 June 1917, 11.40am: City of London

At 9.00am (British time) on Wednesday 13 June, after months of preparation, the *Englandgeschwader* made ready to strike London, the hub of the British Empire. Twenty Gothas fired up their engines at Sint-Denijs-Westrem and Gontrode (see map, p.xiv). One by one they rumbled across the grass airfields and with engines roaring they soared into the sky. Two soon developed engine problems and dropped out but for the rest, as one Gotha commander described, the mood was one of expectation and exhilaration, the culmination of all their hard work.

> We can recognize the men in the machine flying nearest to us and signals and greetings are exchanged. A feeling of absolute security and an indomitable confidence in our success are our predominant emotions.[8]

At about 10.30am, when about 10 miles north of the Kent coast, one bomber left the formation to make a diversionary attack on Margate. Six bombs were dropped over the town and one in the sea. They caused no major damage, smashing 120 windows and injuring four people. Local anti-aircraft guns opened fire and four RNAS aircraft from Manston (two Bristol Scouts, a Sopwith Pup and a Sopwith Triplane) along with a Sopwith Baby floatplane from Westgate, took the bait and pursued the lone Gotha out to sea without result.[9]

From within the main formation, confidence remained high as they neared the British coast.

> We notice our comrades in other machines pointing to the coastline. They nod at each other and seem highly enthusiastic. We pass the cloud bank... and through the hazy veil the mouth of the Thames appears.[10]

News of the attack on Margate and a sighting at 10.50am of the main formation approaching the mouth of the River Crouch had reached GHQ, Home Forces leading to the issue of the 'Readiness' order to the RFC, RNAS and guns, followed by 'TARA' (Take Air Raid Action). The first RFC and RNAS aircraft were airborne a few minutes after 11.00am. Between them the two air forces flew 94 sorties that day but none would be able to climb fast enough to engage the Gothas on their way to London.

On a pre-arranged signal, three more Gothas left the main formation. One engaged in photo reconnaissance to the south of the Thames, while the other two made a diversionary feint towards Shoeburyness. Anti-aircraft guns engaged as they dropped their bombs. Although no damage of note occurred, two people suffered injury. Their job complete, the two Gothas headed back down the Thames Estuary.

The remaining 14 bombers now grouped into what eyewitnesses described as a wide diamond formation. Regular reports on their progress reached GHQ, Home Forces, but with a hazy sky not all aircraft were always in view, leading to a wide variety in estimates of the formation's strength. The great volume of sound created by their engines also added to the confusion, with some reporting the unseen presence of Zeppelins.

At the village of Great Leighs in Essex, the Reverend Andrew Clark stood mending a fence at the rectory when he heard a peculiar sound, as he noted in his diary.

> This forenoon we heard an unusual drumming noise in the E. and S.E. It went on for a considerable time. My daughter heard it about 11.15 a.m. I thought it was drums in Terling Camp, or a regiment on a route-march on the road beyond that. My daughter thought it was an aeroplane, but out of order.[11]

Only later, at 6.15pm, did they discover that the sound had been generated by the Gothas on their way to London.

From Romford, north of the Thames, the first of the guns defending London opened fire at 11.24am, followed three minutes later by the gun at Abbey Wood, south of the river. The commander of one of the Gothas remained unperturbed.

> Suddenly there stand as if by magic here and there in our course little clouds of cotton wool, the greetings of enemy guns. They multiply with astonishing rapidity. We fly through them and leave the suburbs behind us; it is the heart of London that must be hit.[12]

Gunners all over London were now hammering the sky but, estimating the Gothas height at between 12,000 and 14,000ft, most were firing short; *Kagohl 3* approached at around 16,000ft. A few minutes after the gunfire commenced, the first bombs fell between East Ham and the Royal Albert Dock. And the killing began.

A girl who lived in Alexandra Road, East Ham, attended school in an adjoining road.

> We were all busy when I chanced to look out of the window, and saw what appeared at first to be a large flock of silver birds. We all stood watching the aeroplanes, and saw a black object fall from amongst the crowd of them. There was a terrible explosion. Then we realised it was an air raid.[13]

Two bombs exploded in Alexandra Road damaging 42 houses and killing four people. Among them were the girl's mother, Christina Clarke, and her 4-year-old brother, George. At the docks a single bomb claimed eight lives and injured nine other men. Two of the victims, George Larkins and Arthur Simmonds, were amongst a group working in an office at the docks who went outside when they heard the guns commence firing.

With the Gothas back in formation, Brandenburg fired another flare on reaching Regent's Park, and they banked again, heading towards the City of London, the financial hub of the capital. *Kagohl 3* now abandoned its formation, with Brandenburg describing his squadron 'flying back and forth and in circles'.[14] Now to make the raid count.

At last it is time. I give the signal, and in less time than it takes to tell I have pushed the levers. I anxiously follow the flight of the released bombs. With a tremendous crash they strike the heart of England. It is a magnificently terrific spectacle, seen from mid-air. Projectiles from hostile batteries are spluttering and exploding beneath and all around us, while below the earth seems rocking and houses are disappearing in craters and conflagration in the light of the glaring sun.[15]

Vera Brittain, a Voluntary Aid Detachment (VAD) nurse home on leave and staying with her parents in London, had just returned from shopping and saw the sky full of aeroplanes 'as the uproar began': 'I saw the sinister group of giant mosquitos sweeping in close formation over London.' Then, as her family huddled helplessly in the basement, they 'listened glumly to the shrapnel raining down like a thunder-shower upon the trees in the park'.[16]

In the space of two minutes, commencing at 11.40am, the main attack developed with 72 bombs falling within a 1-mile radius of Liverpool Street Station. Despite the danger, not everyone sought shelter, as an American journalist travelling on an open-topped bus reported.

From every office and warehouse and tea shop men and women strangely stood still, gazing up into the air. The conductor mounted the stairs to suggest that outside passengers should seek safety inside. Some of them did so.

'I'm not a religious man,' remarked the conductor, 'but what I say is, we are all in God's hands and if we are going to die we may as well die quiet.'

But some inside passengers were determined that if they had to die quiet they might as well see something first and they climbed on top and with wonderstruck eyes watched the amazing drama of the skies.[17]

Three bombs smashed through the glass roof of Liverpool Street Station, with one exploding on the edge of Platform 9 as the 11.50am train to Hunstanton prepared for departure, blasting apart the restaurant car and causing fierce fires in two other carriages. Another struck a special train opposite where a medical board were carrying out examinations of men for military service, causing it to burst into flames. The bombs killed 16 and injured another 15. One of the victims aboard the departing train, Thomas Ivor Moore, Assistant Director of Barrack Construction at the War Office, died from a wound to his neck, while 27-year-old Francis Reeves, waiting for his medical examination, lost his life in the burning carriage.[18]

On leave and at the station that morning stood the soldier and poet Siegfried Sassoon. He looked on, shocked, and struggled to make sense of it all.

> In a trench one was acclimatized to the notion of being exterminated and there was a sense of organized retaliation. But here one was helpless; an invisible enemy sent destruction spinning down from a fine weather sky; poor old men bought a railway ticket and were trundled away again dead on a barrow.[19]

About half a mile west of the station, at Barrett's Brass Foundry off Beech Street, nine men were working on the roof when the bombing commenced. One of them, C. Murphy, shouted a warning but before they could find shelter an explosion knocked him unconscious. When he came to, all his colleagues were dead.[20]

About three quarters of a mile north-west of Liverpool Street Station, Police Constable Alfred Smith was on duty in Central Street, a road off Old Street. The previous night he had lain awake due to terrible pains in his legs. His wife urged him not to report for work in the morning but he went in because 'it was his duty to go'. Later that morning Rhoda Pipe, one of 150 women working in the basement of Debenham & Co in Central Street, puzzled over a distant noise. When she heard another, however, she shouted 'Bombs!' Everyone rushed to get out into the street.

Outside, PC Smith also heard the thunderous booms. When the door burst open and staff started to emerge, he leapt forward. Rhoda described the policeman putting up his arm to hold them back – as he did so two bombs exploded in the street. The concussion of the blast struck PC Smith. All of those crowded in the doorway escaped injury but Alfred Smith lay dead at their feet. The bombs killed 13 people in the street, including 80-year-old Elizabeth Cain, but the death toll would have been greater but for PC Smith's selfless act.[21]

At 65 Fenchurch Street, about 750 yards south of Liverpool Street Station, more bombs exploded. Thomas Burke, in his office on the third floor, heard 'ominous rumbles', then came 'two deafening crashes' as the building swayed and trembled before half of it came crashing down. Burke crawled to a window.

> Looking out... on to a street that seemed enveloped by a thick mist – the rising dust of debris... Excited shouts of 'Come out!' and 'Keep in!'... Safes, burst open, with their scattered contents, piles of books and papers and other debris, in the roadway... A girl, who had been standing in the doorway of a provision shop, having now lost both her legs... An unknown man lying dead against the wall of an A.B.C. shop opposite... A number of dead (probably having taken refuge in our building) who were unknown to the office tenants... A small cat mewing piteously, with its fur blown away.[22]

From the rubble they extricated 19 bodies, 14 others bore cruel injuries.

About 350 yards north-east of Fenchurch Street a bomb smashed down on Aldgate High Street, shattering the 200ft frontage of the Albion House Clothing Company occupying the block between Minories and Jewry Street. It also wrecked a bus, blowing the driver, J.T. Wise out into the street but, although terribly shaken by his experience, he helped with the removal of his passengers. Bill Goble, a messenger in a shipping office, rushed out into the street.

> A bus conductress lay on the pavement – her leg appeared to be severed from the knee. A policeman sat on a chair, his trouser legs ripped away and one leg covered in blood. To add to the horror of the occasion, a number of [shop] window dummies had fallen out onto the pavement amongst the bodies of the dead and the injured. A... bus stood silently by the kerb, every window shattered; a solitary figure of a man was hunched up in the seat immediately behind the driver's seat. He sat motionless, a piece of glass was said to have pierced his neck and we were told he was already dead.[23]

About 500 yards south-east of Aldgate High Street, a bomb struck a wall at the Royal Mint, partially destroying a mechanic's workshop, killing four people working there – Howard Avery, William Beadle, Albert Crabb and George Cavell – and injuring 30 more.

After the main attack the Gotha formation split into two again, either side of the Thames. Passing over Southwark, the southerly group dropped more bombs, one of which stuck tea merchants British and Beningtons on Southwark Street. About 30 women workers had taken shelter in a basement strongroom which had a concrete ceiling, but the bombs shattered it, burying the refugees. Help arrived quickly but it came too late to save Phyllis Barker (aged 15), Winifred Churchill (14) and another girl, who all died; rescuers pulled the rest from the rubble, although only three escaped uninjured.[24]

The Gothas that kept north of the Thames also marked their path with tragedy. A bomb in Gibraltar Walk, Bethnal Green, caused widespread damage, but at No. 18, the home of bootmaker Joseph Moss and his family, it produced a charnel house. While Mr Moss was away at the market the bomb demolished his home. A soldier on leave, J. Lynch, tried to help.

> On account of the dust it was very difficult to see, but by sheer luck I saw an arm sticking out of the debris. Clearing the dirt away as carefully as I could, I at last uncovered a woman's face. She must have been nearly dead, but she managed to gasp, 'My babies are here, too!' So I again started to pull the rubbish and stuff away with my hands, and had the satisfaction of uncovering her two little kiddies, twins. I could not release their bodies as they were pinned down by the roof rafters and other stuff, so I wiped the dirt out of their mouths and eyes.[25]

Despite Mr Lynch's efforts, the mother, Rebecca Moss, died in the wreckage and the 9-month-old twins, Bessie and Cissie, later died in hospital. The couple's two other daughters, Hettie (11) and Esther (5) also died in the rubble, as did a lodger. In an instant, Joseph Moss had lost his entire family and his home. Outside in the street two other children, out with their grandmother, also died – Annie Stanford (3) and her 9-month-old sister, Ivy.[26]

There were other child victims too. At 35 Woodville Road, Dalston, the home of the Reynolds family, Mrs Reynolds was downstairs with three of her children – Ivy, Hilda and Robert – while the grandmother was upstairs with the youngest, 18-month-old Lilian. Mr Reynolds, a munitions worker, was at work. When Mrs Reynolds heard the sound of explosions she shouted to the grandmother, 'Bring baby down here; they are dropping bombs'. Almost immediately a bomb dropped outside the house. Rescuers recovered the adults, injured but alive, all four children, however, 'crushed with bricks and mortar' were dead.[27]

There were countless more stories of death and destruction in London that day; from Clerkenwell, the westernmost point bombs had fallen, north to Dalston, south to Bermondsey and east to Stratford; they had inflicted 588 casualties (162 killed and 426 injured – the most in any single raid in the war) and inflicted damage estimated at about £125,000. But of the 118 bombs dropped on London, one above all others filled the city's population with horror and repulsion – it wrecked the Upper North Street School in Poplar, in the East End of London.

The crew did not deliberately aim to hit the school, the commander of the Gotha, like all the others, wanted to make sure he had released all his bombs before commencing the return flight. He may have been tempted by the sight of the West India Docks about 500 yards to the south of the school. Whatever the reason for dropping the bomb at that precise moment, fate determined that it struck the school, where the three storeys of the building were packed with children at their lessons. Two older children – Edwin Powell (12) and Rose Martin (11) – were killed as the bomb made its way down through the building before exploding on the ground floor among two classes of 64 young children aged 5 and 6. When desperate rescuers had finished their work, 16 of these infants were dead and 30 others, as well as four teachers, injured. The funeral, a week later, brought that part of London to a halt.

> The East End of London yesterday paid a sorrowful last tribute to the children who were killed in their class-room at school last Wednesday.
>
> A hard life had not hardened the dwellers in dockland. Behind the dingy and often squalid exterior of the East End there lies a rich fount of human emotion. Sometimes it wells up and makes one marvel at the great heart of the toilers in these mean and crowded streets. Yesterday all Poplar and the neighbouring boroughs were charged with an overflowing sympathy for the mothers and fathers whose children have been slaughtered on the alter of German ruthlessness, and while the little ones were being carried to the grave all who were able came out to mourn with the mourners. The pulsing industrial and commercial life of the district was stilled for a

while, and in its place there appeared a throbbing community of sorrow.[28]

The Gothas, heading east, ran the gauntlet of the anti-aircraft guns and Home Defence aircraft. The guns defending London along the Thames and at Margate fired 360 rounds while aircraft flew 94 sorties, but only 11 managed to open fire, without bringing down any of the raiders. At the same time the pilots of *Kagohl 3* claimed two kills although none were shot down. One of the incidents may refer to a Bristol Fighter of No. 35 (Training) Squadron piloted by Captain Con Cole-Hamilton, with Captain Cecil Keevil as his observer/gunner. They attacked three straggling Gothas over Ilford, themselves coming under return fire. A bullet struck Keevil in the neck and killed him, and with his forward-firing gun jammed, Cole-Hamilton dived away – his attackers may have believed him shot down.[29]

Safely back on the Ghent airfields, Brandenburg sent a dramatic report to von Hoeppner. He replied enthusiastically.

> The squadron has fulfilled its mission. That is the highest recognition I can accord to you and your crews. The squadron attack on London has been for years an objective of our fliers and our technology. With the execution of the attack *Kagohl 3* has provided a new basis for air attacks. I thank you and your brave crews... Good luck in future deeds under the symbolic slogan: Brandenburg over London.[30]

That 'symbolic slogan' would be short-lived.

Chapter 4

'The lights of death'

The press releases issued in Germany were greeted enthusiastically. The Gothas had picked up the baton dropped by the Zeppelins and were now effectively carrying the war to the pulsing heart of the British Empire, to 'Fortress London'.

> The objective was the bombardment of docks, wharves, railway establishments, Government stores and warehouses situated in the centre of the town on the banks of the Thames.
>
> Numerous fires broke out and were well nourished by the stores of goods.
>
> The squadron remained over the points of attack more than a quarter of an hour, and, notwithstanding British anti-aircraft measures, all our aeroplanes returned undamaged.[1]

The result of Brandenburg's attack delighted the *Kaiser* who summoned the commander of *Kagohl 3* to Supreme Headquarters at Kreuznach. Brandenburg left Gontrode the day after the raid, flying in a two-seater *Albatros* piloted by *Oberleutnant* Hans-Ulrich von Trotha. At Kreuznach, Brandenburg received the *Pour le Mérite*, Germany's highest military order, known informally as the *Blauer Max* (Blue Max). Brandenburg and von Trotha set out to return to Belgium on the morning of 19 June, but a few minutes into the flight the engine failed and their aeroplane crashed. Von Trotha died and Brandenburg suffered such serious injury to a leg that it required amputation. It would be many months before he could return to command his squadron. The men of *Kagohl 3* were devastated, their commander, the man who had created the squadron now removed at the moment of triumph. Fearful of losing the impetus, von Hoeppner urgently sought a replacement.

***

Back in London a feeling of outrage simmered everywhere; German aircraft had appeared over the capital in the middle of the day without an apparent effective response. Many demanded reprisals against German towns, a feeling echoed in the Press and in parliament. The fact that London had no public air raid warning system also provoked debate.

The War Cabinet met on the afternoon of the raid and again the following day, during which time a proposal for a significant increase in the RFC, almost doubling its size, passed, receiving final approval on 2 July – but that was long-term. Reprisals were also discussed and these were referred to Field Marshal Sir Douglas Haig, commanding the British Army on the Western Front, and Major General Hugh Trenchard, commanding the RFC in the field, who were both in London on 17 June on other business. As to the question of reprisals they made an unequivocal response.

> Reprisals on open towns are repugnant to British ideas, but we may be forced to adopt them. It would be worse than useless to do so, however, unless we are determined that, once adopted, they will be carried through to the end. The enemy would almost certainly reply 'in kind' and unless we are determined and prepared to go one better than the Germans, whatever they may do and whether their reply is in the air, or against our prisoners, or otherwise, it will be infinitely better not to attempt reprisals at all.[2]

Haig ended any further discussions on the subject by adding that the RFC 'had no aeroplanes to spare for such an operation'.

The meeting did, however, agree to the temporary detachment of two RFC squadrons to undertake fighting patrols on both sides of the English Channel. No. 56 Squadron, equipped with the SE5, relocated two flights to Bekesbourne in Kent and one to Rochford in Essex, and No. 66 Squadron, with their Sopwith Pups, moved to the French coast near Calais. But the agreement came with an important proviso; both squadrons were to resume their duties on the Western Front by 6 July.

No. 56 Squadron arrived in England on 21 June. Cecil Lewis, one of the pilots, could not believe his good fortune.

> Agitation in the press! Scandalous neglect of the defence of dear old England! Panic among the politicians! Lloyd George acting quickly! Result: a crack squadron to be recalled for the defence of London immediately. And twelve elated pilots of 56 Squadron packing a week's kit into our cockpits. God bless the good old Gotha![3]

On the day No. 56 Squadron arrived in England, Lieutenant Colonel Simon submitted a plan for increased gun protection on the eastern approaches to London, designed to 'greet the enemy with a shower of shell bursts'. His plan required 45 additional guns but again the response informed him there were none to spare.[4]

Also on 21 June, a meeting took place between the Home Secretary, George Cave, and the mayors of the London boroughs to discuss public air raid warnings for the capital. With the Gothas flying faster than Zeppelins, the warning system introduced between February and May 1916 was found wanting. The meeting concluded that warnings were needed but the War Cabinet rejected the idea. The government maintained its belief that the public, advised of an imminent raid, would congregate in the streets, risking their own safety and hindering the emergency services. Additionally, concerns were raised that if no raid materialised following a warning, people may ignore future alerts, and the risk of disruption to work shifts also seemed likely; evidence showed that workers who dispersed due to raid alerts often did not return when the threat had passed. There would be no public air raid warnings for London – for now.

***

In Germany, while Britain concerned itself with what to do next, Peter Strasser, the naval *Führer der Luftschiffe*, must have felt personal frustration at the success of the army's Gothas over London. He had other concerns to deal with too. On 23 May, Zeppelin L 40 had survived an encounter with the new British threat over the North Sea, the H-12 'Large America' flying boat. The commander had not recognised his attacker as a new unknown long-range aeroplane and presumed his attacker to be a floatplane deployed from a seaplane carrier.

On 5 June, the day of the Gotha raid on Shoeburyness and Sheerness, L 40 again encountered the same H-12 and crew off the island of Terschelling. Although L 40 escaped this time too, her commander, Erich Sommerfeldt, again failed to recognise a new threat. He reported his assailant as 'a biplane resembling a Nieuport', but after an extensive search he could not find the ship that he erroneously believed must have brought his attacker so far out in the North Sea.[5]

Nine days later, on 14 June, the day after the Gotha raid on London, five Zeppelins were patrolling the North Sea. The RNAS crew that had attacked L 40, now flying H-12 No. 8660, discovered L 46 about 45 miles north-east of Great Yarmouth and attacked without success, but the Zeppelin's commander, *Kapitänleutnant* Heinrich Hollender, noted his assailant as an 'English seaplane, biplane'. By the time they had broken off the fight, another Zeppelin had crashed into the sea. H-12 No. 8677 from Felixstowe located Zeppelin L 43 near the Dutch island of Vlieland. After a short engagement, explosive and incendiary bullets fired from the flying boat saw the Zeppelin engulfed in flames before the wreckage smashed into the sea, trailing a great cloud of black smoke.[6] *Kapitänleutnant* Hermann Kraushaar and his crew were killed.

The loss of L 43 did nothing to improve Strasser's mood, but with the new moon due on 19 June and a period of good weather forecast, he ordered 'attack in south, London'. The decision seems odd; in the past Strasser had avoided raiding during the shortest of June's summer nights.[7] It seems a huge risk; did he hope to demonstrate to the Army that the Navy Zeppelins still offered a threat to match the Gothas? This time he did not accompany the raid, instead his deputy, and nominal head of the Naval Airship Division, Viktor Schütze, would join L 48 on its first raid. Schütze would be among friends – the crew had served under him on L 11 and briefly on L 36 before his promotion.

Six Zeppelins set out on 16 June but things did not start well. Strong crosswinds at Ahlhorn prevented L 46 and L 47 from leaving their sheds and engine failures over the North Sea forced both L 44 and L 45 to turn back. Just two, L 42 and L 48, remained on course for England. Strasser also had to face an unconnected setback. A couple of hours after the Zeppelins departed, L 40, which had survived the recent close encounters with the H-12 flying boats, ran into difficulties returning from a scouting flight and crash-landed near Nordholz. The extensive damage inflicted resulted in L 40 being written off.

17 June 1917, 2.10am: Ramsgate

With *Kapitänleutnant* Martin Dietrich in command, L 42 held out to sea off the north Kent coast for some hours as the summer sky only became completely dark around 11.30pm. He then had just 3 hours before it would begin to lighten again. Battling against the wind, Dietrich decided to attack Dover first then, hopefully, continue to London. Struggling with navigation, however, instead of Dover, he attacked Ramsgate.

At about 2.10am, L 42 approached the harbour dropping the first two bombs in the sea as searchlights flickered into action, but they struggled to hold the great bulk of the Zeppelin's black-painted envelope in their beams. The third bomb, however, a huge 300kg monster, reaped dividends. It exploded squarely on the Fish Market, a range of buildings situated on the harbour's Crosswall, which had recently been converted into a naval magazine. Stored inside were artillery shells, machine gun and rifle ammunition, depth charges and a couple of recovered German mines. When the bomb hit, all hell broke loose: 'A sheet of blood-red flame shot upwards and for hours ammunition of all kinds continued to explode with a tornado of fury.'[8] Ernest Cockburn, a Ramsgate resident, awoken by the noise of the first bombs detonating at sea, pondered the cause as he lay in bed.

> I was just wondering whether it was the monitor[9] practising or the 'real thing' when I saw the windows lit up by star shell or searchlight. Heard a loud shrieking as of a shell or aerial torpedo, a terrific explosion and the glass of my bedroom window tinkled out onto the bow window below. I decided that it was the 'real thing'.[10]

With the continuous roar of explosions filling the air, Cockburn initially concluded that a naval battle had commenced outside the harbour. Dietrich, from his lofty viewpoint about 3.5 miles above the town, had a better grasp of the situation.

> With the bursting of a 300kg bomb a gigantic explosion took place, which caused further explosions at intervals of ten minutes, until the whole district, apparently a munitions store, was completely in flames.[11]

The great danger encountered by those who attended the conflagration resulted in 29 firemen from the brigades of Ramsgate, Margate and Broadstairs receiving the British Empire Medal for their work that night.[12]

Coming inland, L 42 laid a bloody trail. Two bombs exploding in Albert Street obliterated four homes leaving a scene of utter desolation. 'A [bomb] fell at the back of our house,' an eyewitness reported, 'I distinctly saw it and heard it hissing through the air... It was terrible to hear the screams, for in a dozen different houses, families were imprisoned, and were crying for help.'[13] Incredibly only three people – neighbours – were killed. For three hours police and soldiers pulled away at the debris from where they could hear a woman's voice: 'Finally they found her [Mrs Thouless] beneath eight feet of debris. Beside her was the dead body of her husband [Benjamin]. They had been standing together when the bombs fell.'[14] Mrs Thouless recovered from her trauma in hospital.

Next door lived Jonathan Hamlin, his wife Eliza and Hamlin's brother. The brother escaped with slight injuries, but not the married couple. Already dead, Jonathan's 'mangled body rested in the ruins', but Eliza still lived.

> [A police officer] could see the head and shoulders of Mrs Hamlin sticking out above the rafters and brickwork of the roof. Her face was saturated with blood, upon which the dust had settled, and it was impossible to recognize her. She was conscious and was crying piteously for her husband. Several tons of rubbish had to be shifted before she could be released.[15]

Although freed from the wreckage, Eliza Hamlin died in hospital of her terrible injuries.

The same two bombs also damaged homes and shops in Ivy Lane and Addington Street, but everyone there escaped injury.

L 42 continued dropping bombs. Damage occurred in Crescent Road and at Southwood House and Nether Court, where a VAD hospital cared for wounded soldiers, but no more lives were lost. Dietrich then neared the RNAS air station at Manston where flares were burning as three aeroplanes had flown from there. L 42, now flying at 19,400ft had little chance of achieving accuracy with her bombs. Three explosive and two incendiary bombs fell in fields about half a mile east of the airfield resulting in just a few broken windows. All the time anti-aircraft guns had kept up a steady fire, joined by the monitor, HMS *Marshal Ney*, in the harbour. L 42 remained overland for 14 minutes before Dietrich wisely decided against making a push for London and commenced the homeward journey.

Ramsgate 'presented an extraordinary picture of devastation and debris'.

> Nearly 700 houses had been damaged – over 40 tons of splintered glass were collected and the material damage amounted at least to £60,000[16] – three people were killed and 16 injured.[17]

17 June 1917, 3.28am: Theberton, Suffolk

The other Zeppelin to come inland, L 48 commanded by *Kapitänleutnant der Reserve* Franz Eichler, had Schütze on board. First located about 40 miles north-east of Harwich at 11.40pm, her movements appeared puzzling and not until after 2.00am did she finally came inland south of Orfordness (see map, p.xv). But trackers were unaware that L 48 had experienced problems with two of her engines and the liquid compass had frozen making navigation difficult. With one engine now restored, but having lost much time, Eichler agreed with Schütze to target Harwich instead of London. Their manoeuvrings for the next 30 minutes were erratic but at 2.42am, when north-east of Harwich, she came under fire from anti-aircraft guns, joined by ships in Harwich harbour and minesweepers moored off Bawdsey. Although reports suggest the guns were firing short, the sheer volume of fire from the land-based guns (434 rounds) appears to have deterred L 48. She turned about, dropping 24 bombs which the crew believed hit Harwich but they landed around the villages of Falkenham, Kirton and Waldringfield with limited result.

L 48 moved away slowly at first but gradually picked up speed as the sky began to lighten. Without her compass, however, L 48 headed north, rather than east towards the sea, before the forward engine failed and her speed dropped again. Following a request for radio bearings, Eichler received advice of a tailwind blowing at 11,000ft and reduced his height to take advantage of it. A lightening sky and descending to an altitude easily within range of all Home Defence aircraft made L 48 incredibly vulnerable.

Among those searching for the intruder were a Canadian-born officer, Lieutenant Loudon Watkins of No. 37 Squadron, who took off in a BE12 from Goldhanger, and two aeroplanes from the RFC's Experimental Station at Orfordness, an FE2b flown by Lieutenant Frank

Holder, with Sergeant Sydney Ashby as his gunner, and a DH2 flown by Captain Robert Saundby.

Despite the early hour, many local people, awoken by the gunfire, scanned the sky for the hunted Zeppelin.

> There were no stars, no clouds, only a rosy flush in the east heralding the breaking through of the sun... it was seen that she was in difficulties. She veered clumsily from one side to the other, suggesting she had been hit by the coast guns. All the time she was relentlessly pursued by aeroplanes, and her demeanour for several minutes... was of a trapped animal searching vainly for some way of escape.[18]

L 48 had travelled north for about 20 miles since dropping her bombs. Although there is no evidence that she had been hit by gunfire, many observers reported that she appeared to be struggling. All three pilots first spotted L 48 near Harwich and now began to close in.

Lieutenant Watkins, flying at 11,000ft, first saw the Zeppelin about 2,000ft higher. As he narrowed the distance he continued to climb, firing two drums at long range without result. He then waited before firing a third, as his matter-of-fact report concluded.

> I then climbed steadily until I reached 13,200ft and was then about 500ft under the Zeppelin. I fired three short bursts of about 7 rounds and then the remainder of the drum; the Zepp burst into flames at the tail, the fire running along both sides, the whole Zepp caught fire and fell burning.[19]

Holder and Ashby in the FE2b were flying at 14,200ft but Holder estimated they were still about 2,000ft below the raider. Both the pilot and observer opened fire but Holder's machine gun jammed and Ashby failed to clear it. They edged up another 300ft, estimating L 48 to be travelling at 50mph and losing height. Ashby continued to fire when the opportunity presented itself.

> About five miles beyond Leiston, the observer fired about 30 rounds at about 300 yds range. I turned for the observer to correct a stoppage, and to avoid fire, which was opened on the FE, and looking round observed the H.A. [Hostile Aircraft] in flames.[20]

Saundby, in the DH2, had also joined the pursuit.

> Followed him and climbed up under his tail firing three drums of Pomeroy and tracer bullets at rapidly shortening ranges. The H.A. was by this time losing height and I was climbing... I saw another machine higher than myself... firing bursts of tracer bullets. In the middle of my third drum the H.A. caught fire at one point and immediately became a mass of flame.[21]

Although all three aircraft had a claim in shooting down L 48, after some consideration the RFC awarded the honour to Lieutenant Watkins of No. 37 Squadron. It has been suggested that the War Office preferred recognition to go to a regular Home Defence pilot rather than the part-time defenders from an experimental squadron.[22]

Whoever had fired the fatal shots, they had sealed L 48's fate. Many watched her final moments in awe.

> The next moment the airship put on her lights – as one observer expressed it. But they were the lights of death. At first there was the glow as of a lighted cigar when it is fanned by a breeze. The glow increased apace, and soon the entire envelope of the airship was illumined. The red gleam gave place to tongues of flame, which assumed fantastic shapes as they shot upwards, lightening up the sky like a blast furnace.[23]

The official report stated that the L 48 descended more slowly than previous airships, 'the fall taking from 3 to 5 minutes'. Newspapers described the moment the Zeppelin hit the ground.

> She... drifted down into a field about four miles from [Saxmundham] settling on her tail. About three-quarters of the vessel was completely telescoped, leaving the framework of the fore-end standing virtually intact. Like the half of a huge egg at an angle of ninety degrees, the extreme point of the nose being fifty feet in the air, with strips of shrivelled envelope hanging to it. Some of the crew had apparently jumped clear just before she struck the ground. A number of bodies were found scattered about the vicinity.[24]

After a seemingly senseless order for an airship attack on Britain so close to the shortest night of the year, and a decision to descend to a height within reach of British aeroplanes, L 48, the latest Zeppelin to be built to the new specifications, had survived just 25 days in the naval service. And among the wreckage lay the remains of Strasser's most determined and experienced deputy, Viktor Schütze, as well as that of Franz Eichler, the commander of L 48, and 14 members of the crew. Although the airship smashed into the ground at 3.38am, in no time people appeared in the field on Holly Tree Farm at Theberton, Suffolk, to see the crumpled wreckage.

> The onlookers had the unpleasant experience of watching the cremation of the wretched Germans, an uncanny spectacle at any time, and especially so in that lonely spot, amidst the mist of dawn.[25]

Another uncanny spectacle then emerged from the mist – a man staggered from the burning wreckage. Heinrich Ellerkamm, an engine mechanic stationed in a starboard midships engine gondola, had climbed up into the body of the airship to check on the fuel supply for his engine when bullets struck the gas bags: 'There was an explosion – not loud, but a dull "woof" as when you light a gas stove.'[26] Horrified, Ellerkamm froze.

> Suddenly I saw tiny blue flames appear in the fifth and sixth bags aft. Oh, Lord! The very next moment came the roar of a mighty explosion, and a couple of seconds afterwards the L 48 was one mass of flames. It was all up with us... I sensed that the ship was beginning to drop.[27]

Ellerkamm wedged himself against a girder and bracing wire to stop himself falling down through the ship, beating out flames that began to catch his fur overcoat. Fortunately for him the draught forced the flames away from where he clung on for dear life as the airship plummeted down.

> One thinks a lot in moments like that – silly things perhaps, but they are all about the bright side of life. I was expecting a fortnight's leave, and Gretel, my fiancée, was waiting to see me. And I was to die here?
>
> ... Suddenly the ship's stern crashed to pieces with a fearful din. I did not know what was going to happen next; I only

> knew that a chaotic jumble of girders, bracing wires, benzine tanks and car fittings were coming down on my head, and that above me a sea of flames was collapsing.
>
> 'Now keep your head,' I thought, ... The shock of the crash must have torn some of my muscles and taken the wind out of my body... But, good Lord! You're still alive! You're still alive, man!

With flames all around him and imprisoned within the Zeppelin's glowing red-hot girders, the mechanic made a desperate bid for life.

> With the strength that such a moment of despair gives one – I pushed against a girder. Another girder gave way in front of me and left a gap free. I crawled along the ground and felt grass; I crept forward. Behind me was a mass of burning oil. I rolled over two or three times in the grass.
>
> Then I found myself in the open air... I collapsed exhausted. I can still see the meadow, with horses and a wild duck flying overhead in the dawn... I saw the horses galloping away madly, scared by the flames of the L 48.
>
> Then an Englishman came running across the field, wearing only a shirt and trousers. He stared at me as if I had dropped from another world. 'You are from the Zeppelin?' he asked.

The man, Chief Petty Officer F.W. Bird, home on leave from the Royal Navy, had run from the village of Eastbridge, about half a mile away. Much to his surprise, Bird found the dazed German wandering around the field.

> He appeared to be totally unhurt and I beckoned him towards me as I ran. He looked very confused and helpless, and, could not or would not speak English. By signs I asked him for any papers he might be carrying, and, not reassured by his actions, I made him put his hands above his head and then searched him. He had a purse containing various coins, some of them English, a railway ticket and a knife. The latter I took from him.[28]

Incredibly, there were other survivors. Those first on the scene pulled the badly burnt and terribly injured Wilhelm Unger, another mechanic, from the wreckage of an engine gondola. He remained a hospital patient for the rest of the war and, poignantly, died on Armistice Day 1918. However, another man did survive, L 48's executive officer, *Leutnant-zur-See* Otto Mieth. Mieth lost consciousness during the descent, but the shock of the crash woke him. Surrounded by a sea of flames and red-hot metal girders, he lost consciousness for a second time. When he came round next he found himself lying on a stretcher.

> I half raised myself painfully, and saw that my legs were in thick, bloody bandages. I could hardly move them, for they were broken. Then I made a new discovery: my head and legs were covered with burns; my hands were lacerated; when I breathed I felt as if a knife were thrust into me.
>
> I thought to myself, 'Am I dreaming or awake?' Just then a human voice interrupted my groping thoughts: 'Do you want a cigarette?' and a Tommy stuck a cigarette-case under my nose with a friendly grin. So it was no dream. I was a prisoner.[29]

All three survivors had been in the forward half of L 48, which fell on its stern, the rear half absorbing much of the shock of the crash. On no other occasion did members of a crew survive the fall of an airship shot down in flames over Britain.

When L 48 began to burn, Martin Dietrich in L 42 was about 20 miles off the Suffolk coast making his way home. He clearly saw the fireball and through binoculars caught glimpses of aeroplanes in the glare. He radioed the shocking news back to Germany. Strasser, out on the landing field at Nordholz, waited impatiently for L 42's return. He immediately climbed aboard and demanded details of what Dietrich had witnessed – that aeroplanes had shot down L 48, the latest of the 'height-climber' Zeppelins. Dietrich later confided that initially Strasser would not believe him and insisted: 'The English have no real defence against our airships!' Dietrich, however, knew what he had seen. 'But it *was* a plane,' he maintained, 'I saw it myself.' Dejected and depressed by the news, Strasser remained isolated for a while but then his spirits lifted, as they always did, and he wrote a letter to Admiral Reinhard Scheer, commander of the High Seas Fleet and Strasser's direct superior, adding a fresh spin to the situation.

The deliberate minimizing of the effects of the attacks by the English press in my opinion is designed, in conjunction with our losses, to cause us to be doubtful of their success.

If the English should succeed in convincing us that airship attacks had little value and thereby cause us to give them up, they would be rid of a severe problem and would be laughing at us in triumph behind our backs.[30]

Despite the loss of his latest Zeppelin and his able deputy, Viktor Schütze, Strasser had no intention of limiting Zeppelin attacks on Britain, but it would be August before they returned. In the meantime, there were high-level changes within *Kagohl 3*.

***

Following the serious injury to Ernst Brandenburg, von Hoeppner selected 30-year-old *Hauptmann* Rudolf Kleine, currently serving as *Gruppenführer der Flieger 1* at Army Corps Headquarters, Reims, as his replacement. Previously a flight commander with *Kagohl 1*, Kleine, although also recovering from a wound, joined *Kagohl 3* in late June.

Since the London raid, bad weather had prevented any further activity. Around this time, *Leutnant* Walter Georgii replaced Cloessner as *Kagohl 3's* meteorological officer. The relationship between the squadron commander and weather officer remained an important one.

As the new commander, Kleine wanted to make his mark but the conditions continued to hinder operations. Keeping a watchful eye on the weather patterns, *Leutnant* Georgii noted an opportunity on 4 July, but a threat of thunderstorms later in the day meant a raid on London could be dismissed. An early start, however, and an attack on a coastal target would be practical. Kleine chose the twin targets of Harwich and Felixstowe, where the rivers Stour and Orwell meet and exit into the North Sea. Both were home to important naval installations.

4 July 1917, 7.10am: Felixstowe and Harwich

Early on the morning of 4 July the airfields at Gontrode and Sint-Denijs-Westrem reverberated to the roar of 50 Mercedes engines as 25 Gothas took to the air. Kleine planned a course that took the *Englandgeschwader* beyond the prying eyes of the Dunkirk squadrons and away from the observant lightship crews. But before long some of those engines developed problems and seven of the force turned back.

At 6.50am, 9 miles north of Harwich, a two-seater DH4 of the RFC Testing Squadron left Martlesham Heath on an endurance test. On board were pilot Captain John Palethorpe with Air Mechanic Jessop as observer/gunner. After about 15 minutes, much to their surprise, the crew saw the widely spread Gotha formation flying at 14,000ft and crossing the Suffolk coast near the hamlet of Shingle Street. Undaunted, and at odds of 18 to 1, Palethorpe, unwisely headed for the centre of the group whereupon his forward firing machine gun jammed and although Jessop's rear gun fired about 100 rounds, a significant number of *Kagohl 3's* gunners returned fire and one bullet pierced Jessops' heart, killing him instantly. Unfazed, Palethorpe returned to Martlesham, picked up another observer and returned to action, but by then the Gothas had gone. His 'great courage and determination', earned him the Military Cross, with Jessop's 'gallant and distinguished' service marked with a posthumous mention in despatches.

Over Ramsholt on the River Deben, *Kagohl 3* divided into two sections, one heading for Felixstowe and the other towards Shotley and Harwich harbour. The first of the Harwich Garrison guns opened fire at 7.10am but clouds made observation difficult as the sections broke up. The attack shocked local people.

> The strange noise and the dropping of the bombs signalised the arrival of the raiders… It was sudden and surprising, for there had been no warning. The [Gothas] had come hidden by the clouds and in a stiff north-easterly breeze. The clouds skidded across the sky, and at intervals the German flyers could be seen between them. Bombs fell in quick succession.[31]

The section heading for Felixstowe dropped a couple of 12kg bombs on Trimley Marshes amid a flock of pedigree sheep, killing 21 immediately with 29 others having to be slaughtered due to their injuries. The farmer estimated his loss at £1,000. Seven more bombs also fell in the area but only broke a few windows. In Felixstowe three bombs exploded near the railway station with little impact, but two in Mill Lane struck a detachment of soldiers from the 3rd (Reserve) Battalion, Suffolk Regiment. Although taking cover behind an earth bank, the bombs killed three of the men, fatally injured two more and wounded 10 others. South of the town 11 bombs buried themselves in waste land, two more landed just to the north of Felixstowe Dock and another four detonated near the Beach railway station but without causing damage. The impact of the final two bombs, however, proved costly in terms of life and materiel. They struck the RNAS air station incinerating one of the new H-12 flying boats, and killing six RNAS personnel and three civilian workmen. Another 18 servicemen suffered injury as did a civilian. Turning back out to sea, five bombs fell in the water off the Spa Pavilion.

The other section of *Kagohl* 3 approached Harwich over Shotley, home to the land-based Royal Navy Training Establishment, HMS *Ganges*. About 200 boys were undergoing physical training on the parade ground, among then 16-year-old Archibald Filmer.

> We were about half-way through the first exercise when we are startled to hear aeroplane engines, and, looking skyward, see many aeroplanes coming towards us... 'All right, lads', yells the P.T.I. 'They're only some of our boys on manoeuvres.' We carry on.
>
> Two minutes later – Boom! – the first bomb drops from 'our boys'... 'Scatter for your lives and lie flat!' the P.T.I. shouts. So we scatter, in every direction, so as not to make a target for the enemy, and lie on our backs looking up at the fleet, yet fearing every minute that a bomb will drop on us.[32]

These bombs only broke windows and dug a crater in the parade ground, but more were falling. The RNAS had a kite balloon station near Shotley Gate. On hearing explosions, the men were ordered to scatter as four bombs exploded close by shattering windows, but the blast also claimed the lives of three servicemen. Another 15 bombs then splashed down in Harwich harbour without doing any damage. In response three light cruisers, *Canterbury*, *Concord* and *Conquest*, fired 31 rounds, added to the 135 fired by the seven guns of the Harwich Garrison, all without success. In Harwich a bomb landed outside the church of St Nicholas but failed to detonate, and two that dropped on Dovercourt inflicted only minor damage while filling the air with, 'a blue-black and very evil-smelling smoke'. The last three bombs fell offshore in the mud. The bombers had gone 'in less time than it takes to have a cup of tea', a special constable recalled. Although quick, the raid claimed the lives of 17 men, injured 29 more, destroyed a flying boat and decimated a flock of sheep.

The Gothas were gone by 7.25am. Frustratingly, the RFC only received the 'Readiness' order at 7.24am, with the squadrons receiving the 'Patrol' order between 7.26 and 7.35am. With all credit, three of No. 37 Squadron's Sopwith Pups from Stow Maries were airborne within three minutes of receiving the order to ascend, but still too late to catch the retreating raiders. The first RNAS aircraft were up a minute later from Covehithe, 30 miles to the north-east of Felixstowe. No. 56 Squadron, brought over from the Western Front for just such a moment, flew 21 sorties but, like everyone else, received their orders too late. And due to an oversight, the other squadron withdrawn from front line duty and relocated to Calais, No. 66, did not receive the 'Patrol' order in time to engage the returning aircraft. A flight of Sopwith Camels from No. 4 (Naval) Squadron at Dunkirk attempted to intercept *Kagohl 3* but, following some inconclusive engagements, all Gothas returned safely to their airfields.

For the men of No. 56 Squadron their 15-day sojourn in England neared the end. They had enjoyed themselves immensely as pilot Cecil Lewis, based at Bekesbourne, confided.

> A large marquee was run up as a mess. The Major scrounged some planking, and very soon there was a regular Savoy dancing floor. Visits were paid to Canterbury to enrol the fair sex. Those lightning two or three day acquaintanceships began to ripen… The squadron stood by, gloriously idle. It was a grand war.[33]

The only interruption to this welcome posting being the fruitless patrol on 4 July. The following morning the squadron prepared to return to France. No sooner had they departed than London found itself once more on the front line.

Chapter 5

'The damned impudence'

In London, Lord French had grown increasingly frustrated by the impending departure of No. 56 and No. 66 squadrons, and on 2 July wrote to the War Office expressing the importance of retaining their services for Home Defence. While acknowledging that new efficient fighting machines were slowly arriving, he observed the squadrons' departure left him 'dangerously weak', and added: '... it cannot be supposed that the danger of attack can be any the less after the 5th instant than it is now or has been in the past. In fact, it is probably much greater.'[1]

Unfortunately, due to a bureaucratic error, the War Office did not see the letter until after the squadrons had been released. Frustrated to have received no reply, French wrote to Sir William Robertson, Chief of the Imperial General Staff (CIGS), on 6 July, emphasising the lack of fighters with which to engage the Gothas. Dismissing the older aircraft, with their slow speed and poor rate of climb, Lord French stated he had just 21 effective aircraft (12 Sopwith Pups, three SE5s and six DH4s) with which to oppose the enemy raids, although the DH4s were currently allocated to an Aircraft Acceptance Park and a Testing Squadron. He acknowledged more Sopwith Pups were expected by 15 July but considered this but a drop in the ocean.

> ... I desire to place on record my most emphatic opinion that even with the addition of twelve Sopwith [Pups]... the aeroplanes which I can dispose of are not sufficient for effective action against raids in force. Such raids may certainly be expected, and if London is again subjected to attack the results may be disastrous.[2]

Even as Lord French penned his letter to CIGS, Kleine received information of an expected break in the thundery weather over the North Sea. It offered a window of opportunity to strike at London on 7 July, three days after the attack on Harwich and Felixstowe. The *Englandgeschwader* made ready.

7 July 1917, 9.29am: Margate

Kleine led the formation of 24 Gothas, but out over the North Sea the curse of engine problems forced two to turn back. At 9.14am, observers on the Kentish Knock lightship saw the bombers at a distance and informed London. As usual, a single Gotha detached from the formation to create a distraction on the north Kent coast. At 9.29am the lone raider approached the Cliftonville area of Margate as the local anti-aircraft guns engaged, firing 115 rounds without result. The Gotha released three bombs. One smashed through the roof and practically demolished a house at 11 Arundel Road, the home of retired London businessman James Marks, his wife Jane and Agnes Cooper, their housekeeper. The two women were killed instantly and Mr Marks died soon after; two women and a child in the damaged neighbouring properties received slight injuries. Another exploded in the back garden at 7 Prices Avenue, wrecking the rear of the house, and one between Crawford Gardens and Northdown Road damaged property nearby, but there were no more injuries. The guns were in action for just three minutes before the Gotha departed.

7 July 1917, 10.20am: London

The 'Patrol' order, issued between 9.24 and 9.33am, saw 15 RFC formations respond (four Home Defence Squadrons, five Training Squadrons, three Aircraft Acceptance Parks, one Depot Squadron, one Experimental Station and a Testing Squadron). The first RNAS aircraft took off at 9.27am, followed a minute later by three RFC aircraft of No. 37 Squadron, but at airfields across south-east England many more were only minutes behind. Between them the RFC and RNAS flew 108 sorties. The Gothas crossed the Essex coast near the mouth of the River Crouch at about 9.45am, engaged by two mobile anti-aircraft guns near Southminster, the first of 56 guns to engage the enemy that morning. About ten pilots encountered *Kagohl 3* on the way to London, but neither they nor the anti-aircraft guns managed to divert the *Englandgeschwader* from its mission.

'The damned impudence'

At about 10.10am the squadron appeared over Brentwood in Essex whereupon it turned towards Epping Forest, the landmark selected by Kleine as the point from where he would head for London. Five minutes later the first of the London guns opened fire. The turning manoeuvre also saw *Kagohl* 3 split into two wings, the left wing heading south from Waltham Abbey towards the City, while the right wing approached from the north-west, observed from Hendon and Hampstead between 10.20 and 10.30am, ready to sweep in behind the first wave.

The left wing dropped the first bombs, these falling near St Pancras at around 10.20am. One killed a man and injured three people when it blasted 12 houses in Wellers Court, Pancras Road. In Shoreditch 18 bombs destroyed two houses, severely damaging several more and inflicting minor damage on around 200 others. These bombs killed 15 and injured 67, and in Golden Lane, just south of Old Street, another killed David Murdock and Frederick Billington while 19 others suffered injury.

As the leading aircraft approached the City, the stragglers dropped bombs at about 10.30am over Chingford, Edmonton, Tottenham and Stoke Newington. Great damage occurred in Edmonton at the works of the Vegetable Oil Company in Angel Road, while in Stoke Newington hundreds of windows were smashed in Cowper and Wordsworth roads. The furious fire of the anti-aircraft guns, however, led to casualties too as unexploded shells or shell fragments fell to earth.

Bombs also claimed lives in Dalston. In Boleyn Road, William Stanton heard someone shout, 'The Germans!' Looking up he 'saw the aeroplanes. People were running everywhere. There was a terrible explosion, and a hundred yards away three houses were blown to the ground'.[3]

Also in Boleyn Road, James Lewis and his wife Rose heard the crash of explosions and piled furniture in the corner of a room, telling their children to stay there. Mr Lewis then went to the door and began talking to a man on the other side of the road when two bombs fell. 'I screamed to him to come in,' Mrs Lewis explained, 'and, getting no reply, ran to the door, to find my husband lying dead.' Distraught, Mrs Lewis gathered her children; she had blood running from her throat and 4-year-old Walter had injuries too. She got him to hospital but his injuries were so bad he died; they buried him alongside his father.[4] Others were killed too.

Lewis had been speaking to Phillip Frantzmann, a naturalised German baker. The blast killed him and his 19-year-old daughter, Elizabeth, and a friend, Henry Hoppe, another German baker. A delivery boy, 12-year-old Charles Summers, passed the spot just as the bomb exploded: 'A youth who was passing on a bicycle was absolutely destroyed, portions of his body being blown into our building as far as the back wall.'[5]

Hearing that her son had been hurt, his mother made a desperate search and found him in hospital, his body covered by a sheet. Mrs Summers asked to see him.

> They told me it would be best if I did not... Whilst they were taking full particulars I snatched the sheet off, and received the terrible shock, for there lay my poor boy almost unrecognisable... After that I collapsed.[6]

Bombs were now falling on the 'square mile' of the City of London; they just missed St Bartholomew's Hospital. A patient, Evelyn McEvoy, described a horrific scene inside.

> That morning will live in my memory always like some appalling unearthly nightmare – the screams of helpless, terrified patients as the bombs fell around the hospital; for we couldn't move or take cover; we just had to lie there.
>
> Afterwards some of the victims of the ghastly slaughter were brought in and laid on the floor of the ward, on mattresses, blankets, anything the nurses could lay hands on. Wounds, blood, burnt flesh – groans, and mothers screaming for their children.[7]

Bombs fell in the narrow streets on the eastern side of the hospital, including Bartholomew Close[8] and Cox's Court. In Bartholomew Close fires gutted two warehouses, killing Ebenezer Bird, Bertram Browning, Edwin Scuse, Leonard Wheatley and William Wigzell, and leaving four injured. In Cox's Court fierce fires raged. William George Woolford left his place of work there as the bombs fell, with one exploding close to him and, despite having 'part of his arm and shoulder-blade torn off' and an injury to his left foot, he retained the presence of mind to stagger across to St Bartholomew's Hospital, but he died there later that day.

Seconds later a bomb exploded on the roof of the Central Telegraph Office at the corner of Newgate Street and St Martin's-le-Grand. The bomb smashed through the roof causing extensive damage there and on the top floor. Michael MacDonagh, a journalist at *The Times*, went out to 'pick up something about what has happened'. He got on a bus and spoke to the conductress.

> 'It was simply awful,' she said in gasps of excitement... 'We were running along Newgate Street and had got near the General Post Office when the 'bus was stopped and we were almost shaken out of it by a terrible explosion. Immediately the place became dark with sawdust, which fell all over the 'bus as we jumped off and ran for shelter.'[9]

MacDonagh made towards the General Post Office but discovered it was the Central Telegraph Office that had been hit, and discovered the source of the sawdust.

> Such was the disrupting force of the explosion that it shattered extensive hutments erected for War purposes on the flat roof of the building, reducing most of the timber to a thick shower of sawdust, some of which fell on the omnibus.

MacDonagh also noted that part of the parapet of the roof had crashed down to the street, killing a soldier on sentry duty, 53-year-old Private John Taylor, of the 103rd Protection Company, Royal Defence Corps.

A City of London policeman, Thomas White, on duty at Mansion House, looked on as the Gothas swept over the Bank of England.

> I stood on the steps and watched them. They were flying quite low, swooping down and up again like crows in flight. They passed over George Yard, Lombard Street and dropped a very heavy bomb which failed to explode.[10]

It appears there were two bombs of which one did explode. It smashed through the roof of the Church of St Edmund the King & Martyr, just a few yards from George Yard, damaging the roof which remained unrepaired until October 1919.

In Leadenhall Street explosions shattered a water main and destroyed offices while by Fenchurch Street, Mr Shardlow watched the Gothas approach.

> A pal and I were standing in Mark Lane... when suddenly we heard the drone of aeroplane engines. There coming

towards us, was a whole flight, flying very low. We watched fascinated. And then suddenly they dropped a bomb clean on Ironmongers' Hall.[11]

Three bombs fell in Fenchurch Street, killing a man at No. 163, while the Ironmongers' Hall, headquarters of the Worshipful Company of Ironmongers, one of the City of London's Great Livery Companies, suffered significant damage. At the same time, a bomb sent up a huge plume of water as it exploded in the Thames alongside Billingsgate Fish Market. Another exploded in Lower Thames Street causing a wall of a pub, The Bell, to collapse onto an alley where passers-by had sought shelter. Four died buried under the rubble with seven others extracted safely but injured.

At Tower Hill a young man, S.H. Goth, worked in an office where about 80 people had crowded into the ground floor seeking shelter; the street now deserted except for three abandoned horse-drawn vans. Then a bomb dropped.

> [It] fell a few hundred yards away, and then – a blinding flash, a chaos of breaking glass and the air thick yellow with dust and fumes… Five men had been struck by bomb fragments, and a boy of my own age… died in the afternoon.
>
> Outside was a terrible sight – the horses twisted and mangled (the carts had disappeared except for a few bits of burning debris); the front of the office next door, which had caught the full force, blown clean away.[12]

The bomb in Tower Hill left eight dead and 15 injured, while out in the street 'a fireman with his axe, put the last horse out of its anguish'.

By now some of the Gothas had crossed the Thames and bombs began to drop near London Bridge station, but none hit the target. In Tooley Street, alongside the station, Police Constable Asquith had already halted two runaway horses pulling a van when he attended a warehouse on Battle Bridge Lane where a bomb had landed but failed to explode. Asked to remove it, the nonchalant constable wrapped it in a sack, hoisted it on to his shoulder and carried it off to Tower Bridge police station where all his colleagues clustered around to see – and touch – the still live bomb! But PC Asquith was not happy with one of them later.

[He] brought his two children to look at it, and then, about two hours afterwards had the impudence to tell me it was dangerous and ought not to have been touched.[13]

Although 21 Gothas reached London it appears that as many as four may have been photographing the effects of the raid, leaving the rest to drop the 87 bombs the British authorities accounted for. Equally as worrying was evidence that 49 anti-aircraft shells crashed down on London. Total casualties were given as 54 killed (10 of those by falling shells) and 190 injured (55 by AA). Estimates of monetary damage settled at £205,202, the second highest total of any raid, by airship or aeroplane, during the war.

After the attack the Gothas of *Kagohl 3* lost all appearance of formation as they straggled back across Essex. About 16 RNAS and as many as 76 RFC aeroplanes remained in the air, working individually to try and intercept the raiders. Machine guns from both sides came into play and in the confusion anti-aircraft guns opened fire on friend and foe alike.

One of those defending London, Second Lieutenant Wilfred Salmon, an Australian based at Joyce Green near Dartford with No. 63 (Training) Squadron, had only received his probationary commission 17 days earlier; now he went into action for the first time. Encountering the returning Gothas, Salmon attacked in his Sopwith Pup, firing 55 rounds, but return fire from Gotha G.IV/406/16, commanded by *Leutnant* Adolf Genth, with *Leutnant* G. Radke and *Vizefeldwebel* Kurt Gaede as crew, pierced Salmon's fuel tank, cut a control wire and slashed across his forehead. He made a valiant attempt to land but lost control and crashed. He died from a fractured skull.

Further east along the Thames Estuary, Captain John Palethorpe, from the RFC's Martlesham Heath Testing Squadron, sat at the controls of the same DH4 he had flown during the raid three days earlier which saw his observer/gunner, James Jessop, killed. Now with Air Mechanic F. James manning the rear gun, Palethorpe engaged the Gothas at 15,000ft, but with the odds again already ready stacked against him, his forward firing gun soon jammed leaving James to make the attack.

> My observer fought three of them, moving in to attack, and moving away again to change drums, three of them firing at us all the while... I got a bullet wound in the flesh of the hip, and the blood ran down to my boots, so in order to get down before I lost too much, I put her down with full engine,

my observer continuing to fire until out of range. I landed at Rochford Aerodrome, the machine being very much shot about.[14]

It appears that a No. 37 Squadron Sopwith 1½ Strutter that took off from Rochford, piloted by Second Lieutenant John Young with Air Mechanic Cyril Taylor as observer/gunner, came under fire from anti-aircraft guns, was hit and crashed into the sea near Maplin Sands, offshore from Foulness Island. Anchored off Shoeburyness, the crew of the monitor HMS *General Wolfe* were straining their eyes trying to follow the aerial battle. One of the crew, H. Bennett, saw an aeroplane hit.

> Suddenly a loud cheer rang out as a machine went into a spin and crashed on the surface a few miles ahead; but what dismay spread around the ship when our steamboat returned after rescuing – a man of the R.F.C., who had a large headwound. His words as he was brought on board I have always remembered: 'Go easy, lads. I'm only 18.'[15]

The crew of the monitor had recovered the badly-injured observer, Taylor, but he died soon after. Young's body sank with the wreckage of the aircraft and, despite an extensive search, they were unable to locate it. He was 19.

As the Gothas headed further out to sea some aircraft kept up the pursuit. One of them, an Armstrong Whitworth FK8 of No. 50 Squadron with Second Lieutenant Frederick Grace at the controls and Second Lieutenant George Murray as observer/gunner, attacked a Gotha off the coast near Harwich. But when three other German crews rallied to its defence the British pair disengaged and turned their attention to a straggler at a lower altitude. The crew of this Gotha, *Leutnant der Reserve* Max Elsner, *Vizefeldwebel* Franz Hölger and *Unteroffizier* Georg Mickel, were in trouble.

Grace opened fire at 800 yards with the forward-firing Vickers gun, then flew a zig-zag course closing on the target. Having almost halved the distance, Murray opened fire with the Lewis gun. Grace watched the action.

> The observer opened fire on it, with good results as we saw black smoke coming from the centre section, and the H.A. dived into the sea... We circled round it at 2,000ft., discerning

its markings and two of its passengers mounted on the port wing. We fired off several Very's lights, but failed to attract any attention to the spot... This machine was visibly sinking. We had to leave the spot owing to our petrol supply running low.[16]

By the time a search vessel arrived all trace of the Gotha and its crew had disappeared.

There were other problems for the returning Gothas too. Having sustained damage in combat one crash-landed on the beach at Ostend while another struggled to land in the strong wind at its home airfield, ultimately crashing and bursting into flames. Two of the crew died in the fire while the commander, *Leutnant der Reserve* Max Röselmüller, terribly burnt, succumbed in hospital three days later.

Back in London the journalist Michael MacDonagh noted the reactions of those around him when the skies cleared of German bombers.

> Large numbers of people had come up from the basements and were now in the streets. Not even the sense that the danger was passed brought calm to their ruffled feelings. There was deep exasperation at the audacity, 'the damned impudence,' of the Germans. Did they not show how they despise our defences by twice coming over in broad daylight and successfully carrying off their raids. So the disputations went on.[17]

As the day wore on the raid remained the only topic of conversation as friends as well as strangers exchanged stories of their own personal experiences and shared danger, as MacDonagh bleakly observed.

> But at the bottom was humiliation at the affront which the Germans had put upon us and resentment at the unpreparedness of the Government to repel or avenge it. But is it possible to devise any effective protection of London against attacks from the air? I doubt it. Perhaps it only remains for us to grin and bear it![18]

Those in power, including Sir William Robertson, CIGS, were equally frustrated.

> We saw Saturday's raid from the War Office windows. Our anti-aircraft artillery was apparently of no use, and our

airmen arrived in driblets and were powerless, but succeeded in getting one machine down. The fact is we have not got enough machines to meet our requirements.[19]

Help for London, however, was at hand.

July 1917: London

On the afternoon of the raid, the War Cabinet met and agreed to redirect a new squadron forming for service in France to Home Defence, to instruct Sir Douglas Haig to withdraw two fighting squadrons from front line duty for Home Defence and to consider a reprisal air attack on the town of Mannheim. Haig, weighed down with preparations for the launch of the Third Battle of Ypres (Passchendaele), blasted back a brusque and damning reply.

> Two good fighting squadrons will proceed to England tomorrow as ordered. Request following facts may be laid before War Cabinet at once in connection with this decision. Fight for air supremacy preparatory to forthcoming operations was definitely commenced by us this morning. Both enemy and ourselves have concentrated fighting machines for this struggle in the air which will undoubtedly be the most severe we have yet had. Success in this struggle is essential to success of our operations. Withdrawal of these two squadrons will certainly delay favourable decision in the air and render our victory more difficult and more costly in aeroplanes and pilots. If raid on Mannheim is undertaken in addition our plans will have to be reconsidered entirely and the operations may have to be abandoned.[20]

Suitably admonished, the War Cabinet reduced its request to one squadron and postponed the requested raid on Mannheim. On 10 July, the nominated squadron, No. 46, left France and established itself at Sutton's Farm airfield in Essex.

On 11 July, another meeting of the War Cabinet took place, which concluded that the whole question of Home Defence needed to be reconsidered and, in a very British way, desired to form a committee to examine:

(i) the defence arrangements for home defence against air raids, and
(ii) the air organization generally and the higher direction of aerial operations.

The nominal head of the committee, the Prime Minister, David Lloyd George, took little part in its work. In fact, the 'committee' comprised just one member, Jan Christian Smuts, the former Boer War guerrilla leader, now a lieutenant general and South African statesman. Smuts joined the Imperial War Cabinet early in 1917 and had impressed with his intelligence and analytical mind; he seemed ideal for the task. Recognising the urgency of the first item, Smuts initially focused on that and, wasting no time, presented his report eight days later. He would return to the second point at a later date. In preparing the report he relied heavily on information and recommendations provided by Sir David Henderson, Director-General of Military Aeronautics.

The report highlighted that the system in place, designed to oppose night attacks by Zeppelins, appeared inadequate to face this new daytime threat from German bombers.[21] The three main elements of air defence – observers, RFC and anti-aircraft guns – were receiving their orders independently of each other from GHQ, Home Forces, resulting in a lack of co-ordination. The report recommended 'a senior officer of first-rate ability and practical air experience be placed in executive Command of the air defence of the London area'. It concluded: 'The unity of command which is essential to any warlike operation, whether of an offensive or defensive character, would thus be achieved.'[22]

Smuts report also called for anti-aircraft guns defending London to form a barrage of fire in front of approaching bombers, a concentration of shells breaking up the enemy formation and allowing attacking aircraft to pick off dispersed raiders. It emphasised that immediate attention should be given to the numbers and disposition of guns, adding:

> ... there is at present said to be an insufficiency of guns for this purpose but... we regard the defence of London as so important as to call for exceptional measures, and special endeavours should therefore be made to provide an adequate number of guns for this purpose.

In addition, the report recommended the continuing independence of the RNAS and called for an increase for the RFC, with pilots trained in formation flying to be added to the defence of London. Plans were already underway for three new RFC squadrons[23] to join the Home Defence roster but Smuts urged a speeding up of the process, and further recommended that the loaned No. 46 Squadron should be held in England until such time as they had secured London's defence. The report received acceptance in principle; Lord French would finally get what he had been demanding, and the search for a 'senior officer of first-rate ability and air experience' began.

Two days before Smuts delivered his report came another announcement of great meaning to the British nation. After the raid of 7 July there had been another upwelling of anti-German feeling and attacks on businesses owned by people with German-sounding names, whether they were actually of German origin or not. The rather awkward matter of the German origins of the British Royal Family and their name Saxe-Coburg and Gotha, which included the despised name of the German bombers now terrorising Britain, came under the spotlight too. The king made a swift and final response, a proclamation issued on 17 July announcing his decision to relinquish 'all German Titles and Dignities' and stating 'henceforth our House and Family shall be styled and known as the House and Family of Windsor'.[24]

The debate on the subject of air raid warnings also came to a head following the raid of 7 July. The government now responded to public demand by employing marine distress maroons to alert of approaching enemy aircraft. These were fired from small brass mortars on fire station roofs and exploded in the air, supported by policemen touring the streets on foot, by bicycle and in motor cars with placards bearing the words 'Take Cover', attracting attention with whistles, bells or car horns. Once the raid had passed, policemen would again tour their districts with placards bearing the words 'All Clear' accompanied by Boy Scouts blowing bugles. The maroons were only to be employed to warn of daylight raids, at night only the police warning would be given. The police tested the new system on the evening of 14 July and it proved effective. The final confirmation on the use of the maroons followed on the evening of Saturday 21 July, and as such few members of the public were aware of their introduction when Gothas appeared over Britain again on the Sunday morning.[25]

22 July 1917, 8.10am: Felixstowe

While Britain had been looking to improve its defences, in Belgium, Rudolf Kleine had been unable to follow up his raid on London.

Although not adverse to taking risks, the weather forecasts for the North Sea were bad, often with gale force winds, forcing him to bide his time. Constantly monitoring the weather, *Leutnant* Georgii informed Kleine that he believed there would be an improvement on Sunday, 22 July. After two weeks of bad weather Kleine authorised a raid, but chose a return to the easier twin targets of Felixstowe and Harwich rather than risk a push on London. He ordered 22 Gothas to take part; this time only one dropped out with a faulty engine.

The senior officer of the Harwich Command anti-aircraft guns received word of the approaching German bombers at 8.04am, but within a minute the gunners on the coast saw the formation appearing out of the early morning haze, approaching the coast north of the River Deben. Estimating the formation's height at 15,000ft, the gun at Felixstowe Golf Course, the first to engage, opened fire at 8.07am; three minutes later the first bomb fell about 50 yards out to sea, east of Bawdsey Manor.[26] At Felixstowe, less than 3 miles to the south-west, the explosions caused consternation to early bathers enjoying a dip in the sea. More guns joined in as the Gothas opened their formation and commenced bombing.[27]

The first two landed in fields to the north-east of St Peter & St Paul's Church in Old Felixstowe, followed by one that struck a cottage at the corner of Quinton's Lane and High Road, demolishing the roof and upper floor of the cottage, leaving only the bare walls standing. The couple who lived there were in the garden at the time and escaped serious injury. A bomb at Maybush House inflicted further serious damage, while another, at Uplees House, about 350 yards west of the Town railway station, caused chaos.

> The extension of a detached house was so badly damaged that the inner bedroom could be seen from the outside. Of the two ladies in the house one was in bed, but both were so seriously injured from falling debris that they were taken to hospital.[28]

A bomb caused significant damage to a house named Wanstead Cottage on Garrison Lane, seriously damaging those on either side. Just a short distance along Garrison Lane, 17-year-old barman Edgar Ludbrook ventured outside the Ordnance Hotel having heard explosions. As he did so a bomb exploded, killing him and ripping through a group of soldiers. Sergeant George Taylor and Private Charles Nash, of the 3rd (Reserve) Battalion, Suffolk Regiment were both killed and two other men injured.

Two bombs exploded in Langer Road, running parallel with the beach, bringing down telephone wires and smashing windows at the HQ of the Army Service Corps, injuring two men there; one, Driver Herbert George Broyd, died of his injuries. Continuing southwards towards the Landguard area, a bomb fell on the beach about 100 yards from Manor Terrace where a group of men from 3rd (Reserve) Battalion, Bedfordshire Regiment were on duty. They took cover in a trench but, as the Gothas drew closer, curiosity led some to stand to gain a better view. Eight, including an officer, Second Lieutenant Frederick Amess, were killed and another officer and 15 men injured. Other bombs fell around Landguard Common but caused only a single injury. However, at the RNAS air station at Felixstowe, previously bombed during the 4 July raid, an explosion obliterated an engineer's shed, injuring two men, one of who, Air Mechanic William Allen, later died.

The Gotha formation had split into two when it first came inland, with the second section flying a wider course and approaching Harwich over Shotley. But the move proved largely ineffective. An estimated 13 bombs dropped in the River Stour/Harwich harbour but they only inflicted a little damage to the minesweeper *Touchstone* and injured two of her Royal Naval Reserve crew. On the Harwich side of the Stour, 11 bombs fell between Parkeston and Dovercourt but had little impact of note.

Just seven minutes after the first bomb dropped *Kagohl 3* had turned for home. The British authorities traced 55 bombs and in response the seven guns of the Harwich Garrison fired 273 rounds, but the gunners found observation difficult with many of the Gothas attacking with the sun behind them.

The defence pilots fared little better. The RFC's No. 46 Squadron, brought back to England in response to the raid on London earlier in the month, were first up, taking off at 8.13am from Sutton's Farm, about 50 miles south-west of Harwich. The first RNAS pilots were airborne from Manston at 8.20am, 40 miles south of Harwich. Many more pilots were in the air by 8.30am, flying 122 sorties, but the raiders were already well on their way home by the time most of the pilots reached patrol height.

The experience of No. 37 Squadron proved an interesting one. Flying Sopwith Pups, pilots of A and B Flights had been practising formation flying under Captain Claude Ridley, and the day before the raid had patrolled along the Essex shore of the Thames to familiarise the anti-aircraft gunners with this new tactic. Ridley could have saved himself the trouble. As the aircraft reached the southern end of their patrol line, over the Thames Estuary near Southend, the gun on Canvey Island opened fire at 9.11am on a 'confirmed' hostile formation. One shell hit Ridley's Sopwith Pup, shooting away the engine cowling. His rather terse report summed up his frustration: 'Formation fired at by anti-aircraft guns near Southend. I saw no hostile aircraft.' The official report hints at how serious the incident might have been when it stated: 'It was only owing to the skill and experience of the pilot that he was able to land in safety.' Two mobile guns at Leigh-on-Sea also opened fire on the British formation – twice – while eight other mobile guns also engaged them between 8.50 and 9.35am as patrols passed over the area.

The guns and defence pilots reported no success against the raiders but, as the scattered bombers neared the coast of Belgium, a patrol of No. 48 Squadron, RFC, from Bray Dunes near Dunkirk, intercepted five returning Gothas and brought down one which crashed on the coast.

Although the raid had limited impact, unknown to the crews of *Kagohl 3*, its effect had reached London, over 60 miles away. At 8.30am, some 13 minutes after the bombers had begun their return journey, the new warning maroons started firing all over London for the first time, whereupon 'the great majority of Londoners mistook the "sound bombs" for shells from our anti-aircraft guns'.[29] According to reports, 237 of the maroons were fired from 79 fire stations, following official guidance for each station to fire three at 15-second intervals. But with each fire station receiving the warning at slightly different times it resulted in an unbroken series of explosions lasting for 10 minutes.

> When the last echo of the last 'maroon' was dying away, nine-tenths of the population were firmly of the opinion that no warning whatever had been given, but that a ferocious raid had taken place over some quarter or other of the metropolis, and that it had been responded to by our guns with a bombardment of unexampled energy.[30]

Half-dressed Londoners, their Sunday morning lie-in disturbed, appeared at their doorways: 'London has never before seen such an exhibition of ladies' haircurlers in use. Others, grabbing dressing gowns and coats, rushed to the safety of nearby Underground stations where they crowded on the platforms to wait out the raid'. But it seems that some Londoners took the inconvenience in their stride, as the *Daily Mirror* reported.

One family party who made their way in dressing gowns on to the platform of a tube station near Maida Vale were accompanied by their servant with a long coat hurriedly thrown around her shoulders, and actually carrying a breakfast tray, with eggs, teapot, cups, and bread and jam complete for four![31]

On this occasion the maroons sounded a false alarm but after some adjustments the system achieved a fine level of efficiency. But the maroons were only intended for raids in daylight hours and paradoxically the Gothas never again appeared over London in the daytime.

Chapter 6

'A senior officer of first-rate ability'

August 1917: London

The man selected to command the new London Air Defence Area (LADA), 45-year-old Major General Edward Bailey Ashmore, at the time commanded the guns of 29th Division on the Western Front. Importantly he had trained as a pilot and had previously held positions at brigade level in the RFC. He perfectly fitted the requirements as outlined in Smuts' report. It seems he also had a sense of humour.

> At the time I was... in the line north of Ypres, and my dug-out... was drenched with gas most nights, so that the change to London had, for me at any rate, some advantages. The bombing on the Army fronts had not up to that time amounted to very much, and I am afraid we of the Expeditionary Force were inclined to look on the troubles of London somewhat light-heartedly. The fact that I was exchanging the comparative safety of the Front for the probability of being hanged in the streets of London did not worry me.[1]

Ashmore took up his new position on 5 August 1917. London, within the context of LADA, extended far beyond the capital. It included all the fixed anti-aircraft guns and searchlights of the London, Harwich, Thames and Medway, and Dover commands, as well as mobile anti-aircraft brigades assigned to the Harwich and Dover commands. At the time of his appointment, Ashmore's authority also included six RFC squadrons (Nos. 37, 39, 50, 51, 75 and 78, plus Nos. 44, 61 and 112 now forming) as well as all Observer Corps companies of the Royal Defence Corps east of a line drawn across the country from Grantham in Lincolnshire to Portsmouth in Hampshire. However, the new LADA commander quickly discovered that the guns were going to be a problem.

Lieutenant Colonel Simon, London's gun commander, had requested more guns in June but had seen his plan rejected. He had put forward another scheme on 16 July, supported by Lord French, proposing a ring of gun stations about 25 miles out from London, to break up approaching bomber formations. This plan, requiring many additional guns, also met with rejection from the War Council, with Lord French informed on 9 August, four days after Ashmore took office, that the priority remained to arm merchant ships for defence against U-boats. With no support forthcoming, Simon reshuffled his pack to boost the guns on the main approaches, moving ten there from other parts of the capital and bringing in another 24 from outside London.

Ashmore also considered ways to deal with an increasing 'friendly fire' problem. In response he introduced his 'Green Line' plan, which specified areas of action (see map, p.xix). In essence the 'Green Line' was an imaginary line drawn about 20 miles out from London and surrounding the capital, creating a border before reaching Simon's 25-mile gun line. Beyond this line the guns had priority, but inside it that priority switched to the defending aircraft. Ashmore admitted that he found it difficult to draft the order, with the resulting wording open to interpretation and leading to some errors of judgement at first.[2]

Ashmore also recognised the difficulty in getting information to pilots once they were in the air. In daylight hours, since the latter part of 1916, the Ingram system had operated. It consisted of a large white T-shaped marker placed on the ground at airfields, with white discs arranged around it, each configuration conveying a different message and directing pilots towards enemy aircraft. Ashmore was not impressed.

> Our pilots had little training in the use of this system, and there was too much delay in setting the signals out to make them of any real value. Practically, therefore, the defenders left the aerodromes without organization, and once in the air received no help from the ground.[3]

Ashmore advocated another system, reverting to an idea promoted but not adopted as far back as summer 1915.

> I arranged for large white arrow signals to be laid out at searchlight positions, and at other points where men were

available to work them. The arrow was to be kept pointing to the enemy aircraft so long as they were in sight... Our pilots, seeing the arrow, would know in which direction to look for the enemy. In clear weather these arrows could be seen from a height of 17,000ft.[4]

Also in early August 1917, pairs of BE12s from No. 37 Squadron and No. 50 Squadron were equipped as wireless telegraphy tracker aircraft. The pilots were able to send back basic messages to ground stations in Morse code giving location, number of aircraft, direction and time, but not height. The trackers, however, could only transmit, they could not receive information.

A week after taking up his new role, Ashmore could report: 'Our new arrangements, so far as concerned the squadrons close to London, were in fair working order by 10th August. We had not long to wait for them to be tested.'[5]

On the first day of the Third Battle of Ypres, 31 July 1917, after a two-week preliminary bombardment, the rains came. They continued for three weeks and turned the shattered, cratered landscape into a morass that shaped for many the enduring hellish image of the First World War. This same weather had curbed the impatient Rudolf Kleine for a while, but on 29 July, ignoring the advice of *Leutnant* Georgii, he authorised a raid. Shortly after crossing the Belgium coast, however, Kleine encountered the bad weather Georgii had forecast, forcing him to turn back.

12 August 1917, 5.55pm: Southend-on-Sea

On Sunday, 12 August, the weather cleared a little during the morning and Kleine decided at short notice to make a raid; it seems unlikely Georgii gave his approval. Due to the lack of recent action many of the men had been granted permission to go into Ghent and Kleine could only muster 13 crews. Kleine's own crew did not take part and he gave command of the raid to *Oberleutnant* Richard Walter, the squadron's senior flight commander. They planned to target the naval facilities at Chatham, with Southend-on-Sea marked as the secondary target. Any individual aircraft forced to fall out near the British coast would target places on the north Kent coast as they headed home. Two Gothas soon dropped out with engine issues, while the remaining 11, encountering strong winds from the south-west, were pushed further north than intended. This would have serious consequences later.

At 5.06pm the formation appeared off Felixstowe, some 20 miles north of the usual line of approach. Flying into the face of a stiff wind, *Kagohl 3* followed the coast southwards, managing about 60mph. On reaching the mouth of the Blackwater at 5.30pm, the squadron, now reduced to ten after another had dropped out, followed the river upstream towards Maldon before turning south again, heading towards the airfield at Rochford near Southend, home to the newly formed No. 61 Squadron.

The first RFC pilots took off in response to the raid at 5.14pm while *Kagohl 3* followed the coast southwards, and were from No. 46 Squadron, on loan to Home Defence. Many more took to the air but most settled into their standard patrol lines, anticipating a raid on London. Ashmore decided to hold back No. 61 Squadron, as they had no chance of reaching the Gothas on their inward journey, planning to send them up later to intercept the raiders when he had information on their return course.[6] But as *Kagohl 3* approached Rochford, No. 61 Squadron's commander, Major Edward Pretyman, took matters into his own hands and sent his squadron up.[7]

Two bombs dropped on Rochford airfield at 5.50pm, injuring two RFC mechanics, but caused no damage to buildings. Another dropped harmlessly near a railway line. But Walter could see heavy banks of rain cloud towards London and, battling against the wind, he abandoned the idea of a raid on Chatham. Nearing Canvey Island he fired signal flares redirecting the squadron to the secondary target – Southend. Guns at Shoeburyness and others of the Thames and Medway Garrison now burst into action as the first five bombs dropped on Leigh-on-Sea where one, in Lord Roberts Road, passed sideways through a house and buried itself 6ft below the foundations. Luckily for the occupants it failed to detonate. In the next road, Cliffsea Grove, seven houses were rocked by an explosion but the occupants escaped unhurt.

Passing over Westcliff-on-Sea seven more bombs dropped but three failed to explode while the others did no significant damage. And then, at 5.55pm, on to Southend-on-Sea.

Southend, about 40 miles from London by train, had long been a popular summer destination for the capital's day-trippers and thousands enjoyed the experience each year: a train journey, a walk along the promenade, the beach, the pier, fish and chips for lunch and home before dark. When the ominous drone of Gotha engines filled the sky, many visitors were making their way back to the station for the homeward train to London, 'others were churchgoers, and a number were making purchases at a newsagent's shop and an adjoining restaurant'.[8] With little cover, those that could crowded into shop doorways. At least five bombs fell within a 200-yard radius of the Great Eastern Railway station off Victoria Avenue, and in the roads leading to the station all hell broke loose.

Alderman Martin of Southend had driven into the town from Rochford.

> He came upon a heap of torn and mangled humanity, 20 people in all being involved, and at once conveyed bodies to the mortuary. In the roadway was a little girl [12-year-old Dorothy Rice] who was on her way to a Salvation Army meeting and who was killed. Another victim was a mother of two children, the latter escaping with injuries.[9]

Walter and Edith Batty had taken their two children to Southend for the day; the parents were both killed and their children injured. Jessie Orton from Bethnal Green died, as did her 5-year-old daughter. Thomas Cornish died too, alongside his 13-year-old daughter Emily, as did a married couple, John and Leah Cohen from Plaistow. It took three or four days before the remains of another woman were identified; Ada Childs was 32 and lived near Regent's Park in London.

Two bombs just overshot the station. The first exploded in Milton Street.

> 'I heard a torpedo whistling through the air,' said a man who did heroic rescue work. 'It fell ten yards off as I lay on my face. Down came another and another quite near. I thought I was a dead man. On the other side of the street a Salvation lassie and an old railway guard [Charles Humphries] lay dead.'[10]

The second of these bombs smashed into a house in Guildford Road and destroyed it. Of the five people inside two, cousins Frederic Hawes (14) and Lena Gooding (7), were killed. About a mile beyond the station an explosion wrecked a house in Lovelace Gardens where a family of three were having tea. Elizabeth West and her daughter Gladys died but Mr West escaped unharmed.

The raid ended by 6.00pm, the final two bombs dropping over Bournes Green and Little Wakering but neither detonated. In the greater Southend area 32 people were dead (17 were from London) and 46 injured. But it could have been worse. Of the 34 bombs that fell between Rochford and Little Wakering, 16 failed to explode.

The official German statement issued to the Press reported:

> One of our aviation squadrons yesterday attacked England. Bombs were dropped with visibly good results on the military works of Southend and Margate at the mouth of the Thames. One of our aircraft is missing.[11]

At the same time Southend's chief constable, H.M. Kerslake, could not fathom the reason for the attack: 'There is nothing that we should consider a military objective in Southend.'[12]

While *Kagohl* 3 headed homewards with RFC pilots in pursuit, notably from No. 61 Squadron, another 12 bombs fell in the sea. But as the German press release confirmed, bombs had also fallen on Margate.

12 August 1917, 5.40pm: Margate

The lone Gotha that dropped out of the formation earlier with engine problems passed over Margate on its return journey. At 5.40pm anti-aircraft guns opened fire and this attracted RNAS pilots who had taken off earlier from Manston, Eastchurch and Walmer, many flying first-class Sopwith fighting machines, such as the Camel, Triplane and Pup. The first bomb fell in the sea before the bomber passed inland and dropped three more in the Cliftonville district. The first wrecked an unoccupied house in Surrey Road, the second landed in the grounds of Laleham School on Lower Northdown Road, the third about 250 yards further south, in the grounds of Surrey House School on Laleham Road. These last two smashed windows, broke down doors and sent ceilings crashing to the floor amidst great clouds of plaster dust. Back out over the sea and pursued by as many as nine RNAS pilots, the Gotha led a charmed life and, despite attacks from at least six of the pursuers, eventually crossed the Belgium coast on one engine at a height of just 600ft, crash-landing near Ostend. Against the odds the pilot had brought the crew home.[13]

Flight Lieutenant Harold Kerby had been amongst the pursuers in a Sopwith Pup, but had not managed to engage and turned back. About 30 miles from the British coast, Kerby saw a group of eight Gothas pursued by British aircraft. He attacked but it came to nothing, then he spied a lone Gotha some 4,000ft below the main group and made his move.

> Attacked from front and drove him down to water where observed him to turn over. Saw one of occupants hanging

on to tail of Gotha. Threw him my lifebelt and did two or three circuits around him and returned to England. On way back observed four Destroyers when at 6000 ft going towards Dunkirk. Fired 3 Very's lights to try and get them to follow [me] back to machine in water but they continued on their course.[14]

Although he failed to draw help to the scene, Kerby received the award of the Distinguished Flying Cross for his actions.[15]

The crew of the downed Gotha were lost: 22-year-old commander *Leutnant der Reserve* Hans Rolin, *Unteroffizier* Rudi Stolle, 25, (pilot) and *Unteroffizier* Otto Rosinsky (gunner), aged 21. But *Kagohl 3* also lost four other Gothas. As well as the aircraft that crash-landed near Ostend, three others also crashed; one had simply used up the very last drop of fuel as the pilot prepared to land. The wind that had pushed the Gothas further up the coast, and the subsequent battle against it, had consumed valuable fuel. Others may have suffered battle damage, adding to the already inherent difficulties encountered when landing a Gotha. Of the 11 Gothas that had taken part in the raid, defenders had shot down one and four crashed; *Kagohl 3* paid a heavy price. The crews of *Kagohl 3* claimed three British aircraft shot down, but all pilots returned unharmed.

In Britain, those senior officers concerned with aerial defence had been surprised by the raid, as is shown in the official – secret – report distributed in October 1917; it made no hesitation in pointing the finger of blame for the German losses.

> One of the most interesting features of the raid is the comparatively unfavourable nature of the weather in which it was carried out. It was hardly expected that a raid would be attempted on 12th August. The reason is to be found in the character of *Hauptmann* Kleine, who is known to be a rash and headstrong officer, obsessed by the desire to raid London. He has on several occasions endangered the safety of his machines by taking them out, or ordering them to be taken out for this purpose, in weather utterly unsuited for long distance raiding purposes, and he is responsible for having caused a large number of them to crash in such weather.[16]

There were also other technical issues that both sides needed to investigate. British pilots were experiencing a great number of gun jams when closing to attack and many of the German bombs were failing to detonate.

August 1917: Germany

While Kleine took stock of his problems, the new moon on 17 August heralded the darkest nights of the month and offered a raiding opportunity for Strasser's Zeppelins. But that date also set a limit on the further development of the Naval Airship Division. Up to this time the division had been receiving, on average, two new Zeppelins per month. The army's *Erster Generalquartiermeister*, Erich Ludendorff, proposed in July an increase in aeroplane production. To facilitate this, he recommended halting airship construction and redirecting the aluminium and rubber to aeroplanes. Admiral Scheer, commanding the High Seas Fleet, leapt to the defence of the Naval Airship Division, pointing out that German bombers were limited to the south-east corner of Britain while Zeppelins could reach the industrial north and midlands. To continue these raids at least one new Zeppelin per month would be needed and, even if the raids were abandoned, a new Zeppelin every two months would still be required to fulfil North Sea reconnaissance duties. On 17 August, the matter reached a conclusion. In future the High Seas Fleet in the North Sea would be limited to 18 Zeppelins with the Naval Airship Division overall capped at 25 and 27 crews, with replacement airships restricted to roughly one every two months.[17]

Although experiencing a favourable phase of the moon, the weather did not immediately suit a raid on Britain, but scouting missions and patrols continued. One took place in the early hours of 21 August when L 23 left Tondern and headed north up the Jutland coast.[18] Some miles in the distance her commander, *Oberleutnant-zur-See* Bernhard Dinter, sighted a British light cruiser squadron with supporting destroyers. One of the cruisers, HMS *Yarmouth*, carried a Sopwith Pup able to fly off a platform fitted over her forward guns. The pilot, 25-year-old Flight sub-Lieutenant Bernard Smart, waited while HMS *Yarmouth* turned into the wind and increased her speed as he prepared for the hazardous take-off. Although some miles off and disappearing behind clouds at times, Smart remained focused on L 23, climbed quickly and closed on the Zeppelin as it turned away from the naval squadron. Dinter transmitted a wireless message: 'Am pursued by enemy forces.'[19] Smart, flying at 7,000ft, had managed to get above L 23, then took up a position to the Zeppelin's rear and attacked.

[I] dived at roughly an angle of 45 degrees getting up a speed of 130 knots [150mph]. One man and machine gun was observed on top of envelope, but I zigzagged slightly until quite near... When within 150 to 200 yards fired burst of 10 to 15 shots, but they went rather high so nose-dived, flattened out and fired continuously until within 20 yards of stern when flames broke out and I made a sharp dive and swerve to avoid ramming Zeppelin. Having recovered myself I looked back to observe effect.[20]

His eyes fixed on the fiercely burning stern of the L 23 as the airship rapidly fell away. The flames spread quickly and by the time it hit the sea only a small part of the forward section remained intact. A column of dense black smoke reached 'an apparently enormous height' as oil and fuel burned on the surface. Dinter and his 17-man crew were all killed. Bernard Smart located the naval squadron and ditched in the sea close to a pair of destroyers. Soaked through and cold, he determinedly clung to the tailplane of his slowly sinking Sopwith Pup as he waited for the rescue boats to pick him up. His achievement saw him awarded the Distinguished Service Order, but the reason for the award remained secret, preventing information on the cause of L 23's destruction reaching Germany.

22 August 1917, 12.30am: East Yorkshire

Later that same day, 21 August, Strasser considered the weather suitable and ordered a raid by L 35, L 41, L 42, L 44, L 45, L 46, L 47 and L 51. Both L 35 and L 51 turned back early, while Strasser accompanied the raid onboard L 46, his deputy, Viktor Schütze, lost in the destruction of L 48 over England back in June.

The remaining six Zeppelins arrived off the Yorkshire coast at about 8.30pm, remaining over 60 miles out to sea for around three hours before making their move. But although the officers variously reported bombing shipping near Spurn Head and raids on Lincolnshire, there are no British reports, either official or in the local press, of any bombs falling in these places. What is clear is that the Zeppelins were all at great height – up to 20,000ft – and in the extreme cold experienced at this altitude, liquid compasses froze, despite adding as much as 44 per cent alcohol to prevent such an occurrence.[21]

Only Kuno Manger's L 41 made an incursion over Britian that night. He appeared intent on attacking Hull but, thwarted by vigilant searchlights and anti-aircraft guns, his movements were restricted to the area east of the city. Due to L 41's great height it proved difficult to hold her in the beams of light and for the gunners to accurately find the range, but their efforts appear to have acted as a deterrent.

L 41 crossed the Yorkshire coast near Tunstall at 12.03am heading inland and, after some meandering, dropped an incendiary bomb over the village of Elstronwick, probably for the crew to estimate ground speed, or perhaps even to determine if they were over land or sea.[22] From there, heading south-west, Manger passed a few miles east of Hull, remaining unseen until heading between Paull and Ryehill at about 12.30am.

> From many points brilliant searchlights were raking a clear starlit sky, and about one o'clock a silvery Zeppelin was revealed in what looked like a circle of fire, and it was quickly exposed to terrific gunfire.[23]

The searchlight at Paull found L 41 first, at about 12.48am; the Zeppelin slowly began to move towards it.

> Now and then flashes would leave the ship, followed by loud explosions; but the noise of the bombardment was so great that it was difficult to distinguish bombs from guns.[24]

L 41 released seven bombs as she approached Paull, but all landed in open country and were ineffective. At the same time guns at Paull, Marfleet and Chase Hill Farm commenced firing. Held by the lights and under fire, Manger turned away from Paull and at 1.00am passed over Hedon where he dropped five more explosive bombs.

Damage on the east side of the town, on Baxter Gate, affected 11 cottages. And more followed.

> All that remains of the Primitive Methodist Chapel are the four walls, which enclose a great heap of debris. The entire building is gutted, the bomb having smashed the pews, pulpit, and galleries to atoms. Across the way, and within a hundred yards, the Roman Catholic Church suffered considerably.[25]

Damage also occurred at a YMCA hut on the Burstwick Road where a man received slight injuries, the only casualty of the raid. Manger continued and just over a mile further on released three explosive and 12 incendiary bombs, which landed a mile east of the village of Preston. Somewhat surprisingly, L 41 then turned about and headed south once more, using cloud cover where possible, but at 1.10am the Marfleet searchlight found her. Five minutes later, L 41 dropped a single bomb over Thorngumbald, a village between Paull and Ryehill, as guns at Paull and Marfleet opened fire again. At 1.19am L 41 reached the Humber, seemingly uncertain which way to go as searchlights and guns on the south side of the river now joined in, as did others onboard the scout cruiser HMS *Patrol* and the destroyer HMS *Nith*. The hunted Zeppelin climbed rapidly, turned away and disappeared into clouds, Manger making good his escape.

RFC pilots from No. 33 and No. 76 squadrons flew 21 sorties that night, but only nine of these took place with L 41 still overland. Yet the aircraft forming the northern squadrons were just not capable of engaging raiders at the heights Zeppelins could now reach. Only two pilots saw L 41, but just one, Second Lieutenant Herbert Solomon of No. 33 Squadron, flying a BE12a from Scampton, opened fire, although he knew the target was beyond the range of his guns.[26]

Although other Zeppelin commanders claimed successful raids, where their bombs fell remains a mystery. There were unconfirmed reports of Zeppelins and explosions far inland, but no bombs were traced and these were dismissed at the time. Strasser, on board L 46, claimed he came inland and saw the lights of a big city which he thought could be Sheffield but turned back as he felt the distance too great. There were reports from Doncaster of the sound of Zeppelin engines; Doncaster is about 15 miles north-east of Sheffield. Strasser then states that L 46 flew back towards the coast, dropping bombs on Louth, but no bombs fell anywhere in Lincolnshire.

The raid proved ineffective, causing damage estimated at just £2,272, but those responsible for Home Defence were beginning to realise that a new class of Zeppelin had arrived, one that could operate beyond the reach of the northern defences.

***

While Strasser had been fighting for the future of the Naval Airship Division and preparing for his latest raid against the north of England, at the Ghent headquarters of *Kagohl 3*, after the disappointment and losses of the raid on 12 August, Rudolf Kleine remained as keen as ever to try again. So keen, in fact, that on 18 August he once more ignored the advice of the weather officer, *Leutnant* Georgii. While Belgium may have been experiencing good weather, it did not indicate the conditions approaching over Britain. Not a single bomber reached England and for *Kagohl* 3 it evolved into the worst single day in the unit's history.

Kleine ordered all available Gothas to take part and 26 departed the Ghent airfields. When well out to sea it became apparent that strong winds had blown the formation far north of its planned course. Kleine ordered *Kagohl* 3 to turn back but they became scattered in the difficult conditions. One Gotha returned direct and only just made the coast before it crash-landed near Zeebrugge. Others passed over neutral Dutch territory and came under heavy fire; two were damaged and, having made emergency landings, their crews were interned by the Dutch. Others managed to reach friendly territory but were forced down or crash-landed when fuel supplies became exhausted. The exact figure is unclear but of the 26 Gothas that took part in the aborted raid, two came down in the Netherlands, one near Zeebrugge and perhaps as many as nine others suffered damage to a greater or lesser extent. Inevitably crews were lost and injured and a least one officer died. Another disaster for Kleine, and one of his own making.

22 August 1917, 10.30am: Margate and Ramsgate

Undeterred by the losses, however, Kleine launched his next raid just four days later. The implications of the previous raid meant only 15 Gothas were available. But with ever present engine malfunctions, five turned back early, including Kleine's own aircraft. Command of the raid again passing to the senior flight commander, Richard Walter. This time the plan did not include London, instead Sheerness or Chatham as well as Dover were the targets.

News of the bombers approach telephoned from the Kentish Knock lightship at 10.06am led to the first RNAS aircraft getting airborne nine minutes later, swiftly followed by the first of the RFC fighters, taking up their patrol lines to protect London. The defenders flew 138 sorties.

The German bombers were again observed at 10.30am as they approached the north-eastern corner of Kent.[27]

> They were moving slowly... like a flock of birds, in the shape of an inverted letter 'V'. Anti-aircraft gunners quickly sighted them, and found the range in a remarkably short space of time. Shrapnel could be seen bursting round the raiders...,

> the invaders appeared like silvery dragon flies glistening in the sunlight. They dodged in and out of the white and black puffs of smoke which appeared just below them.[28]

The anti-aircraft guns held nothing back and blasted 537 rounds into the sky over the next 16 minutes. And RNAS fighters were engaging too. This combined attention of guns and aircraft proved deadly.

> Presently one of the raiders was seen to shudder, and slip sideways. She dropped very slowly, with a spinning motion, then suddenly did something that looked like an attempt to loop the loop. Recovering herself for a moment, she seemed to stand still in the sky, turned completely over, and plunged towards the sea. Margate's cheer nearly drowned the thunder of the guns.[29]

The Gotha came down at sea about three-quarters of a mile off Margate. Her commander *Leutnant* Walter Latowski and the pilot, *Leutnant* Werner Joschkowetz, died but the 19-year-old gunner, *Unteroffizier* Bruno Schneider, survived, found clinging to the tailplane of the sinking Gotha by the crew of the destroyer HMS *Kestrel*. From the confusing aerial engagement three RNAS pilots shared a claim for shooting down the Gotha.

But the remaining Gothas were also in trouble – one shell burst under a Gotha's wing.

> A tongue of fire leapt out from the rear of the aeroplane and it began to descend… The sight of the falling Gotha fascinated and enthralled. Though the machine was rapidly descending the pilot, with a wonderful display of airmanship, managed to keep the keel of his craft fairly even. But as the fire spread the wings fell away and the remainder came toppling down in a shapeless mass.[30]

The bulk of the Gotha fell in a field about 2 miles from the coast. Despite the best efforts of a farmer, *Oberleutnant* Echart Fulda, *Unteroffizier* Heinrich Schildt and *Vizefeldwebel* Ernst Eichelkamp all died.

With two of his ten aircraft already shot down, Kleine fired flares to divert his remaining force to Dover, but the message, unclear or not seen, saw bombs dropped on Margate and Ramsgate before they reached Dover.

At Margate five hastily dropped bombs fell with limited effect. One wrecked an unoccupied house in Windsor Avenue and seriously damaged the neighbouring property, and two that landed in Approach Road smashed windows in about 60 properties in the vicinity. An unexploded bomb smashed through the roof of 42 Cliftonville Avenue and another buried itself in a potato plot near St Mildred's Road. There were no injuries.

A single bomb landed in a farmer's field near Broadstairs before the main attack descended on Ramsgate, where 34 bombs fell over a wide area of the town. A number large buildings, formerly schools, were now occupied by the Canadian military which had a strong presence in the area, being utlised as military hospitals, including Chatham House, which suffered a direct hit, Townley Castle, where three bombs exploded in the grounds, destroying tents and out buildings, and St Lawrence College where three bombs in the grounds smashed numerous windows. The Chatham House bomb crashed through the roof and down to the basement before exploding, causing extensive damage, and killing Private David Crighton of the Canadian Army Medical Corps, working as a butcher/cook, and injuring others. Shortly after the raid the Canadian authorities moved all their hospitals away from the Ramsgate area. A bomb in Church Hill, outside the newspaper offices of the *Thanet Advertiser*, struck another Canadian soldier, Gunner John Paul, who had taken shelter there. '[It] mutilated him so terribly,' the newspaper reported, 'that he died soon afterwards.'[31]

Most of casualties were caused by a bomb that exploded on Military Road at the harbour where granite mooring posts on the quayside 'were snapped off like carrots'.[32] A number of storage facilities cut into the chalk became makeshift shelters, but when the bomb exploded some people were still standing at the entrances. Six men and a 5-year-old girl, Nellie Fox, were killed or died of their injuries, with others badly wounded. One of those killed, Walter Spain, had been out of work for some time but had secured a job earlier that morning. He had gone home, changed his clothes and was on his way back to begin his new job when the raid began. He died while seeking protection at the shelters.[33]

Other bombs narrowly missed the Ramsgate County School, the Public Library and St George's Church where people were sheltering in the crypt. The bomb smashed stained glass windows and damaged neighbouring properties. At Ramsgate Town Station a bomb struck one of the platforms 'shattering a great amount of glass and practically destroying a building which was being used as an emergency canteen to supply the immediate requirements of wounded soldiers' as they arrived from France, but everyone there escaped injury. Elsewhere, in Picton Road, where 'houses were shockingly damaged,' three children were injured.[34] Other explosions ravaged buildings in Prince's Street, High Street, Boundary Road, Alexandra Road, Percy Road, Hollicondane Road, Duncan Road and St Mildred's Road. Casualties in Ramsgate rose to nine killed and 22 injured.

22 August 1917, 11.10am: Dover

The remaining eight Gothas headed south along the coast towards Dover, engaged by anti-aircraft guns and harried by pilots of the RNAS. A bomb dropped harmlessly in a field at Whitfield then, at 11.10am the Dover guns opened fire, which persuaded two of the Gothas to head straight out to sea, leaving the other six to unload nine bombs on the town.

The first of these exploded in the yard of the Admiral Harvey public house on Bridge Street, killing 17-year-old barmaid Lucy Wall. She had been in the yard and had just asked a neighbour standing at a window if the aeroplanes were German. She told Lucy they were and urged her to go inside, when 'something fell like a flame of fire fell past the window, and burst below'. Lucy died before helpers could get her on to a stretcher. One of those first on the scene, Ernest Ewell, described the scene in the yard where he found Lucy lying.

> There was a bad wound at the top of the left arm, and a deep wound below the left breast. She was lying about 10 yards from the hole made by the bomb, and on the wall behind her, at about the same height as the wounds were marks where it had been struck by pieces of the bomb.[35]

A bomb in Priory Hill failed to detonate, but another in the grounds of Dover College caused significant damage while injuring four soldiers and two officers – two of the soldiers later died. At 53 Folkestone Road a bomb that passed right through the house failed to detonate, narrowly missing two of the occupants. And at Dover Castle two bombs near the keep killed a horse and seriously injured a soldier of the Royal Defence Corps; two more fell in the harbour close to the RNAS seaplane station.

A Sopwith Camel piloted by Flight sub-Lieutenant Edward Blake from RNAS Manston, one of those who pursued the Gothas to Dover, received credit for shooting down a third Gotha as the raiders turned for home. Of the ten bombers that had reached Britain, three had been shot down and another crashed as it neared Ghent with the loss of all onboard. Added to the losses during the aborted raid four days earlier and those incurred in the raid of 12 August, the situation appeared unsustainable. Kleine urgently needed to reassess his strategy.

For Edward Ashmore it had been eventful first 18 days in command of the wider London defences. But he had no time to feel complacent because the elements that made up LADA – the aeroplanes, guns, searchlights and observers – would soon be facing a new, more challenging examination.

Chapter 7

'I shall never forget that night'

The resources deployed to oppose the raid on the morning of 22 August were impressive. The Kent anti-aircraft guns fired 1,449 rounds at the ten Gothas, which had quickly been reduced by losses to eight and then seven by the time they set course back to Belgium. In addition, the RNAS had 17 aircraft airborne from the air stations at Dover, Eastchurch, Manston and Walmer, harrying and attacking the raiders. At the same time the RFC flew 121 sorties, despatched from the usual wide-range of RFC formations, an increasing number of which were made by first rate fighters. Most of these aircraft took off in anticipation of an attack on London so did not see action, but it demonstrated how far the defence organisation had progressed in the short time since the daylight raids commenced three months earlier. In addition, aircraft based in France had kept up the pressure on the returning Gothas, and for the first time a BE12 'tracker' aeroplane, flown by Second Lieutenant Leonard Lewis of No. 50 squadron, transmitted a wireless telegraphy message from air to ground giving the position and direction of the Gothas returning past Dover.

Back in July, Lieutenant General Smuts had been asked to prepare a report looking into Home Defence arrangements against air raids and secondly, the air organization generally and the higher direction of aerial operations. He had delivered the first report on 19 July then, on 17 August, came the second part. Again, he had listened to those with expert knowledge, and once more Lieutenant General Sir David Henderson, Director General of Military Aeronautics, proved a big influence. The report's recommendations proved momentous.

Looking ahead, Smuts acknowledged the likely future impact of air power.

> As far as can at present be foreseen there is absolutely no limit to the scale of its future independent war use. And the day may not be far off when aerial operations with their devastation of enemy lands and destruction of industrial and populous centres on a vast scale may become the principal operations of war, to which the older forms of military and naval operations may become secondary and subordinate.[1]

Smuts recommended the creation of an Air Ministry to replace the rather limited scope of the current Air Board, and an air force independent of the army and navy. He advocated '[A Ministry] consisting of a Minister with consultative Board on the lines of the Army Council or Admiralty Board... This Ministry to control and administer all matters in connexion with aerial warfare of all kinds whatsoever'. Within this ministry 'an Air Staff be instituted on the lines of the Imperial General Staff responsible for the working out of war plans, the direction of operations, the collection of intelligence, and the training of the air personnel'.[2]

And then came the recommendation directly affecting the personnel of the RNAS and RFC.

> That the Air Ministry and Staff proceed to work out the arrangement necessary for the amalgamation of the [RNAS] and [RFC] and the legal constitution and discipline of the new Air Service, and to prepare the necessary draft legislation and regulations, which could be passed into operation next autumn and winter.[3]

Smuts' recommendations were accepted by the War Council on 24 August. For now, the RNAS and the RFC continued their separate courses, but on 1 April 1918 a new independent air organisation would take to the skies – the Royal Air Force.

Interestingly, Hugh Trenchard, commanding the RFC in France, and often considered the 'father of the air force' had opposed the change during wartime.

> I thought that if anything were done at the time to weaken the Western Front, the war would be lost and there would be no air service, united or divided... Henderson had twice the insight and understanding that I had. He was prepared to run risks rather than lose a chance which he saw might never

come again. He did so with no thought of self-interest, and it is doubtful whether the R.A.F. or Britain realises its debt to him, which is as least as great as its debt to Smuts.[4]

Britain's air defences had acquitted themselves well in August and plans were in motion to secure a wider, more co-ordinated commitment to the future of air defence. Yet this comfortable position, without warning, now turned upside down – Rudolf Kleine switched *Kagohl 3* from daylight to night-time raids.

The losses suffered by *Kagohl 3* during August could not be allowed to continue. While aeroplanes could be replaced, it took time to train new crews to replace those killed or injured in combat or the increasing numbers injured or killed in landing accidents. After the raid on 22 August, Kleine halted the campaign. The switch to night bombing meant an intense period of training for his crews to acquaint themselves with the very different experience of flying and navigating over the featureless North Sea in the dark. But unlike the Zeppelins, which used the darkest nights of the month to try and hide their great bulk, the smaller and more nimble Gotha aircraft timed their attacks to coincide with brighter moonlit nights.

***

2 September 1917, 11.05pm: Dover

On the night of 2 September, while *Kagohl 3* were completing their retraining, another squadron attacked Dover. That night *Kagohl 4*, generally employed against Allied positions on and behind the Western Front, made an attack on the French Channel ports. A very clear, starry night meant those on the Kent coast could see the anti-aircraft fire. Then, without warning, the action moved closer to home.

> ... at 10.55pm we could distinctly hear Aircraft approaching from S.E. and was over us at 11.05pm, a few minutes later bombs were dropped on Dover... Neither the anti-aircraft guns or searchlights of the Dover defences came into action.[5]

Dover had indeed been caught off-guard. A single aircraft had broken off from the raid on the French coast, its crew making an attack on Dover. It came inland close to Dover Castle where three bombs fell on the camp of the 6th (Reserve) Battalion, Royal Fusiliers, at Northfall Meadow. One of them destroyed a hut, killing Second Lieutenant Henry Larcombe and injuring another officer of the battalion and two men of a Labour Corps company attached to the Fusiliers.

Passing on the north side of Dover Castle, the next bomb, a dud, fell in the grounds of a VAD hospital at Castlemount. The authorities showed much interest in the bomb, an adapted 25-cm trench mortar shell nicknamed by British soldiers the 'Crashing Christopher', weighing in at over 90kg. It appears to have been an innovation limited to *Kagohl 4*. The next three bombs were of the small 12kg type: one damaged a cottage in Castlemount Road, blowing out the side wall and slightly injuring a young girl, before seconds later two fell in neighbouring Leyburn Road damaging two houses. Another exploded at Prospect Cottages, to the rear of Maison Dieu Road, shattering walls and injuring two women. The next two, a 50kg bomb and a 'Crashing Christopher', ripped through Crundall's Timber Yard, located just off High Street, wrecking the sawmill and a timber shed. They also made a huge crater in the rear garden of the Angel Inn on High Street.

> [It] did a tremendous amount of damage by concussion to the backs of the houses in Wood St. and High St. People had to be got out of their bedroom windows so badly were the houses knocked about.[6]

Three bombs fell on the Western Heights, part of Dover's defences dating back to the Napoleonic Wars, leaving craters but causing no casualties. A final bomb fell in the sea. The raid had not been a particularly damaging one, but it gave evidence of a change in tactics about to be embraced in earnest by *Kagohl 3*. Night time raids on Britain, and particularly London, were about to become the norm.

***

Edward Ashmore, the commander of LADA, had received information that *Kagohl 3* pilots were practising night flying and accepted the inevitable: 'I had every reason to expect aeroplane raiding at night.' For him that caused a problem as his improved defences were created to oppose daylight raids.

> To fly the more efficient scout machine at night was not considered possible. This opinion was impressed on me at

the time by the RFC commanders, who were men not in the least likely to underate the possibilities of their pilots.[7]

It meant a return to the older, slower aircraft types that had been successfully deployed against the Zeppelins but which Ashmore realised 'were quite incapable of catching a Gotha, even if they could find one'.

The overall warning system at LADA headquarters, however, worked well, as Ashmore explained.

> The first indication of a raid, generally before the enemy crossed our coast-line, was reported to the duty officer... the staff and telephone operators on duty were summoned to their 'action' positions... The code word 'Readiness' was then issued on the direct lines, to warn for action all guns, searchlights, aerodromes, etc. Scotland Yard were also informed, in order that the police and fire brigades should make their preparations.
>
> As soon as 'Readiness' was received, the fighter squadrons would have machines lined up, and the pilots dressed and waiting in them.
>
> When the approach of the enemy was confirmed, the order to patrol was sent out...
>
> The progress of the raid was reported by the observer cordons and other reporting stations. These had special telephone facilities, known as the 'Airbandit' system, from the code word used to ensure priority.

Once the message arrived at LADA headquarters it passed to Ashmore. The responsibility for civilian warnings principally lay with the Home Office, relying on information provided by Ashmore.

> ... for the sake of speed, the process was made automatic. The warnings were arranged in a colour code as follows:
>
> 'Readiness' – Warning troops, police, etc., for action.
>
> 'Green' – Air raid is threatened.

'Red' – Air raid is imminent.

'White' – Enemy clear of the district.

'Yellow' – Cancel all precautionary measures.

'Turn in' – To all troops, etc.

There was in the operations room a map divided into the various warning districts, with an ingenious arrangement of coloured lamps behind it. When a particular district was threatened, I had only to press a switch, and the district on the map turned green; when attack was imminent another switch turned the district red. These colour signals went automatically to the Telephone Trunks Manager at the G.P.O. [General Post Office], who was supplied with a list of warnings to be issued in each case…

In anticipation of further raiding, probably by night, we had constant rehearsals of the control system… On the evening of 3rd September, during a rehearsal at which Lord Derby – then Secretary of State for War – was present, a real warning came through. With some tact Lord Derby at once withdrew.[8]

***

3 September 1917, 11.12pm: Chatham

In Belgium, Kleine decided the time had come to launch *Kagohl 3* on its first night raid. But for this initial action he chose not to strike London but the closer target of Chatham with its naval facilities. Kleine called for volunteers and selected five crews, including his own. Gone were the formations of the daylight campaign, now the bombers took off at five-minute intervals to avoid the risk of collision in the dark. Shortly after take-off, however, one of the Gothas turned back with engine problems. Some things did not change.

Ashmore received the first report of hostile aircraft at LADA headquarters at 10.35pm when engine sounds were heard from the North Foreland, on the north-eastern corner of Kent. Moments later one of the Gothas turned inland between Westgate and Margate, flying south-east across Thanet, heard but unseen as it searched for a target. The intrusion achieved little.

> It remained for some minutes then proceeded, after dropping two bombs in a meadow. Five more bombs were dropped at a distance of about three-quarters of a mile, two falling in oat fields, two in a potato field, and a fifth on a shed at the rear of an unoccupied house. No other damage was done.[9]

The remaining three Gothas continued their westward course following the Thames Estuary, however, the searchlights sweeping the sky struggled to find them in the bright moonlight.

In Chatham no one expected a raid. Those who had been to the music halls or picture palaces were advised of gun practice taking place that night, and six RFC aircraft were in the air as part of Ashmore's rehearsal, although two had just landed when those first bombs dropped near Margate. Inexplicably the telephone warning for Chatham met with a delay.

The leading Gotha bypassed Chatham before turning back and approaching the town from the west, dropping its first two bombs at Frindsbury and Rochester at 11.10pm without causing any damage, although one landed dangerously close to a gas works.

Across the River Medway in Chatham four bombs fell around the Royal Naval Barracks. Two, falling either side of the huge Drill Shed, caused only minor damage, but the two that hit the building brought tragedy and devastation.

The Drill Hall, about 250 yards long with a glazed roof, served as an overspill dormitory for about 700 sailors, packed close together and sleeping in hammocks. At 11.12pm two 50kg bombs smashed through the glass roof and exploded with terrific force within the hall sending lethal shards of razor-sharp glass arrowing downwards amongst the sleeping sailors. Those outside the Drill Hall rushed to give what help they could. One of them, E. Cronk, witnessed the full horror.

> I shall never forget that night… we of the rescue party picking out bodies, and parts of bodies from among glass and debris and placing them in bags – fetching out bodies in hammocks and laying them on a tarpaulin on the parade ground (you could not identify them). I carried one sailor to the sick-bay

> who was riddled with shrapnel and had no clothes left on him…
>
> It was one of the most terrible nights I have ever known – crying and moaning of dying men who ten minutes before had been fast asleep.[10]

Another of the rescuers, Ordinary Seaman Frederick Turpin, also left an account.

> It was a gruesome task. Everywhere we found bodies in a terribly mutilated condition. Some with arms and legs missing and some headless. The gathering up of the dismembered limbs turned one sick… It was a terrible affair and the old sailors, who had been in several battles, said they would rather be in ten Jutlands or Heligolands than go through another raid such as this.[11]

The final casualty toll of those in the Drill Hall reached 130 killed[12] with another 86 injured – the greatest loss of life in a single incident throughout the German air offensive against Britain. But the raid continued.

Two bombs exploded harmlessly on open ground on the edge of the dockyard, followed by three along the Inner Lines defences of Chatham. A bomb struck Trinity School and another Mansion Row, but one that exploded in gardens about 50 yards from the Sally Port injured five people. Two of them were Royal Navy personnel; one, Engine Room Artificer Claude McIntyre later died of his injuries.

> The jury were taken to the bedside of George Downs, who said he was with McIntyre at the time of the raid, in company with two girls. The girls began to run but witness said 'what is to be will be,' so they stood still, and at once a bomb fell in front of them.[13]

In the garden of Government House, between Chatham Barracks and the Garrison Church, three bombs exploded amongst growing potatoes, and three that dropped on the open space of the Great Lines, between Chatham and Gillingham, exploded about 250 yards west of the Royal Naval Hospital. The explosions shattered numerous windows in the area. Another smashed directly into a house at 2 Church Terrace, Luton, on the outskirts of Chatham, where George Longley, a draper's assistant, and his wife Mary, were in their dining room. Their son, two daughters and a niece were all in bed when Mrs Longley thought she heard an aeroplane so her husband went into the garden to investigate. As he did so the bomb smashed down through the house to explode in the cellar, 'blowing the place to pieces' and damaging the houses on either side. Two policemen saw the explosion, then a great cloud of dust engulfed the house.

> Cries for help were coming from the ruins and [Police Sergeant Ernest Hoare] and others set to work to rescue, and after a time brought out Mr Longley's daughter and niece neither of whom was badly hurt.[14]

All members of the family, except Mary, were eventually pulled from the rubble, bearing surprisingly light injuries. Only on the following day did they find Mary Longley's lifeless body, buried half upright in the wreckage of her home.

South of the naval complex, seven 12kg bombs fell on the town. Two straddled the Town Hall, one exploding on open ground near the Royal Sailors' Home and the other in Town Hall Gardens. A bomb at 139 High Street damaged a house and a pub, then four landed close to Chatham railway station, damaging homes and other buildings but injured only one person. Finally, about 2 miles south-east of Chatham, a couple of bombs dropped in a field at Shawsted and amongst growing hops near Capstone.

One of the Gothas still had bombs on board when, at 11.50pm, it approached the Isle of Sheppey and began dropping 12 bombs around the village of West Minster inflicting only minimal damage, although there were near misses at a gasworks and an isolation hospital. The final three bombs on Sheppey landed closer to Sheerness: one on the Naval Recreation Ground and two on the Royal Naval Balloon Ground, but this only resulted in damage to a garage.

Although no anti-aircraft guns opened fire from Chatham, at 11.48pm the first of the guns on the Isle of Sheppey briefly engaged a fleeting target, joined by others, but none were in action for more than 90 seconds as the last Gotha headed back down the Thames Estuary. Other guns, at Whitstable and Herne Bay, also engaged briefly at 11.57pm. The last bomb dropped near the North Foreland at 12.17am but failed to detonate.

The handful of RFC pilots involved in the raid rehearsal were joined in the air by seven others from three night-flying squadrons: Nos. 37, 39 and 50. They saw nothing of the enemy, but there were also three other pilots – surprisingly – in the air. No. 44 Squadron based at Hainault Farm in Essex flew Sopwith Camels but were considered a daylight squadron, due to concerns over the perceived danger of flying an aircraft with such sensitive handling at night. The squadron commander, 22-year-old Captain Gilbert Murlis Green was a skilled pilot with victories to his credit in Macedonia, and felt aggrieved to be denied this chance of action. He contacted Home Defence Brigade and eventually gained permission to take off, accompanied by Captain Christopher Brand and Second Lieutenant Charles Banks.

Cecil Lewis, now a flight commander with No. 44 Squadron, had never flown at night and offered observations on the problems these pilots faced in the Camel.

> Most of the pilots had no experience of night flying. None of the machines were fitted with instrument lights, so to go up in the dark meant flying the machine by feel, ignorant of speed, engine revs, and of the vital question of oil pressure. If this gave out, a thing which happened quite frequently, a rotary engine would seize up in a few minutes, and the pilot might be forced down anywhere.[15]

Undaunted, Murlis Green, Brand and Banks took off. They saw nothing but all touched down again safely, as Captain Brand delightedly recalled.

> We patrolled for about 40 minutes then returned for news, and incidentally to find out if we could effect a safe landing. This successfully accomplished convinced us of the delightful qualities of our machine (Sopwith Camel), and the exhilaration of our new adventure created the most intense excitement and eagerness among the other pilots.[16]

Ashmore shared their excitement: 'This was perhaps the most important event in the history of air defence.'[17]

While Ashmore delighted in this development, Kleine could also express his happiness with the outcome of the *Englandgeschwader's* first night raid. They had found their target and bombed it, while facing little in the way of opposition. Keen to strike again with the moon still full, Kleine called for volunteers and ordered a raid on London for the following night. Eleven crews stepped forward.

4 September 1917, 10.25 – 11.00pm: Orfordness, Margate, Tiptree and Dover

As on the previous night, the Gothas took off at five-minute intervals but two aborted the mission after engine problems developed. The first Gotha appears to have lost its course and reached the Suffolk coast at about 10.25pm near Orfordness, about 50 miles north of the Thames Estuary. Flares burning at the Orfordness Experimental Station airfield attracted the Gotha which quickly dropped seven bombs before turning back out to sea. None found the target.[18]

At 10.38pm, a Gotha approached Margate's Cliftonville district and, keeping close to the coast, also dropped seven bombs. One, in Oval Gardens, failed to explode and two in Eastern Esplanade smashed windows in ten properties. Two falling in Surrey Road practically demolished No. 13 but five women inside were fortunate to suffer only minor injuries. These bombs also significantly damaged No. 5, injured a young couple walking past the Hotel Florence, and affected properties in Cornwall Gardens. In all, the bombs damaged about 29 buildings and injured eight people.[19]

Another lone Gotha strayed into rural Essex at about 11.00pm, dropping 11 bombs near Tiptree where a searchlight flickered across the sky. All fell on farmland, breaking windows to the value of a little over £3.[20]

At 10.40pm, while these individual Gothas dropped bombs over Kent, Suffolk and Essex and the remaining aircraft continued towards London, a single Gotha from *Kagohl 4* made another sudden attack on Dover. As on the previous occasion, amongst its bombload were adapted 25cm 'Crashing Christopher' mortar shells. Three bombs fell in Dover harbour before the Gotha flew a straight course, east to west, over the town. Bombs fell on Pencester Meadow in the centre of the town, on a nearby timber mill and at the rear of a property in Biggin Street, with much of the force striking homes in Queen's Court, but everyone involved escaped injury. The next two bombs, mortar shells, struck houses in Priory Hill but failed to detonate, although flying rubble killed the unfortunate Henry Long. Another of the 'Crashing Christophers' exploded with great force behind two houses in Widred Road. Both were wrecked, killing Edward Little, aged 73, and badly injuring his married daughter, Minnie Smith. She finally succumbed to her injuries in October. Her husband and three others were also hurt. Two bombs in Odo Road resulted in the lower half of No. 14 being wrecked, the upper floor only held in place by the houses on either side. The family, who were fortunately in the upper part at the time, escaped. Of the final three bombs, one in a back garden in Edred Road caused no damage, another exploded on the roof of 56 Union Road, blasting the occupiers down the staircase, and the last exploded at the end of Union Road on the local Corporation's refuse tip. The attack lasted about a minute. No one sighted the raider, although they heard it; the local defences had no time to come into action.

The confused information flooding into Home Defence headquarters from observers with little experience of tracking aeroplane sounds at night, resulted in an official statement that a force of 26 Gothas were over south-east England with ten reaching the capital, whereas there were only nine raiders and just five over London.

As soon as LADA headquarters believed the raiders were heading for London, the warning system swung into operation. 'The warning was received between 11.15 and 11.30pm. Special Constables and Red Cross VAD units were mobilised, and police appeared on cycles with the 'Take Cover' notice.'[21] But no maroons exploded in the sky – they were only to be used as a daytime warning. Those who lived close to Underground stations gathered their children and sought subterranean safety, as did many theatregoers emerging into the cool night air from their evening's entertainment. London did not have long to wait for the main act.

Chapter 8

'Am I dead or alive?'

In bright moonlight over south-east England, five widely-spaced Gothas pressed on for London. A slight haze hindered observation but from 11.02pm guns along the Thames commenced firing at the engine sound as they progressed westwards. Not all Gothas got through. At 11.27pm a searchlight found one after which the 3-inch, 20cwt gun at Borstal, south-west of Chatham, immediately opened fire. '[The Gotha] was apparently disabled by our gun fire,' reported the commander, Second Lieutenant Charles Kendrew. 'A direct hit was then scored and it was observed to fall almost perpendicularly for a short distance turning over and over.' For *Oberleutnant* Helmuth van Zanthier, *Unteroffizier* Theodor Fries and *Vizefeldwebel* Hans Hansen-Beck, these were their final moments. The doomed Gotha came down in the Thames Estuary but they found no trace of the three men.

The first of the Gothas to reach London approached over the eastern outskirts.

> Shortly after 11.30 the hum of aeroplane engines was heard. The noise became louder, and soon the anti-aircraft guns opened fire, and searchlights sent silver pencils of light flashing over the sky in an endeavour to pick out the enemy aircraft. Guns were firing from all directions, and above the sharp detonations heavier bangs, caused by falling bombs could be heard.[1]

4 September 1917, 11.25pm: London

That first Gotha announced its arrival by dropping a couple of bombs on allotments in Barking before releasing six more that fell on

Wanstead Park at about 11.25pm, where they damaged an eighteenth-century 'temple', smashed windows and damaged railings. In Stratford two bombs fell: one smashed the glass roof of a disused jute factory in Carpenter's Road, which until very recently had housed interned German nationals, and the other, in Gibbins Road, inflicted widespread damage and injured two men. Three bombs landed in West Ham. As the first smashed down at the junction of Henniker Road and Leytonstone Road, a policeman heard 'a whirring in the air, then suddenly there was a flash and loud explosion,' as it wrecked 60 shop fronts. By the smoking crater lay the body of telegraphist William Gibson. He suffered terrible injuries and died shortly after arrival at hospital.[2] The second bomb smashed windows and doors in Gurney Road, then came the third. Mrs King and her husband were standing by their back door in Ravenstone Road listening to the ominous sounds in the sky. After a few minutes they went back in to check on their children. Moments later the bomb exploded, smashing their back door, demolishing the backs of three houses and damaging many more. 'We just had time,' Mrs King recalled, 'to throw ourselves across the bed to cover the children when the window, frame and all, came all over us.'[3]

A second Gotha dropped a couple of bombs over Millwall Docks before crossing to the south of the Thames and, at 11.42pm, released five bombs that crashed down between Foyle Road and Coleraine Road, just over 600 yards east of Greenwich Park. The explosions damaged only windows, doors and ceilings, but in one of the affected houses 64-year-old Rosa Hannell awoke to the sound of distant explosions and got out of bed. As she stood on the upstairs landing a 'violent explosion' occurred behind the house and a lethal shard of glass from the bathroom window dug into her throat. Her sister found her lying in a spreading pool of blood. The deep incision had severed two arteries and fractured the bone.[4] Rosa died before help could arrive.

Three minutes later seven bombs fell on Woolwich Common, between the Royal Artillery Barracks and Royal Military Academy, injuring a woman but causing minimal damage. East of the Common three bombs landed in parallel roads – Manor Street and Jackson Street – damaging three houses and injuring two children.

The third Gotha appeared over London's West End at 11.52pm. Approaching from the north it dropped five 50kg bombs. The first caused extensive damage at Bourne & Hollingsworth 'drapers' in Castle Street East, on the north side of Oxford Street, which also impacted on other premises in the street as well as in Wells Street, Wells Mews, Castle

Mews and Berners Street. Passing over Soho and Covent Garden, the next bomb exploded with deadly effect in Agar Street, opposite the entrance to Charing Cross Hospital, smashing windows there and in 24 nearby shops.

A gentleman, H. Stockman, walking along Agar Street heard the anti-aircraft guns resume firing after a lull, causing him to seek cover. He noticed two men sheltering in the doorway of a small temperance hotel opposite the hospital.

> As I made to join them, a woman [Eileen Dunleary] came up with terror written on her face. There was only room for one more in the doorway... and we three men looked at each other. I signed to the woman to take the place. She did so with profuse thanks.[5]

An army officer listened as the bomb fell. 'It made a loud swishing sound,' he said, 'and it became louder and louder as it neared earth... There was a blinding flash, and I heard a woman shriek.'[6] Mr Stockman turned and saw Eileen Dunleary lying dead on the ground by a hole in the roadway. Beyond the shattered doorway of the hotel chaos reigned.

Two Canadian soldiers from Ontario – Sergeant Bartley Lumley and Private Albert Bond – in London on leave, were sitting near the front window of the hotel when the bomb exploded. Although blown off his feet by the blast, Stuart Lewis, an RFC officer, rushed to help.

> Going into the lower room, I found two Colonial soldiers sitting dead in their chairs. One [Private Bond] had been killed by a piece of the bomb, which went through the back of his head and out at the front of his Army hat, taking the cap badge with it.[7]

Helpers carried the injured Sergeant Lumley across to the hospital still in his chair but he died moments later. Ten others with injuries emerged from the wreckage of the hotel, including three soldiers, a US Navy sailor, a police constable and Admiralty clerk, George Brabham. A one-inch square piece of the bomb casing had struck him in the chest and, although he remained in hospital for almost four weeks, he eventually died of his injuries.

Just seconds later the next bomb detonated at the rear of the Little Theatre, which backed on to Durham Street. The explosion wrecked the theatre, utilised as a canteen by the Canadian YMCA, but there were no injuries, neither were there any when the following bomb exploded in the normally tranquil setting of Victoria Embankment Gardens. Then the last bomb arrowed down towards the Victoria Embankment, running alongside the Thames. At the same time a single-decker tram, having crossed Westminster Bridge, now headed along Embankment towards the Kingsway Tunnel. The conductor, Joseph Carr, said his driver, Alfred Buckle, had a presentiment that evening. 'I'd give anything,' he had told Carr, 'not to do this last journey.'

As the tram rattled along the Embankment, Buckle heard the explosions nearby and accelerated to get clear but, as he drew level with the ancient obelisk known as Cleopatra's Needle, the bomb exploded on the pavement directly between it and the tram. The blast seared through it, killing the two passengers – Amy Cuthbert, a tea shop waitress, and Richard McCaughlin, a postal sorter. Amy's sister managed to identify her only by her clothes and a ring she wore. McCaughlin, on his way to work, suffered a terrible injury to the left side of his body and doctors pronounced him dead on arrival at hospital. The blast sent the conductor, Joseph Carr, flying from one end of the tram to the other before he staggered bewildered into the street. The driver, Buckle, however, took the full force of the bomb.

> [He] was very severely injured, his leg being practically blown off and broken in two places. He managed, however, to muster sufficient strength to pull up the vehicle, and when the vehicle was inspected it was found that he had jammed on the brakes tightly.[8]

Two American army surgeons attended Buckle but they were unable to save him.

The explosion also injured nine people walking along Victoria Embankment, where the force of the blast burst through the pavement, smashing open a large gas main below as well as scarring the base of Cleopatra's Needle and one of its guardian bronze sphinxes.[9]

The fourth and fifth Gothas were located by searchlights at 12.30am over Edmonton, North London. One dropped three bombs in the Edmonton/Tottenham area, damaging a school in Montagu Road, before turning south. Approaching Hornsey, about five bombs fell, injuring a soldier but they inflicted little damage. The next slammed into the laundry of the Islington Workhouse on St John's Lane, Upper Holloway, and wrecked it. After dropping a final bomb on West Hill, Highgate, the Gotha departed.

The other Gotha headed south from Edmonton, dropping its first bomb in a brick yard in Lamble Street, Gospel Oak, followed by two over Kentish Town. In Vicar's Road one of these damaged 15 houses before, seconds later, the other created havoc in Wellesley Road, with tragic consequences. Awoken by the noise of the raid, many of the residents were out in the street as others gathered by open doorways.

William Thompson told a reporter that he saw a flash in the air, immediately followed by an explosion in the road and dense smoke. He heard screams and ran to see if he could help.

> He saw Mr Allen crouching in the passageway with one foot partially blown away. The little girl [Elsie Allen, aged 5] was lying on her face in a pool of blood, and her mother [Mary Allen, 45] was lying… a little further in the passage. She was dead, and the child died almost immediately.[10]

Home on sick leave, William Calow, a gunner with the Royal Garrison Artillery, stood at the front door with his widowed mother and fiancée, Florence Gibbon. Mrs Calow said her son reacted when they heard a gun fire.

> He saw the flash from the next shot and, taking me by the shoulder, he said, 'Mother, get inside.' As he pushed me in he fell on his face. I turned around and saw him lying dead.[11]

The blast also knocked Florence down but she and Mrs Calow escaped injury. Nine others in the street, however, were hurt, some of them seriously and two of these – Thirza Darwood and Maria Verity – later died in hospital.[12]

Continuing for three-quarters of a mile, the Gotha then dropped two bombs together. They landed at the corner of Oppidans Road and Ainger Road in Primrose Hill. Although one failed to detonate, it still injured seven people as it crashed through the house at 47 Ainger Road.

A bomb in the middle of Regent's Park followed before the Gotha approached Edgware Road, where three 50kg bombs hurtled down. They fell within 150 yards of each other, one in Norfolk Crescent and two in Titchborne Street. Writing some 18 years later, Mrs M. Davies, recalled that as an 11-year-old child she had lived with her family in

Titchborne Street. They had heard no bombs and were waiting for the 'all clear' to sound. Thinking they might have missed it, she and the family's lodger walked towards Edgware Road to find out. They stopped a passer-by.

> As we stood there talking to a stranger we heard a terrible explosion [Norfolk Crescent]. I remember turning to run home, but nothing further until I found myself lying on the kerb about 50 yards down the street. All was dark but I could hear voices. I distinctly remember saying to myself, 'Am I dead or alive?' And as my voice convinced me of being alive, I got up and found my way home.
>
> There my mother was waiting for me. I could see she was bleeding from the mouth and she could see I was injured. I had a hole through my knee. Also, the frock I was wearing had 15 holes in it where I had been whirled along and struck by shrapnel... The stranger we were talking to was killed outright.[13]

The 'stranger', 33-year-old violinist Henry Over Parsons, died when a bomb exploded about 12ft above the ground. The other bomb in Titchborne Street seriously damaged eight houses, leaving three in a dangerous condition. The tally of injured in the street rose to 15.[14]

In Norfolk Crescent the bomb had fallen on a conservatory at the back of No. 27, obliterating the structure and destroying the basement rooms below, killing the cook, Mary Hayes. Witnesses described how her bed 'had been twisted into a most fantastic shape' by the explosion.[15]

By about 1.00am the raid had ended, the attack lasting about 90 minutes. It claimed the lives of 19 and left 71 other people bearing the pain of injury.

Anti-aircraft guns had fired 800 rounds, most of these by guns positioned outside London. The RNAS kept their aircraft grounded as the Admiralty had not approved night attacks on aeroplanes. The RFC flew 18 sorties, the majority by the BE types which were unsuitable for the job, however No. 44 Squadron sent up four Sopwith Camels this time, and again all returned without mishap.

For Londoners the horror of raids in the darkness had returned to haunt them once more; almost a year had passed since the last menacing Zeppelin had dropped its bombs on the city.

'Am I dead or alive?'

***

In the morning a meeting of the War Cabinet again called on Lieutenant General Smuts, this time 'to hold an investigation into the last two "nights" raids and favour the War Cabinet with his views as to the provision of protection for the civil population,' and also to consider proposals for carrying the air war to Germany. Smuts did not waste a moment and the following day, 6 September, presented a memorandum entitled 'Night Air Raids on London'. His findings were bleak.

> So long as we are adopting defensive measures, however, it will be most difficult to prevent these raids, and they may even assume larger proportions and inflict more damage and destruction than hitherto. Our aeroplanes afford no means of defence at night as they find it impossible to see the enemy machines even at a distance of a couple of hundred yards. In recent night raids they have been sent into the air but to no purpose, and they might just as well have remained on the ground... On moonlight nights our anti-aircraft guns are not much use either, as the moonlight neutralizes the searchlights and makes it very difficult for them to pick up the enemy aeroplanes.[16]

Smuts recommended the introduction of more powerful searchlights, which he hoped might dazzle the Gotha crews and affect their navigation, and recommended the creation of a balloon apron from which dangling steel cables might entangle unwary pilots – already under Ashmore's consideration. But he believed these methods and others were not the ultimate answer to the problem. 'The only proper defence,' he emphasised, 'is offence.'

> We can only defend this island effectively against air attacks by offensive measures, by attacking the enemy in his air bases on the Continent and in that way destroying his power of attacking us across the Channel.[17]

The speed with which Smuts produced the report meant he had been unable to consult a wide range of experts, and the giant leap into the dark undertaken by the Sopwith Camel pilots of No. 44 Squadron appears unknown to him at the time.

Ashmore, however, remained optimistic; he held great hopes for the night-flying fighters.

> As a result of these raids, it appeared to me that, although we should have to rely mainly on the gun barrage for a time, it would only be for a time, and that, after some training and practice, a large number of pilots would follow the pioneers of 3 September and fly scout machines at night. If the scouts could find the bomber, it should be possible to repeat the 1916 success of the aeroplane in night defence.[18]

In the meantime, Ashmore continued with the development of his 'Green Line' plan and began repositioning those guns still located between the outer gun line and London.

> At night, when our patrols were up, it was plain that, as it was not possible to distinguish friend from enemy, these guns must remain silent. I therefore began to clear this patrol zone of guns, and I filled it with searchlights... In this zone, our pilots could fly on their patrol lines, without risk from gun-fire.[19]

The outer gun line stretched in a great crescent extending from Hatfield in the north, around the east side of London, to Redhill in the south. By removing guns from the aeroplane patrol zone, they could be redeployed to extend this line and, with the addition of mobile guns brought in from other parts of the country, this would eventually result in a complete circle around the capital, but with greater strength on the eastern side.

For the LADA guns, Lieutenant Colonel Simon and Captain A.R.F. Kingscote, Royal Garrison Artillery, developed a new system of barrage fire giving 'curtains' of shellfire with a depth of about 2,500ft from top to bottom, targeted at heights anywhere from 5,000 up to 17,000ft. The map used by Simon's command had numbered squares and, as enemy aeroplanes were plotted about to enter a particular square, the controlling officer could direct a 'curtain' of barrage fire on the face of it. As the bomber progressed from square to square, they would be met by successive barrage screens.[20] In time these pre-set barrages were given codenames with the controller able to bring concentrated fire on such quaintly named locations as 'Cosy Corner', 'Dandy Dick', 'Noisy Norah' and many more.

Following that first Gotha night raid on London, bad weather set in lasting for almost three weeks, allowing time for these developments to be introduced. During this period Ashmore found time to visit elements of LADA, and on 15 September arrived at Hainault Farm, home to No. 44 Squadron and its darkness-defying Sopwith Camels. The visit did not go exactly as Ashmore expected.

Shortly before his arrival the pilots had received a keg of ale and as lunchtime approached decided to sample a pint or two. Suitably 'refreshed' one of the pilots shouted, 'Let's go up for a flip!', and with that some of them embarked on aerial follow-my-leader flying low over the Essex countryside. After about half an hour the pilots began to return, but as Second Lieutenant Charles 'Sandy' Banks prepared to land three figures walked across the airfield. Frustrated, and presuming them to be an annoying group of air mechanics, Banks decided to give them a scare. Unfortunately for him the three figures were Major General Ashmore, escorted by the squadron commander, Captain Murlis Green and another officer.

Cecil Lewis recalled that Banks, one of the night pioneer Camel pilots and an exceptional flyer, swooped down like a hawk.

> [Ashmore] was at first amused, screwing his monocle tighter into his eye; but soon he became alarmed, and finally sat, panic-stricken, in the mud while the undercarriage of the Camel shrieked by about a foot above his head and the slipstream from the prop blew his beautiful brass hat off... But Sandy was not satisfied with this... and dived again. The result was precisely the same, except that... this time the seat of his trousers was sopping, his dignity had been outraged, and he was altogether a very angry General.[21]

Still not satisfied that he had taught the 'air mechanics' a lesson, Banks swooped again. 'This time he shaved them even closer than before, so that the General thought his hour had come and lay flat on his back cursing!'

Cecil Lewis claimed, rather dramatically, that Murlis Green had Banks hauled before him, deprived him of his Sam Browne (officer's belt) and put him in irons for three days. Banks own entry in his log book reads: 'Zoomed at General Ashmore by mistake. Trouble!'

***

The extended period of bad weather prevented *Kagohl 3* from resuming its campaign until 24 September, when they embarked on an intense period of bombing, later dubbed in Britain as 'The Harvest Moon Offensive', with six raids taking place over eight nights.

In Belgium, Rudolf Kleine had been waiting impatiently for deliveries of a new version of the Gotha – the G.V. He had hoped that its anticipated superior performance would allow him to raid by day and night, with the older G.IV types continuing at night and the new G.V taking on the role of daylight bomber. Frustratingly, however, the G.V failed to deliver any significant improvement in performance and bombing remained restricted to the dark hours. But support for *Kagohl 3* was at hand.

Kleine received notification of a new squadron about to join him in the assault on London. After serving on the Eastern Front in early versions of the R-type, *Riesenflugzeug*, literally Giant aeroplane, *Riesenflugzeug Abteilung (Rfa) 501* transferred to Berlin in July 1917 and commenced training on the new R.VI type, built at the Zeppelin works at Staaken near Berlin. Commanded by 30-year-old *Hauptmann* Richard von Bentivegni, the squadron began arriving in Belgium in September.

The Giants had an enormous wingspan, measuring just over 138ft, dwarfing the Gotha (78ft) and had a greater wingspan than either the Lancaster or B-17 Flying Fortress of the Second World War. The R.VI type had four engines, two mounted in tandem either side of the fuselage between the biplane wings, driving pusher and tractor propellers, and could carry a bombload of up to 1,000 kilos. Individual R.VI type aircraft were numbered R25 to R39. *Rfa 501* also had two earlier single-aeroplane prototypes, the R.IV and R.V, with different engine arrangements, the R.IV prototype identified as R12 and the R.V model as R13. With the squadron's establishment set at six of these massive aircraft, the first Giants of *Rfa 501* landed at *Kagohl 3's* airfield at Sint-Denijs-Westrem on 22 September.

24 September 1917, 7.09pm: Kent

On 24 September, Kleine launched 16 Gothas in what he hoped would be a major attack on London. Shortly after take-off, however, three returned with engine problems. The rest reached England but only three penetrated to the capital. The others dropped their bombs over Kent and Essex. It appears that six targeted Dover, where a warning siren sounded at 7.09pm. The first of 42 bombs (35 explosive and seven incendiary) fell six minutes later.

At 10 Folkestone Road six girls were attending a shorthand class when a bomb exploded in the front garden. All six and the teacher were struck and one, 17-year-old Dorothy Wood, died of her injuries. Another bomb demolished two houses in Crabble Hill. It killed Ellen Kenward who lived at No. 75 when she went next door to help a bedridden neighbour. Only the following morning did rescuers pull her body from the rubble, 'cut in two and fearfully mutilated'. Her father, Edwin Kenward, badly hurt in the explosion died of his injuries. At Glenfield Road a bomb wrecked the back of a house, home to the Keates family. They had moved there after being made homeless in a previous raid. Annie Keates and her 12-year-old daughter, Annie Evelyn, were at home with Annie's sister while Mr Keates, a train driver, had gone to work. The explosion killed Annie Keates and fatally injured her daughter, and although also injured, her sister survived. The police report succinctly summed up the damage in the town: '6 cottages demolished. 1 chapel demolished. Gas Works damaged, but work not stopped. Railway line damaged. Many houses slightly damaged.'[22]

Beyond the town another 12 bombs fell at Guston, Martin Mill, Ringwould, Oxney and West Cliffe, but without inflicting any significant damage.

Elsewhere in Kent, at about 8.10pm, five bombs exploded harmlessly on farmland on the Isle of Sheppey, but 35 minutes later two men of the Lincolnshire Yeomanry were killed at Leybourne Camp, south-west of Chatham, when 11 bombs fell there. Those bombs also injured another ten soldiers and wrecked part of the camp's infrastructure, while also causing damage at the neighbouring villages of West and East Malling. Also in Kent, near Cliffe on the Hoo Peninsula, an incendiary bomb fell dangerously close to an explosives factory before the Gotha crossed to the Essex side of the Thames, releasing three more incendiaries in the vicinity of Coalhouse Fort, East Tilbury. Also in Essex, a 50kg bomb exploded on farmland about 500 yards west of No. 37 Squadron's Goldhanger airfield, and three bombs fell on the foreshore at Leigh-on-Sea.

24 September 1917, 8.05pm: London

The three Gothas that reached London passed over the city between 8.05 and 8.40pm. They met a heavy response from guns employing the new curtain barrage.

> The gunfire was at times intense... The anti-aircraft forces were in operation for the whole time, and during the three

> attacks hundreds of shells... were fired. Even though no good targets are seen... such fire is calculated to have a good effect, for it acts very much like a vertical barrage and keeps the raiders at a height from which they are unable to see their targets clearly.[23]

When policemen toured the streets giving the air raid warning they 'emptied with remarkable rapidity' and many people sought safety at Underground stations.

> The subways and steps leading to the platforms were lined two and three deep by people of all classes, and hundreds more sat on the platforms. Women and children were in the majority, some of the women nursing infants in arms.[24]

The government estimated that 100,000 people sheltered on the Underground that night; a trend that continued to grow.

The first Gotha appeared over Poplar, East London, at 8.05pm, releasing four incendiary bombs. These smashed windows in Lodore Street, Vesey Street and Perry's Close, and one that fell on East India Dock Road, damaged the roof, ceiling and storeroom of the United Reform Church. Crossing over the Thames, another incendiary fell on a roadway at the Surrey Commercial Docks, before an explosive bomb crashed into a garden in Lower Road, Rotherhithe, but failed to detonate. The final three bombs dropped in Deptford: two in Trundley's Road and one in Crooke Road. The explosion at the rear of 105 Trundley's Road ripped the backs off four houses, injured a man and left many other houses without windows. The bomb in Crooke Road had a similar effect.

The second Gotha came in over north London at about 8.35pm, dropping seven incendiaries and one explosive bomb between Stoke Newington and Islington, although limited damage ensued. Five minutes later the Gotha approached King's Cross Station but its bomb fell about 150 yards short, in King's Cross Road.

At 144 King's Cross Road, 15-year-old James Sharpe had returned home to the family's tenement above a shop and told his mother he had heard an air raid warning. James' younger brothers and sisters were in bed so he helped dress them and carried them to a cellar on the other side of the road. At the subsequent inquest his mother recalled her conversation with her son.

> 'Grandfather has put out the light. Stop here, mum, I will not be long. I am going to see how grandfather is.'

> 'His grandfather is an invalid,' added the mother. 'He can only walk from his chair to the bed with a stick, and I knew that my boy would not leave him after he had seen all the children into safety.'[25]

A neighbour saw the boy cross the road; as he got to the door of his home the bomb exploded: 'I saw Jimmy picked up off his feet and thrown over and the debris fell on top of him.' James Sharpe died, six others were injured and the upper portion of the building demolished, but James' grandfather survived.

The Gotha now turned east, dropping bombs in Garrett Street, off Old Street, and Great Eastern Street, damaging numerous buildings and injuring two people. A final incendiary fell without effect in Foster Street, Bethnal Green.

The third Gotha also approached north London about five minutes after the previous raider and began dropping incendiary bombs. Two, in Highgate and Chalk Farm were followed by three in Bayswater, but in all cases little damage occurred. The Gotha now banked around and headed back towards the centre of London. The next bomb proved the deadliest.

A doctor, R.D. MacGregor, had left his surgery on Roseberry Avenue, planning to go the Bedford Hotel on Southampton Row, Holborn, for supper. Aware of the raid threat, he made his way gingerly along the darkened streets. When he reached Southampton Row a policeman advised MacGregor to shelter with him in a doorway, but after ten minutes he had waited long enough.

> I said to him, 'I'm going to risk a bolt across to the hotel.' He advised me not to, as the noise above was very loud.

> However, pulling my hat well down, I said, 'Here goes! Good-night,' and made a dash. I was within 20 yards of the door when a terrific screeching from above nearly paralysed me. I knew it was a falling bomb. With one spring from the pavement I cleared the steps through the doorway of the hotel. The door at that moment was being cautiously opened by some of the porters, waiters, and guests of the hotel.

> I shouted: 'Get in!' and barged in, coming in contact with one of the men, knocking him down and falling on top of him just as the torpedo exploded. That fall saved his life and mine.[26]

The bomb exploded outside the hotel's main entrance. When the smoke and dust cleared 11 people were dead, two others fatally injured and 22 wounded. Most of the dead were at the entrance, but one of them, promising 19-year-old actress Elsie Clarke, had sheltered in a doorway on the other side of the road. Dr MacGregor survived the bomb but the concussion of the blast affected his hearing and two years later 'serious deafness' forced him to give up his successful medical practice.

The Gotha pilot then banked again. Now heading towards Piccadilly, a bomb wrecked the back of three houses in Edward Street (now Broadwick Street) and damaged others before another smashed through the glass roof of Burlington House on Piccadilly, home to the Royal Academy of Arts. The worst damage occurred in No. 9 gallery on the first floor and to the anatomical school on the floor below. Moments later a bomb exploded at the north-east corner of Green Park, near The Ritz Hotel. Windows there and in many other large properties crashed to the ground. At that moment the Minister of Munitions, Winston Churchill, stood in a room at the rear of Wimborne House (21-22 Arlington Street), just 50 yards from the point of detonation. The windows in the room all blasted in leaving Churchill shocked but unharmed; it had been a close call. The final two bombs straddled the Houses of Parliament, one in Dean's Yard, Westminster Abbey and the other in the Thames, sending a huge spout of water cascading into the air.

All the Gothas returned to Belgium although one crashed on landing at Gontrode, killing the commander and the gunner. They had all evaded the intense barrage of 3,358 shells blasted into the sky by LADA guns all over south-east England, but few gunners ever saw more than a fleeting glimpse of the raiders. In London, falling fragments or unexploded shells were responsible for damage in 73 incidents and caused injuries to 13 people.

Again, the RNAS pilots remained grounded during the raid although the RFC flew 30 sorties, but the majority of those were by the older BE-types; only three Sopwith Camel pilots from No. 44 Squadron were in the air – 'Sandy' Banks not one of them. Also that night, a BE12a of No. 39 Squadron, its flight recently relocated to Biggin Hill in Kent, flew the first operational sortie from the airfield that later became synonymous with the Battle of Britain in the Second World War.

However, not only the Gothas troubled Britain that night – Peter Strasser chose to send out his Zeppelins too. An earlier attempt, on 12 September, had not got off the ground due to strong winds, so when a break appeared in the extended period of bad weather on 24 September, Strasser grabbed the chance. The moon had reached the first quarter, later in the cycle than he routinely selected, but he ordered his crews to avoid London, targeting the less well-protected North and Midlands instead. Eleven Zeppelins set out but only six crossed the English coast, and one, L 44, departed again without dropping any bombs, deterred by the combination of low cloud over Norfolk and strong winds.

25 September 1917, 12.15 – 2.51am: Lincolnshire and Yorkshire

Strasser accompanied the raid onboard L 46, commanded by *Kapitänleutnant* Heinrich Hollender. Crossing the Lincolnshire coast at 1.20am, Hollender also struggled with navigation but believed he had found a target when about 8 miles south-west of Grimsby. He saw what appeared to be a large illuminated angular structure, suggesting a factory or industrial site. This 'factory', however, was the flare pattern laid out at the RFC ELG at Cuxwold. At 2.35am six 100kg explosive bombs and three incendiaries hurtled down, crashing into the earth west of the village of Beelsby, followed a minute or so later by 16 explosive bombs that pummelled fields south of the flares.

Landing flares also proved an attractive target for L 53. *Kapitänleutnant* Eduard Prölss appeared over southern Lincolnshire at 1.00am, dropping an explosive bomb in open countryside at Surfleet Seas End, a few miles north of Spalding. Just over 3 miles away the flares at Gosberton Fen Landing Ground convinced Prölss to release eight bombs at this target, but they only stripped tiles from a cottage roof and smashed windows. Turning north, L 53 headed for more flares burning at Ruskington Fen Landing Ground, dropping bombs on the way near Aslackby, Ewerby and Anwick. None of the five bombs then aimed at the flares inflicted any damage. There is no indication what target Prölss had in mind when he released his final six bombs over the open landscape of Walcot Fen.

Having come inland at 12.15am over Bridlington on the Yorkshire coast, *Kapitänleutnant* Hans Kurt Flemming, making his first raid, spent 90 minutes laboriously working L 55 up the coastline, apparently seeking a regular Zeppelin target, the Skinningrove Iron Works. His bombs fell at Boulby, 3 miles short of the target. Six fell on the seaward side of the cliffs as a searchlight found L 55 and the gun at Skinningrove opened fire, with gunboats at sea joining in. Flemming dropped four more bombs in the sea off Staithes as he turned away and set course for home.

Zeppelin L 35, commanded by *Kapitänleutnant* Herbert Ehrlich, crossed the Lincolnshire coast just after midnight, intending to push into South Yorkshire to attack Sheffield. A strong headwind proved problematical but, when near Pontefract, Ehrlich observed distant lights and having identified them as 'blast furnaces and railway yards', he set course towards them; the lights were shining brightly at the Park Gate Iron and Steel Works, just north of Rotherham. The raid warning only reached the area at 2.30am, with all lights extinguished within five minutes. The area plunged into darkness with L 35 still some miles off but, at 2.45am, Ehrlich began dropping a string of 25 bombs (20 explosive and five incendiary), believing he had reached the now obscured target. The bombs fell near Thurnscoe, Highgate, Bolton upon Dearn, Swinton and the Ryecroft district of Rawmarsh, the final bomb exploding about a mile short of the works. The bombs smashed windows, cut telegraph wires and smashed a school boundary wall, but hit nothing of great importance. At 2.51am the gun at Ryecroft opened fire towards the sound of L 35's engines after which the Zeppelin turned back to the coast.

The last Zeppelin to come inland, L 41 commanded by *Hauptmann* Kuno Manger, had Hull as its target, as it had done the previous month. Manger crossed over Hornsea at 1.27am, just 12 miles north-east of Hull, but it took over an hour before he passed over the city from north-west to east, dropping seven explosive and nine incendiary bombs. The explosive bombs shook buildings in Crystal Street, Lansdowne Street, South Parade and Lister Street, damaged wagons and telegraph poles on a railway goods line between Albert Dock and Neptune Street, with two more landing at Albert Dock. Of the incendiaries, two fell on the tracks by Paragon Station, two in Short Street, one at the junction of Hessle Road and St James's Street, and a group of three in Nile Street and Commercial Road. Most damage occurred in Lansdowne Street, extending to the Naval Hospital between Lansdowne Street and Argyle Street. Even so, that damage generally remained restricted to smashed windows and broken roofs. East of Hull, four bombs fell in fields at Marfleet before the gun at Paull opened fire at 2.43am and L 41 moved away, dropping four final bombs in fields at Preston where they exploded harmlessly.

This raid by five Zeppelins had little to show for the great effort involved. British officials estimated the value of the damage at only £2,210, with a handful of people injured. Flying at heights above 16,000ft

(3 miles and above), in the dark with cloud cover meant the chances of accurately hitting any target were significantly reduced. The RFC squadrons in the Midlands and North flew 32 sorties and this time the RNAS sent up four aircraft, but only three pilots saw a Zeppelin, two of those only fleetingly, as searchlights struggled to find the black-painted undersides of the high-altitude raiders.

One of those who did see a Zeppelin, Second Lieutenant William Cook, a New Zealander, observed L 55 on its way to Skinningrove, but the searchlights lost her. Flying a No. 76 Squadron BE2e, he later saw L 41 near Beverley, about 2,000ft higher than his own aircraft, prior to its attack on Hull, but again the searchlights lost contact. Cook then headed out over the coast hoping to pick up homeward bound raiders and saw one but, unable to get closer than 800 yards, fired four drums of ammunition as the Zeppelin climbed away. Of the other RFC pilots, six returned early with engine problems, two curtailed their patrols because of the bad weather, three crashed on landing and a No. 33 Squadron FE2d returning to Elsham, Lincolnshire, hit trees as it came in, resulting in the death of the observer, Lieutenant James Menzies. And two second lieutenants, Harold Thornton and Cuthbert Moore, crewing an FE2d of No. 36 Squadron, never returned from patrol; it is presumed they were lost at sea. Neither side emerged from the night with much to be proud of.

The defenders of the Midlands and North of England could now evaluate the response at their leisure. It appeared clear that the Zeppelins had settled into a pattern of one raid per month, and with the moon cycle now about to enter its brightest period nothing more would be expected until mid-October. But in the south of the country the LADA defences had no time to relax because raiding was about to become a nightly event.

Chapter 9

'If only we had had a warning'

Encouraged by *Kagohl 3's* raid over London on 24 September, Rudolf Kleine ordered a repeat the following day. The squadron mustered 15 Gothas but one dropped out with engine problems. Alerted to an approaching raid, the Home Defence organisation went to 'Readiness' at 7.02pm with the first of 18 RFC pilots taking off seven minutes later. This time, with Admiralty approval, the RNAS sent up two BE2cs from Manston. Although 14 Gothas crossed the British coast, most progressed no further than Kent.

25 September 1917, 7.15pm: Kent

The first bombs dropped in north-east Kent at about 7.15pm. Eight fell in the sparsely populated area between Minster-in-Thanet and the hamlet of Ebbsfleet, but other than injuring a soldier near an army ammunition dump at Weatherlees Hill, they achieved little. Just to the south, however, lay the top secret Richborough Port on the River Stour from where men and supplies were despatched to France. By chance, four bombs fell just to the south of the port, narrowly missing three shipping berths, with three other bombs landing near a searchlight and anti-aircraft gun on the coast. Another Gotha released seven bombs hoping to hit the gun but they all overshot and fell in the sea.

It is not clear how many Gothas were circling over this corner of Kent, but at 7.35pm two bombs smashed cottage windows south of Garlinge, while 300 yards away another exploded close to the Thanet Isolation Hospital (Haine Hospital) although it inflicted no damage. A third bomb followed as the Gotha returned towards the coast, anti-aircraft guns firing blindly at the sound of its engines. It damaged buildings and killed a horse inside a stable at a farm near Northwood, west of Broadstairs.

About 10 minutes later another Gotha approached Folkestone overland, announcing its arrival with a bomb on farmland near Hawkinge. A good deal of ground mist in the area made observation difficult and the Gotha's next two bombs slammed down on Caesar's Camp, a hill overlooking Folkestone. They fell 200 yards apart and were followed immediately by one or two more that landed in a reservoir on the west side of the hill. The local water company deemed it appropriate to shut off the supply while they sent off a water sample for analysis to ensure it had not been poisoned. It received the all clear. Two mobile 13-pdr, 9cwt guns at Cheriton engaged the Gotha before it passed out to sea, when guns at Dover opened fire too as it headed up the Channel.

While the skies over Kent had been full of circling Gothas and exploding shells, one Gotha attempted to reach London over Essex, its engine first heard at 7.15pm. After passing Shoeburyness and Southend, at least three anti-aircraft guns opened fire when the Gotha appeared south-west of South Benfleet. The commander of the Gotha had seen enough, turned away and flew back along the Thames Estuary, dropping his bombs at sea about 3 miles south-east of Southend. There is a possibility that a chance shot hit the Gotha and damaged a fuel tank as many newspapers carried a story of the discovery of a large amount of petrol over a wide area in the eastern part of an unidentified Essex town.

Three of the Gothas approached London via Kent. At 7.30pm they were observed from Chatham when the local guns opened fire. About 10 minutes later a bomb dropped on the banks of the River Medway at the Cuxton Brickfield, about 3 miles west of Chatham, followed by another at Lower Luddesdown, but neither caused any damage. The outskirts of south-east London lay about 20 miles ahead.

25 September 1917, 7.40pm: South-East London

The first of the London guns opened fire at 7.40pm, followed by an order for barrage fire along a 5-mile line extending from the Thames at Blackwall south to Grove Park. Soon exploding shells thundered into the sky. For those in south-east London this came as a shock – the police had not issued a warning. This chilling curtain of shellfire proved too much for one of the Gothas; it turned away from the capital, hurriedly dropping one explosive and three incendiary bombs over Blackheath before returning the way it had come. The bombs fell in Coleraine Road, Beaconsfield Road and two in Glenluce Road, but all failed to detonate or ignite.

The two remaining Gothas crossed the barrage line near Lewisham, heading towards Peckham. One carried six 50kg explosive bombs and the other about 15 incendiaries. The first explosive bomb landed in Goldie Street, Camberwell, but failed to detonate. The pilot followed a straight line for half a mile, dropping the rest of his bombs as he headed towards the huge Bricklayer's Arms Railway Goods Yard. The attack probably lasted just 30 seconds.

The second bomb exploded in Cobourg Road, severely damaging eight houses and leaving a great crater 4ft deep in the pavement and roadway. Many other houses in the road and in neighbouring streets suffered from the effects of the explosion, and there were casualties too. The blast slammed Martha Avery against a wall and killed her, while four others were injured. One of those, John Stripple, had been recently discharged from the army following the loss of an eye. With his wife shopping in the Old Kent Road when the guns started, he went out to look for her as she had 'a weak heart'. Unable to find her, he turned back only to be caught by the explosion in Cobourg Road. Bleeding from his injuries, he staggered to a house. 'For God's sake, let me in,' he begged, 'I went to go to a doorway to lie flat, but the bomb caught me.'[1] He died in hospital a week later. His wife arrived home safely.

In Odell Street, off Cobourg Road, the next bomb smashed into the garden at the rear of a house, the explosion causing the backs of six houses to collapse, wrecking the interiors and injuring a woman. Many other houses there and in Domville Grove felt the force of the explosion.

Passing over Albany Road, a bomb crashed down in Mina Road. The explosion partly wrecked a building under construction and created havoc at the premises of a leather manufacturer, while also damaging ten houses in the street and smashing windows in many others there, in Amery Place and in Smyrks Road. Mina Road joined Old Kent Road – the next bomb fell there.

At a bakery at 269 Old Kent Road, the Tew family were just about to sit down to supper when Mr Tew heard a double boom.

> Suddenly I heard two guns go off, and I went to my backyard... Seeing the searchlights, I concluded there was a raid and shouted to my wife: 'Get the children down at once to the dugout'.

Mr Tew then turned to his staff.

> I called the bakers out of the bakehouse… I directed them to the storeroom, where I had some time before placed a number of sacks round the walls as high as the ceiling. The man last to leave the bakehouse was only just in time to escape the bomb. He was knocked down but not hurt. It was all a matter of moments, and yet seventeen people, young and old… were gathered into the storeroom while the house crashed down about our heads.[2]

His daughter, Gladys, confirmed that the family had a narrow escape.

> There was a terrifying crash, and we knew the house had been struck.
>
> The dreadful noise and the sudden darkness; the choking dust; the screaming; the continuous tumbling of the ruins above us, we shall always remember; and soon, to our horror, we heard the shouts of men and clanging of the fire-bells – we thought the wrecked part of the house, under which we were buried, had caught fire. The fireman dug us out more dead than alive.[3]

Gladys' father, however, took a more positive view.

> It was a most terrifying experience, and you can imagine how thankful I am that my forethought prompted me to provide such a nest of sacks, which enabled me to save eight children, four girl assistants, two bakers, my mother, my wife and myself – my entire household, without one receiving a scratch.

The bomb struck the rear of the bakery but all along Old Kent Road the effects of the explosion were felt. Around 74 shops and homes were damaged, the pavement glistening with a thick coating of shattered glass. And even before the falling glass had settled, the final bomb exploded in Marcia Road, a narrow street running behind Old Kent Road and just 30 yards from the bakery. It smashed down on the roadway fracturing a gas main and shocking a passer-by.

> In such a narrow street the effect was tremendous. It seemed as if the whole place were coming down about my ears. The dust raised was blinding, and it was a long time before it

settled. The tinkling of broken glass and the rending of house beams had a most weird effect, but it was all mixed up in one terrific crash.[4]

A woman in one of the houses related her experience to a reporter.

> They came quicker than ever this time. I was upstairs when I first heard the booming of the gun. I turned out the light, picked up my baby and rushed down to the passage. My other children were there and my husband, and an old lady and her son who lodges with us. We had only just shut the door when the crash came. Then the door blew in right on top of me, and we were all thrown in a heap from one end of the passage to the other. Afterwards, when we got the door open, we saw a young fellow who lived a few doors away lying dead on the pavement in front of the house.[5]

The 'young fellow' was Andrew Gebbett, a driver with the Royal Field Artillery, home on leave with his wife Sarah and two children. The couple were returning to their house when the guns began firing. Sarah 'wept bitterly' as she gave evidence at the inquest.

> He told me to run home as fast as I could, and he would follow me. I had just got into the house when a bomb fell in the roadway opposite the door. I saw my husband lying dead on the pavement a few moments after.[6]

Another man lay dead in the street. William Sanger, 67, had been to a pub with his daughter-in-law, leaving her children at home. They and his son all lived together in Marcia Road, but that night his son was working. When the guns burst into action the frightened children came to the pub and, together, they all ran back home. Sanger reached the house last, just as the bomb exploded; he died by the front door.

Inside another house in Marcia Road, Sarah Gill, her husband and five children were all together in one room. Her 10-year-old son bravely spoke at the inquest.

> There was a flash like lightning, a bang, and the ceiling came down. Mother was lying on the floor and I couldn't awaken her. I got hold of the baby and ran out of the house.[7]

The boy and the baby were the only ones to escape unhurt. Sarah died and her husband, two sons and daughter were all removed to hospital with serious injuries.

There were 15 others injured in Marcia Road and one of those, William Probert, died in hospital.

The confines of the street intensified the effects of the blast resulting in severe damage to the 12 houses nearest to the explosion, with most of the rest suffering to some extent. The rear gardens on the north side of the road backed on to the Bricklayer's Arms Railway Goods Yard. If the Gotha commander had delayed dropping his bombs by 30 seconds all may have struck this valuable target. But with his bombs now gone he turned to the east, passing over Bermondsey and Rotherhithe, heading towards the docks on the Isle of Dogs.

One woman, who escaped from her wrecked house, expressed the thoughts of all those living in the area: 'If only we had had any warning.'[8]

The second Gotha of the pair that passed through the barrage parted company with the first over Peckham, turning to the east and dropping a string of incendiary bombs as it headed towards Deptford, but they had little impact. Of those of note, one fell by the laundry of the South Eastern Fever Hospital on Avonley Road, where only the prompt actions of a member of staff saved the building: 'With great courage and presence of mind, [he] immediately rushed to the spot with buckets of water, which he applied to the missile until it was rendered harmless.'[9] A school in Monson Road sustained damage as did a building at New Cross Station goods yard. In Wotton Road three bombs crashed down then another damaged tram tracks in Evelyn Street. Now approaching the Thames, the Gotha released two bombs that fell on the Army Service Corps' No. 1 Reserve Depot, located in the old Foreign Cattle Market alongside the river, breaking windows and setting fire to about 20 cases of milk powder. Other bombs simply burnt out in gardens or on roads, doing little or no damage. Having crossed the Thames, a final incendiary bomb started a small fire at Sufferance Wharf on West Ferry Road, Isle of Dogs, before the two Gothas reunited and made off together over Essex.

The guns defending London fired about 1,000 shells during the raid, of which the London Fire Brigade concluded 85 were responsible for damage on the ground. One, at Royal Albert Dock, exploded on the deck of SS *Stockwell* a freighter plying her trade in the Indian Merchant Service. When the guns began firing, an officer ordered the crew to take cover but one of them replied, 'I don't care', and almost immediately an anti-aircraft shell exploded on the ship, tearing a hole in the after deck.

Four men were cut down and removed to hospital. Doctors pronounced Karimullah Nizamuddin, an oilman or 'greaser', dead on arrival, another, Second Steward Joaquin Fernandes, died the following day, and the chief cook, Jonas Pires, failed to recover from his injuries and died two weeks later.

Of the 20 British aircraft searching for the raiders, only two recorded sightings and opened fire, but both lost contact during their attempted pursuits. *Kagohl 3* did, however, lose one Gotha, which crashed at Zuydcoote, just east of Dunkirk, apparently brought down by anti-aircraft guns. The commander, *Leutnant der Reserve* Franz Rahning, and pilot, *Leutnant der Reserve* Alfred Herzberg, were killed, but the gunner, *Vizefeldwebel* Wilhelm Wienecke, survived the landing to be taken prisoner.

If Kleine hoped to raid again the following night, he faced disappointment as a period of rain and heavy cloud set in for the next 48 hours. In London, fear of further raids saw thousands flock needlessly to the safety of the Underground stations. They went again on Friday, 28 September, but although the raiders returned to England that night, they did not reach the capital. Even so, a panic broke out at Liverpool Street Underground Station when the warning sounded, resulting in a crush and the death of a 68-year-old woman, Doro Kopitko, and possibly another woman and a child.[10]

28 September 1917, 7.52 – 8.55pm: Kent, Essex and Suffolk

Leutnant Georgii, *Kagohl 3's* meteorological officer, had given Kleine the news he wanted to hear: on 28 September he believed the thick cloud cover would dissipate at low level. Just prior to take off, however, the latest information suggested a possible change and crews were advised to turn back if they encountered solid cloud. Kleine mustered 25 Gothas, the most so far, and, for the first time, two Giants of *Rfa 501* were ready to take part. But once out over the North Sea towering thick cloud threatened and 15 Gothas aborted; another returned with engine problems. The remaining nine Gothas and two Giants pressed on, climbing higher to discover a beautifully clear, star-filled sky, as they flew on over 'a milk-white sea of clouds', as *Oberleutnant* Fritz Lorenz recalled.[11]

The beauty of the scene, however, did not help the mission. The cloud completely obscured any sight of the ground. Lorenz continued.

> Where a devil's cauldron of bursting shrapnel had never let
> a machine pass without inflicting at least some hits, there

prevailed this time in this silvery solitude a peace which was like something out of a fairy tale. On the white blanket beneath, the moon cast a silhouette of our machine.[12]

With the sky obscured by thick cloud, the anti-aircraft gunners were forced to fire blindly at the droning engines. And the great noise produced by the multi-engined Giants led to wild reports of a far greater number of bombers overland than there were. It appears that a significant number of bombs were dropped offshore with the crews unable to determine whether they had crossed the coast. Evidence suggests only three Gothas and one Giant, the six-engined R12 (the sole R.IV type), dropped bombs on land, with about 50 being traced. Based on dead reckoning, Fritz Lorenz believed he had bombed London. 'A few twists of the levers, a slight shudder of the machine, and the long, torpedo-shaped missiles silently find their way down through the clouds.'[13] Not a single bomb, however, landed anywhere near London. There were three concentrations of bombs, in Kent, Essex and Suffolk.

The first bomb landed on the north Kent coast at 7.52pm, on the foreshore near Whitstable where it did no damage, a result matched by bombs at Frindsbury and Rochester, after which anti-aircraft guns prevented any further progress towards London. Over the next 30 minutes at least 15 bombs dropped in this part of Kent, but at Cuxton, Cobham, Luddesdown, Meopham and between Birling and Snodland they failed to inflict any harm. Only two bombs that exploded in Gillingham, in fields alongside Barnsole Road, had any effect, smashing windows in Barnsole Road, Carlton Avenue, Albany Road, Louisville Avenue and Livingstone Road, to the value of £120.[14]

In Essex, although they could not see the target, anti-aircraft gunners at Billericay opened fire at 8.35pm, joined by guns at Burstead and Ingatestone. The raider, which may have been Giant R12, immediately abandoned any attempt on London and began dropping 18 explosive bombs on open land from Hutton, north-east of Brentwood, to Laindon, west of Basildon. Only at Great Burstead did the bombs have any impact, as outlined in the police report: 'Windows broken and roofs damaged by fragments of bombs and ceilings broken by force of explosion. Estimated damage £8.'[15]

Over Suffolk, guns of the Harwich Garrison opened fire at an unseen enemy at 8.43pm. It seems likely that the single Gotha, deflected away from Harwich by the guns, followed the River Deben inland and at 8.55pm dropped 11 explosive bombs on the airfield at RFC Martlesham

Heath where they damaged telegraph wires to the value of about £1.50. As the bomber headed back to the coast it dropped four more bombs near Bucklesham but three proved faulty and they inflicted no damage.

Despite the thick cloud, RFC pilots still flew 23 sorties, but saw nothing, while the RNAS remained grounded. The anti-aircraft guns blasted over 1,400 shells into the sky and although no Gothas were shot down, one G.IV may have been damaged; it crashed into the Dutch waters of the Zuiderzee on its return, and when the bodies of the crew were recovered the following month, bullet wounds were discovered on the commander, *Leutnant der Reserve* Martin Emmler. Two other Gothas made emergency landings in the Netherlands, their crews interned by the Dutch authorities. But they were not the only losses. Exhausted pilots coming in to land through thick cloud and rain while low on fuel contributed to disaster when six of the returning bombers crashed. From the 25 Gothas that had set out to raid England, nine had been lost or wrecked, their bombs causing damage estimated at just £129.

Notwithstanding these considerable losses, Kleine ordered *Kagohl 3* back to England the following night – 29 September. Only seven Gothas were available but they were joined by three Giants: R25, R26 and R39, all of the R.VI type. Cloudy conditions and extensive areas of ground mist outside London hampered them again. Only four Gothas and three Giants dropped their bombs on British soil, but the huge noise generated by the Giants baffled ground observers whose reports estimated 18 or 19 Gothas overhead. Some reports even concluded that Zeppelins were involved. Those crews that did attempt to complete their missions flew into a storm of anti-aircraft fire as guns in 101 locations across the southeast combined to fire 12,700 rounds, almost all of them fired blind in barrage fire.

There is much confusion in the observer reports but it appears that incoming aircraft were heard approaching the coast from Essex to Kent at various times between 8.00 and 10.30pm. One, which approached Dover, did not survive for long. At 8.12pm the crew of a mobile 13-pdr, 9cwt gun, taking part in barrage fire, only saw the Gotha after a shell hit it: 'it burned for about five minutes and then fell zigzag in flames' out to sea.

29 September 1917, 9.25pm: London

Others heading towards London initially made a determined approach over Kent and Essex but the fierce barrage fire they encountered forced three to turn back. The only bombs to fall in this early part of the raid were at Uplees, north of Faversham, when at 9.00pm four landed in the mud close to the local gunpowder works.

It appears that two Gothas and one Giant reached London. A report on the raid by the commander of the LADA guns, Lieutenant Colonel Simon, suggests that three bombers penetrated across London to Hyde Park where they were all turned by the barrage fire, one turning south, one north and one back the way it had come.[16]

The bomber that deflected south reached Putney in south-west London where a searchlight on Putney Common attracted two bombs but they fell short, landing about 200 yards apart. One landed on Barnes Common, just south of Lower Richmond Road, and the other on a footpath off Queen's Ride alongside the Common. The second bomb smashed windows in St Mary's Grove but the first, not only damaged 27 houses, but also claimed lives.

George and Elizabeth Lyell, married for 18 years with two children, had decided to go for an evening stroll on the Common. The children were at home with their grandfather. The couple were sitting on a bench when the bomb exploded just yards away. Sub-Divisional Inspector Barrett of the Metropolitan Police visited the harrowing scene.

> The man was lying in the centre of the road six yards from where the bomb had dropped. The woman was on the opposite side of the road, also about six yards from the bomb crater. Both were quite dead. In each case the right leg was blown off, the body was disembowelled, and the left leg nearly blown off. The woman had both forearms blown off.[17]

Mr Lyell's watch had stopped at 9.25pm.

Keeping to the south of the Thames, the bomber headed back towards central London, appearing to target Waterloo Station. Over Kennington an explosion ripped the back off a house at 18 Renfrew Road, injuring a man and damaging 88 other houses. Moments later a bomb exploded in the grounds of the Bethlem Royal Hospital on Lambeth Road (now home to the Imperial War Museum). Numerous windows were smashed and doors broken but no inmates or staff were injured. A few seconds later a bomb exploded outside 10 Mead Row, injuring five people and damaging most buildings in this short road connecting Kennington Road and Westminster Bridge Road. With Waterloo Station directly ahead two bombs dropped. One exploded on the tracks between the station and the railway bridge on Westminster Bridge Road, the other on sidings close to York Road. Railway tracks and rolling stock were damaged but there were no injuries. This bomber may have headed north now and been responsible for dropping bombs in the grounds of a secondary school on Highgate Road in north-west London and in a field at Caen Wood Towers on Hampstead Lane, Highgate, killing a grazing sheep.

The bomber that turned back east from Hyde Park may have followed the line of the Marylebone and Euston roads before dropping its first bomb in Islington where it destroyed two houses in Alwyne Road before nine 12kg explosive bombs fell along a line 1,000 yards in length. The first four fell west of Kingsland Road, close to De Beauvoir Square, with one exploding with lethal force at the rear of 34 Mortimer Road.

Mabel Hall, the wife of a serving soldier, had rooms at the house and her six children were with her in the kitchen as she nursed the youngest, just a baby. Mrs Hall had her back to the window when the bomb exploded 12 yards away. She took the full force of the blast and fell to the ground, dead. Her 6-year-old son Percy also died but the baby and other four children were left untouched.[18]

The next bomb, in Kingsland Road, had limited effect, as did one in Trafalgar Road, but between them a bomb that exploded opposite 46 Lee Road, Haggerston, injured nine people with one of those dying of his injuries three weeks later. The final two bombs of this group exploded in Shrubland Road. One, outside No. 14, injured a man, but a tragic outcome followed when the other bomb smashed in the end of the house at No. 31, home to Mr and Mrs Lee and their four children.

> The father was wounded in one arm, his wife was seriously wounded, and two children were slightly injured. The father ran across to a neighbour and shouted, 'I've copped it; give me some help,' and the neighbour went over and found the house in total darkness, with a strong smell of gas about. He removed the injured to his own house, but found that the girl [Ethel, 6] was dying, while the boy [William, 11] was already dead.[19]

The bomber banked to the south and, when over Bethnal Green, released two more bombs; one in Canrobert Street failed to explode but still caused damage as it crashed down through a house, and the other landed 170 yards further on, exploding at the back of 39 St Jude's Street, wrecking the house, seriously damaging the two on either side and causing lesser damage to others nearby. Remarkably there were no injuries. The final bomb, an incendiary, inflicted only minor damage at a house in Studley Road, Forest Gate.

The third of the bombers that turned over Hyde Park, did so in a clockwise direction. At about 9.45pm it dropped a 50kg bomb over Notting Hill, in gardens to the rear of Nos. 11 and 12 Ladbroke Gardens, where damage affected 61 houses but there were no casualties. The raider then probably followed a similar course to the previous crew, initially along the Marylebone and Euston roads before turning north towards the Highbury area of north London, towards a vast complex of railway depots, sidings and the main lines running north from the capital, occupying an area of land between Holloway Road and Seven Sisters Road.[20] Two bombs fell on Benwell Road, just short of the railway complex.

At 62 Benwell Road the O'Hara family and some friends were sheltering on the ground floor when a bomb exploded on the roof. Mr O'Hara and his daughters were sitting against one wall as the building collapsed around them, killing 10-year-old Kathleen, injuring her father and two other children. The other bomb smashed into a yard at No. 56, the site of P&J Arnold's Ink Factory. The managing director, E.W. Brown, feared the worst.

> [The explosion] blew down the entrance gates, scattering the fragments across the road. It was in the adjacent part of the factory, where our machines for manufacturing carbon paper were installed, that the damage was done; the walls and roof were severely damaged, and the machinery covered with debris to such an extent that it seemed impossible to expect a re-start of working for a very long time.[21]

Although the damage appeared severe at first, the factory returned to production four weeks later. The situation, however, had a more lasting effect for the Butterfield family who lived above the factory. They had been out shopping but went to a shelter when they heard the warning. After the raid ended Mrs Butterfield heard someone calling their name.

> They said our home had been smashed to ruins, and so it had... It was some time before I managed to get in, to get a few papers and policies which were important to me. Inside it was awful... Everything was gone – the bedstead like twisted iron, the bedclothes rags; and the shopping we had

taken home had been blown to smithereens. My husband and I stood looking at the remains of the home we had worked so hard for for years... it was practically gone; nothing was of much use now.

We had to walk about to find a place to sleep.[22]

The next bomb fell half a mile away, at the corner of Hornsey Road and Seven Sisters Road, on The Eaglet public house.

When Edward Crouch, the landlord of the pub, heard the raid warning he took his pregnant wife, Janet, down to the cellar with their children and nurse. Some customers went home, others stayed and sheltered in the cellar too. Mr Gooch had been playing snooker with William Kyte. When he heard the warning, he went home to be with his wife while Kyte remained. Henry Slark, home on leave from the army's Labour Corps, planned a night at the Finsbury Park Empire with his fiancée, Kate, seemingly unaware of the earlier raid warning. As they approached The Eaglet someone bundled them inside and moments later Kate 'heard what seemed to be a loud pop inside my ears. I remember putting my hands to my face'. After that she blacked out. Ellen Rose and her married daughter, Mary Ling, had left home to find more secure shelter but on hearing bombs nearby had huddled in the entrance to pub's saloon bar. The bomb smashed down through the cellar flap in the street and exploded below ground. Upstairs in the bar Edward continued diligently counting the takings 'when the whole of the ground floor,' he recounted, 'was blown to pieces'. Outside, 68-year-old Ellen Rose and her daughter were both knocked unconscious by the blast. Mary awoke in hospital to find her mother had died of her injuries. In the carnage of the cellar, Edward Crouch, himself only slightly injured managed to help get his children, their nurse and his staff out, but not his wife. She had left the others to turn off a dripping tap just as the bomb exploded. Oliver Cousins, a Special Constable, worked tirelessly in horrendous conditions to rescue those in the cellar for which he later received the British Empire Medal. Part of his citation reads: 'He subsequently extricated, with considerable difficulty the mutilated body of the landlord's wife, with the remains of her unborn child, and removed same on stretcher to Ambulance.'[23]

Slark's fiancée, Kate, regained consciousness while still in the shattered ruins of the cellar: 'The next thing I heard was a man calling out, "There's another one here," and, realising I was buried, I screamed.'

Slark, terribly wounded, and Kate were removed to hospital; her family told her he called out, 'Katie! Katie!' just before he died.[24]

Also badly injured, William Kyte had a leg amputated in hospital but he died from gangrene. The explosion also injured 32 other people sheltering at the pub.

While the dust settled at The Eaglet, the next bomb exploded just over 200 yards away, behind 1 Orpingley Road, wrecking the building and injuring four women and two children. The last bomb on London had fallen.

Throughout the attack on the capital the anti-aircraft guns kept up an intense fire and inevitably unexploded shells, shell cases and fragments rained down; they killed one man and injured 23 others. The victim, Thomas Weight, had been visiting his son-in-law, home on leave from the army, when the raid began. His son-in-law explained that Thomas decided to go home before the raiders got too close.

> On his way home he had had to pass a coffee-stall, and while he was helping the woman to shut the stall up, so that she could take cover, one of our own shells fell on the pavement outside the Wheatsheaf public house in Goldhawk Road, Shepherd's Bush, making the public house look like a pepper-box full of holes, and killing my father-in-law. A bit of the shell nearly took his leg right off as if it was cut off. The woman was more fortunate; she only had two toes taken off.[25]

The raiders that had reached London, and those turned back by barrage fire, made their outward flights over Essex and Kent, running the gauntlet of the anti-aircraft guns. Two bombs dropped near the village of Bapchild, south of Sittingbourne, at 9.50pm and five minutes later flares burning at RFC Throwley, south of Faversham, attracted a load of ten bombs, but none struck the target. Also in Kent, Edith Owers had taken cover behind the door of her cottage in Deal when an anti-aircraft shell exploded and blasted it off its hinges; struck by the door she died from her injuries.

Just when it appeared the attack had finally come to an end, another raider, apparently one of the Giants, appeared off the coast at Broadstairs at 10.38pm. The great noise generated by its engines led observers to believe there were three aircraft. Heading up the Thames Estuary, people in Sheerness heard it at 11.08pm when it crossed the river to be engaged by guns on the Essex side between 11.24 and 11.31pm. The ferocity of their fire forced the commander back across the river to the Kent side where he turned for home. As the huge aircraft passed over the Isle of Sheppey it released 14 of its 50kg bombs. They injured a soldier, killed 11 horses and two cows, damaged railway tracks and cut military phone lines. Another 50kg bomb dropped at Whitstable from where an anti-aircraft gun opened fire, but it caused no damage. A final bomb landed in a field at Minster-in-Thanet at about midnight resulting in some damage to crops.

British aircraft flew 33 sorties but some were short-lived due to the poor weather conditions. Three pilots caught glimpses of enemy aircraft but none were able to engage. Back in Belgium one Gotha made a bad landing, resulting in the death of the gunner, *Gefreiter* Friedrich Egener.

This latest raid had drawn to a close, but the Harvest Moon Offensive had not.

Chapter 10

'A growing confidence'

The raid on the night of 24 September had heralded the beginning of the most concentrated period of bombing throughout the war. After mounting further attacks on 25, 28 and 29 September, Rudolf Kleine's crews were now exhausted, but he ordered them back into action on the night of Sunday, 30 September as the Harvest Moon Offensive continued.

In London, attitudes to the raids were changing. On the first night about 100,000 Londoners sought shelter in the depths of the Underground railway. But that increased each night with the number officially given as 300,000 by the end of the week.[1] The system had not been designed for this and people came with or without a raid warning; they greatly valued the protection provided by the tunnels and platforms deep below the ground.

> People took up their places as soon as darkness set in, or even before, prepared to camp out until all possibility of danger had passed. They blocked the stairs and the platforms, and the majority of them, it was said did not prove amenable to the efforts of the railway officials to distribute them to the best advantage.[2]

So packed did the stations become that in many cases it proved impossible for passengers to alight from trains or exit stations, while sanitary arrangements were makeshift, often just a bucket on the platform shielded by a curtain. An official who saw the reality of the situation for himself had this to say.

> The crowds mostly consisted of women and children. Rugs and shawls were carried in evident preparation for a long

> stay. Several had baskets of food and bottles, but from many quarters I heard plaintive enquiries where they could get water. The babel of talk was like a parrot house. The people seemed of the poorest class.
>
> There was no rowdyism, but a number of boys were larking (where there was room) and it was noticeable how many of the younger ones were smoking cigarettes.
>
> The atmosphere was heavy and unpleasant. Streams of urine were trickling from where the little children sat or lay on the floors. The railway staff told me that these have to be washed with disinfectant every morning.[3]

Kleine allocated 11 Gothas for the raid of 30 September, accompanied by one of *Kagohl 3's* two-seater C-type aeroplanes, carrying eight small 12kg bombs, but no R-type Giants took part this time. Inevitably one of the Gothas turned back early with engine problems and, once again, the night attack confused the British trackers who initially thought 30 aircraft were involved, but later downgraded that figure to 'not more than 25', still slightly over double those taking part. Although London remained the main target, some crews, perhaps the less experienced ones, made for Margate, while the C-type ventured no further than Dover.

30 September 1917, 7.00pm: Margate

The first attack on Margate commenced at 7.00pm when two incendiary bombs fell in Byron Road (now Byron Avenue) and Clifton Street but failed to make an impact. Heavy anti-aircraft fire greeted every incursion over the town.

> The general impression given by this two hours of spasmodic sound and fury was that of stray invaders – singularly purposeless and undirected, wandering in a maze and being peppered whenever they gave a chance, rather than that of a determined and well controlled attack.[4]

At 7.45pm bombs caused significant damage in Helena Avenue and at 36 Buckingham Road, vacated just minutes before by the occupants; one smashed through the roof before exploding inside, creating havoc there and next door, where seven people sheltering in the cellar had to be rescued. The blast also seared across the road killing Alice Coleman who, with her husband, had gone to visit friends; his legs were fractured by the blast. The explosion also fatally wounded William Walker.

About 30 minutes later another Gotha appeared, dropping three explosive bombs on Elmwood Farm, 700 yards west of the North Foreland lighthouse, killing a cow and injuring three others, before four more fell on the open space of Dane Park. Another explosive bomb and seven incendiaries dropped as it passed over Northdown and headed back to the coast. A final incendiary crashed through the roof and landed on a bed at a house in Percy Avenue, Kingsgate, but failed to ignite.

The final intrusion over Margate took place at about 9.10pm with bombs in Trinity Square, Cliffe Terrace, Edgar Road, St Paul's Road and Sweyn Road. Living above her greengrocer's shop at 82 Trinity Square, Annie Emptage and her mother, Eliza, were at home with neighbours, Thomas Parker and his wife. Annie had opened the front door to look out just as the bomb exploded. At the same time a soldier, Driver William Hollins of the Army Service Corps passed by. The explosion shattered the shop front and wrecked her home. Annie Emptage and William Hollins both died, while inside Eliza and the Parkers were badly hurt; all were recovered from the ruins but Eliza and Thomas Parker later succumbed to their injuries.

The bomb that exploded in Cliffe Terrace, alongside a row of shops with homes above, 'shockingly mutilated' three soldiers: Thomas Armstrong, John McGratty and Frank Williams. They were friends serving together in the Royal Engineers' Inland Waterways and Docks section. They had missed the last train back to camp at Richborough and were on their way to report to the local military headquarters. The explosion, 'wrecked all the shops, and blew in the windows of the upper rooms, tearing down ceilings and displacing furniture'. In one of them, Jane Lee and her husband were at home with her elderly parents. Standing close to the window, Jane died instantly when glass slashed into the room. Her badly injured husband and parents were taken away to stay with friends.[5]

Bombs in Edgar Road and St Paul's Road damaged 'forty of fifty houses' and claimed another victim, Private Benjamin Farnhill of the Yorkshire Regiment. He had sought shelter in a doorway in St Paul's Road but a bomb exploded close by and killed him. The attack on Margate resulted in 11 deaths and left 11 injured, as well as demolishing two houses, seriously damaging 25 shops, houses or business premises and smashing windows in about 450 properties.

The C-type aeroplane, flown by *Leutnant der Reserve* Immanuel Braun[6], whose Gotha suffered damage in a previous raid, came inland at Deal at 7.50pm, evading the anti-aircraft guns in the Dover area which had been in action intermittently for about an hour. Five minutes later three bombs fell at Guston, north of Dover. One, a few yards from the hospital at the Duke of York's Royal Military School, only broke windows, and two others dropped into a field 200 yards from the airfield at RNAS Dover. Once over Dover, the crew released three small explosive bombs. The first damaged the roof of an engineering works in Bridge Street, followed by one that wrecked 59 Peter Street, injuring a man out in the road. The third dug itself into an allotment on Castle Avenue before a final bomb fell in the sea.[7]

Other bombs in Kent struck the western part of the county, mainly near Chatham. At about 8.00pm three landed near the village of Borstal, another near Cuxton and, half an hour later, one hit Chatham cemetery and another exploded in a turnip field at Walderslade. Later, at 9.15pm, two more fell just east of Borstal with a final bomb dropping in the sea north of the village of Graveney. The only damage – three broken telegraph wires.

The sound of aeroplane engines also reverberated in the sky over Essex, but only three bombs fell, all at Thorpe Bay, setting fire to a house at about 9.15pm.

30 September 1917, 7.45pm: London

In London, determined policemen toured the streets warning of approaching raiders; it had the desired effect.

> London anticipated the visit, and when the warning was issued there was no consternation, but a hastening to places of safety or shelter. Traffic continued until the gunfire came close at hand and shrapnel was whizzing through the air. About 7.30 the first metropolitan guns began to bark, and through the preliminary firing omnibuses and taxi-cabs scurried to and fro. When the formidable barrage fire commenced, however, discretion became the better part of valour, and the drivers and conductors took shelter. None too soon in many cases, for dozens of shells were soon hurtling through the air and bombs were heard exploding.[8]

A railway line separated the East London cemetery at Plaistow from a large expanse of railway sidings, works and depots of the Midland Railway. At 7.45pm the first London bomb exploded in the cemetery, followed by three more at the railway complex. Following the railway line to the east, another exploded at a goods siding at Plaistow Station. These bombs damaged three locomotives and the roof of a cleaning shed as well as impacting on 170 other properties. A final bomb in this area, an incendiary, fell in Queen's Road, running alongside the railway between Plaistow and Upton Park stations.[9]

A second Gotha appeared about 15 minutes later, this time over north London. It appeared to target the railway at Hornsey Station where a bomb ripped up a section of track at a coal siding. Heading south-west for about 1.5 miles, the next bomb exploded in the grounds of St Aloysius College on Hornsey Lane, smashing windows there and in 28 other houses. Crossing Highgate Hill, another exploded dramatically in the grounds of St Pancras Infirmary on Dartmouth Park Hill.

> A bomb dropped just outside the lodge, and a little girl was struck by a piece of glass. The bomb was heard whistling through the air, and the explosion was preceded by a bright red flash. The lodge was completely wrecked and every window in the infirmary shattered, but only one person was cut... The lodgekeepers were having supper when the guns began. Hearing a machine overhead, they decided to rush for the infirmary. As they were running along the gravel path the bomb fell, knocking them over. Though suffering from the effects of the concussion, they got up and ran to the building and escaped injury. A man named Green, who was standing near the lodge, was blown through a door, which was forced off its hinges. He escaped with bruises.[10]

Besides smashing infirmary windows and wrecking the porter's lodge, the blast also smashed down a section of wall and damaged iron railings. Two bombs on Swain's Lane ruptured a gas main and shattered windows in 32 homes before the Gotha ended its bombing run over Parliament Hill, an area of parkland and part of Hampstead Heath, where three bombs exploded on a cricket pitch, causing an eruption of the precious turf up into the air.

Although this appeared to be developing into a serious attack, none of the raiders penetrated to central area of the capital. The next Gotha reached east London at 8.15pm. 'In a narrow thoroughfare of two-storeyed residences,' a newspaper reported, 'a bomb fell squarely on a house.' The ill-fated house stood at 3 Fairfoot Road in Bow.

> The whole of the upper storey was cut clean away as though by a knife, nothing being left except a chest of drawers protruding from the debris and two pictures facing each other on the walls. Furniture was blown into the street and scattered in all directions. The road was littered with broken glass and remains of chairs, tables, and miscellaneous furniture... Many people living in the street had taken refuge in some arches nearby and escaped.[11]

However, others did not fare so well. The explosion injured five and 79-year-old former carpenter, William Simmons, died from a 'violent fracture of the skull'. Remarkably, only Simmons' death that night could be attributed to the bombs, but two others – Walter Douch in Southwark and Thomas Ransom in Stratford – died when struck by falling anti-aircraft shells.

A bomb in Weston Street, about 500 yards south of Fairfoot Road, caused no damage, before two fell close together in Poplar. They injured nine people in Southill Street, wrecked a dairy in Kerbey Street while also damaging over 150 properties. The final bomb is this area landed in Newby Place, about 300 yards south of the previous pair, smashing windows at a rectory and at Poplar Police Station.

Another Gotha came in north of London, dropping an explosive bomb on the playing fields of Pymmes Park in Edmonton at 8.36pm, smashing windows in surrounding houses. Heading south-east for 5 miles, a bomb exploded in front of a house at 16 Cambridge Park, Wanstead, injuring two people. Three incendiary bombs followed, one in Fords Park Road, Canning Town, and two that straddled Victoria Dock, but all burnt out harmlessly.

Having crossed the Thames, the Gotha approached the western edge of Woolwich at about 9.00pm, dropping another incendiary close to Siemans Electrical Works on Bowater Road. A following explosive bomb struck the adjoining road, Trinity Street, damaging the roof of the GPO's Submarine Cable Depot in Woolwich's Royal Dockyard as well as several outbuildings and nearby properties. An incendiary inside the Dockyard burnt out before the flames could spread, with the final bomb in Woolwich exploding with great force on railway tracks running between George Street and Prospect Row. The line reopened a few hours later once the rubble and debris were cleared away.

At 9.00pm, just as those bombs were falling in Woolwich, the night's final attack commenced east of London, but only eight incendiary bombs were recorded. These fell in Lichfield Road, East Ham, two at the East Ham Isolation Hospital on Roman Road, in King Edward Street and Howards Road, Barking and three in a field alongside Movers Lane, also in Barking. Other than a little damage to the hospital roof, the effects of the attack were negligible.

The police accounted for 26 explosive bombs and 17 incendiaries in the London area. They also calculated that around 200 anti-aircraft shells, or large fragments, fell on the capital, reinforcing the government's message to stay indoors during raids. Across London and south-east England, the LADA guns fired 14,000 rounds, but many of the pilots flying that night's 37 sorties reported that the shells were bursting too low to threaten the raiders.

Without hesitation, Kleine ordered another raid the next day, 1 October, despatching 18 Gothas, however it appears only 11 reached south-east England, supported by a Giant. From 6.46pm aeroplane engines were detected from the Kent coast and one of those manning the North Foreland lighthouse reported: 'All machines coming in... as soon as within range were subject to very heavy gunfire all round... the guns keeping regular barrage of fire all round them as they disappeared in the direction of London.'[12] The stream of incoming Gothas spread over a period of two hours.

1 October 1917, 7.19pm: Kent

The first bomb, an incendiary, dropped at 7.19pm, landing harmlessly about 200 yards from Sandwich Station. Two explosive bombs immediately followed, apparently aimed at an anti-aircraft gun at Richborough, but they failed to find their target. About 10 minutes later two concentrations of bombs fell north of Broadstairs. One group of 12 incendiary bombs at Kingsgate, between Percy Avenue and Fitzroy Avenue, caused no damage in an area largely undeveloped at the time. Of the second group of seven bombs, two exploded in fields on Elmwood Farm, also bombed the previous evening, an incendiary landed on Kingsgate golf course and two bombs that exploded close by in Convent Road smashed open a water main. The most damage occurred at the unoccupied Victoria Convalescent Home on Stone Road. A fire started by an incendiary bomb gutted the upper floor but the determined efforts of the fire brigade, willing soldiers and civilians prevented the flames spreading to the rest of the building.

Other bombs in Kent fell at Herne Bay on the north coast at 7.57pm, along 1.5-mile line from west of Hampton Pier to Eddington. Most either fell in mud on the foreshore or in fields. Of the rest, one exploded on a building plot 100 yards from the sewage works pumping station, another 150 yards west of Herne Bay's gasworks, with the final bomb damaging a shed at Eddington.[13]

1 October 1917, 8.04pm: London

Those bombers not offloading their cargoes over Kent made for the capital.

> It was shortly after 7 o'clock when the first warning was circulated, and within a few minutes the streets were deserted. The approach of the raiders was heralded by the distant booming of the guns in a northern direction at about 7.45, and within a short space of time a strong barrage fire was sent up.
>
> The demeanour of the people was again remarkably calm, not the slightest sign of panic being seen. There is evidently a growing confidence in the ability of the anti-aircraft guns to keep the raiders at bay.[14]

In London the bombs fell in three main concentrations: in the south-west, the north and north-east. The 'distant booming' came in response to the appearance of the first Gotha to reach the city, which dropped a bomb close to gasworks on Dysons Road in Edmonton. This Gotha then continued for 8 miles on a south-west course across the capital until it reached Hyde Park where at 8.04pm a bomb exploded in the Serpentine lake, the concussion reportedly killing all the fish. Otherwise, only park railings and gas lamps were affected. The Gotha then turned to the south-east, heading towards the Thames, dropping four bombs on Belgravia and Pimlico.

The first exploded in South Eaton Place, creating a great crater and damaging a gas main. Two people were taken to hospital. The next struck the rear of 11 Little Ebury Street, severely damaging the property and affecting others in the area. Then, in Sutherland Street, an explosion on the roof of the St George's Row School caused severe damage, as a newspaper described.

> A bomb fell on a L.C.C. [London County Council] school, wrecking the roof, which was of reinforced concrete. Usually on Monday nights there are continuation classes held there, but these had been discontinued, and no injury to life or limb was sustained. The front of the building was sagging dangerously early yesterday morning owing to tons of masonry being suspended over it.[15]

The final bomb of this group exploded with shocking effect in Glamorgan Street. A group of teenage friends, members of a football team, were talking outside a house in the road where one of them, 17-year-old kitchen porter Frederick Hanton, lived with his parents. When they heard the preceding explosions, they moved inside.

> Mrs Hanton said... they all crowded into the passage. Her son said, 'Mother, if we are to go we will all go together.' The bomb fell on the house opposite and the street seemed full of flames.[16]

The force of the blast smashed open the door behind which the friends were sheltering and vicious jagged bomb fragments found easy targets in the confined space. Frederick Hanton died, along with three of his friends: Henry Greenway (17), a fitter's mate, and two munition's workers, George Fennemore (17) and Leo Fitzgerald (18). Seven others in the house sustained injuries.

As the Gotha made off, rescuers appeared as 'ambulances, motor-cars, and fire engines made their way over a prickly carpet of broken plate glass'. Of the 198 properties affected by the bomb, which included many shops, 15 were demolished or seriously damaged.[17] The raid here ended by 8.10pm, just as bombs began to fall in north London.

The first of these bombs, probably the dud that dropped on 31 Melton Street, narrowly missed Euston Station. The next, about 2 miles to the north-east, smashed into the pavement outside 38 Highbury Hill, resulting in numerous shattered windows. About half a mile further on another exploded with terrific force outside 38 Canning Road where a man stood in the doorway with 78-year-old Harriet Sears and a child.

> I heard the bomb coming, and thought it was a falling aeroplane. The noise was terrific. I saw a fearful flash a few yards away. I pushed a little girl into the open door, but the woman was knocked down and received terrible injuries, her head nearly being blown off.[18]

Miraculously the man escaped with just a scratch to his face.

The next bomb dropped 500 yards further on, in Digby Road, killing a woman and injuring another, before the last struck a garage at 208 Green Lanes, Stoke Newington.

The sky above London now remained quiet until the final concentration of 19 bombs descended at 9.58pm in north-east London, along a half-mile line from Haggerston to Hoxton.[19] In an area of poor-quality houses many of the occupiers, very aware of the scanty protection their homes offered, had sought shelter elsewhere.

The first three bombs dropped at Haggerston Wharf on the Grand Union Canal, at Laburnum Street and in Mansfield Street.[20] Damage spread over a wide area, striking industrial property at the wharf, a school, and a great number of homes, shops and two pubs. Keeping on the east side of the North London Railway, four connecting roads, Shap Street, How's Street, Pearson Street and Ormsby Street, were pounded by seven explosions.

In How's Street a bomb shattered neighbouring houses. In one the occupiers had stayed at home. The building collapsed burying them under an avalanche of bricks, plaster and rubble. William and Amelia Singleton, Charles Hollington and Emily Harper were all together in one room when the bomb hit; there they died. A direct hit on this type of housing could be devastating: 'All that is left,' one witness commented, 'is a heap of bricks and woodwork a few feet high.' These seven bombs damaged over 200 buildings, with some demolished and others partially so, but as so many of the occupants had sought alternative shelter, beyond the four deaths, only four others were injured.

Another group of three bombs dropped as the raider approached Cremer Street, which crossed the railway. Damage affected homes in St Nichol Square and ten houses in Maria Street, as well as businesses located in railway arches, while also wrecking a section of railway track. As many as 85 properties were affected and nine people injured. In Caesar Street, running alongside the railway, bombs reduced at least three houses to rubble, wrecking many others and leaving six people injured.

Early in 1917 the RNAS took delivery of new Curtiss H-12 'Large America' flying boats. It enabled patrols to extend far out into the North Sea, and its initial deployment caught Zeppelin crews off guard. On 14 May 1917, a 'Large America' shot down Zeppelin L 22. (CCI)

The development of the G-type bomber, the *Grosskampfflugzeug* or 'large battle aeroplane', better known as the Gotha, brought London within range of squadron bomber attacks launched from Belgium. The image shows ten Gothas of *Kagohl 3* prior to an attack on England, the first raid taking place on 25 May 1917. (Colin Ablett)

Hauptmann Ernst Brandenburg (left) was given a blank sheet of paper and orders to create a bomber squadron to take the war to England, and London in particular. He succeeded spectacularly on 13 June 1917. Injured a few days later, command of *Kagohl 3* passed to *Hauptmann* Rudolf Kleine (right), who earned a reputation as a risk taker. (Author's Collection)

An aerial view of the Gotha G.IV in the pale daytime camouflage. The commander occupied the circular nose position and an off-set passage allowed him to move back and communicate with the pilot who sat behind him. Just to the rear of the upper wing the rear gun position can be seen, and the inverted v-shaped opening that allowed the gunner to fire down through the fuselage. (Author's Collection)

The funeral procession through the East End of London of the children killed at the Upper North Street School in Poplar. The names of the 18 victims are commemorated on a monument located in Poplar Recreation Ground. Procession image (David Marks Collection), monument images (Author's Collection)

This image of school children lying down during air raid drill at their school is dated just four days after the bomb exploded at the Upper North Street School. The original caption says: 'At a given signal all lie down flat.' (Author's Collection)

On 17 June 1917, just after 2.00am, Zeppelin L 42 bombed the coastal town of Ramsgate in Kent. Two bombs falling on Albert Street obliterated four houses and left a scene of utter devastation. Looking at the image it is hard to understand how only three people were killed. (Author's Collection)

The wreckage of Zeppelin L 48, which was shot down over Theberton in Suffolk in the early hours of 17 June 1917. The burning wreck plummeted to the ground tail first, the rear part crumpling on contact with the ground and absorbing the force of the impact, leaving the nose untouched. This enabled three of the crew to survive the fall. (Author's Collection)

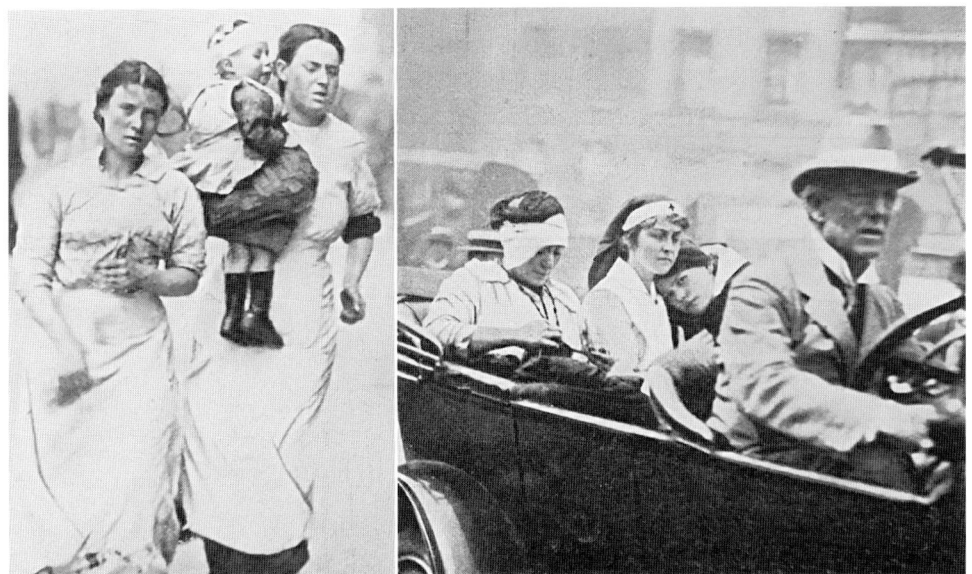

Casualties of the second London Gotha raid on 7 July 1917. Taken completely by surprise, when *Kagohl 3* appeared over London on the Saturday morning, casualties quickly mounted, with 57 killed and 193 injured. (Author's Collection)

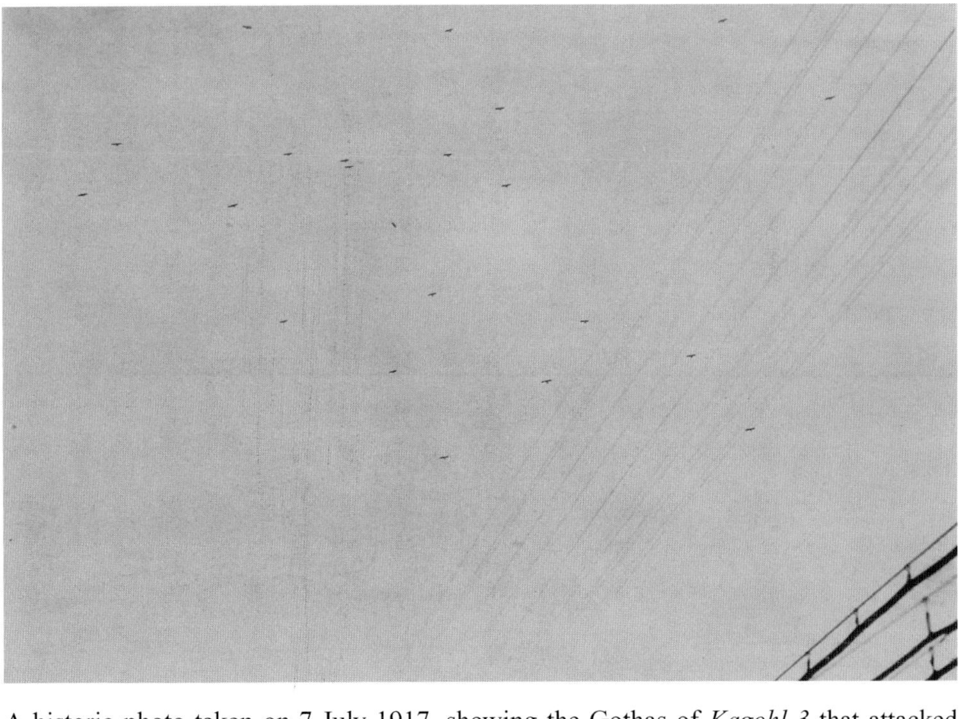

A historic photo taken on 7 July 1917, showing the Gothas of *Kagohl 3* that attacked London, the formation now broken up after dropping their bombs and commencing the homeward journey. The photographer took the image through telegraph wires and power cables. (Author's Collection)

Having previously blocked all attempts to introduce public air raid warnings in London, after the Gotha raid on 7 July, the government authorised a system of police warnings. Police officers toured the streets on foot, by bicycle and car, bearing placards with the words 'Take Cover' while blowing whistles, ringing bells and sounding car horns to attract attention. (Left: Author's Collection; Right: Colin Ablett)

At the same time as the police warnings, marine distress maroons were fired from small brass mortars fixed on fire station roofs. Initially these warning maroons were only to be employed during daylight hours but later, when the raids switched to night time, they were also employed after dark. (Author's Collection)

Jan Christian Smuts (left) had fought against Britain in the Anglo-Boer War but was now a Lieutenant General and South African statesman. He joined the Imperial War Cabinet in early 1917 and was appointed to analyse Britain's air defences and make recommendations for the future. One recommendation led to the appointment of Major General Edward Bailey Ashmore (right) to the newly created role of head of the London Air Defence Area (LADA). (Author's Collection)

For the first night raid by *Kagohl 3*, on 3 September 1917, five volunteer crews targeted the Chatham Naval Base in Kent. Two bombs exploded at the vast drill hall, employed as an overspill dormitory for around 700 sailors. The explosions killed 130 men and injured another 86; the greatest loss in a single incident during the German bombing campaign. (Author's Collection)

Developed in autumn 1917 by Lieutenant Colonel Maximilian St Leger Simon, commanding London's AA guns, and Captain A.R.F. Kingscote, Royal Garrison Artillery, a new system of barrage fire resulted in 'curtains' of shellfire at pre-set map-based locations, directly in the path of incoming raiders. (Author's Collection)

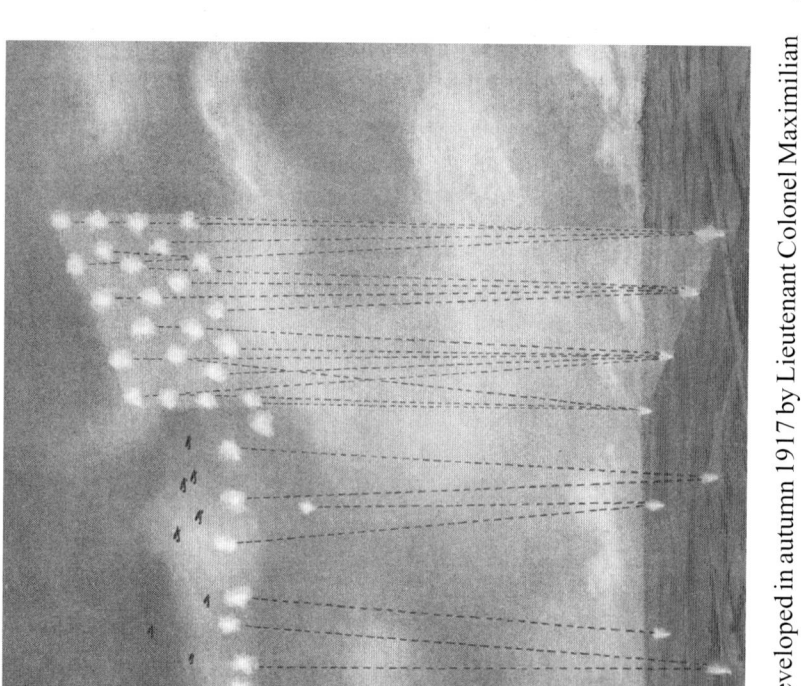

Another of Smuts' recommendations saw the creation of a balloon apron protecting London's eastern approaches. Ten apron sections were raised, each comprising three balloons 500 yards apart and linked by cables, ascending to 10,000 feet. From these cables, 1,000-foot-long steel wires hung down at 25-yard intervals, creating a threatening aerial barrier and forcing raiders to approach at more predictable heights. (Author's Collection)

The 'Silent Raid' of 19/20 October 1917 was a disaster for the German Naval Airship Division, with five Zeppelins lost. One, L 44, was shot down in flames by French AA guns near Chenevières, only about 10 miles from safety. Earlier in the raid, L 44 had dropped bombs in Norfolk, Essex and Kent, but they had little effect. No one survived the crash. (Author's Collection)

Like many of the Zeppelins lost in the 'Silent Raid', L 45, was blown across France by strong winds, following the failure of three of her engines. Unable to get back to Germany, her commander ditched her a few miles north-west of Sisteron, on an island in the shallow River Buëch. The crew survived, but earlier their bombs had killed three in Northampton and 35 in London. (David Marks Collection)

During the Gotha raid on 6 December 1917, anti-aircraft guns damaged two of the raiders, forcing them down. One (left) crash-landed north-east of Canterbury in Kent where the crew surrendered to two Special Constables. The other Gotha (right) crashed on the RFC airfield at Rochford, but was accidently set on fire. When Cecil Lewis, one of the pilots at the airfield, went to see the crashed bomber in daylight, 'only the charred iron-work of the fuselage, the engines and wires were left'. (Author's Collection)

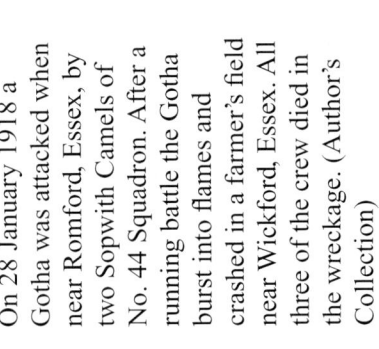

On 28 January 1918 a Gotha was attacked when near Romford, Essex, by two Sopwith Camels of No. 44 Squadron. After a running battle the Gotha burst into flames and crashed in a farmer's field near Wickford, Essex. All three of the crew died in the wreckage. (Author's Collection)

The devastation at Ahlhorn Zeppelin base after the disaster there on 5 January 1918. Little remains of Shed III 'Alrun' and IV 'Alix', or L 46 and SL 20, which were inside. In the top right corner of the image are the uncompleted Sheds V and VI. (Sourced by Harry Redner)

Just after midnight on 29 January 1918, Giant R12 dropped a 300kg bomb that exploded at Odhams Printing Works on Long Acre, Covent Garden. The basement of the building served as a public shelter during raids. The destruction caused by the explosion was immense and it took six weeks before the final bodies were recovered. In total 38 died at Odhams, with 85 injured, the most casualties in London caused by a single bomb. (Author's Collection)

The full range of PuW high-explosive bombs used by German bombers. In Britain, due to their shape, they became popularly known as 'aerial torpedoes'. From left to right: 50kg, 100kg, 300kg, 1,000kg; the soldier in the centre is holding the 12kg bomb. (Author's Collection)

A Gotha, showing the night-camouflage 'lozenge' pattern, being loaded with 450kg of PuW bombs, a fairly typical load for a night raid: 2 x 100kg and 5 x 50kg. (David Marks Collection)

R39, the *Riesenflugzeug* (Giant) commanded by *Hauptmann* Richard von Bentivegni, who also held command of *Rfa 501*. R39 was the only R-type adapted to carry the 1,000kg high-explosive bomb. (Collection DEHLA)

On the night of 16 February 1918, Giant R39 dropped a 1,000kg bomb when over south-west London. It struck a wing of the Royal Hospital Chelsea, home to the Chelsea Pensioners, obliterating quarters occupied by the Captains of Invalids and their families, and killing five of the occupants. (Author's Collection)

A close-up of the cockpit area of Giant R25. On 29 January 1918, R25 returned from a raid on England riddled with 88 bullet holes, and on 17 February made a solo attack on London, succeeding in dropping a close concentration of five bombs on St Pancras Station. (Author's Collection)

During the last air raid on Britain, two bombs exploded in Avondale Square, off Old Kent Road, just before midnight on 19 May 1918. These photos show two images of one of the houses damaged in the square and its neighbour. (Author's Collection)

The very last bomb dropped on London by a Gotha struck St Clement's House in Bolsover Street, a women's hostel and training college, at about 12.20am on 20 May 1918. The explosion injured three women and a Canadian army officer. (David Marks Collection)

Zeppelin L 70, the largest and most powerful airship to see service in the war, joined the Naval Airship Division on 8 July 1918. Surprisingly, command went to the relatively inexperienced *Kapitänleutnant* Johannes von Lossnitzer. (Author's Collection)

On 5 August 1918, *Führer der Luftschiffe* Peter Strasser ordered a raid on Britain, and participated on board L 70 to observe his new airship in action. Following an encounter with British aircraft, L 70 was shot down in flames. Strasser, 'the father of the Naval Airship Division', and all on board, were killed. (David Marks Collection)

Zeppelin L 64. At the end of the war, after the scuttling of the German Fleet at Scapa Flow, loyal Zeppelin crews destroyed seven of the remaining front-line Zeppelins. Only three survived; one of them, L 64, was handed over to Britain as part of the war reparations. (David Marks Collection)

The final bombs demolished a house at 15 Union Walk, wrecking the property next door and damaging 52 houses on Long Street, struck a factory at 70/72 Kingsland Road and damaged Hoxton House school, between Hoxton Street and Kingsland Road. Countless other buildings experienced lower levels of damage.

London had been under attack for about two hours but now, at 10.00pm, the raid ended as the last bomber departed. The sound of the guns provided Londoners with a constant reassurance that something was being done – but that came at a price. The guns in London fired 4,900 rounds but there are reports of at least 225 incidents of property damage from falling anti-aircraft shells and the death of 43-year-old Ada Parker. She lived with her parents in East Dulwich in south-east London, far from any of the bombs. The three were sitting together in a room at the back of the house when Ada went to another room to look out of a window.

> A shell-case came through the top bay window of the bedroom, penetrated the floor, and struck her, fracturing her skull. Hearing the crash [her father] went into the room and found his daughter lying on the floor dead. A doctor said the right side of the skull was fractured, and there was a laceration of the brain.[21]

About 20 minutes before the last bombs fell on London, an attack had developed off Felixstowe on the Suffolk coast, probably made by a couple of Gothas returning or turned away from the capital. At 9.40pm the Harwich and Felixstowe guns burst into action when bombs exploded at sea. The combination of barrage fire and searchlights drove the Gothas away but about 12 minutes later seven bombs fell near Stone Point, to the north of Walton-on-the-Naze, either in the sea or on the salt marshes.

The raid on the 1 October proved to be the last of the Harvest Moon Offensive. The weather had turned during the raid, with banks of mist hampering the defence aircraft, and brought an end to the intense period of aerial attacks. It had certainly proved a testing time for the anti-aircraft gunners as Lieutenant Colonel Alfred Rawlinson recalled.

> Several of our guns on [30 September] fired over 500 rounds apiece during the two hours the 'action' lasted. In many instances the guns were red-hot, and 'fire' had to be temporarily 'ceased' to allow them to cool, in spite of the constant streams

of water which were poured over them. Everything breakable in gun-stations quickly succumbed to the constant concussion; the men, in many instances, were temporarily 'blinded' by the flashes of the guns, and 'deafened' by the incessant concussions, until they became entirely bewildered and practically useless.[22]

As well as the gunners exhausted by their nightly exertions, the same could be said for the guns. The estimated life of a 3-inch, 20cwt gun stood at around 1,500 rounds and intense firing during the recent raids had determined that 'some guns were already useless'. In response, the Minister of Munitions, Winston Churchill, undertook to re-line twenty gun barrels per month and increase their dangerously depleted stocks of ammunition. In addition, guns were transferred from the Admiralty to Home Defence to bolster numbers, reversing an earlier decision to move them in the opposite direction.[23]

An interesting technical development also took place during this period. On 1 October, for the first time during the war, there is a report of the use of a sound mirror. Following earlier experiments, in 1917 the Munitions Invention Department had a 15ft diameter acoustic dish carved into the chalk cliff at Fan Bay (also known as Fan Hole) near Dover. Rendered with concrete to provide a smooth reflective surface and fitted with a 3ft pivoted trumpet connected to a stethoscope, a trained operator could pick up reflected aeroplane engine sounds and gauge their bearing and direction, earlier than with the naked ear. After the raid on 1 October the anti-aircraft gun commander at Dover reported: 'An experimental sound detector has been erected at Fan Hole... this post promises to be of great value in obtaining information.'[24]

***

The Harvest Moon Offensive had drawn to a close. Six raids in eight days being the most intense period of aerial attacks on Britain throughout the war. Even so, the results from a German point of view – if they had known the truth – were disappointing. These raids inflicted total damage estimated at the time at £137,547 (83 per cent of that in London), with 69 people killed (71 per cent in London) and 260 injured (88 per cent London).

There were, however, other effects that were meeting the German strategy. Munitions production at Woolwich Arsenal suffered significantly during the raids. Taking .303-inch rifle ammunition as an example, each shift – day and night – targeted production of 850,000 rounds. On the night of 24/25 September, the first night of the offensive, production plummeted to 140,000, while the following day-shift produced 640,000, and the night shift on 25/26 September resulted in a reduction to 283,000 rounds.[25]

All this information remained secret and none of the detail reached Germany. There the effectiveness of the raids could only be estimated, usually extremely optimistically. On 4 October, Rudolf Kleine received Germany's highest military order from *Kaiser* Wilhelm II, the *Pour le Mérite*, in recognition of his outstanding leadership of *Kagohl* 3 and the six recent raids on England.

The weather that had begun to turn during that last raid heralded a period of difficult conditions, preventing any further attempts by the *Englandgeschwader* until the end of October. Peter Strasser, commanding the naval Zeppelins, however, saw an opportunity to strike a heavy blow against Britain's industrial output and ordered a strike against the Midlands and North of England to coincide with the new moon on 16 October. His decision resulted in the greatest disaster suffered by the Naval Airship Division during the war.

Chapter 11

The Silent Raid

With the introduction of the high-altitude Zeppelins, 'height-climbers' as the British authorities referred to them, missions became ever more testing for their crews as they battled the debilitating effects of anoxia – altitude sickness – which starves the brain of oxygen, and extreme cold. Zeppelins were issued with supplies of compressed oxygen to help the crews breathe but there were incidences of contamination resulting in some refusing to use it and becoming incapacitated as a result. Later, flasks of liquid air replaced the compressed oxygen.[1] There were also increased instances of engine failure due to the thin air at very high altitudes. And critically, German meteorologists were unable to predict weather conditions at the great heights Zeppelins now flew to bypass Britain's defences.

On the morning of 19 October, Strasser ordered 13 Zeppelins to prepare for departure. Intense activity followed at Ahlhorn (six Zeppelins), Tondern (two), Nordholz (three) and Wittmundhafen (two) as the ground crews made final preparations and checks. Their orders highlighted targets in the industrial areas of the North and Midlands. With departure time for most set between noon and 1.00pm, strong cross winds at that time prevented two of the Nordholz Zeppelins – L 42 and L 51 – leaving their sheds. And unknown to Strasser, a deep weather depression surged towards Britain from Iceland, heralding fierce gales of up to 50mph.

Strasser, of course, remained as confident as ever, sending a message before departure to the commander of L 45, *Kapitänleutnant* Waldemar Kölle: 'The weather conditions are good, Kölle; go right into the interior, and good luck.'[2]

19 October 1917, 6.45 – 7.45pm: East Coast of England

One of the more experienced commanders, *Kapitänleutnant* Freiherr Treusch von Buttlar Brandenfels, now commanding a new Zeppelin, L 54, became concerned as he crossed the North Sea.

> Everything went quite smoothly. At least at first. Only when I rose to 12,000 feet did I discover that a gale was blowing from the north. We were completely taken aback. There had not been a word of warning in the observations sent out from Ostend at 4.00pm… It was quite unaccountable.[3]

Once at the English coast, von Buttlar joined the battle for wireless bearings, the system overwhelmed by the number of requests from disorientated commanders. When he did receive bearings, von Buttlar realised the strong winds were pushing him south. Even so, he filed another of his impressive reports, this time claiming attacks on Derby and Nottingham. In fact, he never penetrated more than 15 miles inland from the East Anglian coast. He aimed a couple of bombs at landing flares burning at RFC Hadleigh from where two aircraft of No. 75 Squadron had taken off earlier. Nine bombs then fell between Hadleigh and Raydon, but without causing any damage, and four in Essex, at Wix and at Little Clacton, smashing glass at a commercial greenhouse. Returning across the North Sea at a height of no more than 5,000ft, Von Buttlar kept below the gales and became the first of the raiders to return home, his mission lasting just under 21 hours (see map, p.xvii).

L 47, commanded by *Kapitänleutnant* Michael von Freudenreich, came inland at Sutton-on-Sea on the Lincolnshire coast at 7.45pm, 60 miles further south than he had estimated. He reported bombing Nottingham but those bombs were aimed at RFC Wittering near Stamford in Lincolnshire, over 70 miles from Nottingham, and all overshot. Carried south-east by the gale, L 47 dropped bombs at Ramsey in Huntingdonshire then, like L 54, tried to bomb RFC Hadleigh, but failed. Later a concentration of ten 50kg bombs near the village of Great Wenham, 6 miles west of Ipswich, damaged some farm buildings and a cottage. Von Freudenreich reported the target as a blast furnace. L 47 also kept low over the North Sea, but engine failures left her drifting over the neutral Netherlands at one point from where she came under rifle fire, but made it back to Germany just over 24 hours after departure.

Although flying at 19,400ft, *Kapitänleutnant* Heinrich Hollender, commanding L 46, recognised the wind had pushed him south and abandoned his plans when he reached the Norfolk coast. Hollander claimed a successful raid on Norwich but he only remained overland for about 20 minutes and never ventured more than 2 or 3 miles inland. His 20 explosive bombs landed between the villages of Walcott and East Ruston where they smashed windows, damaged a few roofs and ceilings, wrecked farm buildings and killed two horses. The wind also carried L 46 over the Netherlands but, flying at a greater height than L 47, she remained unseen by the Dutch defences and reached Germany safely.

Hauptmann Kuno Manger brought L 41 inland at 7.15pm over Cleethorpes, Lincolnshire and set a course for Manchester, unaware of the effect the gales were having on his progress. He made his main attack on 'Manchester' at 10.50pm, but at the time British trackers logged him 60 miles away, west of Birmingham, over Rowley Regis. From there Manger observed lights about 7 miles away which he correctly identified as a factory and foundry. He dropped 25 bombs (five explosive and 15 incendiaries) between Rowley Regis and Bartley Green, breaking a few windows, as he closed on the lights which marked the Austin Motor Works at Longbridge, now manufacturing artillery shells, guns, aeroplanes, aero engines and trucks for the war effort. Eight more explosive bombs whistled down towards the target but, fortunately for those at the works, three failed to explode and three overshot. The other two damaged the Heating and Boiler House, smashed a glass roof over the Aeroplane Shop and damaged a temporary engine house, but only injured one man. The attack had little effect on output. Carried south-east with the wind, Manger dropped his last two bombs as he passed over the village of Field Burcote, north-west of Towcester, but neither detonated. The gale carried L 41 across the English Channel and behind Allied lines in France. Continuing the battle against the wind for nearly three hours, L 41 finally crossed over the Western Front near La Bassée, about 7 miles north of Lens. Low on fuel she reached the base at Ahlhorn but a bad landing resulted in damage to the forward gondola.

Kapitänleutnant Eduard Prölss, commanding L 53, came inland over The Wash near Boston at 7.30pm.[4] He believed he bombed a big city, presuming it to be Birmingham, but it proved to be Bedford, about 65 miles to the south-east of that city. L 53 appeared before the town received a raid warning and lights were shining brightly on the south side of the town, through the glazed roof at the Elstow works of Saunderson & Mills. Ten explosive bombs fell in a line from Elstow towards Kempston, straddling the works and railway tracks. They all exploded in open fields but the concussion shattered glass at the works and injured two men.

Propelled by the wind, Prölss thought he had found another city but the ten bombs he dropped fell near the village of Heath and Reach, just north of Leighton Buzzard, breaking a few windows. Prölss released more bombs as he passed over Kent, aimed at landing flares burning at RFC Detling. All three bombs overshot the target by a considerable distance, smashing a few windows and doors at Bearsted and at the village of Leeds. Once over France, Prölss continued his battle with the wind and at about 3.30am crossed the Western Front near Lunéville and reached Nordholz safely after being airborne for a little over 27 hours.

Oberleutnant-zur-See Kurt Friemel, commanding L 52, arrived over Mablethorpe on the Lincolnshire coast at 7.30pm and, like other commanders, struggled with navigation. He dropped a 100kg bomb at Gosberton in Lincolnshire, which caused no damage, and at 9.45pm dropped a huge 300kg bomb at Kensworth near Dunstable but it only smashed a few cottage windows. Friemel soon realised he had reached London's northern outer defences and, passing south of Hertford, released 14 explosive bombs between there and Hoddesdon, injuring a man and damaging a few cottages. Fifteen minutes later Friemel released 13 incendiary bombs as L 52 approached Waltham Abbey but, even though five fell in the grounds of the Royal Gunpowder Mills, they caused no damage of note. After a long struggle over France, L 52 finally managed to cross the Western Front at 5.30am, when about 30 miles south-east of Lunéville. Lacking the fuel to get back to Wittmundhafen, L 52 fortunately found a safe berth at Ahlhorn.

Six of the 11 Zeppelins that had set out on the raid were now safe back in Germany after long and difficult journeys. They were the last to do so, although another almost made it.

20 October 1917, Morning: France

Kapitänleutnant Hans Kurt Flemming, commanding L 55, had come inland over the Lincolnshire coast at Anderby at 7.30pm, but claimed attacks on Mappleton and Hull in Yorkshire, whereas his first six bombs landed near a railway line in open country at Holme, about 6 miles south of Peterborough. Flemming believed he then attacked Birmingham but the 16 bombs fell around six or seven villages between Hitchin and Hatfield in Hertfordshire where they caused only minor damage and injured just one man. Carried over France by the strong gale, L 55 suffered severe engine problems and lost the use of the radio, but having underestimated the strength of the winds, Flemming believed they were still over England. When guns on the Western Front opened fire he presumed the fire came from Dover. Later, when the crew spotted aeroplanes, Flemming ordered L 55 to climb rapidly and in doing so reached 24,000ft, breaking the existing altitude record. Flemming eventually got L 55 back over Germany but, receiving confusing instructions from the now restored radio, and with his fuel running dangerously low, he accepted he could not get back to any of the Zeppelin sheds and made an emergency landing in a woodland clearing at Tiefenort, about 165 miles south-east of L 55's Ahlhorn base. Badly damaged on landing and beyond repair, the crew helped dismantle the wreckage. Others were not so lucky.

Kapitänleutnant Franz Stabbert, who had survived the crash-landing of Zeppelin L 20 in Norway in May 1916, then absconded from internment to return to Germany and the war, now commanded L 44.[5] Stabbert came inland on the north Norfolk coast at 6.45pm but the results of his attack were inconsequential. A 100kg explosive bomb fell in a field at West Bradenham, 6 miles east of Swaffham, and four incendiary bombs dropped in fields at Rivenhall in Essex; police reports show that they had little effect. Crossing the Thames Estuary to Kent, five bombs fell near Reculver, but only inflicted some minor damage to the King Ethelbert Inn. Three others fell harmlessly on marshes at Chislet and in fields at Sarre. Swept across France behind Allied lines, L 44 found herself just 10 miles from the Western Front at 6.15am when French anti-aircraft guns caught her. Stabbert increased speed, zig-zagged and climbed rapidly as shells arrowed up towards the Zeppelin. Then, just as it appeared she might escape, an incendiary shell struck home, engulfing L 44 in a ball of fire. The burning wreck smashed into the ground at Chenevières. Stabbert's luck had run out; everyone onboard lost their lives.

Zeppelins L 49 and L 50 came inland over the north Norfolk coast and, following parallel courses, roughly 18 miles apart, both dropped their bombs along lines about 16 miles in length. Both commanders were over Britain for the first time.

Kapitänleutnant Hans-Karl Gayer, commanding L 49, came inland at 8.00pm, his 42 bombs (18 explosive and 24 incendiaries) bombarding farmland between East Dereham and Forncett St Peter, resulting in a sprinkling of smashed windows, a handful of damaged houses and farm buildings, and three horses killed. Gayer believed his bombs fell in East Yorkshire, between Flamborough Head and Hull.

To the west of L 49, *Kapitänleutnant* Roderich Schwonder, commanding L 50, released his 30 bombs (25 explosive and five incendiaries) at 8.20pm, over villages between Downham Market and Thetford. Unlike Gayer, Schwonder knew he had found Norfolk, but his bombs were even less effective; only at Oxborough were a few windows broken. The last bomb at Thetford may have been aimed at landing flares burning at the RFC's landing ground at Snarehill.[6] Both Zeppelins were carried to France by the gale.

A thick haze below hindered ground observation and when L 49 reached France, with the radio out of action, Gayer and his officers concluded they were over the Dutch coast. He attempted to steer a course that would take them back to Germany, but with only two engines working, the powerful wind carried them deeper into the French interior. In the pre-dawn light, however, Gayer noticed another Zeppelin in the distance – Stabbert's L 44 – and began to follow it – until it suddenly burst into flames. Believing Dutch anti-aircraft guns had shot it down, Gayer turned away and headed west, but when near Neufchateau, to his horror he saw five French aeroplanes closing in. The Nieuport fighters of *Escadrille N.152* were not armed with the explosive and incendiary bullets necessary to bring down a Zeppelin, but the commander of the squadron, Lieutenant Charles Lefévre, had a cunning plan.

For the crew of L 49, who had been in the air for nearly 18 hours, much of the time in sub-zero temperatures, with only two working engines, things could not have appeared worse. Gayer tried to wriggle free, however, each time he climbed, the pursuing aircraft opened fire, but he noted they stopped firing if he descended. Lacking the engine power to get away from his assailants he decided to ground L 49 before they too were shot down in flames, unaware that his assailants lacked the means to do so.

L 49 crashed in woods in the valley of the Apance river, about 3 miles from Bourbonne-les-Bains. The relieved crew scrambled clear but, before they could carry out the destruction of their Zeppelin, an angry mob of French civilians armed with shotguns and farming implements confronted them. The crew, somewhat relieved, surrendered to the resourceful Lieutenant Lefévre who had landed close by, but the failure to destroy L 49 handed this latest Zeppelin design, virtually intact, into the Allies' hands.

L 50 crossed the French coast near Dunkirk, the crew having had a similar experience to others that night, with failed engines, navigation issues and altitude sickness, and now had little idea of where they were. For hours Schwonder wandered hopelessly over France, trying to fix his position then, horrified, he too saw the burning outline of L 44 lighting the sky about 40 miles away. He turned away and, when over Tonnerre, he descended until with binoculars he could read a sign in a town below – *Café du Centre*. He now knew for sure that he was flying over France.

Returning eastwards again, at about midday the grounded hulk of L 49 came into view, with aeroplanes nearby. Assuming he had finally reached friendly territory, Schwonder prepared to make an emergency landing, but as they descended, L 50 came under rifle fire and with horror he realised the aeroplanes were French. He began to climb again but with only three engines working they could not escape. In desperation Schwonder took the decision to crash-land, hoping to cause serious structural damage to the Zeppelin to prevent it from being of use to its captors. L 50 subsequently hit the ground at Dammartin-sur-Meuse, about 8 miles west of L 49, but rather than crashing into the ground she struck trees, smashing in the nose, tearing off the control gondola and crushing the rear gondola.

Schwonder tumbled clear, others were thrown upon the ground, while those in the engine gondolas leapt overboard. Now lightened, the ship shot back up into the sky with four men still aboard; they may have been killed or incapacitated during the rough landing. The grounded crewmen tried unsuccessfully to shoot L 50 down with signal flares as the wind picked her up and tossed her about as if it were a discarded toy balloon. The uncontrollable wreck soared into the sky, carried away by the wind with French aeroplanes in pursuit. The 16 members of the crew were taken prisoner by the French; in interviews some 'were deeply incensed with their commanding officer on account of his bad leadership'.[7] At about 6.30pm on 20 October, Zeppelin L 50 passed Fréjus and out over the Mediterranean Sea, the last anyone ever saw of the abandoned ship and the four men left onboard.

Zeppelin L 45, commanded by *Kapitänleutnant* Waldemar Kölle, the last of the raiders that night, made a greater impact on Britain than

19 October, 10.50pm: Northampton

L 45 crossed the coast near Withernsea in Yorkshire at about 8.30pm, intending to strike at Sheffield but, climbing to 19,000ft, the wind took hold as did the cold, the crew recording a temperature of minus 26 degrees Celsius. Although steering westwards, 'the navigation,' according to rudder man, Heinrich Bahn, 'was getting more and more uncertain.' Continuing on their tentative course, Bahn added: 'We dropped a few bombs at some faint lights, but providence alone knows where they went.'[8] The population of Northampton, however, knew exactly where they fell.

The first three bombs landed at 10.50pm to the north of the town, between Dallington and Kingsthorpe, exploding alongside the main railway line. Switching to incendiary bombs, three dropped either side of Spencer Bridge Road before three more descended on the St James district. One fell harmlessly in Victoria Park, one in a garden in Park Road, which the occupier quickly extinguished, but a third smashed through the roof of a house at 46 Parkwood Street, the home of Henry Gammons, a bricklayer for the London & North West Railway, and his wife Eliza.

There were seven people in the house that night: Eliza Gammons and her twin 13-year-old daughters, Gladys and Lily, her married daughter, Elizabeth, and son-in-law, Albert Bazeley, home on leave from the Army Veterinary Corps, as well as the couple's two sons, Walter aged 6 and 3-year-old Charles. Henry Gammons was working the night shift but the rest were all in bed when L 45 approached.

Bazeley and his family were sleeping in the front bedroom when he and his wife awoke to an odd noise – the sound of exploding bombs. Elizabeth Bazeley asked her husband what had made the noise, to which he drowsily replied, 'Oh nothing, girl, go to sleep'. Moments later an incendiary smashed through the roof of the house, bursting into flames in the room where Eliza and the twins were sleeping.

Shocked into action, Bazeley and his wife leapt from their bed; Albert tore off the blankets, threw them out the window and shouted for help. Two neighbours quickly responded and together they held out one of the blankets into which Bazeley unceremoniously threw his two young sons. He then dashed to the other bedroom. The bomb had struck his mother-in-law's head, setting fire to her bed and filling the room with smoke and acrid fumes as fiercely burning liquid flooded across the floor. Eliza's head – the face charred beyond recognition – rested on the floor while her legs were still on the bed. Through the smoke-filled room she appeared beyond help, but Bazeley found the twins and managed to carry them to the front bedroom. Both the girls were severely burnt but Bazeley recalled how they screamed, kicked and struggled as he threw them out of the window into the blanket held out below. Then his wife jumped. Bazeley tried to return to his mother-in-law's bedroom but the landing wall, now burning fiercely, appeared about to collapse. With no other choice he too jumped from the window.[9]

While they waited for an ambulance, the desperate Bazeley smashed down the front door with the help of others and together they extinguished the fire with buckets of water. But despite Arthur Bazeley's heroic efforts to save the twins, they both succumbed to their terrible burns: Gladys died in hospital at 7.30am the following morning and Lily two days later.

Oblivious to the terror below, Kölle released another batch of three incendiaries over the southern edge of the town but they caused no further damage, before six explosive bombs fell near the Hunsbury Hill railway tunnel where they smashed a few farm windows. Carried south-east by the wind, L 45 dropped two more ineffective bombs over the Northamptonshire countryside, but 30 minutes later the crew made a surprising discovery, as Heinrich Bahn, the rudder man relates.

> We began to see lights below and as the lights continued so it suddenly dawned upon us that it could only be the city of London... Even Kölle looked amazed... as Schultz suddenly shouted, 'London!' It was then that we first realised the fury of the savage tempest that had been driving us out of our course.[10]

Bahn and the rest of the crew were surprised there were no searchlights sweeping the sky over the city and that the anti-aircraft guns did not open fire, concluding that the fierce winds had also created havoc on the ground. But not so. Realising Zeppelins were over England but at a great height and with their engines barely audible, the Home Defence organisation took the decision not to engage. Firing at the Zeppelins when beyond the range of the guns would just serve to indicate possible important positions and so the defences remained quiet. With L 45's engines rarely heard and the guns muzzled, the attack became known as the 'Silent Raid'.

19 October 1917, 11.25pm: London

Now aware they were approaching London, the crew of L 45 prepared to drop their remaining bombs. Heinrich Bahn described the moment.

> It was misty or so it seemed, for we were above a thin veil of cloud. The Thames we just dimly saw… but the speed of the ship running almost before the gale was such that we could not distinguish much. We were half frozen too, and the excitement was great. It was all over in a flash.[11]

The first four explosive bombs landed in north-west London at 11.25pm. One caused damage at Hendon aerodrome, the location of an RFC Aircraft Acceptance Park, and another to cottages nearby on Colindeep Lane. Of the other two, one fell at the Midland Railway yard at Cricklewood Station, damaging tracks, five railway trucks and smashing a great number of windows. The other bomb also fell by the railway, in front of Haberdashers' School in Westbere Road, smashing the windows at the front of the building and those of about 100 other properties, however there were no casualties. L 45 now had just three bombs remaining.

London had received warning of a raid two or three hours earlier, but the sky had remained quiet and impatient Londoners began to return to the streets despite no 'all clear' having sounded. About 3.5 miles above the city, the crew of L 45 released their next bomb. They could not have hoped to find a more symbolic target in the heart of London. The 100kg bomb exploded outside Swan & Edgar's fashionable department store at Piccadilly Circus, the pulsing heart of London's West End.

May Trotter, a 'nippie' waitress at the Lyon's Corner House on Coventry Street, had left work to start her journey home. As she passed a cigar shop she had a shock.

> … the form of a man darted out from the side-door. He flung his arm across my chest… and as I bumped against the window there was a terrific hissing sound, a volume of light and an explosion. The ground was rocking and I was

swaying backwards and forwards, seeing only that blinding light. There was a stinging pain under my left arm.[12]

As May gathered her senses, she saw a huge hole in the road and at her feet lay the body of an army officer, Lieutenant Harold Prew. By shielding May from the blast, he saved her life; it was his birthday, and also the day he died. Six others were cut down.

A farmer's wife from Dorset, Kate Phripp had come to London to see her 23-year-old son Arthur, an army officer back in England on leave. Both were killed. Another soldier, gunner Walter Dudley, died, as did 23-year-old engineer, Christopher Wildman, and shop porter James Canavan, aged 18. The final casualty, 25-year-old Mabel Barrington must have been very close to the bomb when it exploded because it left her body unidentifiable, her 'identity' only established from her clothing and jewellery.[13] Eighteen others were removed to hospital for treatment to their injuries.

The bomb smashed two gas mains and telephone cables below Piccadilly and inevitably caused extensive damage at Swan & Edgar's, with shattered windows in all the roads surrounding Piccadilly Circus.

A female Army Service Corps driver, although home on leave, received orders to take out an ambulance when the police issued the warning.

> I was worming my way in the darkness down Regent Street, when – bang!... a sound I knew so well. I could see a sort of ground-fog coming up from Swan & Edgars Corner.

She stopped her ambulance by the wrecked department store.

> Was that a groan I heard? I fumbled about in the darkness. A police officer said 'Hello driver! You're a cheerful sight. Let's see if anybody's hurt.' He was covered in dust and mortar. Slowly we felt clothing that littered the pavement. Yes! – I could feel a woman's leg. Feverishly we worked away the bricks and wreckage. 'Pull!' said the officer. We both pulled, sick at heart, and the leg came away in our hands. The constable shone his dim lantern on it – and I really think even Jerry would have joined in our laughter could he have seen us... sitting on the pavement holding a dummy's leg which had dropped from the window of Swan & Edgars.[14]

19 October 1917, 11.30pm: Camberwell, London

L 45 now had just two large 300kg bombs left. The first of these hurtled down towards Camberwell in south London just after 11.30pm, where it exploded with shocking force.

When the raid warning had sounded, people without basements or cellars had left their homes to seek more secure shelter. In Camberwell, Dr Whitelaw at 103 Albany Road, had made his cellar available to local people. The building next door, at No. 101, a fish and chip shop owned by Mr Skelton and managed by Edward Brame, also had a cellar but it remained private.

Mr Brame and his 19-year-old daughter, Ivy, were working in the shop. The owner's 15-year-old son, Stephen Skelton was there too. Crowded into Dr Whitelaw's cellar were 18 people, among them Henry and Nellie Balls, with their young family, Reginald, aged 6, Leslie, 4, Edwin, 3, Greta, not yet 2, and a baby, Joan, born earlier that year.[15] On the floor above, the Glass family remained at home except for the son, Stephen, on leave from the Royal Navy. A shipmate, Alfred Fowler, had joined Stephen and the two friends spent the evening with 22-year-old Jessie Martin around a piano in the cellar beneath the fish and chip shop.

The 300kg bomb landed on the party wall between 101 and 103 Albany Road. Henry Balls, standing outside, heard the eerie sound of the falling bomb and dived back into the cellar where his family were sleeping. In the fish and chip shop Edward Brame heard a whizzing sound then a bang as the building collapsed around him. A policeman described seeing the front of Brame's shop blown into the street. And a police inspector vividly recalled that the two buildings were simply swept away.

Inside the doctor's cellar Nellie Balls instinctively threw herself across her children to protect them as falling timber and rubble crashed down around them, but it was all to no avail. Two of the boys, Reginald and Edwin, suffered fatal injuries as the building collapsed. But rescuers worked desperately to save the others entombed in the cellar. Policemen bored through a door and managed to pull 16 people to safety, including a distraught Mr and Mrs Balls and their three surviving children.

Next door, the house had collapsed, burying Edward Brame under the debris, but his ordeal only lasted 45 minutes before firemen managed to dig him out. One of his rescuers heard a cry from beneath the rubble and hacked away floorboards with an axe until he found Ivy Brame.

We could not extricate her, as her feet were caught by some heavy timber, but I got a fireman to remain with her, to prevent any more debris from covering her. A doctor was called, and the girl was given some tablets. She was extricated about 8 o'clock, after sufficient debris had been cleared away.[16]

Ivy Brame had remained buried under the rubble for over eight hours by the time rescuers brought her out. She did not survive, neither did young Stephen Skelton. The work parties remained hard at work through Saturday and that afternoon recovered the battered body of a dead sailor, then found two more bodies in the wreckage. Jessie Martin and shipmates Alfred Fowler and Stephen Glass were all dead.

The night proved a tragic one for the Glass family. As well as Stephen's death, his mother Emma also died in the wreckage, as did her daughters, 21-year-old Alice and Emily, just 8. At about 4.00am Saturday morning rescuers had discovered Emily and a younger sister buried in their bed under rubble and debris. The younger daughter survived but Emily, severely injured, died as they brought her out. In all ten people lost their lives in Albany Road, with 22 injured.

19 October 1917, 11.35pm: Hither Green, London

High above, L 45 continued its wind-blown south-east course. About 4 miles on they dropped the last bomb at 11.35pm, another 300kg monster. The unfortunate recipients were asleep in their beds in Glenview Road, Hither Green.[17]

The Kingston family had spent the evening with friends on the other side of the street and returned home to 17 Glenview Road at about 11.00pm. The widowed Mrs Kingston looked after her seven children, but that night a nephew, 13-year-old William Turner, had also come to stay.

The Milgate family, next door at 15 Glenview Road, were all in bed; the mother Mary, father Samuel, three daughters – Beatrice, aged 20, Edith, 18, Elsie, 13 – and a son, 8-year-old Leonard.

The Jenner family lived at the next house, 13 Glenview Road. Mrs Jenner slept in a room with her four children, and a friend and her child were staying. Also living there were an elderly couple, Edward and Emma Dorey. And in one of the three houses slept Frances Grant, a 32-year-old widow and sister of the neighbour who the Kingston's had spent the evening with.

A police sergeant heard a whistling noise rushing through the air before the bomb struck. It simply obliterated the three houses in Glenview Road. At No. 15, Beatrice Milgate also heard the whistling sound and sensed the house collapsing around her. She remembered nothing more until she awoke in hospital where she remained for six weeks.

The explosion blasted everyone at No. 15 out into the street. The bodies of the children, Elsie and Leonard Milgate, were lying on the other side of the road. Elsie suffered a serious head injury, probably caused when flung against a fence. Both children were dead. Hearing moaning, a police constable climbed over a high wall where he found 18-year-old Edith Milgate, physically thrown by the blast over the opposite house. She had a fractured skull, a broken right ankle, left thigh and left arm. She died a few hours later. Samuel, the children's father, remained in hospital for a week but died the day after they buried his three children. Only Mary, his wife, and Beatrice, the eldest daughter, survived.

Frances Grant's sister, living opposite the bombed houses, ran out and struggled to make sense of the shocking sight, seeing Mrs Kingston standing alone amidst the rubble that been her home just moments before. With blood running down an arm, Mrs Kingston just stood there repeating to herself, 'I know they're all dead, I know they're all dead'. Helpers took the distraught woman to a neighbour's house, but there she sat in a rocking chair in the window looking on as rescuers brought out one-by-one all seven of her children and her nephew, either already dead or dying. When Mrs Kingston's married daughter, Joyce, arrived she found her mother rocking to and fro, calling her children's names. Although needing hospital treatment, Mrs Kingston attended the funeral. Carried to the graveside by a friend, she said a final goodbye to her family with Joyce by her side, the only one of her eight children now alive.

Frances Grant died too, buried beneath the rubble. Edward Dorey lost consciousness when the bomb exploded. His only memory of the incident being an odd 'squeak' made by his wife, Emma. Edward regained consciousness in hospital only to discover Emma, aged 72, had died. He told the inquest, 'I have lost everything'.[18]

A final desperate story of survival emerged from No. 13. Mrs Jenner heard the rush of air before the bomb exploded and the house crashed down around her. As the rubble settled, a beam slanted across the room creating a gap where she and six others were crowded. Mrs Jenner, summoning all her strength, held back a partition with her shoulders and one by one the rest were able to crawl to safety – except 8-year-old Edith. Mrs Jenner tried to look for Edith but her strength failed, she collapsed and the partition fell. Rescuers pulled Mrs Jenner clear, but when they eventually found Edith, life had ebbed away.

The families in Hither Green became the last victims of the Zeppelin campaign against London. Zeppelins would not return to the capital.

High above, Zeppelin L 45 continued onwards but at about 11.40pm descended and escaped the worst of the wind. Flying on a homeward course, Kölle reached the mouth of the River Medway, but there, L 45 came under a long-range attack by Second Lieutenant Thomas Pritchard of No. 39 Squadron. Determined not to be shot down, Kölle immediately climbed but as he did so the wind caught him again and swept him towards France.

Events now began to conspire against the crew of L 45. They lost the use of one engine while still over England and two more when over France. Despite determined efforts to push east over the next few hours, the lack of engine power prevented L 45 breaking clear of the gale's grasp. And so it continued. With the Mediterranean coast now just 70 miles away Kölle resigned himself to the fact that he could not get L 45 home and took the decision to bring her down.

They landed in a wide, almost dry riverbed just north-west of Sisteron, but as she hit the ground a gust of wind forced L 45 over, ripping off the port engine gondola with two men inside; another two men jumped from the rear engine gondola. Thus lightened and uncontrollable, L 45 began to rise, but another gust of wind dashed her down onto an island about 600 yards further on in the very shallow River Buëch where the rest of the crew scrambled clear of the wreckage. A crowd of angry French farm workers set upon the first four men ejected from L 45, but the others were able to set fire to the Zeppelin and surrender at a nearby village.

Eleven Zeppelins had left their bases in Germany, determined to cause havoc and destruction over the industrial north of England. Estimates for the damage they inflicted came in at £54,346 of which £48,205 resulted from L 45's London bombs. The damage attributed to the other ten Zeppelins, and L 45's attack on Northampton, amounted to just over £6,000. For this, Germany lost five Zeppelins, each costing the government in region of £150,000 to construct, and four crews.[19] It could not be considered anything other than a disaster for Germany's Naval Airship Division.

Yet it could so easily have been a huge success, a fact not lost on those responsible for Britain's defence. Eleven Zeppelins of the most modern type had appeared over Britain at heights beyond the reach of the Home Defences. Britain had nothing capable of preventing the completion of their mission if the powerful winds had not taken a hand. As the official historian of Britain's air war remarked: 'The fact remains, however, that had the Zeppelins come and gone without let or hindrance, as they well might, the airship menace would, once again, have become a very live one.'[20] But it did not.

Peter Strasser remained bullish, blaming the disaster on the metrological service for the absence of high-altitude information, but he also highlighted problems with transmitting and receiving wireless bearings, engine breakdowns and altitude sickness. The Zeppelins would come again, but in those last thirteen months of war there would be only three more Zeppelin nights.

The time for the Gothas and the Giants to take up the baton once more had arrived; they alone would carry it for the next five months.

Chapter 12

'Got it!'

The poor weather that brought the Harvest Moon Offensive to a close on 1 October still held sway at the end of that month. Keen to take advantage of the full moon, which the bomber crews favoured, Rudolf Kleine ordered a raid for the night of 29 October but, due to the conditions, targets were limited to coastal areas with just three volunteer crews taking part. Once in the air two of the crews aborted due to heavy cloud, unloading their bombs on Calais before returning. Although only one Gotha reached England, appearing over Essex, the official report claims there were four separate detachments of which only one dropped bombs; the other 'detachments' were in fact Home Defence aircraft unsuccessfully searching for the raider.

At 10.22pm, as the Gotha headed south-west, the first bomb exploded on farmland about half a mile north-east of Burnham-on-Crouch. About 10 minutes later the anti-aircraft gun at Bowers Gifford opened, followed by the Canvey Island gun. This turned the Gotha, which then dropped a line of ten bombs between Rayleigh and Hockley, close to the railway line leading to Southend. They smashed a water main and damaged two cottages in Rayleigh, and in Hockley broke windows and killed a turkey.

Two days later another brief 'hit and run' raid took place on Dover at 4.30am. It is unclear who made the raid but it does not appear to have been *Kagohl 3*. The speed of the enterprise prevented any aerial response and the anti-aircraft guns were in action for just 45 seconds. Explosive bombs brought down telegraph wires at the RFC's Swingate Down airfield, while others smashed windows at a farm at Guston, used by the RFC as a sergeants' mess, before the final bombs fell in Admiralty Harbour and in the sea.

31 October 1917, 10.37pm: Kent

Later the same day, the weather and the moon combined to give Kleine the chance he had been impatiently waiting for and he readied 22 Gothas. A new incendiary bomb, weighing just 4.5kg, had just been introduced meaning great numbers could be carried by individual aircraft. It gave new hope to the long-held goal of setting great fires burning across London. Kleine planned a staggered approach over Kent towards London but, as the night wore on, freshening winds pushed some of the raiders north to come in over Essex; for once, none of the raiders dropped out. Although London remained the principal target, 183 of the 274[1] bombs dropped during the raid fell on Kent as intense anti-aircraft fire turned back some of the Gothas; others were content to restrict themselves to attacking coastal towns. The extended attack on Kent lasted for about three hours but, despite the number of bombs, they killed only one person, injured two others while causing only minimal damage.

The first bombs dropped on Dover at 10.37pm (one explosive and 22 incendiaries), all close to the sea front.[2] They started a fire at the RNAS seaplane station at East Cliffe, and another onboard a cross-channel troop ferry, but these were quickly extinguished. The sole explosive bomb detonated near the Prince of Wales Pier, under which two men were sheltering. The explosion injured one of them but killed the other, Walter Gibbs of the Royal Naval Reserve. Thirty minutes later three bombs fell at Guston but they only broke a couple of telegraph wires.

Shortly after 11.00pm a Gotha appeared over Herne Bay on the north Kent coast, dropping seven explosive bombs and three incendiaries on the town, damaging walls, ceilings and windows in 62 houses. At neighbouring Edington, breaking glass injured a woman, but at Whitstable an incendiary bomb failed to ignite.

At 11.30pm an incendiary fell at South Preston, followed 25 minutes later by an explosive bomb at Fawkham, near an anti-aircraft gun and searchlight, which also attracted more bombs later. Others landed at Dartford, Southfleet, Cuxton and Darenth, but all failed to cause any damage.

Between 11.40 and 11.50pm, 16 incendiary bombs fell around villages to the south of Canterbury, where the army had established camps, but again they caused no damage. A similar result ensued from the six incendiaries that were dropped over Westgate and Garlinge at 11.50pm. Bombs followed at East Northdown and Kingsgate, with one house damaged at the latter place. And at 12.30am a single incendiary at

Walmer burnt out without effect. Over the next 10 minutes an incendiary fell at Wormshill near Frinsted, followed by 18 of the 12kg explosive bombs on villages north-west of Ashford, but all failed to wreak any damage.

At about 12.20am an explosive bomb struck a bakery in Canterbury Street, Gillingham, damaging machinery and stock to the value of £5,000, but 17 other bombs between 12.40 and 1.15am at Ridley, Longfield and Ash, near Wrotham, failed to have any impact, and a 50kg explosive bomb at Linton failed to detonate.

Between 1.15 and 1.30am, returning Gothas passing over north Kent dropped bombs at Dartford, Swanscombe, Northfleet, Gravesend, Denton and another at Gillingham. Only at Gravesend did the bombs make their mark, damaging two houses and a school. Another returning Gotha offloaded five bombs over Ramsgate as it headed out to sea. Two struck the gas works in Boundary Road, damaging the purifier, with bomb fragments piercing one of the gasometers 'in nearly a hundred places'. The escaping gas caught fire, creating 'blazing jets which illuminated the whole district'.[3] Ten houses in Boundary Road, as well as a pub and six shops were damaged in the blast, while another bomb damaged properties in South Eastern Road.

In Essex a Gotha came under anti-aircraft fire from Canvey Island at 12.25am, soon joined by three other guns. It retaliated by dropping an explosive bomb at Corringham and seven incendiary bombs, at Mucking, West Tilbury, Stifford, West Thurrock and Rainham. They all burnt out on marshy or open land.

Now attention turned to London.

Although these days Slade Green and Erith form part of the great urban sprawl of south-east London, at the time they were both considered part of Kent, but Erith's large engineering works produced guns and ammunition for the war effort. Two Gothas encountering spirited barrage fire as they approached Woolwich turned away and released their bombs. At 11.49pm 13 bombs (six 50kg explosive and seven incendiaries) were released over Erith, followed a minute later by 22 incendiaries at Slade Green, but these later bombs inflicted no damage. At Erith, a bomb sliced a house in half at 63 Alexandra Road, wrecking those on either side and killing bricklayer George Jarvis and an 87-year-old widow, Caroline Sutton; two other women and a child were injured. In the same road an incendiary bomb at No. 71 failed to ignite but still damaged the roof and upper floor. At 3 East Terrace, Crayford Road, three people were hurt when a bomb demolished the house, two that exploded in Queen's Road injured a man, another smashed a water main in Park Crescent and at 58 Crayford Road an explosion injured a policeman and damaged two houses.

To the west, the population of London waited nervously.

> London slumbered beneath a silvery radiance. The warning had been received, and between then and midnight sounds of distant gunfire indicated that the outer defences were keeping the enemy at bay.
>
> A long silence ensued, until a quarter or ten minutes to one, when the duel between batteries and aircraft was suddenly transferred to the London area.[4]

1 November 1917, 12.45am: London

Those first London bombs – incendiaries – dropped silently at about 12.45am in Silvertown, close to the Royal Victoria and Royal Albert docks, before the Gotha crossed the Thames and the first explosions reverberated in East Greenwich. Passing over the Isle of Dogs, incendiary bombs fell in Manchester Road followed by West Ferry Road, where a fire caused some damage to the Seamen's Institute. Recrossing the Thames, four incendiary bombs fell between Deptford Green and Blackheath – one close to the historic Royal Observatory in Greenwich Park – but none caused any damage. At Charlton the Gotha returned to the Thames, dropping bombs along the industrial river front, but the only significant damage occurred at a storehouse of the Silicate Paint Works.

At least one Gotha struggled in the face of London's fierce barrage.

> The curtain of fire drove it relentlessly from district to district, from end to end of the Metropolis, refusing to allow it to return by the way it came, until the occupants must have completely lost their bearings… From one locality the barrage forced the aeroplane towards the curtain of shells from the next district, which in its turn drove it further afield.[5]

This intense barrage fire drove one Gotha as far as Richmond Park in the south-west of the capital before it could turn back east. Unfortunately for those living in Tooting, it dropped its first three bombs there at 1.30am, two in Dafforne Road and one in Romberg Road.

At 39 Romberg Road the Page family were asleep when the warning sounded, but Alfred Page woke his family. One of his sons, H.J. Page, recalled: 'I can remember my father shaking my brother and me into wakefulness that night and saying, "Quickly boys! The raiders are coming nearer."'

> Half-dressed and more asleep than awake, we were hustled downstairs and took shelter in the drawing room under an improvised dug-out constructed by Father, which consisted of a settee inverted upon two chairs. A similar shelter had been made in the dining room for Mother, my sister and a woman friend.
>
> The droning of the enemy aeroplanes became louder and louder, while the shrapnel from our anti-aircraft guns could be heard thudding on the roof.[6]

Mrs Page heard the explosion in Dafforne Road and shouted to her husband in the other room, before hearing 'a dull whine, a crash and then oblivion', as their house collapsed. In the dining room shelter the explosion killed the family's friend, Sarah Statt, but after three hours' painstaking work, rescuers extricated Mrs Page and her little daughter from the rubble, their lives saved by the makeshift shelter.[7] The drawing room shelter, however, proved less successful. Alfred Page and a son, also called Alfred, both died, but the other son, H.J., escaped with injuries to his foot and side. The bomb also wrecked the houses on either side where a woman and two children suffered injury. Mrs Weddell, the mother-in-law of one of the neighbours, greatly relieved that her family had survived, looked on respectfully when rescuers pulled the body of 13-year-old Alfred Page from the rubble.

> The house adjoining was completely destroyed and three people were killed in it, one a Boy Scout, who was fully dressed in his uniform when he was found, and had near him his bugle all ready to sound the 'All clear' when the time came. He was completely buried upside down, only his feet being visible.[8]

All along Romberg Road and Dafforne Road windows were smashed, and the next bomb, which detonated on allotments in Avoca Road, resulted in more broken glass, but no casualties. Those first four bombs had been dropped at intervals of around 100 yards, but now the Gotha reached Streatham before the next six fell, although they only caused light damage with the lone significant building affected being the Tate Library on the High Road.

The final Gotha appeared over Plaistow in east London at about 1.40am, dropping bombs in Woodside Road and Cumberland Road, damaging over forty houses, mostly of a minor nature, and injuring a woman. Continuing a south-west course for 2 miles, the Gotha's next bombs fell over the docks on the Isle of Dogs but these were generally ineffective, except for one in Maria Street which caused widespread damage, but everyone escaped injury.[9] Crossing over the Thames, a bomb landed in Greenland Dock at the Surrey Commercial Docks, followed by one in Deptford Park where the RNAS operated a searchlight, damaging a building used by the crew and industrial premises. The Gotha headed south-west for about 6 miles, no doubt engaged by the gun barrage and, at 1.50am, found itself over Tooting where it dropped three explosive bombs, the first just 700 yards from where the previous bombing run over Tooting had commenced.

At 31 Crockerton Road, a large house converted into upper and lower flats, Frank Marwood, an aeronautical engineer, lived in the upper flat and had a housemaid, Maria Carter. The owner of the ground floor flat invited them both down when the raid warning sounded. They were joined downstairs by the Elston family and an army officer, Second Lieutenant David Douglas of the East Lancashire Regiment. Marwood, Mr Elston and Douglas stood in the hallway looking out through the open front door as Maria Carter came down the stairs; she noted that the gun firing became very heavy before a bomb fell outside: 'I was dazed and glass covered me,' she told the inquest. 'When I recovered I saw Mr Marwood falling, and Mr Elston was lying near the stairs, while Douglas was lying nearby,' adding, almost apologetically, 'I did what I could, I gave them water.'[10]

Rescuers found Mrs Elston lying across a bed, both she and her husband were badly injured and removed to hospital, but Marwood and Douglas died.

In Brenda Road, running parallel to Crockerton Road, Harold Greenwood and his wife lived in the upper flat at No. 23 but they were also sheltering downstairs. They were in the hallway when Mr Greenwood said he could hear an aeroplane, to which his wife replied, 'I don't like this music,' and made towards the kitchen. As she did so, a shattering explosion occurred no more than 5ft from the front door.

Looking back in horror she saw her husband face down on the floor near the stairs – dead.[11]

The Gotha dropped a final bomb 200 yards further on, in the back garden of 2 Langroyd Road, smashing windows but claiming no more lives.

By 2.40am the last bomber had cleared the coast. Although the anti-aircraft guns had made conditions difficult for the Gotha crews, they failed to damage any of the raiders, but in London five people were injured by falling shells and a woman in Hammersmith, Anna Silcocks, died when one struck her house. The five RNAS aircraft and 45 of the RFC that patrolled the sky were also unable to intercept any of the raiders. Even so, the German plan to start fires burning across the capital had come to naught – British sources calculate the impact of the raid at £22,822. And as the returning crews of the *Englandgeschwader* neared Belgium they found the region shrouded by a cloak of thick grey fog. With fuel running low the returning pilots had no choice but to descend blindly through the murk to reach safety; five of them were wrecked.

Bad weather then dominated the whole month of November and prevented further bombing attempts. With many new crews being assigned to *Kagohl 3*, Kleine used the time to introduce a new intense training programme for all his men.

Only on 5 December did Kleine receive news of a possible break in the weather, offering a chance to strike London. But to make sure, a Rumpler C.IV reconnaissance aircraft fitted with a two-way radio telegraph preceded the attack, able to send back updated weather information. The message Kleine received gave positive news.

6 December 1917, 2.15am: Sheerness

Britain's defences received the first intelligence of approaching bombers at 1.40am from lightships at the mouth of the Thames Estuary, and at 2.04am LADA issued the 'Readiness' order. A procession of 16 Gothas (three had already dropped out) and two of *Rfa 501's* Giants crossed the English coast between 2.00 and 4.30am, predominantly loaded with 4.5kg incendiary bombs.[12]

The sound of aeroplane engines soon reached gun crews on the Isle of Sheppey and at 2.15am the gun at Barton's Point opened fire. Three minutes later bombs began to drop on Sheerness, but another 12 minutes passed before the air raid warning sounded in the town. By then people were dead and buildings wrecked.

The first bomber may have been one of the Giants and carried at least eight explosive bombs which dropped in a straight line starting in Cavour Road and all along Invicta Road before reaching the Thames again, where more may have dropped. The area had suffered previously during the 5 June raid on the town. The first of the bombs injured four people, the second added three more to the list. The fourth bomb, at 141 Invicta Road, became the first to claim lives. In a letter, Walter Bateson, a fitter at the dockyard, explained to his wife, staying in Cornwall with their daughter Murial, what happened.

> One of our fitters [James Hubbard] was killed with his mother [Mary] in the same house but his little girl about Muriel's age, after the roof falling in, both walls front and back falling out, the partition walls demolished and the bedstead through the ceiling on the ground floor, all smashed up, when they turned back the counterpane she was not even scratched and only passed the remark 'Daddy. I do feel so cold'.[13]

It took about an hour to rescue the child, her bed exposed to the chill night air, but her Daddy could not help. The bed, which had come through the ceiling, had broken his neck – and her mother bore injuries too. Bateson concluded, 'It was something horrible.'

At 133 Invicta Road another bomb injured a mother and her two children, while one at No. 129 killed 37-year-old Laura Cox in her bed. She and her husband had been asleep when debris crashed down and buried them. Rescuers found her husband sitting upright but unable to move. He explained at the inquest that his wife managed to say a few words to him after the explosion but died minutes later.

About 80 yards further along the road, an explosion at No. 97 killed a Royal Navy shipwright, Horace Mouatt. At home with his wife and awoken by the guns, Mouatt had gone downstairs and opened the front door to look out into the street. He had just shut it again when the bomb exploded, blasting the door inwards, and killing him. The final bomb injured a woman living at No. 44. The string of bombs all dropped within the space of about 10 seconds.

But the raid was not over. About 18 minutes after the first attack, a Gotha appeared over Sheerness dockyard loaded with an entire cargo of the new incendiary bombs. The official report identified 17 of the bombs on land but inevitably others dropped over the Thames Estuary.

The first three landed in the dockyard but damaged only one building. The next four landed at or close to the Dockyard Station, damaging the roof of the engine house while another smashed into a passenger carriage. No one noticed at the time as it had failed to burn. Later, the train departed and only when it stopped at Sittingbourne and a passenger opened the door of the damaged compartment did the bomb, resting on a seat, come to light. The remaining bombs fell in a line, some on open ground, others failed to detonate, with only a couple of houses suffering minor damage. The final incendiary bomb fell in Cavour Road, just 40 yards from where the first of the explosive bombs had detonated. In the time between the first and last bombs, four people had died with at least 12 more injured.

As with the previous raid, the main route towards London passed over Kent, where, in addition to those in Sheerness, more bombs dropped. Three in the Dover area at 3.35am resulted in damage to a hut at Connaught Barracks and a paint store set on fire at the docks. At the same time about 20 incendiary bombs dropped between the airfield at Manston and Margate, but all without effect. At 4.00am two bombs fell on marshland between the village of Graveney and the sea then, 20 minutes later, an incendiary set fire to a house in Margate at 2 Oxford Street, occupied by Mrs Yeomans, a soldier's wife, and a lodger Amelia Roberts. Both were trapped inside the burning building and although rescued from the flames, Mrs Roberts later died from her injuries.

At about 4.30am a raid developed near Ramsgate when an explosive bomb landed in a field at Minster-in-Thanet followed by a 100kg bomb on the foreshore at Pegwell Bay, then 28 incendiary bombs tumbled down but the only damage occurred at the porter's lodge at Westcliff Terrace on Pegwell Road. A bomb smashed through the roof of the portico and began to burn, but water that had pooled on the roof poured through the hole and extinguished the flames.

Ten minutes after the bombs near Ramsgate, another attack commenced on the north Kent coast, between Seasalter and Herne Bay, via Whitstable. Although it appears the bomber kept close to the railway line, and at Whitstable bombs fell at the station and in the town, an estimate of the damage amounted to just £5. At 4.45am nine incendiaries that dropped over Herne Bay failed to find any targets, before the same Gotha dropped 27 incendiaries and a single explosive bomb on Margate. Two houses, in Buckingham Road and Norfolk Road, suffered damage and a large fire broke out at the Auction Mart at 120 High Street.

6 December 1917, 4.45am: Rochford

North of the Thames three Gothas tried to approach London over Essex. At 4.35am one dropped two incendiary bombs aimed at the Tunnel anti-aircraft gun at West Thurrock as it headed for east London. Ten minutes later another Gotha dropped 15 incendiary bombs on open ground at Purfleet before crossing the Thames and making a sortie across south-east London. The third Gotha had a very different experience.

The crew of the Gotha G.V, *Leutnant* R. Wessels, pilot *Gemeiner* J. Rzechtalski and gunner *Vizefeldwebel* O. Jakobs, came inland over Canvey Island at about 4.20am but, pushing westwards, ran into barrage fire from the guns at Bower's Gifford and Hawkesbury Bush, which shattered a propeller. The pilot turned away from the guns but it quickly became apparent they were in trouble. Having observed flares burning at No. 61 Squadron's Rochford airfield, north of Southend, the crew decided to try their luck and land there, rather than crash into the sea. By pure chance the crew fired a green flare as they came in to land, which happened to be the pre-arranged signal colour of the day for the airfield. Able to make an unharried approach, Rzechtalski prepared to land but, unfamiliar with the airfield's layout, the Gotha hit a tree and crashed on the neighbouring golf course at 4.45am. Presuming the aircraft to be British, RFC personnel dashed over to help but were amazed when three Germans emerged from the battered aeroplane.

Police Sergeant Rennett also heard the crash.

> [I] found a German aeroplane on the Golf Links about 600 yards south of Rochford Church. It was on the ground surrounded by members of the Royal Flying Corps who had one man (a German) on the stretcher injured and two other Germans under arrest... The machine was at the time only apparently slightly damaged... Some 68 incendiary bombs and 2 aerial torpedoes had been taken from the machine and laid on the grass also two machine guns and some machine gun ammunition.[14]

Captain Cecil Lewis, now with No. 61 Squadron, had flown an earlier patrol that evening and had retired for the night.

> There was a knock on the door... I half woke up. 'What is it now?'

> 'There's a Gotha down, sir. Crashed on the edge of the aerodrome, sir. The crew are prisoners in the guardroom, sir.'
>
> It was exciting news enough; but I was too sleepy and tired after that patrol. The thing would still be there in the morning. I grunted and went to sleep again.
>
> Thus it happened that I never saw a Gotha, for the thing was not there in the morning.[15]

No intact Gotha had yet fallen into Allied hands and this unexpected prize promised to reveal the aircraft's secrets. Pilots were aware of rumours that a tunnel through the fuselage allowed the rear gunner to fire down below its tail, the favoured position when attacking an enemy aircraft. The intact Gotha lying out on the airfield could explain that mystery and offer insights into its weaknesses. But while Lewis returned to blissful sleep the prize went up in flames.

> Some officers turned out to inspect the wreckage and remove the bombs… They also took out the Very Light pistol… The machine was pretty well smashed up and the tanks had burst, flooding the ground with petrol. The Equipment Officer, who had taken the Very Light Pistol, slipped it into the pocket of his mackintosh. As he walked away, he pulled it out to show to one of the others. The trigger had no guard, caught in his pocket flap, and the pistol went off. The white-hot magnesium flare bounced along the ground, reached the petrol, and instantly the whole wreckage was in flames.[16]

When Lewis strolled out in the morning, now keen to inspect the grounded Gotha, he found only 'the charred iron-work of the fuselage, the engines and wires'.

For the six Gotha crews that battled their way through the barrage, London now lay ahead. Their bombs dropped over the capital between 4.38 and 5.43am.

> The first action of hundreds of people who were awakened yesterday morning by the firing of the guns was to take a glance at the time…

This 'cock-crow' raid on London came after an interval of more than a month of undisturbed nights, and dispelled from many minds the comfortable theory that the enemy would not send his aeroplanes over in cold weather. At midnight on Wednesday the frost seemed to have become more keen, and with ice on the window-panes a raid was not generally expected, although the stars glittered brightly in the sky, and there was not a whisper of wind. Those that looked out at the time the raid was in progress saw that the roofs were white with rime, and that a half-moon was ringed with a faint halo, which promised mist later in the morning.[17]

6 December 1917, 4.38am: London

The first Gotha arrived over south-east London, releasing six incendiaries on Sydenham with very limited effect at 4.38am. The outcome was different, however, when an incendiary and two explosive bombs hit Dulwich four minutes later. One of the bombs exploded on a building in College Road owned by the Red Cross. Adam Howie, the caretaker, lived in an annexe with his wife Edith, and had their 12-year-old niece, Edith Callaway, staying with them. Adam had gone downstairs to light the stove when he disappeared under a cloud of plaster as the ceiling collapsed and injured him. Having also heard a crash from upstairs, he dusted himself down and returned to the bedroom but could find no sign of his wife or niece amidst the wreckage.

Help quickly arrived and, hearing voices, they began pulling away the debris, but found no one. Yet they could still hear voices. Carefully listening, they traced the sound to a field outside; the explosion had blasted Edith and her niece out through the roof. They carefully dug away at a mound of earth to discover the pair underneath. They were still alive, barely, but died shortly afterwards.[18] They were the only people killed by bombs that early morning.

The Gotha continued dropping bombs: seven over Clapham, where an explosion in Paradise Road injured three children and caused widespread damage, three in Chelsea, four in Kennington and 11 around Brixton. Considerable damage resulted in some places, particularly in Kennington Road and in Burgoyne Road, Brixton.

The second Gotha also came in via south-east London, dropping 15 incendiaries over Lee and Brockley at 4.45am, with little damage recorded, before the raider steered towards the City, with four more incendiary bombs damaging a chemist's shop in Holborn and a rubber goods merchant in Farringdon Street. One of ten then released over Clerkenwell started a significant fire in Exmouth Street (now Exmouth Market) before the Gotha banked to the south, dropping 13 incendiaries between Holborn and the Strand. One caused a major fire in Henry Street (now Roger Street), off Greys Inn Road, completely burning out the Acorn Brush Works. Crossing back over the Thames to south London, the last incendiaries fell in Lambeth (nine), Kennington (one), Brixton (eight) and Dulwich (two and two explosive bombs). Only one of these, at 120 Oakley Road, Kennington, developed into a serious fire.

The Gotha that had earlier dropped 15 incendiary bombs over Purfleet, crossed the Thames and released nine more and two explosive bombs between Blackheath and Chislehurst. One of the bombs exploded outside 14 Blackheath Park seriously damaging roofs and house frontages.

At about 5.00am a single incendiary dropped in Chelsea heralding a new attack as a Gotha headed north-east over the capital, dropping 50 incendiaries over Hoxton, Shoreditch, Finsbury, Stepney, Hackney and Dalston. In Curtain Road, Shoreditch, a huge fire engulfed the premises of a cabinet makers, where an estimate of the damage reached £45,000, with the flames spreading to Worship Street and the factory of Rose & Co, producers of lime cordial. Another burnt out a cigar box manufacturer at 21 Hanbury Street, also affecting a nearby brewery, and one caused a large fire at 393 Commercial Road.

At 5.06am another Gotha began dropping 60 incendiary bombs on Islington, St Pancras, Kensington, Westminster, Bloomsbury, Bethnal Green, Whitechapel and Hackney, but serious outbreaks of fire were restricted to 113 High Street, Whitechapel and 5 Columbia Road, Bethnal Green.

At around 5.30am a sixth Gotha made an appearance, dropping its load of incendiaries on Sydenham, Dulwich, Brockley, Clapham, Stockwell and Battersea, before looping around over the Thames and dropping more on Peckham Rye, Lewisham and Chislehurst. The Gotha also dropped a single explosive bomb at Stockwell, which caused significant damage to a school and brewery on Lingham Street and to neighbouring houses.

All the Gothas that had reached London were now on their outbound flights, hoping to avoid the barrage and the patrolling British aircraft. But one had found trouble.

> A correspondent in a London suburb states that the gunnery there was exceptionally good, and a series of shell-bursts culminated in one which apparently struck a raider. Loud

cheers were raised, and cries of 'Got him!' The enemy machine was seen to wobble and descend slowly to the north.[19]

A shell had damaged the Gotha's port radiator causing the engine to overheat. The crew nursed their aeroplane back over Kent but, when the engine caught fire, they had no choice but to crash-land. Although two of the crew were injured when the Gotha came down in a field at Hackington, between Canterbury and Sturry, they were still able to set it on fire and deny it to the enemy. The crew of *Leutnant* Franz Schulte, pilot *Vizefeldwebel* B. Senf and gunner *Leutnant* P. Barnard then surrendered to the Reverend Philip Somerville and G. Haimes, two special constables who had heard the crash and rushed to the spot.

Another Gotha failed to reach home, possibly due to damage inflicted over England. It crashed into the sea off Dunkirk with the loss of the three-man crew. In addition, another broke up when landing at its airfield and two more made forced landings in Belgium behind German lines, including Kleine's own Gotha.

The raid had taken British defences by surprise; no previous attack had commenced around 5.00am before. But despite the large number of bombs deployed, the damage they inflicted was small in comparison. British records show 276 bombs (267 incendiary and nine explosive) in the London area, with 148 (129 incendiary and 19 explosive) across the rest of the south-east. Those bombs caused damage estimated at £103,408, the highest total since the second daylight Gotha raid on 7 July, which suggests the raid and the new bombs were successful, but these figures are misleading. The London Fire Brigade estimated the damage in the wider capital area at £92,257, but with £75,285 of this attributed to just three fires, in Curtain Road, Whitechapel Road and Henry Street. In his report, Rudolf Kleine commented that only two or three fires were observed and he questioned the effectiveness of the new 4.5kg incendiary bombs.

> From the present experience it cannot be assumed that the dropping of even larger quantities of incendiary bombs of the present type will have the desired effect. In any case in no locality were a larger number of fires observed than during previous raids when [explosive] bombs were used. The incendiary bombs lacked the great morale effect of the [explosive] bombs.[20]

A German historian, *Major* Freiherr von Bülow, later condemned the effectiveness of the bombs.

A great deal of time was spent over the design of these incendiary bombs, on whose effect on the densely populated London area such high hopes were based. The bomb was a complete failure. During two night raids on England, on 31st of October and the 6th of December, 1917, large numbers of these bombs were dropped, both times with no success. The sound idea of creating panic and disorder by numbers of fires came to nothing owing to the inadequacy of the material employed.[21]

If Rudolf Kleine intended to press his objections to the continued deployment of the new incendiary bombs, we will never know. Six days after that last raid, *Kagohl 3* took part in a short-distance daylight raid on military camps near Ypres. Five Nieuport fighters of No. 1 Squadron, RFC, pounced on the formation of 17 Gothas. Bullets raked Kleine's Gotha, which burst into flames and crashed in 'No Man's Land'. A German soldier found the commander of *Kagohl 3* still sitting in the aircraft, killed by a bullet through his head. Brought back to Ghent, he received a full military funeral, attended by the recuperating Ernst Brandenburg, Kleine's predecessor as commander of *Kagohl 3*. *Kogenluft* Ernst von Hoeppner, heaped praise on Kleine, describing him as 'one of whom I expected much. His name, and the air raids he led against England, stand indelibly inscribed in the annals of this war and the honour roll of the *Luftstreitkräfte*'.[22] In Britain, however, the authorities considered Kleine a risk-taker: 'There is little doubt that the vigorous personality of this officer has been instrumental in leading raids over England on occasions when the weather conditions would have deterred other men.'[23] The losses for *Kagohl 3*, in both aircraft and experienced crews, were stacking up.

Chapter 13

'I'll shoot the first man to light a match'

In Belgium, Ernst von Hoeppner, the commander of the *Luftstreitkräfte*, wasted no time in announcing a new leader of *Kagohl 3*, appointing *Oberleutnant* Richard Walter, the squadron's senior flight commander, as acting squadron commander the day after Kleine's death. Hopes remained high that Ernst Brandenburg, the squadron's original commander, would soon be able to return to duty after completing his rehabilitation following the loss of a leg in June. But for now, command of the squadron lay in Walter's hands.

A few days later, notification reached Walter of a favourable break in the weather forecast for 18 December, but the moon cycle conspired against him. Whereas the Zeppelins favoured the dark nights of a new moon, the Gothas timed their attacks to coincide with brighter nights around the full moon. On 18 December the new moon was just four days old, but a fresh fall of snow ensured the dark winding path of the River Thames stood out starkly against the white-blanketed countryside. Because of the phase of the moon and the weather, no one in Britain anticipated a raid.

That same day also saw a reorganisation of Germany's *Kampfgeschwader*. Concern over the arrival of American troops on the Western Front led to a demand for increased bombing flexibility and capacity. To achieve this, the existing *Kampfgeschwader* were doubled in number by reducing each from six flights to three. However, because of its specific role, *Kagohl 3* remained at full strength. On 18 December, however, they were all renamed *Bombengeschwader*, with *Kagohl 3* now identified as *Bombengeschwader 3 der Obersten Heeresleitung*, abbreviated to *Bogohl 3*.

On that day 15 Gothas set out, with two forced to turn back before reaching Britain; they were followed by a single Giant, R12, the six-engined R.IV type. For incendiary bombs, the squadron reverted to older types due to Kleine's dissatisfaction with the new 4.5kg version used on the two previous raids.

Before the main attack developed on London, bombs dropped, as usual, over Kent and Essex.

18 December 1917, 6.25pm: Essex

One of the first Gothas that passed over Essex dropped four explosive bombs at the village of Hutton (12kg) and five at Shenfield (50kg), between Billericay and Brentwood. Broken windows crashed down and a woman fell fatally injured. Madeline Elsie Bates, a nurse home on leave from France, had come to stay at an aunt's house in Shenfield. The sudden appearance of a Gotha at 6.25pm caught the warning system off guard and only the sound of exploding bombs announced the raid. The victim, unaware of the approaching danger, stood outside on a veranda. A doctor noted she had been hit either by a bomb fragment or a stone thrown up by the explosion. It struck her right temple, smashed her skull and exposed her brain. She never regained consciousness and died in hospital four days later.[1] About 15 minutes later three bombs dropped at Kynochtown, near Corringham, where many of the workers at the Kynoch Explosive Works lived. One of the bombs wrecked a hut and injured three men. More activity also occurred on the Kent coast at about the same time.

18 December 1917, 6.05 – 7.57pm: Margate

At about 6.05pm a Gotha dropped 12 explosive bombs – a mixture of 50kg and 12kg – south of Margate, from Hengrove golf course to St Peter's. In Glencoe Road about 20 houses had windows broken, as did 12 cottages near Twenties Farm, and a house in Lister Road lost its windows and sustained internal damage.

Fifteen minutes later another Gotha dropped a line of 16 bombs (nine explosive and seven incendiaries) east of Canterbury, at Patrixbourne, Bekesbourne, Littlebourne and Westbere. None caused any damage even though six of the bombs were aimed at No. 50 Squadron's Bekesbourne airfield where all the aircraft were on the ground.

A third attack on Kent developed over Margate at 6.22pm when 16 explosive bombs (6 x 50kg and 10 x 12kg) fell on the town with damage recorded at 146 properties. An imposing building on Byron Road attracted six bombs, the Gotha commander no doubt believing it to be of some military or civil significance. The gothic-style building, however, housed the Deaf & Dumb Asylum. Fortunately, there were no injuries. Other bombs damaged property in Addington Road and the surrounding district, including at the Foresters Hall, the Emmanuel Church and its schoolroom, and the cricket pitch at Margate College.

At 6.40pm a couple of 50kg bombs landed in open countryside about 2 miles north of Deal before, at 7.57pm, a final attack on Margate took place. The only bomb to cause damage exploded at Clifton Baths on the seafront. It demolished an office and cottage at the Baths, as well as damaging 43 shops and homes in Cliff Terrace and neighbouring streets, with one woman injured in the chaos. The value of the damage inflicted on Margate reached £12,000. But the main impact that night would be felt in London.

18 December 1917, 7.15pm: London

The raid on the capital took the population by surprise.

> [The] raid was the first to be made on London by heavier-than-air machines while the moon was so young – a thin sickle cut clear in an inky sky. Stars twinkled brightly overhead, partially obscured now and then by a light mist, which hung over the river and the riverside districts.
>
> The anti-aircraft guns came into action shortly before 7 o'clock, and firing continued fitfully for upwards of two hours. City offices had already been closed before the bombardment began, but many of the workers in West-End establishments had barely left work for home.
>
> As usual the underground platforms and passages of the tube railways quickly filled, and wherever a building offered solid cover people sought refuge from the danger of the open street. Though some motor-omnibuses and other vehicles continued their journeys during the early part of the raid, pedestrians quickly disappeared.[2]

Between 7.15 and 8.30pm, six Gothas bombed the capital. The 41 explosive bombs (26 x 50kg and 15 x 12kg) and four incendiaries fell across a wide area: Kentish Town, Charing Cross, Walworth, Lambeth, Bermondsey, The City, Farringdon, Clerkenwell, King's Cross and Islington.

One of the first, a 12kg bomb, exploded alongside the Thames on the Victoria Embankment, just a short distance from Cleopatra's Needle, which had been scarred in a previous Gotha raid in September. People were quietly waiting at a tram stop when the bomb exploded without warning. The injured were taken to hospital but four people lay dead: Beatrice Bowen, Minnie Constantine, Edith Maubon and Henry King. The inquest revealed a little of their backgrounds.

> Beatrice Bowen was a cook at a dairy company; King was sub-editor of the 'Church Times'; Miss Constantine was employed at a bookshop, and... had been caught in two previous air raids; Mrs Maubon was married to an Australian soldier six weeks ago, she was a barmaid.

Henry King also served as a Special Constable and had left his office earlier than usual to report for duty. 'He was,' said an inspector, 'a splendid type of man.'[3]

Other bombs fell in the Thames, the explosions injuring two men working on the river. About 10 minutes later five more fell in Spa Road and Southwark Park Road, Bermondsey. In Spa Road the Canadian Army had taken over a large building owned by the Salvation Army, using it as a store. It also served as an air raid shelter. Mrs Gibbons was there with her children.

> It was a sad sight to see youngsters crowding in whose parents were at work: they looked pitifully lost.
>
> After a little while a loud explosion occurred and the lights went out; the suspense was awful as we waited, expecting the roof to fall in. In the midst of the confusion a voice shouted. 'No lights! I'll shoot the first man to light a match.' We afterwards learned that a gas main had burst.[4]

The bombs injured one of Mrs Gibbons' children who had to be taken to hospital.

Ellen Tullemach, just 5 years old, also went to the shelter with her family; her 14-year-old sister explained what happened to them.

> I heard a bang, and something hit me on the head. I was stunned for some time, and then found myself covered with blood. My other little sister had Ellen in her arms, but she was killed. My mother is in hospital with broken fingers and shrapnel in her arms, and my little brother has shrapnel in his arms.[5]

The injured numbered 24, and one of them, Mary Johnson, died in early January.

At 7.25pm, one of the handful of incendiary bombs dropped on London struck a five-storey building in Farringdon Road, the warehouse and offices of John G. Murdoch & Co, piano manufacturers. The remaining employees still on the premises took shelter in the basement. A fire quickly took hold, fuelled by the great amount of highly flammable material there. Two of the employees, Thomas Littlefair and Thomas Crawley, rushed to man a fire appliance, with Crawley taking the hose while Littlefair climbed a spiral staircase to turn on the water. Flames quickly engulfed the staircase. The intensity of the blaze shocked one of the attending fire officers.

> Sub-officer Perrott... said that as his engine was approaching flames were stretching right across the road. It would have been a hopeless chance for anyone. The upper part of one side of the building fell into the road, and flames poured from every window. The fire was so fierce they could not get within 30ft or 40ft of it.[6]

Littlefair escaped the blaze, but firemen later found Crawley's body lying near the bottom of the spiral stairs, still holding the hose.

> A doctor said that deceased body was frozen, and had the appearance of having been in water for some time. Death was due to shock from burns followed by the exposure, the night being very cold.[7]

At 7.33pm a cluster of bombs landed east of King's Cross Station. One, in Wicklow Street, blasted a large hole and damaged a number of buildings.

Mrs Russell, the wife of a policeman, had taken shelter with her two daughters and others in the passageway of a building a few yards away. When he heard his home had been bombed, Constable Russell rushed there to find it wrecked. Neighbours told him his family had gone to the hospital; there he found 3-year-old Violet dead and his wife and other child badly hurt. Louisa Bird had been with the family.

> We were sheltering in the passage – about six of us… Suddenly there was a loud noise, and the next thing I remember was seeing Mrs Russell get up and pick the deceased up.[8]

Ada Brock, another of those in the passage, explained that 'they were all badly knocked about' by the blast, then she heard Mrs Russell cry out, 'My baby is killed'. The explosion also badly injured one of Mrs Brock's children.

Elsewhere in the street, widowed Mrs Whelan had gone to seek shelter with her two young sons and their elder brother, John, aged 15.

> [John] devoted himself to assisting the women and children into safety, and was still doing this when a bomb fell. [Mrs Whelan] was thrown down on top of her two children and the boy was blown through the door. At the hospital he said to her, 'They have hurt me. I am in terrible agony.'[9]

John Whelan died in hospital; seven others in Wicklow Road were injured. And there were up to 20 more injured by another explosion just a few yards away in King's Cross Road.

A few minutes later bombs fell in Clerkenwell. One struck 28 St John's Lane, ripping away the upper stories of a warehouse and offices. Debris cascaded down to the street, burying 76-year-old Daniel Pulham. Two passers-by heard groans and found the victim under a mass of rubble and concrete. His injuries were serious and he died in hospital.[10]

After the earlier bomb on Farringdon Road, another fell there at 8.10pm. It exploded on tram tracks outside No. 109, one of many tall buildings utilised as warehouses. A group of people 'a good distance away' were sheltering on a stairway in one of the buildings, but even so a metal fragment dug deeply into the thigh of textile worker Herbert Mainwaring.[11] He died before reaching hospital. Another man had a narrow escape when flying debris just missed his throat. Six other people in the area were injured.

This bomb had been one of the final ones dropped by the Gothas, but Giant R12 had only crossed the Essex coast at about 8.25pm. Approaching London from the north, R12 only began releasing bombs on reaching Westminster. All but one of them were incendiary, the exception being a single 300kg explosive bomb – the first of this size dropped by an aeroplane. It landed with a shattering crash in Lyall Street, Belgravia, ripping out a crater in the road about 30ft in diameter and 7ft deep; it smashed a gas main, two water mains and the main sewer. Damage spread to many buildings beyond Lyall Street, including the Russian Embassy in Chesham Place.

Of the 43 incendiary bombs attributed to R12, 31 fell between the garden of Buckingham Palace and the Thames at Millbank. Bombs shattered the glass roof over platforms seven to nine at Victoria Station but otherwise damage was remarkably light. Crossing the Thames, four more fell in Lambeth. A couple of these landed very close to Lambeth Palace, the London residence of the Archbishop of Canterbury, and of two in Southwark, one struck the cathedral, but with only minimal damage, while in Whitechapel the final two bombs also had a limited effect.

The anti-aircraft guns defending the capital had been in action throughout the raid, firing 6,962 shells; inevitably leading to damage on the ground. Police reports show 240 houses in London were affected in this way, mainly through damaged roofs and ceilings. There were, however, casualties. In Tottenham a falling shell killed a 60-year-old man, George Parker, in Park Lane. In London Fields, Hackney, families in Blanchard Road took shelter in a pub, the Lord Napier. Daisy Hope huddled there with her 3-year-old daughter, Lilian. 'A missile came through,' the widowed Mrs Hope explained, 'and the child was hit on the head with a flying fragment of some description.' Her daughter died from her injuries, which included a fractured skull, a broken arm and collar bone. The shells also injured 17 other people. Outside London the guns blasted another 3,090 shells at the raiders.

The RFC provided the only aerial opposition to the raid. New, more effective aeroplanes were now finding their way to the RFC squadrons charged with Home Defence: Sopwith Camels, Sopwith 1½ Strutters, the SE5a, Bristol Fighters and Armstrong Whitworth FK8s joined the BE2e, BE12 and new BE12b in opposing the raiders. One of the Camel pilots claimed a 'first' that night.

Captain Murlis Green of No. 44 Squadron took off from Hainault Farm airfield at 6.43pm to patrol between Woodford and Goodmayes in Essex. About 30 minutes later, flying at 10,000ft over Goodmayes,

Murlis Green saw the twin exhaust flares of a Gotha and set off in pursuit.

> When about 30 yards away and directly underneath the machine I was drawing closer but a searchlight beam caught me and the hostile machine together. I fired a few rounds from my top gun, several tracers appeared to go into the underneath of the fuselage of the hostile machine, but only about 12 rounds could be fired owing to the flash of the gun temporarily blinding me.[12]

Onboard the Gotha were the commander, *Oberleutnant* Gerhard von Stachelsky, with *Leutnant* Friedrich Ketelsen as pilot and the gunner, *Gefreiter* A. Weissmann. After firing this burst, Murlis Green noted that the Gotha began dropping bombs; one of these being the one that exploded in Spa Road, Bermondsey. Murlis Green banked away and then made two more attacks. Each time the gun-flash blinded him and, again caught by the dogged searchlight, the Gotha returned fire but 'his tracers were always wide of the mark'. On his final attack, the searchlight lost contact, enabling Murlis Green to fire 50 rounds. 'The machine then dived sharply in front of me,' Murlis Green recalled, 'I pulled up to avoid it, got into its "backwash" and "spun". When I came out of the "spin" I could not see the hostile machine.' But his attack had reaped its reward.

The Gotha's starboard engine began to struggle and then, when about halfway back to the coast, it burst into flames. Although now losing height, the crew hoped they might be able to limp back to Belgium on one engine, but that proved impossible and they ditched in the sea off Folkestone. The crew scrambled up onto the upper wing to await their fate, but an armed British trawler loomed up and prepared to rescue them. Von Stachelsky and Weissmann successfully transferred, but Ketelsen slipped from his precarious perch and disappeared beneath the waves. The trawler attempted to take the downed Gotha in tow but suddenly a huge explosion ripped it apart – probably caused by one of the Gotha's bombs. The blast killed one of the trawler's crew, Frank Gee, Royal Naval Reserve. The surviving members of the Gotha crew confirmed the engagement with a British fighter had been the cause of their descent.

It is appropriate that the recognition for being the first pilot to shoot down a Gotha at night went to Captain Murlis Green; he, back in September, had defied the official line and proved it possible to fly the Sopwith Camel at night, and returned to tell the tale. The other Gothas all returned to Belgium, as did Giant R12, but there were more losses. Two of the Gothas burst into flames after crashing near Ghent and five others were damaged as they came in to land. The mournful level of attrition continued.

The attack inflicted the second highest estimate of material damage of any raid during the war, only surpassed by the Zeppelin raid on central London on the night of 8/9 September 1915. Police records confirm a total of £225,358 for the capital, plus another £12,000 for damage inflicted in Margate.[13] And this time, with little use of incendiary bombs, an increased number of significant fires broke out, with 13 recorded in London; Gotha crews reported one remained visible from 50 miles away.

22 December 1917, 6.00pm: Hartsdown Farm, Margate

While London recovered, four days later activity off the coast of northeast Kent caused an alarm. Strong winds and snow clouds over the English Channel may have disrupted a raid on the French channel ports. No bombs dropped on England but a significant number of explosions sounded out to sea as bomber crews lightened their loads before returning to Belgium. One, however, did not make it.

Having battled through stormy conditions, the crew of one Gotha found themselves close to the Kent coast when an engine failed. The commander, *Leutnant* W. Döbrick, released his bombs at sea, then ordered the pilot, *Unteroffizier* G. Hoffman, to make an emergency landing, as the gunner, *Vizefeldwebel* H. Klaus, prepared for impact.

Just inland, between Westgate and Margate, the officer commanding the Hengrove anti-aircraft gun, returning from checking on the searchlight that supported his gun, looked up amazed to see the Gotha passing directly over him at just 500ft. 'He endeavoured by shouting to bring his Machine Guns into action but failed to make himself heard.' At about 6.00pm the Gotha crashed into a ploughed field on Hartsdown Farm. The crew survived the landing, although Hoffman, the pilot, dislocated his arm. They wasted no time in setting fire to their aircraft with a flare gun. Within minutes police were on their way – by taxi – to arrest the crew. By 7.25pm they were under escort and on their way to London by train.[14]

Late December 1917: London

After the London raid on 18 December, the air raid warning system came in for much discussion. When introduced in July 1917, the warning maroons, used alongside the police alerts announced by placards, bells, whistles and motor horns, were only to be fired during daytime raids. As such, on 18 December, when the raid took the defences by surprise, the police were unable to react and deliver the warnings before the bombs began to drop. This led to a change. In future the maroons would form part of the night-warning system too, but only up to 11.00pm, with the public notified of the change on 10 January 1918. But the following month, in response to demands from local authorities, the cut-off extended to midnight, before a final decision in March saw the employment of the maroons at any hour.

There were also other developments underway too. In his September 1917 memorandum, 'Night Air Raids on London', Smuts made a recommendation for a balloon apron covering the north-eastern to south-eastern approaches to the capital. Plans for 20 of these aprons gained approval, each one held aloft by three balloons 500 yards apart and linked by cables, reaching up to 8,000ft (later increased to 10,000ft). From these cables, 1,000ft-long steel wires hung down at 25-yard intervals. Once aloft the aprons would force raiders to fly at more predictable heights, because any that attempted to come in below 10,000ft risked becoming ensnared in the dangling steel wires. In a report given in January, Lord French confirmed that three were in place and hoped that the remaining aprons could be completed at a rate of four per month, but in the end only ten were raised.

A restructuring of the Observer organisation, part of the Royal Defence Corps, also took place. These men watched and tracked incoming raiders, passing the information on to the Warning Controllers, with many physically unfit for more strenuous roles, a problem when they were required to 'exercise quick and cool intelligence' after long periods of inactivity.[15] In December 1917 these men were replaced by the police, who manned the posts on receiving warning of a possible raid. The military, however, continued to man observer posts 24 hours a day on the coast where aeroplane attacks could develop at any time without warning.

There were also new technical developments. The Neame illuminated ring gunsight, fitted to aeroplane machine-guns, entered service towards the end of 1917. At 100 yards, the wingspan of a Gotha fitted exactly within the ring. Work began on developing a flash eliminator to overcome temporary night-blindness in combat and a new bullet, the R.T.S. (Richard Threlfall and Son), joined the pilots' arsenal. The R.T.S. had both incendiary and explosive properties, the bullet exploding on contact and spreading its incendiary composition on the target. Tests showed the bullet to be very accurate and more effective than the Buckingham incendiary bullet that had preceded it.[16]

A period of bad winter weather now set in, preventing any further raids for over a month.

***

Peter Strasser's Naval Airship Division had suffered badly during the so-called 'Silent Raid' on 19/20 October, with the loss of five Zeppelins. Although the 'height-climber' Zeppelin classes were able to attain heights in the region of 20,000ft, beyond the reach of Britain's defences, the engines were still the same that had been in use since 1915 – the 240hp Maybach HSLu. They were simply unable to operate at full power at high-altitude due to the depleted oxygen content of the atmosphere, reducing them to a speed of just 45mph in perfect conditions, and much less in the face of fierce winds encountered at these new heights. Finally, however, a new altitude engine received approval, the Maybach MB IVa.

It took time to replace the five Zeppelins lost in the 'Silent Raid'. L 58 joined the naval service on 3 November, fitted with five of the new engines. On the same day Strasser also took delivery of L 59, but this retained the older engines. Tests of the new engines at 19,700ft produced speeds of 60mph; Strasser could not hide his delight. But they were slow to produce, with ten due to be ready by 15 December, enough for two more Zeppelins. They were allocated to L 60 and L 61. The latter Zeppelin entered service on 19 December, but problems delayed L 60 and she did join the airship fleet until 1 April 1918.

Strasser launched a five Zeppelin raid on 12 December against the north of England. He flew with the new L 58, but a fierce 45mph wind roaring down from the north caused Strasser to abort the mission. After that a series of winter storms kept the Zeppelins in their sheds.

5 January 1918, afternoon: Ahlhorn, Germany

Ahlhorn had become the headquarters of the Naval Airship Division on 25 July 1917, superseding Nordholz. Its four double-berth sheds – built at great cost – could house eight airships, and two more were under construction. These massive sheds were erected in pairs, each pair about 50 metres apart. At the beginning of January 1918 there were five airships at Ahlhorn: L 46, L 47, L 51, L 58, and the latest wooden-framed

Schütte-Lanz, SL 20. All sheds were traditionally given names beginning with the first two letters of the name of the base. Due to a lack of AH names, Ahlhorn used AL. L 47 and L 51 were berthed in Shed I *'Aladin'*, the new L 58 in Shed II *'Albrecht'*, L 46 in Shed III *'Alrun'*, and SL 20 in Shed IV *'Alix'*.

Late in the afternoon of 5 January 1918, *Korvettenkapitän* Arnold Schütze, commander of L 58, dropped into Strasser's office.

> We had just exchanged a few words and happened to be looking through the window across to my shed ['*Albrecht*']. Suddenly from the neighbouring shed ['*Aladin*']... with the deafening crash of thunder a huge broad flame rose up to the evening sky. The words: 'Whatever is that?' had not left my lips before the same thing happened to my shed and about ten seconds later two mighty explosions followed. Strasser, outwardly calm, rose slowly as if crippled. What was passing through his mind, only he who knew him could imagine.[17]

Oberleutnant-zur-See Heinrich Bassenger of the ground handling troops shared his shock.

> My gaze was drawn to the window by a sudden bright glow... What was it? A fire had broken out! A vast column of flame burst through the roof of the shed and rocketed upwards into the night sky. It grew and grew, colossal, gigantic, until it reached a height in excess of 200 metres. It lit up the entire airfield, bathing it in a blindingly bright, lurid red glow... 'The airships in Shed I are on fire!' came the first shout. The column of flame began to subside... Next instant came the dull thud of an explosion... A great glare followed! It was coming from Shed II, next to Shed I. They disappeared from view in a cloud of smoke and dust...
>
> 'Treachery!' my first thought. 'Someone's sabotaged us!'... There was another explosion, even more powerful than before. Shed III burst asunder in a vast sheet of dull flame, its giant iron frame shattered like matchsticks. Stones and burning fragments were strewn across the airfield. Shed IV was still standing. Would this at least be spared?...

The horror had not yet finished. Once more a terrible explosion shook the air, even more powerful than any previous ones... debris tore through the air; pieces of roof panel flew in all directions. Shed IV had ceased to exist. It was like an earthquake. Thick swathes of smoke, rent with garish plumes of fire marked the spot.[18]

With the new moon rising on 12 January and a break in the weather forecast, each airship stood ready, gas cells inflated with hydrogen and petrol tanks brimming with fuel, ready for action at a moment's notice. Destruction at Ahlhorn was absolute. The stark exposed framework of Sheds I and II still stood but of Sheds III and IV, little remained but scattered brickwork and twisted metal. And inside those great sheds, all five airships were destroyed. There were casualties too: 10 men of the ground crews were killed and 134 injured, while four civilian workers in Shed IV, carrying out repairs to SL 20 were also dead. Amongst those injured, *Kapitänleutnant* Heinrich Hollender, commander of L 46, suffered a bad break to his leg and never flew again. Ahlhorn, another disaster for the Naval Airship Division, just 11 weeks after the grievous losses of 19/20 October.

An inquiry followed, which dismissed claims of sabotage, leaving a great question mark over the cause of the disaster and how Sheds III and IV, situated about half a mile from I and II, also caught fire. Men in Shed I were busy cleaning L 51's engine gondolas when a fire broke, the inquiry believed this may have been caused by a piece of the shed roof coming loose, falling through L 51 and damaging a fuel tank, after which a spark ignited the escaping benzine from where the fire spread rapidly through Shed I to Shed II. Many witnesses reported a huge blast wave, which rolled powerfully over the airfield, smashing windows at Shed III. The inquiry believed this wave had initially compressed the hydrogen bags of L 46 in Shed III, which then expanded violently, damaging them and allowing hydrogen to valve. Flying debris travelled long distances and burning material filled the air. A burning ember would be enough to alight any escaped hydrogen, allowing the process to repeat itself at Shed IV.[19]

There is no doubt that Ahlhorn added another serious setback for Strasser, but outwardly he remained positive.

It was terrible to see the proud Ahlhorn base collapse in wreckage before my eyes in the space of a minute. But we can overcome it. We have sheds and ships to fill the gap, and the determination is there to triumph over all difficulties with head held high.[20]

For now though, Ahlhorn could no longer function and on 10 January Strasser moved his headquarters back to Nordholz. Work continued on the two Ahlhorn sheds under construction; they were completed in April and July 1918.

It had been an inauspicious start to 1918, but the air raids on Britain – by Zeppelin, Gotha and Giant – were set to continue.

Chapter 14

'A desperate struggle for life'

After those appearances by German bombers in the days before Christmas, there were no further raids in 1917, and the New Year skies remained free of hostile aircraft too. The pattern continued through January and the population began to settle back into their normal daily routines. No Zeppelins, Gothas or Giants appeared over Britain for 40 consecutive nights – but that all changed on 28 January 1918.

Bogohl 3 planned a big raid, but after the first 13 Gothas set off, a thick fog rolled over the airfields around Ghent and curtailed any further departures. Later, a Giant of *Rfa 501* managed to get airborne. The testing weather conditions, however, proved too much for six of the less experienced crews and they aborted the mission.

28 January 1918, 8.20pm: Ramsgate

As in so many previous raids, the first bombs were dropped on the north-east corner of Kent. At 8.20pm a Gotha came inland near Ramsgate harbour and roughly followed the course of High Street, turned over Ellington Park and headed back out to sea along the line of Grange Road. '[T]he noise was so horrible that it was impossible to distinguish the guns from the bombs.' The area had suffered before and some houses undergoing repairs in Picton Road and Dundonald Road were struck again.[1]

A bomb smashed windows at St Catherine's Hospital on High Street, and another severely damaged a house in South Eastern Road. The frequency of air raids in this part of Kent had prompted many to take steps to provide for their own safety and at 18 South Eastern Road, Percy Solly had constructed a dug-out to provide shelter for his family and friends. They were playing cards when the bomb hit.

> When the tremendous crash came there was severe concussion experienced by those in the dug-out; but the occupants did not realise the proximity of their peril until they found difficulty in extricating themselves from their shelter. It was then discovered that a bomb had fallen... about four yards away from their dug-out.[2]

Bombs followed in Ellington Park, Dundonald Road and at 126 Crescent Road, where the Reverend Hancocks, his wife and daughter were in the cellar, which he had shored up with sand bags. The bomb exploded at the back of the house.

> The effect was remarkable. The rear of the home at once became a heap of ruins, the whole of the back wing was blown upside down and was viewed with interest by hundreds of people the next morning. The inverted bathroom had the appearance of hanging on a mere brick or two.[3]

Picton Road felt the Gotha's wrath next. A bomb outside No. 52 demolished several house fronts, and another exploded at the rear of No. 57, giving the occupant, Mrs Finch, 'a severe shaking'. But although over a hundred houses were damaged in this attack, not a single person suffered injury.[4]

Five minutes later, about 4 miles south-west of Ramsgate, a second Gotha dropped a string of seven bombs over Richborough, but they all fell in fields where they uprooted some fruit trees and smashed a few windows.[5]

28 January 1918, 9.05pm: Sheerness

Further to the west, a Gotha approached the dockyard town of Sheerness on the Isle of Sheppey. After a previous raid in December, a meeting of the town's residents sent a resolution to the government protesting at 'the continued refusal of the military authorities to provide suitable bomb-proof shelter and a greater measure of protection against enemy action'. A meeting of the War Council on 11 January dismissed the resolution, stating that the provision of air-raid shelters required local authority support, adding the following comment.

> A house offered a good protection against bomb splinters, and the risk of heavy casualties was not so great when people

remained at home as when they were crowded in shelters which could not be made proof against a direct hit.[6]

That official view proved horrifically prophetic when the bombers reached London later that night. But in Sheerness, the population could only hunker down in their homes when the anti-aircraft guns opened fire at 9.05pm. This time the docks took the brunt of the attack.

The first bomb exploded on the eastern side of the Great Basin, damaging the destroyer HMS *Violet*.[7] On a northward course, a second bomb wrecked steam pinnace *No. 121*, at the north-eastern corner of the Basin, killing a launchman, Albert Winmill, and Charles Hibbins, a stoker serving on HM Torpedo Boat *No. 19*. Seconds later a bomb in the Small Basin damaged the lighter *Winkle*. A shattering explosion followed near the impressive Boat House, breaking nearly all the windows there and others in the vicinity. One man, Cook's Mate Walter Munday, suffered superficial injuries from flying glass.

The fifth and final bomb exploded at the War Department's Gun Wharf. It demolished explosive stores and small arms ammunition storerooms, resulting in many thousands of grenades, detonators and rounds of small arms ammunition scattered over a wide area. The bomb also partially demolished two workshops, destroyed a section of boundary wall between Gun Wharf and the Dockyard, and badly damaged offices and storehouses, but willing hands quickly extinguished a fire.

The same bomb injured three army officers and also damaged the War Department's vessel, *Swale*, and a cutter, while the Customs boat, *White Rose*, sank. Beyond the dockyard, the concussion of the blasts smashed windows at Admiralty House, and in Blue Town, bordering the dockyard, windows were also broken at various business premises and at the Crown & Anchor pub, which had also been damaged in the raid of 5 June.

Turning for home, the Gotha retained one bomb which it dropped at 9.37pm on a playing field on Laleham Road as it passed over Margate. No more bombs fell on Kent that night, but other Gothas had already reached London and an attack on the capital was underway.

28 January 1918, 8.00pm: Shoreditch, London

With no raids since 18 December, some sense of normality had returned to London. People were more relaxed and in the evenings the music halls and other places of amusement were doing good business. In Shoreditch, people were anticipating a good night out.

> A crowd of about a thousand people had lined up outside two neighbouring music-halls, and were waiting for the doors to open for the second house. A similar crowd was outside picture palaces in the neighbourhood.[8]

Back on 18 December no warning had sounded prior to a raid, taking London by surprise. In response the rules for the warning maroons to be used alongside police alerts had been extended to include night raids. It seems many were not aware or had forgotten this change of policy, because when the warning maroons exploded in the sky around 8.00pm, people in the huge queues panicked, thinking a raid had begun. A policeman at one of the music-halls noted that the happy mood evaporated in an instant.

> 'Gun!' said a woman, and 'Guns!' travelled all along the line. As loudly as I could I told them it was not guns, but already the crowd was breaking up. A third loud report quite close, and from every side street, picture palace and music hall the people poured into the main road, rushing for shelter. Other maroons went off all round, and each report added to the panic of the people.[9]

Just a short distance away stood the vast Bishopsgate Goods Station which, with its underground levels and brick arches, served as a public shelter when needed. The panicked crowds rushed towards it. The policeman continued his story.

> Several other policemen, with some specials and myself tried to stem the rush, but it was like fighting a wave. In the heart of the crowd women fainted and fell; others stumbled over them and trampled them underfoot… For a long time the crowd stuck, wedged between the walls. Then it suddenly broke and swept down the slope to the safety of the shelter. As soon as we could get at them, the dead and injured were got out.

When the bodies were recovered they found 14 dead and many more injured. A common reaction – echoed in the Press – to demonstrations of unruly behaviour such as this was to blame 'foreigners or persons of foreign extraction'; Russian Jews living in the East End were an easy scapegoat. Amongst the dead were Fanny Bodie, her two young daughters, Cissie (5) and Hetti (18 months), and her mother, Millie Cohen. Lily Kutcher tried to help them.

> One family was wiped out except for the husband (who was on aeroplane work)... in the terrible crush. I was with them when they went down, and tried to get the baby away from the mother, but had to abandon it. The elder girl was shockingly injured about the top of the head.[10]

A similar incident occurred less than a mile away at the Midland Railway's goods depot on Commercial Road,[11] also used as a shelter. Lewis Greenbaum witnessed the panic there.

> When the warning was given people rushed to the gates and fought and grappled to gain admission. [Jane Rosa Ferminsky[12]] fell, and several other people fell on top of her. Immediately the panic increased, and men and women screamed and fought, and it was only with difficulty that they were quietened.[13]

Initial reports stated that two women were only injured in the crush, but Jane Ferminsky later died.

28 January 1918, 8.37pm: London

At 8.37pm the first Gotha reached London, with bombs falling in the City, at Lime Street and at Cannon Street Station. They damaged some offices and a market, wrecked a railway carriage, damaged tracks and injured a railway worker. Heading east, the Gotha released five bombs over Stepney: three exploded in Jubilee Street, one in Dempsey Street and one, which failed to detonate, in Smith Street. Two men, Isaac Kamanovitz and James Day, died in Jubilee Street, with two others injured. The bomb also demolished three houses and damaged many others. In Dempsey Street another hit a school wrecking the gymnasium, but there were no casualties.

At the same time a second Gotha appeared, its first two bombs also landing in east London.[14] The first, at about 8.50pm, fell in Garford Street, Poplar. Exploding in the street, it damaged at least 32 houses, ten of them seriously, and killed two labourers, John Newman and Frederick Myhill. A fatal bomb fragment smashed into Myhill's chest just as he prepared to leave his house to seek shelter elsewhere.[15]

The next bomb exploded in Commercial Road, opposite Branch Road, where people were still in the street. The blast wrecked ten houses and damaged many more. When a policeman recovered his senses after being knocked down by the blast, he found four men lying on the ground near him. Three of them died of their injuries: Charles Smith (17), William Seager, a 15-year-old messenger boy, and a labourer, John Wall (65).

Now following the Thames upstream, a bomb dropped by the Gotha sunk a barge moored at a wharf on Lower Thames Street and damaged two other boats. More bombs dropped at about 8.55pm as it reached Vauxhall. The first of these fell in the Thames close to Vauxhall Bridge, depositing a huge splat of river mud on the Albert Embankment. Seconds later another exploded at the South Metropolitan Gas Company, close to Vauxhall Bridge, destroying a retort house. Then came a huge explosion in a courtyard behind Lennox Buildings, a council tenement block at the corner of Wandsworth Road and Parry Street. The explosion ripped through the building and Clare Cottages, part of the same housing complex, inflicting devastating damage.

Madge Maindonald was 11, her brother Reginald five years older. Their mother had died in 1915 and they lived with their father at Clare Cottages, helped by family friends, Mr and Mrs Gower. When a raid threatened, the Maindonald family would shelter at Lennox Buildings with the Gowers. But with everything still quiet, Reginald went to get some cigarettes, taking his sister with him and leaving the Gowers chatting with a Mr and Mrs Walker and their son. While they were away, they heard 'this dreadful bang' as the bomb exploded at the gas works. The siblings were sheltering at Vauxhall Station when the next bomb struck Lennox Buildings. The scene that greeted them when they returned deeply shocked Madge.

> The blast caught Mr Gower and Mr Walker and killed them both... The boy wasn't hurt... Mrs Walker, she'd been injured and taken away, but Mrs Gower was still there. She was always a very prim lady, always very clean and well-dressed, but she stood at the gate, holding on to keep herself up. She'd lost a shoe, her clothes were torn and dirty and bloody. Her hair was down over her face because her hat had been lost and

I can see her now... this very neat woman in such a terrible mess, blood everywhere.[16]

Nine others were injured at Lennox Buildings, but even as the flying glass settled on the ground, another bomb exploded no more than a hundred yards away, on the bottling store of brewers Plowman, Barrett & Co. at 66 Bond Street. The London Fire Brigade estimated the value of the damage caused by this bomb at £15,122, the second highest incurred that night.[17] A final bomb in the roadway outside 49 Wandsworth Road wrecked one house and damaged nine others. At No. 53, a licensed beerhouse, a policeman found the owner, George Witten, lying dead in a pool of blood.

A third Gotha arrived over South Hackney at 8.15pm, dropping a 12kg bomb in the back garden of 36 Gore Road, which damaged eight houses. Five minutes later two bombs fell in Holborn, ravaging businesses in Parker Street and Newton Street, and injuring two people. The Gotha then turned north, dropping two bombs between the stations at Euston and St Pancras. The first, in Ossulston Street, struck Agincourt House, a four-storey building let out as flats. It destroyed about half of the roof and third floor but remarkably only two children suffered slight injuries. The second, in Purchase Street, hit a Midland Railway coal station, but resulted in only limited damage. A bomb in Cantelowes Road also had little effect before the final bomb, about 1.5 miles to the east, wrecked a house at 94 St Paul's Road.

The fourth raider, a Gotha G.V crewed by *Leutnant* Friedrich von Thomsen (commander), *Unteroffizier* Karl Ziegler (pilot) and *Unteroffizier* Walther Heiden (gunner), approached London over Essex. That night a new type of barrage fire exploded in the sky. Whereas previously the 'curtain barrage' had put barriers of bursting shells at varying heights in the path of incoming raiders, the new 'polygon barrage' aimed to surround raiders with an irregular screen of shell bursts. Once caught by the barrage, whichever way the Gotha turned it risked flying into danger. The gunners fired 14,722 shells that night.[18]

Passing over north London, the Gotha held its bombs until releasing them at 9.50pm between Kilburn and West Hampstead in north-west London. They all fell within a space of 600 yards. At 186 Belsize Road, a large house of 14 rooms, the explosion left only the front of the house standing. An 80-year-old woman living there, Caroline Thorpe, died in the building with another woman injured. The next bomb exploded at the corner of Belsize Road and Abbey Road, outside the Princess of

Wales pub. It killed 50-year-old George Marchant, badly damaged the pub and other buildings in the two streets, and dangerously exposed broken water mains, a gas main and electrical cables. Another bomb damaged three houses in St George's Road (now Priory Terrace), and at 175 Belsize Road one exploded on the roof, having a wide impact and injuring two people. Bombs at 19 Mortimer Crescent and 33 Greville Road completed the attack but only resulted in light damage.

28 January 1918, 9.58pm: Wickford

The Gotha headed out over Leyton, but at 9.58pm, near Romford, searchlights held it in their beams. The RFC had 41 aircraft patrolling and two of them, Sopwith Camels of No. 44 Squadron, had spotted the Gotha's exhaust flames. The pilots, Captain George Hackwill and Second Lieutenant Charles Banks, closed in; the same 'Sandy' Banks who had been disciplined back in September after he 'buzzed' Major General Ashmore during his visit to the squadron's airfield. Those on the ground followed the dramatic duel in the sky as the two Camels closed in.

> One swooped down from above, crossed over the top of the raider, and took up a position on his left – behind and below, and probably no more than 25 yards away. The other climbed up and got below the Gotha's tail.
>
> The height was probably 9,000ft, or 10,000ft. Tremendous machine gun fire broke out immediately from all three aeroplanes. There was a constant succession of flashes of flame as the guns blazed away.[19]

Another eyewitness takes up the story.

> The German was a fighter – give him his due. He responded in kind, so far as firing went. He made a desperate struggle for life. The issue was in doubt, with the odds decidedly against the enemy up to the last minute.[20]

The engagement hung in the balance. After a while Banks' Camel developed an engine fault and he broke away, but Hackwill continued to press his attack. At Wickford a farmer and his family peered up at the night sky.

We saw lights from the British aeroplanes dodging about, and then the rapid firing of their machine guns, followed by the mysterious sound of something rushing through the air, and before we had time to think a bright ball of flame was seen high up in the sky and it fell with a crash 400 yards from my house.

I ran to the spot and found it was a huge Gotha, well ablaze... Many people were soon on the spot. I had not been there many seconds when an explosion occurred, and all stood back in case more should follow. Within a few yards of the machine we could see by its light the charred body of a German, and two others were observed burning in the aeroplane.[21]

The Gotha crashed at Friern's Farm,[22] to the west of Wickford. *Leutnant* von Thomsen (24) and *Unteroffiziers* Ziegler (19) and Heiden (22) were dead; Hackwill and Banks received the Military Cross for their actions.

Back in London the guns fell silent at 9.50pm, but the 'all clear' did not follow. Although the Gothas had either crossed the coast on their outbound flights, or were heading towards it, the danger remained. At 10.25pm Giant R12 of *Rfa 501* came inland and set course for London.

29 January 1918, 12.15am: London

R12 passed over Suffolk and Essex, engaged by anti-aircraft guns and, at one point, attacked by a Bristol Fighter of No. 39 Squadron, flown by Lieutenant John Goodyear with Air Mechanic Walter Merchant as his gunner. Goodyear made two attacks, but both times the slipstream from the Giant's huge propellers knocked him off course, while the German gunners returned fire. Goodyear made a third attempt, manoeuvring so Merchant could use the rear gun, but bullets raked the Bristol, ripping into the fuel tank and wounding Merchant, forcing the determined pilot to break off the engagement. Now free from attack, R12 passed Chelmsford at 12.10am, then 5 minutes later bombs began to drop over Bethnal Green in east London.

Those bombs fell in Maidstone Street, Nelson Street, Florida Street, St Andrews Street and Nicholl Street, inflicting extensive damage. Nine houses were wrecked (Maidstone Street), three demolished (Nelson Street) and four more badly damaged (Florida Street). In addition, at least 274 others experienced lesser damage. There were casualties too:

nine injured in Maidstone Street, four in Florida Street, three in Nelson Street and one in Nicholl Street. In addition, a bomb fragment killed Edward Ewington as he sought shelter in a doorway in Florida Street.

Maintaining the same course, R12 crossed the Thames between Tower Bridge and London Bridge, then swung around to re-cross it by Waterloo Bridge, dropping a bomb in the river. Moments later a 100kg bomb smashed into Savoy Mansions on Savoy Hill. The Air Board had occupied the premises until superseded by the new Air Ministry at the beginning of January. The explosion burst a gas main in the road and smashed the basement wall of the building, thereby undercutting three supporting piers. With that the whole front of the building collapsed like a house of cards. Seconds later a bomb smashed into Covent Garden Flower Market inflicting damage there and in Wellington Street and Tavistock Street. Bombs followed at Long Acre, then Bedford Place in Holborn, followed by Hatton Garden, then Long Lane near Smithfield Market, with two final bombs on Bethnal Green, close to where the raid had begun. The explosion in Bedford Place caused widespread damage, as did the one in the jewellery quarter of Hatton Garden, while in Long Lane a four-storey cold storage facility had the top two floors demolished. And in Bethnal Green a bomb exploded on brewer's Truman, Hanbury & Buxton's bottling stores in Wilkes Street, while the other detonated close to railway tracks between Bratley Street and Fleet Street Hill, damaging ten houses in each street and 50 more in Weaver Street and Pedley Street. These bombs only caused injuries to one person, but a very different situation had engulfed those back at Long Acre.

After the bomb on Covent Garden Market, the next smashed down at 93 Long Acre, a substantial four-storey building occupied by printers and publishers, Odhams Ltd. Most of the floors were built of concrete giving the building an appearance of strength. The owners made the large basement area available to local people as a shelter during air raids and it became popular as people knew they would be well looked after and provided with refreshments. Hundreds had made their way there when the warnings sounded earlier in the evening.

The bomb dropped on Odhams weighed 300kg. It missed the building, exploding just outside on Wilson Street, close to the corner with Arne Street. Tragically, it smashed through pavement lights to explode in Odhams' basement directly among those seeking safety. A man named Cripps had made it to the shelter.

> Children were running about the basement singing, laughing and playing. I had not been there very long when there was a terrific flash, an awful concussion, and a dead silence. Then there was complete darkness... The first thing I remember was the shrieking of a woman and the cries of the children. I got through the door somehow, and found that the place had burst into flames, but the fireman had already got their hoses there. They got a lot of the women out. Some tottered out, some were carried out, and one man came out with his trousers all on fire... In no time the place was a furnace.[23]

The explosion had a catastrophic effect on the building. A technical investigation reported that:

> ... the whole force of the explosion going directly into the basement, undercutting and blowing to pieces the lower part of main walls, and the two adjacent supporting piers of the building, so that the immediate superstructure simply collapsed or subsided, and in doing so pulled out the upper floors.[24]

Following the initial collapse, fire quickly took hold amongst the huge rolls of newsprint stored there and an external wall gave way, trapping many of the injured in the wreckage. For some, those injuries were life-changing.

Mrs McClaskey had sought shelter at Odhams with her two-year-old daughter, Ellen. The explosion set her clothes on fire and blasted the baby from her arms. Ellen died. Mrs McClaskey wrote about her experience some year later.

> I was buried, and had all the fingers blown off one hand, a leg taken off, the top of my head injured (I have to wear a plate), and my body burnt all over. I am just a piece of the woman I was before the air raids came. All I have to do is sit in a chair day after day with people waiting on me, because I am useless for anything. I was in hospital for two years.[25]

For those unused to the effects of bombs in cities, the sight could be over-powering. One woman, who signed herself, Miss M, described how her brother-in-law, 'a big, bluff 16-stone man' had come to visit from Lincolnshire: '"Newspaper talk" was how he dismissed the raids.'

> As my duties meant I had to see most of the horrors of the raids I took him [to Long Acre] the next morning and we were able to pass the barriers where doctors, nurses and firemen were working like trojans to rescue trapped men women and children.
>
> 'What are those?' he asked, pointing to objects stacked against a wall. 'Coffin shells,' I replied. 'They are filling them with all that remains of so many – a leg, an arm, and so on.'
>
> 'These men?'... 'Doctors. They are trying to keep trapped, injured people alive, feeding them through tubes.'
>
> 'And these men? ... they are carrying –'
>
> But big, bluff, scoffing brother-in-law had seen enough; he had fainted.[26]

Giant R12 evaded the anti-aircraft guns and aircraft on its way back to the coast, the red glow from the Long Acre fire still visible to the crew from 60 miles away. They landed safely back in Belgium, but the return proved more testing for the Gothas of *Bogohl 3* – four were wrecked in landing crashes.

The enormity of the devastation at Long Acre meant that it took six weeks before the last bodies were accounted for. The final toll reached 38 killed and 85 injured; the most in London throughout the war from a single bomb.

The London defences, however, had no time to rest and recuperate. German bombers returned the following evening, but this time *Bogohl 3* remained on the ground, the constant losses having an impact on the effectiveness of the squadron and the men's morale, leaving *Rfa 501* to attack alone. Four Giants took part, R12, R25, R26 and R39. Shortly after take-off, however, R12 turned back with engine problems, no doubt the ground crew had not had enough time to complete a thorough overhaul after the previous night's exploits.

29 January 1918, 11.31pm: West London

The commander of *Rfa* 501, Richard von Bentivegni, also commanded R39, and he crossed the coast first, appearing over the mouth of the

River Blackwater at 10.05pm. About 10 minutes later Captain Arthur Dennis, flying a No. 37 Squadron BE12b, saw R39 at about 12,000ft and attacked. His opponent took evasive action and returned machine gun fire but, as Dennis loaded a fresh ammunition drum, he flew into the fierce spiral slipstream produced by the Giant's huge propellers, which twisted him around and he lost visual contact. Dennis felt convinced his bullets had hit the target, but when he landed, he also found holes in his own aircraft. The Giant kept to the north of London, reaching Hertford at 10.56pm then, passing around the west of London, appeared over Isleworth at 11.31pm. At a height of about 2 miles, von Bentivegni caught a glimpse of the towers of Hammersmith Bridge in the distance, which he mistakenly identified as Tower Bridge, leading to his claim that his bombs fell from Charing Cross to West India Docks, whereas they fell in south-west London, between Richmond and Chiswick.

With a bomb load in the region of 1,000kg, von Bentivegni commenced his attack over Richmond's Old Deer Park and the Mid-Surrey golf course, where 13 bombs (two 50kg explosive and 11 incendiary bombs) fell. They smashed windows at the eighteenth-century King's Observatory and excavated an unwelcome bunker on the golf course's 14th green. Passing over the Thames, seven more incendiaries dropped in and around Syon Park but inflicted no damage of note. R39 now headed towards Brentford and Kew.[27]

As George Bentley walked home, he saw an aeroplane held in a searchlight beam. 'At the same moment,' he explained, 'a man a few yards in front of me dived to the ground and shouted to me to lie down, which I did.' Three 'deafening thuds and flashes' followed. Bentley dashed to his home nearby and, having ascertained his family were safe, went on to Whitestile Road where the family of his friend Herbert Kerley, a sergeant major serving in the Middlesex Regiment, lived. When he got there a horrified Bentley found a great cloud of dust hanging above the wreckage of his friend's house. He did not hesitate to act when he heard a groan from the rubble.

> I pulled and wriggled my way into the cellar, which was full of gas and water, and in the darkness came across a young woman, only just alive... With help I managed to get her to the surface, but by that time she was dead.[28]

The young woman was 22-year-old Hilda Kerley, Sergeant Major Kerley's niece. Not until 16 hours later did rescuers carefully extricate the last body from beneath the rubble. The explosion killed Kerley's wife, May, and all their children: Florence, aged 12, Henry, 8, Lilian, 5, Daisy, 3, and little Ellen, just 3 months old. And another died there too, 70-year-old Catherine Berrows, the Kerley's lodger, bringing the death toll to eight; the bomb had wiped out Herbert Kerley's entire family in an instant.

As the tragedy unfolded at Whitlestile Road, von Bentivegni noted his next target as the West India Docks, but they were some 12 miles away in east London. It appears that the large reservoirs and filter beds at the Metropolitan Water Board's Kew Bridge Works convinced him he had found the docks, based on his earlier error in misidentifying 'Tower Bridge'. Ten explosive bombs dropped over the water works with six landing within the boundaries of the site, damaging two reservoirs, and the engineering shop. Another exploded just outside the entrance where the works' foremen had their office. It killed two foremen, Frederick Finch and George Bentley,[29] and injured nightwatchman William Pickton. The explosion also damaged the pumping station, smashing windows there and cutting telephone and power lines. Working in the pitch black and unable to contact anyone, Ernest Gluyas, kept the pumping engine working in extremely difficult circumstances, for which he earned promotion to foreman and later received the award of the British Empire Medal 'for conspicuous courage and presence of mind during an air raid'.[30]

Three final bombs dropped in Chiswick, two on the High Road and one in Park Road, and although no buildings suffered a direct hit, lesser damage affected many properties, but there were no more casualties.

On the outward flight, when about 5 miles south of Gravesend, a pilot spotted R39. Captain Francis Luxmore, flying a No. 78 Squadron Sopwith Camel, swooped down and made two attacks, firing off 100 rounds. With great misfortune, however, one of his tracer bullets stuck the propeller of his own aircraft and the burning bullet flew back, the intense light temporarily blinding him. By the time his eyes had readjusted to the darkness, R39 had melted into the night sky. She continued to run the gauntlet of south-east England's anti-aircraft defences until passing back over the coast near Walmer at 12.50am.[31]

29 January 1918, 10.44pm: Essex

The other two Giants that crossed the coast that night, R26 and R25, had little to show for their endeavours. R26 came inland at 10.44pm but struggled over Essex with two of her four engines giving trouble.

Near Billericay the crew decided to turn back, but at about midnight a searchlight at Rayleigh caught the Giant, at which point the crew released their entire load of 50kg bombs to gain height rapidly. They reported attacking Southend but six of the bombs fell at Rawreth, eleven at Rayleigh and one on a farm between Rayleigh and Thundersley with damage consisting of nothing more than smashed windows.

R25 crossed the coast near Foulness at 10.50pm and headed west. Picked up by searchlights, five British aircraft made attacks on the huge bomber, which zigzagged to evade them. At about 11.25pm a bullet put one of R25's engines out of action, but the crew bravely persevered with reduced speed although they were gradually losing height. A section of the balloon apron between Southgate and Woodford suddenly looming up in their path, however, appears to have been the final straw. The crew released the entire bomb load to gain height and returned to the coast.[32] All 20 bombs landed within 300 yards of each other at Redbridge Lane, Wanstead. Most fell on allotments or a golf course and, other than a few broken windows, this ton of explosive bombs caused little damage.

The crew of R25 returned home safely, but on inspecting their aircraft they found it riddled with 88 bullet holes. Clearly the attacking British aircraft had hit the target, but why had this concentrated attack by five fighters, four of them highly-rated Sopwith Camels, failed to bring the Giant down?

Chapter 15

Giants in the Sky

The failure to bring down Giant R25 on 29 January, following attacks by four Sopwith Camels and a BE2e provoked much discussion amongst the pilots. The first to attack, Second Lieutenant Frank Kitton of No. 37 Squadron in the BE2e, fired a whole drum of ammunition but he lost sight of R25 when reloading. Next came Second Lieutenant R.N. Hall, No. 44 Squadron, the first of the Sopwith Camel pilots, but his jamming machine gun restricted him to short five-round bursts.[1] Another pilot from the squadron, Second Lieutenant Henry Edwardes, spotted R25 when over Brentwood in Essex. 'I climbed towards him,' Edwardes reported, 'and sat under his tail about 40 yards behind him and fired three long bursts into his fuselage.' But then his left-hand gun jammed, and when the synchronising gear on the right-hand gun failed, he damaged his own propeller. Undaunted, Edwardes switched on his lights and took up a position above R25 to highlight its presence to other pilots. He watched three other Camels make attacks, one of them Hall as he continued to harry the Giant. Another pilot, Second Lieutenant T.M. O'Neill, found R25 when just east of London.

> Dived on him firing with both guns. He kept turning sharply to the left and right losing height. I got under his tail and fired another burst into him, when my left gun stopped. As he was just firing at me with his rear gun I pulled slightly away to rectify the stoppage. I got on his tail again, but my left gun would not fire, so I carried on with my right. After about 200 rounds it stopped.

By the time O'Neill cleared the jam he had lost sight of the elusive raider. No. 44 Squadron's commander, now Major Gilbert Murlis Green, made the final attack. When he found R25, Edwardes and O'Neill were pressing home their attacks, but when O'Neill peeled away to clear his jam, Murlis Green manoeuvred into position, encountering 'short and accurate bursts' of machine gun fire. Bullets fired by another Camel then whizzed past him – probably O'Neill returning to the fray. Murlis Green's guns were loaded with the new R.T.S. ammunition.

> I fired at him only intending to use a series of short bursts, but all my R.T.S. looked as if it was detonating on the fuselage of the hostile machine. I kept my triggers pressed and fired one complete double drum [97 rounds] of R.T.S. and three quarters of a drum from my second gun. At any moment I expected the hostile machine to burst into flames.

But R25 did not burn.

After the raid, Murlis Green discussed the engagement with his pilots. When he made his own attack, he estimated the distance at 50 yards, but other pilots disagreed, suggesting his position seemed more like 150 yards from the enemy aircraft. 'From other pilots reports,' he discovered, 'it appears that the R.T.S. was bursting prematurely at about 100 yards.'

But the real cause of the problem could be found in their understanding of the new illuminated Neame gunsight. Pilots knew a Gotha filled the sight at 100 yards. The squadrons had little if any information at this time about the Giants and as such, when attacking R25, they were treating it as a Gotha. But when a Giant filled the gunsight, due to its great size, it was much further away than if it had been a Gotha. The bullets were not bursting prematurely, many were being fired from too far away to be effective.

***

At the airfields around Ghent, the mood amongst the crews of *Bogohl* 3 remained downbeat, this only exacerbated by two training accidents on 17 February. One Gotha smashed almost vertically into the ground shortly after take-off, while the other, apparently a flight for future Gotha commanders, with three 'observers' and the pilot onboard, violently exploded when making a crash landing at Landegem near Ghent. The accidents claimed seven lives. Two of the 'observers' were members of noble families, one of whom was *Oberleutnant* Wilhem Siegfried, *Graf Adelmann von und zu Adelmannfelden* of Württemberg, and a relative of

Count Zeppelin. The King of Württemberg ordered his body brought home, but the 450kg of bombs onboard the Gotha at the time of the crash all exploded and 'all they found of the entire crew were one piece of a shoulder and one arm'.[2]

The day before *Bogohl 3* suffered these losses, *Rfa 501* launched another raid on England, sending five Giants to attack London, each carrying a bomb load of about 1,000kg. Strong winds over the English Channel, however, forced three of the crews to seek secondary targets. R33 had a particularly fraught night. As she approached the Kent coast the forward port engine failed. The crew rapidly released their bombs over the sea and turned back, but then the rear port engine failed too. Shortly after that the rear starboard engine dropped to half power and R33 lost height. The crew jettisoned excess weight while a mechanic worked on the problem. Discovering that the oil had started to congeal in the pipes due to the cold weather, he cut open the oil tank and began to painstakingly transfer the oil to the engine in his cupped hands. He did just enough to keep the engine going, allowing R33 to crawl home.[3]

There is little information on the involvement of R36, other than it experienced trouble with the bomb doors, the crew claiming to have dropped just two bombs, both on Dover, but none fell on the town. R25 also claimed an attack on Dover, however, all 20 bombs fell about 3 miles to the north-east, in a line from St Margaret's Bay to St Margaret-at-Cliffe. The impact, though generally light, did see damage to the laundry at the Convent of the Annunciation on The Droveway, as well as breaking windows at the Convent and cottages nearby.

The other two raiders were able to battle through the strong winds. R12, the single version of the R.IV type had six engines, while R39 mounted four 245hp Maybach MB IVa engines, which although rated less than the four 260hp Mercedes D.IVa engines fitted as standard to the R.VI type, produced more power above 6,500ft. Besides the new engines, R39 also underwent alterations to enable it to carry a single 1,000kg explosive bomb – a metric ton – the largest type dropped from the air during the war. These two Giants crossed over the Essex coast at 9.40pm, close enough together for the plotters and observers on the ground to conclude that just one had passed overhead and on towards London.

16 February 1918, 10.10pm: Chelsea

R39 continued to evade the observers and only when von Bentivegni released the 1,000kg bomb at about 10.10pm, and the huge missile,

13ft long, hurtled down towards the ground, did its presence become known. The crew thought they were to the east of the City, but they were over Chelsea in south-west London.

Helen Banon sat in her dining room at 156 Sloane Street writing a letter when the bomb fell. 'I was literally lifted off my seat,' she noted, 'by the terrific percussion of a huge shell.' The bomb exploded 700 yards away, at the Royal Hospital, Chelsea, home of the Chelsea Pensioners. It smashed through the roof of the north-east wing, where the Captains of Invalids and their families had apartments, down through two floors to explode on the stone floor in the cellar. An eye-witness reported that the building was 'sliced in half... and literally crumbled to dust'.[4] Ernest Ludlow, a former Grenadier Guards officer, his wife Jessie, their five sons, and Jessie's niece, Alice Copley, occupied one of the apartments.

Captain Ludlow and his wife died, as did Alice, buried in the wreckage amidst the smoke and dust and fumes. Two of the boys, 10-year-old Ernest, and Bernard, aged 4, also died – reports state one of them, blasted from the house, had been found impaled on railings along Royal Hospital Road. Miraculously the other three boys, Gerald (aged 9), Lawrence (6) and the baby, Basil, just 6 months old, although injured, were pulled alive from the rubble – but now all three were orphans.[5]

When dawn broke the following morning hundreds gathered to see the extent of the damage. 'Every window in the court was smashed,' Mrs Banon recalled, 'and many windows in Burton Court and even some windows in King's Road [460 yards away] were broken or cracked... [and] the whole courtyard of the East Gate was several inches deep in finely powdered red brick.'[6]

16 February 1918, 10.20pm: Woolwich

Giant R12 had crossed the Thames and at 10.20pm approached Woolwich. The commander, *Oberleutnant* Hans-Joachim von Seydlitz-Gerstenberg, may have also misjudged his position because a section of the balloon apron suddenly veered up dead ahead. Only the skill of one of the two pilots saw the crew through their ordeal, as von Seydlitz-Gerstenberg confirmed in his report.

> The aircraft was first pulled to starboard then port and finally side-slipped out of control...The first pilot, Lt Götte, immediately throttled-down all engines, then opened up the throttles on only one side, whereby the aircraft regained

equilibrium once again after having fallen 300 metres. The impact of the balloon apron was so severe that the starboard mechanic fell against the glowing exhaust stacks, which severely burned his hands, and the port aileron control cables sprang from their roller guides. The aircraft itself remained intact with the exception of minor damage to the leading edge of the starboard wing, propeller and mid-fuselage section.[7]

It had been a narrow escape, skilfully executed, but the rough-handling of R12 had shaken loose two 300kg bombs, which plunged down towards Woolwich. They exploded about 300 yards apart, either side of the Royal Artillery Barracks. A couple engaged to be married, Gunner Eric Munro, Australian Field Artillery, and Gertrude Keyworth, a VAD nurse, were strolling along Grand Depot Road when the bomb struck. A witness heard the explosion but could see little in the darkness. Moving carefully, he found heavy paving stones thrown asunder.

> His legs became entangled in a telephone wire. He disentangled himself, and noticed a live electric wire. This he dodged, and got on to the pavement, when he saw something lying on the footway near a church. On approaching it he discovered it was the body of a man lying on top of something which turned out to be the body of a woman.[8]

Eric Munro and Gertrude Keyworth were dead. Beyond the spot where the couple fell, St George's Garrison Church had suffered significant damage, with many windows also shattered at the Royal Artillery Barracks.

The second bomb smashed down onto a greengrocer's shop in Artillery Place, where John Gregory, his wife, their son, also named John, their married daughter, Alice Cull, and her 2-year-old son, Henry, were all sheltering in the basement. Two shops above collapsed, entombing the family. Rescuers pulled John Gregory, senior, alive from the wreckage but no one else survived. A soldier of the Royal Field Artillery, John Ferguson, walking past the shop at the time died too.

Relieved to have survived their close encounter with the balloon apron, the crew of R12 dumped the rest of their bombs, which fell around Farnaby Road, Shortlands, about 5 miles from Woolwich. Five of the 50kg explosive bombs fell on a golf course and three on allotments.

The RFC flew 60 sorties but only three pilots made brief attacks, all to no avail. The anti-aircraft guns in London and the south-east also blasted 4,519 rounds into the sky without success, but were responsible for damage to 40 properties on the ground.

With a promise of good weather again the following night, von Bentivegni wanted to attack again, but *Rfa 501*, with a full strength of six Giants, could not mount a squadron raid. Although only one, R25, passed all the checks, von Bentivegni did not hesitate to send it out against London alone.

17 February 1918, 10.50pm: St Pancras Station

R25 made its initial approach along the Thames Estuary, engaged by anti-aircraft guns for much of the way. After taking evasive action, R25 reached Swanley then turned towards the outer south-eastern districts of London.

The Giant followed a gently curving north-west course that ran for just under 8.5 miles, making regular bomb drops on the way. The first fell in the rear garden of a house at 30 Newstead Road, Lee, at about 10.45pm, wrecking the back of the property and damaging 29 other houses in the vicinity. Less than a mile further on two bombs in Hither Green caused damage at St Swithun's Church and in the area around Hither Green Lane. Another 260 yards and an explosion at the corner of Lewisham Park and Thornford Road smashed the fronts of four houses and injured two people.

In Lewisham a bomb fell in Vicar's Hill, followed by one in Waller Road, New Cross, and another in Pennethorne Road, Peckham. All exploded in back gardens preventing the complete destruction of any of the properties, but still caused considerable damage, and the explosion in Pennethorne Road also injured three people. The next two fell in a garden in Glengall Terrace, Camberwell, and in Searles Road, Southwark. The first damaged the premises of a metal merchant and the second narrowly missed a school where 500 people had taken shelter. Even so, it killed a discharged soldier, John Bannister, and injured three others, all out in the street, with many properties sustaining damage. The last bomb south of the Thames exploded amongst industrial premises on Bear Lane, Southwark. The police reported: 'Crane smashed, engines and machinery displaced and metal in yard damaged.'

R25 now crossed the Thames, its next bomb landing just off Fleet Street, home of London's newspaper and publishing industry. It struck Dunston House in New Fetter Lane, the offices of Cambridge University Press, but failed to detonate. A bomb in Doughty Mews, a quiet, narrow road off Guilford Street in Bloomsbury, wrecked two properties, one of them a stable, where it killed two horses.

Just over a mile ahead, the commander of R25 now saw a tempting target, the railway station at St Pancras, marked by the tall tower of the integral Midland Grand Hotel. The sounding of the warning had led a rush of people to seek shelter at the hotel, while others crowded under an archway at the station, which led through to the ticket office. Some of the hotel staff were outside hoping to catch a glimpse of the raiders. Edith Gooday and her family were amongst those sheltering at the hotel.

> Hundreds of people were crowded there – strangers, friends, neighbours – singing, and making as much noise as possible for the benefit of the kiddies; but my mother was strangely restless and kept saying she was not going to stay in the hotel itself, for she could feel something awful was going to happen. Friends told her not to be silly; but she took our hands and led us through a long passage and down a flight of stairs, until we found ourselves in what must have been a disused coal-bay.[9]

After a while a family friend went to see if the 'all clear' had sounded. 'Then,' Mrs Gooday continued, 'there came a terrific crash, and darkness descended.' The friend staggered back. 'It's awful outside!' he gasped. Mrs Gooday remembered, 'showers of splintering glass,' and that 'coal dust fell, it seemed, by the ton,' as she and her family cowered in their filthy subterranean refuge.

The crew of R25 released six bombs at 10.50pm – one overshot and exploded in Midland Road, by the wall of Somers Town Goods Station, but the other five fell within 50 yards of each other, on the hotel and station. One exploded in the roadway where taxis exited the station, two on pinnacles on the roof of the hotel (one failed to explode), sending lumps of stone and masonry cascading down into the street, one outside the entrance to the station arch and one by the booking hall on the other side of the archway. Those under the arch were caught between two blasts.

Winifred Coates and Maud Sugars, two maids from the hotel were there. They came from Derbyshire, where a newspaper succinctly summed up their lives: 'They were cousins, went to school together, worked together, and died together.'

Another maid stood on the hotel steps.

> We had heard guns firing for some time, but they did not seem to be at all near... I had got half way down the steps when there was a terrific report and I was lifted off my feet and blown back through the door.[10]

Also on the steps were 18-year-old Herbert Robinson and his father; they had just run to the hotel. Having got their breath back, Robinson senior, suggested they go inside but as they did so the bombs exploded. He pulled his son into the hotel where fumes now filled the corridor.

> We had run about 120 steps when [Herbert] said, 'Dad, I think I've been hit in the back.' I saw he had a wound there, and that his coat and trousers were torn. I gave him first aid, and he was taken to the hospital, where he died.[11]

Also amongst the victims were two brothers, Charles and Albert Harriman, who were sheltering under the arch, and a married couple, Edward and Ada Close. They had come to London to visit their soldier son and were now on their way home. They both received fatal injuries. In Ada's pocket they found a postcard she had already written, ready for posting. It told her son they had arrived home safely.[12] The bodies of many of those caught by the double-blast under the archway were unrecognisable. E. Lilley, serving with the National Ambulance and Nursing Corps, rushed to the scene.

> About ten bodies lay there, terribly mutilated; and two or three soldiers must have been among the victims, for we found two caps, three swagger canes and a limb with a puttee on it – all that remained of them so far as I could see.[13]

One of the military victims, Flight Sergeant Fred Darlington, RFC, suffered terrible wounds and died six days later. A taxi driver, however, considered himself very lucky. Having just dropped off a fare, he left his cab to go to a refreshment room when he saw a flash.

> As soon as I saw that I fell flat on my face, and I reckon that that saved me... If I had been on the cab I must have been killed, for several hundredweight of granite fell on it.[14]

George Jellicoe, RNVR, a guest at the hotel, arrived on the scene just after the bombs had exploded. He described the scene as 'pandemonium', with 'fire engines, people, and police racing about in all directions'.[15]

Edith Gooday and her family remained in the coal-bay throughout, too scared to leave.

> Those of us who were not lying on the ground bleeding and groaning were practically choking. From all sides came cries for water, but no water was to be had... Suddenly a ray of light descended, and framed in a doorway was a man in uniform with a pail of water. He told us... the raid had been over for some time so we tried to leave... When we moved we seemed to be ankle-deep in broken glass; and as we left the ruins matches flickered, and in their light a ghastly sight met our eyes. Dead and injured lay everywhere.[16]

At St Pancras 20 people died with another 22 injured. The London Fire Brigade estimated damage caused by the raid at £39,898, with St Pancras accounting for £25,000 of the total. Beyond the obvious horrors of the incident, amongst military men the skill displayed by the German crew drew a cool, professional appreciation, as highlighted in a report written six days later.

> This bombing of St Pancras represents up to the present by far the most accurate and concentrated fire ever yet brought to bear on any target in London, either by day or night and was a fine piece of shooting by the man responsible for it.[17]

R25 dropped a final 12kg explosive bomb in the grounds of a YMCA training centre in Mildmay Park, but it failed to detonate. Taking a south-east course, R25 crossed the Thames again. That night the RFC flew 69 sorties, but only three pilots saw R25 on its outward course. One, Second Lieutenant Noel Chandler of No. 78 Squadron, observed it when patrolling near Dartford. 'I challenged a large machine in the vicinity of Joyce Green,' he reported, 'and receiving no reply fired at it. The flash was so dazzling that after a burst of about fifty rounds I lost the enemy aircraft.'[18] Two other pilots had unsuccessful fleeting engagements and anti-aircraft guns over a vast area blasted the sky with 7,375 rounds. But many of these rounds were fired at Home Defence aircraft as the confusion created by just one enemy aircraft became widespread.

One of those pilots, Captain Cecil Lewis of No. 61 Squadron, flying a SE5a, came under fire from anti-aircraft guns when over Benfleet in Essex. Despite the danger it put him in, he took it all very calmly: 'Shooting very good. Burst exactly at my height (11,000 feet) and put several holes in my machine.'[19]

As far west as Eton, 20 miles from St Pancras, guns were in action. This reaction did not go unnoticed by the crew of the German bomber.

> An attack by a single R-plane is sufficient to alert the entire British defence system and to cause the expenditure of vast quantities of ammunition. It is seemingly from nervousness that not only anti-aircraft guns in the vicinity of our aircraft but also some 30 km distant were being fired blindly into the air. For example, on our homeward flight a great barrage was being laid-down from Sheerness while we were still south of Rochester [12 miles away].[20]

The following night that nervousness still gripped the defenders when a series of reports detailing hostile aircraft over south-eastern England led to a major false alarm, with the RFC flying 55 sorties and 47 anti-aircraft guns coming into action, firing around 4,000 rounds – at British aircraft.[21]

***

The same day that Britain's defences were chasing imaginary German aircraft around south-east England, *Bogohl 3* welcomed back the much-missed figure of Ernst Brandenburg. Following his crash-landing back in June 1917, resulting in the amputation of a leg, he had been recuperating for the last eight months. But now, although walking with difficulty on an artificial leg, he rejoined his squadron. Although aware of the significant losses, he had not appreciated how much this had impacted on his men's morale. With *Bogohl 3* only able to muster about half its strength, he immediately informed von Hoeppner that he had suspended all operations until he could rebuild the squadron. He estimated it would be ready to return to the fray by late March. Circumstances, however, dictated it would be much later before they resumed their campaign against Britain. In the meantime, the baton remained firmly in the hands of von Bentivegni's *Rfa 501*, but Peter Strasser's Zeppelins were also hoping to return soon, when the weather conditions allowed. But for now, that main thrust remained with *Rfa 501*.

***

After a hiatus lasting 18 days, *Rfa 501* returned to the attack on 7 March. That same morning the squadron re-located to a new airfield at Scheldewindeke, just south of Ghent. Unusually for an aeroplane raid, the moon had entered its last quarter, meaning a dark night. But a light did shimmer in the sky; the Aurora Borealis or Northern Lights were faintly glowing in the heavens. And for the first time all six Giants of the squadron were available. Von Bentivegni led the raid in R39, again carrying a single 1,000kg bomb. Amongst those waiting to take off, *Hauptmann* Arthur Schoeller, First Pilot on R27, completed his preparations.

> At exactly 8 pm *Hauptmann* von Bentivegni fires the starting flare and the first of the R-planes strains forward with an ear-deafening roar. We are next to taxi to the take-off strip and ten minutes after the first aircraft, with full throttle R27 heads into the clear dark night.
>
> Slowly the heavily-loaded machine rolls over the ground; finally it is airborne, and... we head in a direction along the pin-marked course on our maps. Inside the fuselage the pale glow of dimmed lights outlines the chart-table, the wireless equipment and the instrument panel, on which the compass and other navigation instruments are mounted to help guide us through the darkness.
>
> We approach the coast; the night is so dark that the coastline below is but a mere suggestion. Under us is a black abyss, no waves are seen, no lights of surface vessels flicker as we head for the Thames estuary at Margate. On our right, in the distant north, is our only light, the weak pulsating glow of the aurora borealis. Ahead of us a black nothingness – are we on the correct course? We have neither a weather report from the high seas nor wind measurements to go by.[22]

7 March 1918, 11.55pm: Warrington Crescent, London

One of the raiders never reached England – engine problems forced it to return to Scheldewindeke – but the remaining five Giants crossed the coast, two coming inland over Kent and three over Essex. At 10.56pm von Bentivegni's R39 passed over Kent, half an hour before the first RFC aircraft took-off, although anti-aircraft fire marked its progress towards the capital. In London the gun at Tower Bridge opened fire at 11.47pm, then eight minutes later von Bentivegni released his metric ton of destruction. It is not clear what target he aimed at, if any, but the bomb fell about 1,000 yards north of Paddington Station.

The Reverend William Kilshaw, curate of St Simon's Church, Paddington, and his family were at home in Marylands Road. When the guns began to bark, they had moved down to the basement. Now they heard the haunting whistle of a falling bomb.

> Suddenly the darkness of the room was broken in upon by a vivid flash, as bright as a fierce lightning flash, and a terrific roar caused the whole house to tremble. Our top window panes fell to the ground with a shattering noise... After the bombardment we cautiously went to the window, to behold a scene reminiscent of what one reads of the Great Fire of London. The sky to the east was lurid with flames...
>
> When we ventured forth the broad roadway of Sutherland Avenue was littered with splintered glass. Not a window remained intact. It was much as though one were walking over a shingle beach, so thickly did glass cover the road. In Warrington Crescent, where a terrace of four-storey houses had been, there remained but a gap. It was as though a giant had cut the houses clean away from the foundations.[23]

The Reverend Kilshaw was right, a giant had caused the scene of devastation laid out before him, but this one had wings. The huge bomb exploded on the dividing wall between 63 and 65 Warrington Crescent, a quiet 'well-to-do' residential street in Maida Vale. Both houses collapsed, as did those on either side. Another 20 properties suffered substantial damage, with over 400 more in the surrounding streets impacted by the blast wave. Those inside the collapsed houses were buried under the rubble, but a rescue operation soon swung into action. One of the first on the scene, Dr Edward Wright, a Divisional Surgeon with the Metropolitan Police, 'smothered in dust and wearing a shrapnel helmet', worked tirelessly throughout the night. The efforts of Sapper Harry Landregan of No. 2 Emergency Section, Royal Engineers, were noted too, as well as his courage and devotion to duty while spending long periods upside down while administering oxygen to those who desperately needed it. Both men received the British Empire Medal, while much praise also recognised the sterling efforts of 17-year-old Boy Scout, Arthur Nice, during the rescue operation. But there were others too, from the police, fire brigade, ambulance service, Royal Engineers and local people who worked tirelessly for the next few days keeping those trapped under the rubble alive, or working their way through the debris to rescue them. Despite their best efforts, however, 13 died at Warrington Crescent, with over 30 more injured. Among the dead lay a 47-year-old American woman and her son; her name, Lena Guilbert Ford. In 1914 she had penned the words to Ivor Novello's score for the hugely popular wartime song, 'Keep the Home Fires Burning'.

R39 returned safely back to Ghent, but there were four more Giants preparing to play their part that night.

8 March 1918, 12.15am: Belsize Park and St John's Wood, London

The second Giant came inland over Broadstairs in Kent at 11.00pm and later crossed to the north side of the Thames. At 12.05am observers at Potter's Bar reported her heading south and, about 10 minutes later, two bombs fell in the Belsize Park area of north-west London. One exploded in the garden of a large house at 15 Lyndhurst Gardens, damaging the building and smashing windows all around. The second bomb caused severe damage to the upper floors of 31 and 32 Belsize Square, and broke windows in 58 other houses. The next four bombs fell in the St John's Wood area. Two in gardens in Townshend Road (one a dud) caused significant damage to houses at Nos. 37, 39 and 41, and affected 31 neighbouring properties. The next destroyed adjoining houses at 11 and 12 New Street (now Newcourt Street). Frederick and Edith Chick, along with their daughter Marjorie, and Harry and Lilian Hulse with their son, Clifford, were all killed. About ten people were in the houses either side but, incredibly, some of them did not grasp what had happened.

> There was a crash, but we did not realise in the darkness what it was, and we went on talking. Then I pulled the curtains aside to look out, and I saw a great pile of bricks and timber and a policeman clambering over it. He said, 'Is anyone alive here?' and we all came out.[24]

The last of the four bombs exploded about 400 yards away, outside Lord's Cricket Ground in St John's Wood Road. Lieutenant Colonel Frederick Wollaston, Rifle Brigade (attached to the Suffolk Regiment, commanding 1/5th Battalion), back in London on leave from Palestine, occupied a room at the Lord's Hotel. 'He had expressed a wish to see a raid,' a newspaper reported. 'He stood looking out of a window, and hearing a machine overhead, remarked, "I am sure that is a Boche machine."' Seconds later the bomb exploded outside the hotel and a fragment killed him. It also killed a soldier in the street, Driver Sidney Reeves, Royal Horse Artillery, while on his way back to barracks. Hit by bomb splinters he cried out, 'Oh, my poor legs,' as he fell. He died a few hours later.[25] The blast also damaged the main gate of the cricket ground.

Heading south, the Giant crossed the Thames and 5 miles on dropped a bomb at 12.25am in Burland Road, between Clapham Common and Wandsworth Common. It partially demolished three houses, but everyone emerged unharmed. A child explained that she, her mother and two sisters had gone downstairs when the guns began to fire and were huddled in the hall.

> A few moments later we were thrown in a heap on the floor. A bomb had fallen directly outside and the whole of the front, and part of the back, of the house was demolished. Our beds which we had occupied only five minutes before, were twisted into scrap-iron. Still very dazed we were assisted by a constable who, helped by others, lifted us over the debris. It was terribly hot as the bomb had exploded on the gas main in the road and flames were leaping high.[26]

Besides the gas main, the explosion also fractured a water main and damaged 25 other houses in the street and 77 more in the local area. The raider dropped a final bomb in a wood near the village of Hayes in Kent at around 1.00am and passed out to sea near Dover 50 minutes later.

8 March 1918, 12.25am: Finchley and Whetstone

Only one other Giant reached London, but its bombs were confined to the northern outskirts. Running the gauntlet of anti-aircraft fire from the Kent coast, after crossing the Thames, the raider appeared over north-west London. At 12.25am three 100kg bombs fell in fields behind Addison Way, between Golders Green and Finchley, causing some damage to 30 houses. But rather than heading towards the centre of London, the Giant turned north and within a mile dropped a 50kg bomb in the garden of a house in Dollis Avenue, Finchley. The police recorded: 'Severe damage to premises in the vicinity; in all 72 houses damaged.' Another bomb fell just over half a mile further north, in a field on Frith Lane, Mill Hill, smashing windows in two houses. The Giant then dropped a final bomb in the rear garden of 16 Totteridge Lane, Whetstone. A well-known professional golfer, Harry Vardon, living next door, had a narrow escape. He and his wife heard the bomb falling.

> It was a curious sound – a soft, hissing sound, like the falling of sand from a pail. Then came a tremendous explosion, and everything about the place was thrown hither and thither. We were absolutely helpless, standing in the middle of the bedroom, not knowing what was going to happen. Within a minute the place was a wreck. Pictures, ornaments, furniture were flying around, yet we were fortunate enough to escape injury.[27]

Houses close to the point of impact suffered considerably, resulting in the death of one man and injuries to ten other people. Heading back out across Essex, the Giant crossed the coast near Bradwell at about 2.00am.

8 March 1918, 12.35am: Hertfordshire

Two of the raiders failed to reach London. One came inland near Foulness in Essex at 11.10pm, but anti-aircraft fire deflected it north of London, and by midnight it was over Bedfordshire. This may have been Arthur Schoeller's R27. His account of the raid does not tally with official reports but he states they dropped four explosive bombs aimed at flares on an airfield.[28] No airfield came under attack that night, but a group of four bombs did fall close together in Luton Hoo Park. Now heading towards London, anti-aircraft fire turned it away from the capital, and forced numerous changes of course. At about 12.35am a bomb dropped in a field at the village of Great Munden in Hertfordshire before ten more streaked down to explode around the village of Much Hadham. These appear to be the bombs that Schoeller reports were dropped on London. But rather than doing damage among the docks or warehouses of the capital, they wrecked a disused brick kiln, smashed the roof of a cattle shed and a few windows, and blasted crops across a Hertfordshire field. After dodging more gun fire, R27 eventually went out to sea near Harwich.

8 March 1918: 1.02am: Herne Bay

The last of the five Giants came inland at 11.18pm near Southend-on-Sea, Essex. Heavy anti-aircraft fire forced it away from London, but more guns opened fire. At 12.20am a 100kg bomb landed in a field at Tillingham before the aircraft crossed the Thames Estuary to the Kent side of the river, from where more guns engaged the fugitive. Over Herne Bay at 1.02am the Giant dropped a 100kg bomb on the beach near Hampton Pier. The blast seriously damaged five houses and the St George's Hotel, but there were no injuries. Another bomb fell a couple of miles inland in a meadow near Broomfield Hall. The raider then went out to sea near Broadstairs at about 1.25am.

The five Giants kept the anti-aircraft guns busy as they fired off 9,737 rounds. Two people were killed in Leyton and Eltham by falling shells which also inflicted significant damage on 41 houses in London and left another 70 needing basic repairs. The RFC flew 42 sorties attempting to intercept the raiders but none were located. Sadly, two pilots – Captain Alexander Kynoch (37 Squadron) and Captain Henry Stroud (61 Squadron) – died near Rayleigh in Essex when their aircraft collided shortly after take-off. But a Giant failed to make it home too. Water-contaminated petrol caused the fuel pipes on Schoeller's R27 to freeze as they neared the Belgium coast. Schoeller skilfully crash-landed behind German lines allowing the crew to walk away from the wreck. Arrangements were made to recover the engines but Allied artillery bombardments destroyed the hulk of R27.

***

Britain's defenders had every reason to expect the regular bomber raids on London to continue, but suddenly they came to a halt. After this raid in early March the night skies remained calm, no aeroplanes appeared over the capital, no bombs dropped, no booming anti-aircraft guns rudely woke the bleary-eyed population from their slumbers. Could it all be over?

Chapter 16

The Zeppelins Return

After the raid on the night of 7/8 March, no German bombers appeared over London and the south-east for ten weeks. The crews of *Bogohl 3*, however, were not able to use this time to train new pilots and build up the strength of the squadron. The German Army High Command had set the date of 21 March for the launch of their great spring offensive on the Western Front, the *Kaiserschlacht* or Emperor's Battle. Germany hoped to break through the Allied lines and push the British Army back to the coast. All bombers were required to support the attack, targeting Allied supply hubs and railway communications. Although London and the south-east would be free from attack, it opened the door once more for Peter Strasser to launch the Zeppelins of the Naval Airship Division against Britain, with their focus on the industrial regions of the North and Midlands.

There had been no Zeppelin activity over Britain for five months, not since the 'Silent Raid' in October 1917 when the Naval Airship Division lost five Zeppelins. In January, they lost five more in the Ahlhorn disaster. Since October only five new Zeppelins joined Strasser's command, two in November (L 58 and L 59), two in December (L 61 and L 62) and one in March (L 63), but L 58 had been one of those destroyed at Ahlhorn while L 59 had special orders to prepare for a long-distance – ultimately aborted – mission to deliver supplies to German forces operating in East Africa. Therefore, in March 1918, Strasser had eight Zeppelins available for operations against Britain.[1]

On 12 March, Strasser ordered five of his crews to prepare for action. Those selected were L 53, L 54, L 61, L62 and L 63, the last of which had only joined the division three days earlier; Strasser accompanied the mission on board L 62. Initially the weather seemed favourable, but as the force neared the British coast, at heights between 16,000 and 18,000ft, they found the country concealed under a thick layer of cloud. With little or no view of the ground, and inaccurate wireless bearings, the commanders struggled with navigation throughout.

The first noted by British trackers was *Kapitänleutnant* von Buttlar's L 54. Von Buttlar, the longest serving Zeppelin captain, owed his longevity more to a determination to avoid risks rather than his skills as a commander. The British authorities, who regularly tracked his movements, held a low opinion of him and in the summary report of this raid referred to him as the 'notorious Kapt.-Leutnant v. Buttlar', that notoriety based on the fact that he rarely pushed far inland, or even crossed the coast.

Von Buttlar claimed an attack on the port of Grimsby, but that did not happen. A section of Grimsby fishing trawlers, when 80 miles off the coast and under the protection of Lieutenant Higman, RNVR, caught a glimpse of three Zeppelins at great height. Higman concluded that two continued to the west but one, L 54, changed direction. To protect his section of trawlers, Higman ordered them to move location. About 10 minutes later bombs dropped in the area just vacated. This, it seems, formed von Buttlar's attack on 'Grimsby'. In his later memoir, von Buttlar gave a dramatic account of coming under fire from 'anti-aircraft batteries', but although Higman cleared his gun for action it appears he did not open fire.[2]

Even so, L 54, had problems; one, possibly two midship gas bags were emptying of hydrogen. The journey back to Tondern became tense but L 54 made it. Later, a report concluded that the holes in the gas bags were most likely caused by ice thrown back from the propellers. That, however, did not have any impact on von Buttlar's status within the Naval Airship Division. His regular 'creative' raid reports earned him the highest respect and a couple of weeks later von Buttlar received a telegram from the *Kaiser*.

> Since the beginning of the War you have, with five of my airships, successfully carried out innumerable reconnaissance flights and fifteen air raids on important military centres in England, the last of which was 12th – 13th of March. In recognition of these services, I invest you with the order *Pour le Mérite*, and take this opportunity of expressing my warmest thanks to your brave crew.[3]

Another of the Zeppelins, Eduard Prölss' L 53, also failed to cross the coast. Prölss reported bombing Hull, but the cloud cover prevented ground observation and all his bombs fell at sea. On the return journey four engine mechanics in the rear gondola were rendered unconscious by carbon monoxide poisoning, caused by a cracked exhaust pipe, and two died.[4]

12 March 1918, 8.55pm: Hull

The first Zeppelin to cross the coast, the new L 63, had *Kapitänleutnant* Michael von Freudenreich as her commander, his previous ship, L 47, being one of those destroyed in the Ahlhorn disaster. He passed over Hornsea on the Yorkshire coast at 8.30pm, believing he had already penetrated inland, because when he released six bombs near Hull at 8.55pm, von Freudenreich concluded they fell on Bradford and Leeds, 60 and 50 miles to the west respectively.

All the bombs fell on the eastern side of Hull. The first three – one of 100kg and two of 50kg – all exploded harmlessly in fields between Oak Road and the River Hull, as did one that fell in a field between the Hull and Barnsley Railway and the Hornsea branch of the North Eastern Railway. Seconds later another 50kg bomb detonated on a railway embankment in Montrose Street, badly damaging a house, causing lesser damage to others, destroying a workman's cabin and damaging a signal box. A final bomb smashed roofs, broke ceilings and shattered windows along Southcoates Avenue. Sarah Masterman had left home with her family to seek safety in the open spaces of Hull's Pickering Park but she died of shock when the guns came into action. Those at Marfleet and Sutton fired first, followed by guns at Paull, Harpings and Hessle, and south of the Humber from New Holland and Chase Hill Farm. Von Freudenreich blindly retaliated but the six bombs that fell at Sutton, and ten at Swine, all exploded in fields. L 63 left the coast near Tunstall, sent on her way by a section of two mobile guns at Hornsea.

12 March 1918, 11.15pm: Seaton Ross, Yorkshire

About a minute after the Hornsea guns engaged L 63, a mobile gun section at Flamborough, about 13 miles to the north, opened fire on another Zeppelin. Their target, *Hauptmann* Kuno Manger's L 62, had Strasser on board. Manger later claimed a fanciful attack on Leeds but L 62 spent about half an hour north of Bridlington before pushing inland, passing over Driffield towards Pocklington and manoeuvring around Yorkshire. At about 11.00pm trackers believed that L 62 might head for the RNAS airship station at Howden but, engaged by four anti-aircraft guns, she shied away to the north-west. At 11.15pm, Manger claimed to have bombed Leeds, but his 23 bombs (4 x 100kg, 9 x 50kg and ten incendiaries) mostly fell in fields or woodland near the village of Seaton Ross, located between York and Beverley. Of the rest, three or four of the explosive bombs fell either side of the Black Horse Inn in the village, smashing all the front windows, damaging the roof and ceilings, and tearing doors from their hinges, but everyone inside escaped without injury. Just over 2 miles further on, L 62 dropped four more explosive bombs in fields around the village of Melbourne. Turning back towards the coast, L 62 went out to sea near Barmston at 11.40pm, from where a section of mobile guns opened fire as she disappeared into the gloom.

The last Zeppelin, *Kapitänleutnant* Herbert Ehrlich's L 61, failed to drop any bombs. Ehrlich crossed the coast at 10.10pm after his first three attempts were repulsed by the mobile gun sections at Hornsea and Barmston. Once over Yorkshire, however, Ehrlich travelled over a similar area to L 62, but failed to locate any targets through the cloud cover. He left the coast at Filey at 11.10pm, later reporting that he attacked a 'heavily fortified place on the Humber'. As no bombs were traced on land it seems likely that they dropped at sea.

This first Zeppelin attack since October 1917 had little to show for the efforts of the crews, with damage inflicted estimated at just £3,474 and only a single casualty. It had provided the northern Home Defence squadrons with their first action for five months, but the three squadrons ordered to patrol were defeated by the weather. Two pilots of No. 33 Squadron went up to assess flying conditions in their area but soon returned. 'It was impossible to send machines on patrol,' the squadron commander concluded, 'mist, rain, and low clouds prevailing'.[5] Three aircraft of No. 36 Squadron and four from No. 76 Squadron, however, did get airborne. A clearer sky further north allowed No. 36 Squadron to patrol, but no Zeppelins appeared there. Over Yorkshire, the experience of Second Lieutenant S. Hill, No. 76 Squadron, appears typical of the night. He reported that at 13,000ft he could see nothing, the weather being 'very thick'.[6]

Unusually, Strasser, ordered another raid the next day, selecting the three Zeppelins that had not participated in the previous night's raid: L 42, L 52 and L 56. Orders specified an attack on the industrial Midlands but, before they reached Britain, Strasser recalled them, much to *Kapitänleutnant* Martin Dietrich's frustration.

> We received a wireless order: 'All airships to turn back; danger of contrary winds.' All over! Finished! We grind our teeth with rage. We knew that if the wind veered round to the east our return journey would be risky. And – orders are orders. But – not to attack England – to turn back when so near our goal – that was too much![7]

L 52 and L 56 followed orders, while Dietrich decided to take out his frustration on a shipping convoy.

> Just as we are about to attack, the English coast looms into sight. There was hardly ever a day when you could have seen it so plainly – it looked as if you could almost touch it... A hundred different thoughts whirl through my brain. 'If you raid England against orders and anything goes wrong, you can pack up. You'll have to retire from the service. Your career will be finished. More than that: you are responsible for your ship and crew... Germany needs every man and every airship. You are an officer; you have to do your duty.'

While Dietrich considered his responsibilities, he received a status report from the crew; everything on L 42 was working perfectly. He succumbed to temptation: 'We will carry on, come what may. We will trust in our lucky star.'

13 March 1918, 9.20pm: Hartlepool

At 7.52pm, those tracking the Zeppelin's movements noted L 42 about 50 miles off the Northumberland coast but that she made no attempt to come inland. There appeared to be little chance of a raid and, in the town of West Hartlepool, lights at the station, in the factories, docks and streets shone brightly.

At 9.15pm, having waited for the skies to darken sufficiently, Dietrich brought L 42 inland just to the north of Hartlepool. No one tracked him crossing the coast. Once overland, Dietrich approached the town from the north-west, and only when the first four bombs exploded five minutes later did the Zeppelin's presence became known. They exploded in fields near the Hartlepool Union Workhouse, north-west of the town, and were followed by one near Amberton Road, close to the tracks of the North Eastern Railway (NER). The Hartlepool searchlight flickered into life a minute after the first explosion and began sweeping the sky, while the anti-aircraft gun defending the town burst into action at 9.23pm, but the police did not receive the TARA order for another eight minutes. By then the worst was over.[8]

From Amberton Road, L 42 passed over Hartlepool Docks, dropping nine 50kg bombs. One exploded on the edge of No. 4 Timber Pond, carrying away part of the bank, followed by two that erupted in Central Dock. Two more fell in the water close to Dockgate Cottages, breaking a few windows, then one in West Harbour, and another in the mud by a graving dock. To the south of Coal Dock, two bombs exploded about 20 yards apart in the NER sidings, damaging about a dozen coal trucks.

South of the docks lay the closely packed workmen's cottages of West Hartlepool. Here Dietrich's bombs began to claim victims. In South Street, one destroyed an empty house, damaged others and practically wrecked the Normanby Hall public house, but all seven people inside escaped unharmed. The next, exploding on the pavement in Mainsforth Terrace, knocked down part of a wall close to the railway. The last four bombs fell close together, in Temperance Street, Frederick Street and Burbank Street. In Temperance Street the bomb exploded outside No. 23. About ten people from three families were inside at the time. A baby and a little girl had been put to bed in the front downstairs room where everyone congregated when they heard explosions.

> Almost immediately a bomb fell in the street outside, and the front of the house was blown in. All the inmates were buried in the wreckage, but soldiers were soon on the scene, and began the work of extrication.[9]

Inside was carnage. The first two bodies recovered were those of Joseph Middleton, aged 11, and Helen Readman (4). Later they found the body of Eileen's baby sister, Mary, just 13 months old. The force of the blast had thrown her across the room. Also recovered were the bodies of Henry and Louisa Harrison, both in their sixties. Four others were injured. Just about every house in the street suffered damage to some extent. Two bombs that smashed down in Frederick Street left No. 27 in ruins with damage evident all along the street. The full force of the final bomb seared though the houses at 106 and 108 Burbank Street, where every building in the street bore witness to the force of the blast. These bombs claimed three more lives: they found Jane Ann Fordham (67) buried in the debris of her kitchen; John Bamlett (40), a discharged soldier died in the street; and Harry Kershaw (8) at home.[10] The boy's father explained to the coroner what had happened.

> As he was taking his elder son into the kitchen, followed by his wife, who carried the deceased child, there was a terrific explosion just outside the front door. Something struck the little boy full in the face and knocked the mother down. There was a heavy fall of debris. He picked his wife up and took the boy out of her arms only to find that he was dead.[11]

Besides those killed in Frederick and Burbank streets, there were also three others badly injured and 11 who received immediate first aid on the spot for their wounds.

Martin Dietrich continued heading south for just over a mile before turning out to sea at Seaton Carew, under fire from guns at Hartlepool, Seaton Carew and Tees Mouth, and attacked by an FE2d of No. 36 Squadron. Although unable to claw their way up to the Zeppelin's height, the crew opened fire at long-range before pursuing L 42 out to sea with more hope than expectation of being able to catch her. Another No. 36 Squadron aircraft, an FE2b piloted by Sergeant Arthur Joyce, patrolling between Cramlington and Easington ran into difficulties and crashed into Pontop Pike, a hill near Annfield Plain, County Durham. His aircraft burst into flames and Joyce died.

On the homeward journey, Dietrich prepared to face the music for ignoring orders. The fierce wind from the east, which had prompted the earlier recall order, made the journey a difficult one, and fuel supplies began to run low. But, after a tense North Sea crossing, they made it.

> We brought her safely back. With the last drops of our... fuel we reached Nordholz after a trip of twenty-one hours... When we landed, Strasser was not there. This was contrary to his usual custom, and things looked ominous for us... Strasser's adjutant, Captain v. Lossnitzer... squeezed my hand sympathetically. 'The chief is simply boiling over,' he said. 'If I'm in for three days cells, I'll at least get some sleep first,' I replied. In the afternoon I reported to Strasser. But he did not put me in the cells; he stroked his little moustache, smiled his peculiar smile, and christened me the 'Count of Hartlepool'.[12]

***

Strasser's fleet of eight Zeppelins operating over the North Sea increased to nine in mid-March with the delivery of L 64, and to ten on 1 April following the delayed arrival of L 60. But elsewhere another was lost. On 7 April, Zeppelin L 59, based at Yambol in Bulgaria, exploded over the Adriatic during a mission against Britain's naval base on Malta.

On 12 April, Strasser despatched L 52 and L 53 on reconnaissance flights over the North Sea in foggy conditions. In Germany, however, weather conditions appeared promising and Strasser issued orders for five 'v-class' Zeppelins (L 60, L 61, L 62, L 63 and L 64) to prepare for a raid on the industrial Midlands. Each carried a bomb load of just over 3 tons. But favourable weather conditions in Germany soon gave way to thickening cloud and heavy rain squalls over the North Sea. Three of the raiders, discovering that Britain lay hidden under a blanket of cloud, did not venture far inland.

12 April 1918, 9.26pm: The Humber

Kapitänleutnant Hans Kurt Flemming, commanding L 60, reached the Humber Estuary at about 9.20pm, but only remained overland for a little over an hour. He claimed an attack on Leeds but never passed within 40 miles of the city. As L 60 passed up the Humber, anti-aircraft guns opened fire at the sound of her engines and at 9.26pm, when over East Halton, Flemming dropped 13 bombs (4 x 100kg, 8 x 50kg and one incendiary). Three of the larger bombs and the incendiary failed to detonate, limiting damage to a railway signal box and two dead sheep. L 60 continued to drop bombs as it headed west, with 21 (11 explosive and ten incendiary) falling around the villages of Thornton Curtis, Burnham, Saxby All Saints and Horkstow, breaking a few windows and bringing down telegraph wires. Now west of Hull, L 60 crossed to the north bank of the Humber, passed around the north side of the city and returned to the coast.

12 April 1918, 10.35pm: Metheringham, Lincolnshire

Kapitänleutnant Michael von Freudenreich, commanding L 63, also struggled to identify his position after coming inland at 10.05pm. He crossed the coast near Skegness and progressed to the west, but at 10.29pm an anti-aircraft gun opened fire from Brauncewell and von Freudenreich turned north-west. About 5 miles further on he released a 100kg bomb that fell in a field at Blankney Park. Five minutes later, von Freudenreich released 18 bombs (2 x 300kg, 15 x 50kg and an incendiary) which all smashed down about a mile east of the village of Metheringham. This, von Freudenreich claimed, as an attack on the busy port of Grimsby at the mouth of the Humber, which lay about 30 miles away. According to the police, these bombs, weighing about 1.5 tons, resulted in a 'few windows broken'. Von Freudenreich then followed a south-east course for about 30 miles until, at 11.10pm, he dropped incendiary bombs at Fleet and Little Sutton before turning out to sea over The Wash.

12 April 1918, 10.28pm: West of Lincoln

The new L 64, commanded by *Korvettenkapitän* Arnold Schütze, crossed the coast at 9.45pm near Saltfleet, Lincolnshire, and headed south-west. She dropped an incendiary bomb at Biscathorpe at 10.02pm before skirting around the north side of the darkened city of Lincoln. An anti-aircraft gun at Burton Road opened fire at 10.28pm, but L 64 passed around the west side of Lincoln, drawn towards the villages of Skellingthorpe and Doddington, where the air raid warning had not reached and consequently lights were still shining. Two 300kg bombs fell close to Skellingthorpe Station, damaging a railway engine and a shed, and bringing down telegraph wires; three men were injured by an anti-aircraft shell. At Doddington, 12 explosive 50kg bombs rained down but these only resulted in a few broken windows and a shaken chimney. Schütze believed he had bombed Hull, almost 40 miles away. He now swung L 64 onto an easterly course, attracted by landing flares burning on a training squadron airfield at Waddington. A 50kg bomb exploded in a field close to the airfield and three more at the village of Mere, but without effect. At 10.54pm, the gun at Brauncewell, the same one that had earlier engaged L 63, opened fire on L 64 as the raider set a course back to the coast, passing out to sea just south of Skegness.

While these three raiders has achieved little, the other two Zeppelins, however, penetrated deep inland, coming tantalisingly close to Birmingham and Liverpool.

12 April 1918, 11.45pm: Coventry

Having previously commanded L 14 and L 41, Kuno Manger took command of L 62 in January 1918. Coming inland over the Norfolk coast at about 9.30pm, he struck a south-west course, but near Downham

Market a searchlight caught his attention (see map, p.xviii). Changing direction to the north-west, Manger dropped two 100kg bombs but they missed the searchlight by about a mile, falling on the open country of Tilney All Saints Fen. Flying at 18,000ft, L 62 then homed in on landing flares burning at No. 51 Squadron's airfield at Tydd St Mary, but the three 100kg bombs dropped fell in fields about 1,000 yards away. Resuming a south-west course, and when west of Peterborough, L 62 dropped a 50kg bomb aimed at another searchlight; it exploded in a field about a mile east of Nassington, smashing a shop window.

Maintaining his course, at 11.42pm Manger approached Coventry from where anti-aircraft guns defending the city at Radford and Wyken engaged. Three minutes later, as L 62 passed down the east side of the city, Manger dropped four explosive and nine incendiary bombs. At Whitley Abbey Park a 300kg bomb exploded in a field smashing a few windows while the others struck Baginton: two of the explosive bombs and all nine incendiaries landed around the sewage works and in neighbouring fields, killing a bullock, a heifer and a lamb, while one exploded in Baginton Lane but without causing damage.

Passing north of Kenilworth, L 62 approached Solihull on the southeast side of Birmingham. At around 11.53pm two bombs fell in fields at Packwood, followed by two more in fields north of Hockley Heath. Another pair dropped over Monkspath; one landed at Mount Cottage Farm, the other about half a mile to the west, at Mount Lane. Directly ahead of L 62 now stood the city of Birmingham, but at 11.57pm antiaircraft guns at Lodge Hill, South Yardley and Brandwood End opened fire, with two of them using 'Anti-Zeppelin' incendiary shells. Although falling short, they seemingly unsettled Manger because he immediately released two 300kg bombs and shied away from the city. One, falling in Shirley, smashed windows of six shops and 24 houses, the second exploded on Gospel Farm at Hall Green. This damaged farm buildings, smashed windows at Broom Hall, broke more windows in homes near the church and caused some damage to the Ladies Room at Hall Green golf course.

Manger passed to the east of Birmingham, then returned north of Coventry from where the guns at Wyken and Radford opened fire again, as she headed back towards the coast.

Near Peterborough, two pilots from No. 38 Squadron, both flying FE2bs, saw L 62 but were unable to reach her. Both pilots crashed on landing, with Lieutenant Cecil Noble-Campbell reporting a head wound received while pursuing L 62. The crew of the Zeppelin did not report seeing any British aircraft so there is a possibility that the other pilot, Lieutenant William Brown, accidently shot Noble-Campbell, certainly the police reported the incident that way.[13] However, in his report of the night's action, Brigadier Thomas Higgins, commanding VI (Home Defence) Brigade, stated, '[Brown] is in hospital; his report therefore is not very complete'. Regarding Noble-Campbell, he added: 'It would appear this officer was hit by a shell burst.'[14] It seems unlikely the exact truth will ever be known.

On the outbound journey, guns at Pulham St Mary and Yarmouth engaged L 62. The crew later discovered that one of the gas bags had been holed and a large quantity of hydrogen lost.

Weather conditions over the Midlands had prevented some defence aircraft from getting airborne and L 62 reached the industrial Midlands and had the target area at its mercy, yet the damage inflicted by her bombs proved inconsequential and there were no casualties. The official historian of the air war, however, recognised that it could have been much worse.

> The L 62, which had come within striking distance of Coventry and Birmingham and of the congested industrial area in between, had dropped 2½ tons of bombs with no effect, and we were, it must be admitted, fortunate to escape so lightly.[15]

12 April 1918, 11.30pm: Wigan

The final Zeppelin involved that night, L 61, also had an experienced commander, *Kapitänleutnant* Herbert Ehrlich, having previously commanded L 5, L 17 and L 35. Ehrlich crossed the Yorkshire coast near Withernsea at 9.30pm, shortly after which guns of the Humber garrison opened fire at the sound of his engines. Crossing to the south of the Humber, Ehrlich headed west, passing a few miles south of Doncaster and Sheffield. The latter city earmarked as his target but, with thick cloud and Sheffield under blackout, Ehrlich passed it by, unaware of the strength of the tailwind pushing him westwards. At 10.42pm, when about 10 miles west of Sheffield, ground observers lost contact with the raider, her movements untracked for 28 minutes. She reappeared at 11.10pm, having turned north over the River Mersey near Widnes, and dropped two 50kg bombs near Bold, between St Helens and Warrington in Lancashire. One fell on the main road at Bold Heath, damaging a milestone[16] and a water main, while the second exploded in a field on Abbots Hall Farm, breaking windows about 150 yards away in an office at the Clock Face Colliery.

Dr Henry Baker Bates, the Mayor of St Helens, lived nearby. Asleep, his wife woke him because she heard noises and thought someone might be trying to break into the house. Bates listened but could hear nothing unusual, then his wife heard the sound again.

> To gratify her I made a search of the whole place and opened the front door but could not detect anything wrong. Went back to bed, in five minutes she roused me again saying both the door and windows were being tried. I got up and opened the window to listen. The telephone rang and a message came that Zepps were in the neighbourhood and Air Raid action must be taken. This was about twenty minutes after my wife heard the first explosion. She told me altogether there were two very loud ones which shook the doors and windows and about 10 or 11 explosions in the distance.[17]

His wife's keen ears had heard the whole raid.

As Ehrlich continued northwards, a red glow lit the night sky about 10 miles distant. He believed he had finally located Sheffield, but that city now lay about 50 miles to the east.[18] The red glow marked blast furnaces in operation at the extensive works of the Wigan Coal and Iron Company where no air raid warning had reached the industrial town. Unknown to Ehrlich, the city of Liverpool, long on Strasser's list of important targets, lay just 17 miles away. This port city, a major destination for American goods entering Britain, never came under Zeppelin attack during the war, despite German claims to the contrary.

At about 11.30pm, L 61 reached Ince on the southern edge of Wigan where Ehrlich commenced his bombing run. An incendiary smashed through the roof of 7 Frederick Street but failed to ignite then, 25 yards away, another crashed through the roof of 12 Preston Street, down through the floorboards at the foot of a bed to the kitchen where it burst into flames, setting the house aflame and destroying all the furniture. More bombs landed near the railway.[19]

Joseph Ashton was on duty at Ince Hill Siding. Some years earlier, the 57-year-old signal box operator had lost his right leg below the knee when run over by a goods train. High above in the sky he saw a light.

Immediately afterwards a high explosive bomb crashed through his signal box roof and through the floors into the basement, but did not explode. It splintered the wood in the cabin, broke one lever and twisted several others. He felt something hit him on the temple, which bled freely. Ashton sent a fireman to Ince Railway Station for the ambulance box, and although he was aware he was standing above a live bomb, he continued to attend to his duties.[20]

Another bomb exploded between the signal box and Ince Station, damaging a section of track and destroying two trucks loaded with coal. But Ashton remained on duty throughout the raid and, after his injuries received attention, finally went off duty at 2.20am. An army officer who later inspected the bomb reported, 'it was in a very dangerous position and liable to explode'. His employer at the Lancashire and Yorkshire Railway Company, reported that Ashton had, 'acted with great courage, and for his heroic devotion to duty, and the calm, cool judgement he displayed, which no doubt averted a railway accident, I am of the opinion his good services are worthy of special recognition'. Joseph Ashton received the award of the British Empire Medal.

After the bombs on the railway, L 61 crossed the Leeds & Liverpool Canal, with four bombs falling around Hartley Avenue. One of these destroyed three houses in Harper Street. Samuel Tomlinson, a gas meter inspector, and his wife, Jane, were killed by the bomb, blasted out of their house on their bed. Four more bombs tumbled down; two exploded at the junction of Hardybutts, Birkett Bank and Scholefield Lane. The explosion blew in doors up to 50 yards away and smashed windows 100 yards off. The other two exploded either side of Cecil Street, damaging many properties.

Now over Platt Lane, Ehrlich released three more bombs. Two landed harmlessly on waste ground but the other killed 34-year-old Margaret Ashurst. Two weeks earlier her husband, a miner, took a job in another district and Margaret and their four children were waiting to join him. Margaret lay in bed with their 4-month-old baby when the bomb exploded outside the house. A local newspaper offered its thoughts on what had happened.

> It would suggest that the woman raised her head in bed, no doubt in astonishment of the noise, when a fragment of bomb or splinter shot across the room, cut away her face and killed

her immediately. The infant, however, escaped with just a scratch.[21]

None of the other children were harmed, nor were any of the other eight people in the house.

Ehrlich's course roughly followed the line of the main road towards Aspull and, about 650 yards beyond Platt Lane, his next bomb exploded at the rear of 181 Whelley, opposite the gates to the Lindsay Colliery. Bomb fragments smashed into the house, striking Walter Harris as he carried his 5-month-old son, Alfred, downstairs to safety. Both were killed. Another exploded in the Lindsay Pit Yard but only destroyed a coal truck in the sidings, and one struck a stone wall on Whelley just before it becomes the Wigan Road, injuring a man. Just to the west of Wigan Road four more bombs exploded in a line along a brook at New Springs, injuring four people. They smashed greenhouses, broke doors and windows and set a fierce fire burning that destroyed the Crown Brewery.

L 61 turned away from Wigan on an easterly course and, about 8 miles on, dropped an incendiary bomb at Little Hulton, south of Bolton, where it burnt itself out in a field at Peel Hall. A similar result occurred when L 61's final bomb fell in a field at Outwood, south of Bury. Occasional fire from anti-aircraft guns punctuated L 61's return flight, but at 1.25am, north of Hull, the Zeppelin came to a halt while the crew rectified an engine problem. Although engaged by guns of the Humber garrison they did not manage to hit L 61. She moved off again at about 2.00am, passing out to sea near Spurn Point at 2.38am. Ehrlich remained convinced he had bombed Sheffield.

A careful analysis of the damage inflicted by the raid resulted in an estimate of £11,673. Five people in Wigan died, and another woman injured in her home, Mary Cumberbirch, died in hospital eight days later.[22] There is also the report of the death of an unnamed woman in the Midlands attributed to 'shock caused by Zeppelin bombs'.[23] These results were not much to show for a raid that had seen two of the latest Zeppelins penetrate deep into Britain's industrial heartland. But again, a combination of testing weather conditions and the great heights Zeppelin raiders were forced to operate at to evade Britain's defences conspired to make the attack largely ineffective.

Although no one knew it at the time, this had been the last Zeppelin raid on Britain. There would be one more attempt in August 1918, but there would be no final incursion over British soil, no more Zeppelin terror for the population to endure. The last Zeppelin bomb to fall had been the one dropped by L 62 on farm land at Hall Green, south-east of Birmingham. Like so many others dropped during the campaign it had achieved little.

That night those Home Defence aircraft that took to the skies, flying 27 sorties, also faced a difficult task, as Brigadier General Higgins recognised:

> Taking into consideration the adverse weather conditions, low cloud and mist, it is evident that the pilots who took part put up a very fine performance, showing extraordinary courage and determination.[24]

Those courageous pilots were making history. Following the amalgamation of the RFC and RNAS on 1 April 1918, they flew into action for the first time as the Royal Air Force.[25]

Chapter 17

'Dawn of a fine spring morning'

In April 1918, Peter Strasser had ten Zeppelins under his control in the North Sea theatre of war. Their work, however, for the rest of April and into May focused on naval reconnaissance patrols. On 3 May, Strasser added L 65 to his roster, but a week later the loss of L 62 reduced it to ten again. On a marine patrol, L 62 entered a towering cumulous cloud formation, then followed a huge explosion. Only five bodies were recovered from the sea. *Hauptmann* Kuno Manger, the stalwart former army airship commander, and his crew were lost in an instant.[1]

While Strasser pondered the cause of the explosion, by the middle of May activity increased substantially at the headquarters of *Bogohl 3* and *Rfa 501* as both Ernst Brandenburg and Richard von Bentivegni prepared for a resumption of their raids on London and south-east England.

Following the launch of Germany's spring offensive on the Western Front on 21 March 1918, both squadrons had been bombing targets in France. Losses amongst the Gothas continued but replacements managed to keep *Bogohl 3* up to full strength. *Rfa 501*, however, found it harder to replace their losses. During a raid on the night 20/21 April, R34, a R.VI type Staaken Giant, crashed as a result of combat with the loss of all on board. Then, on the night of 9/10 May, after a raid on Calais and Dunkirk, three of the four Giants involved were lost when thick fog over their home airfield at Scheldewindeke caused havoc on their return. Approaching blindly, R32 hit trees on the approach and crashed, causing an unreleased bomb to explode which destroyed the aircraft. Giant R39 got down safely but R26 and R29 ran into problems when they arrived back later. They were recommended to re-route to Ghistelles airfield, which had better visibility, but both ignored the advice. R26 flew straight into the ground while R29 crashed after clipping tree tops. From the three Giants that were lost, 15 out of 21 crew were killed.[2]

Brandenburg, keen to launch *Bogohl 3's* first raid on London since his return to the squadron in February, needed a promise of good weather. On 19 May, with *Bogohl 3* now back at full strength, six flights each of six aircraft, plus two additional Gothas attached to headquarters, he got the news he wanted. Despite having made three raids on targets in France over the previous five days, Brandenburg issued orders for his crews to prepare for the largest raid of the war. A pair of two-seat Rumpler C.VII aircraft received orders to precede the bombers and ascertain weather conditions over the British coast. Von Bentivegni, however, could only muster three Giants after his recent losses.

Sunday, 19 May marked the Whitsun Bank Holiday weekend in Britain, with the population of London and south-east England in a relaxed mood after two months without the night time horror brought by the air raids. At 10.17pm observers noted an aircraft – a Rumpler – circling off the North Foreland in Kent. After a few minutes the crew fired a signal flare; there would be no turning back. At the same time, acoustic mirrors cut into the cliffs at Joss Gap, near Broadstairs and Fan Bay, near Dover, picked up the sound of aeroplane engines.[3] At 10.42pm a Gotha approached the North Foreland; this information immediately passed by telephone on to LADA headquarters in London. The bombers were on their way.

Since appointed to command LADA in August 1917, Major General Edward Ashmore had pressed on with improving the response to night raiding aircraft. By the end of April 1918, he had 10 squadrons of the RAF operating in the LADA area, alongside 266 anti-aircraft guns and 353 searchlights. Ashmore described LADA as a 'highly centralized intelligence and command system' overseeing the 'gun-stations, searchlights, aerodromes, balloon aprons, emergency landing grounds, coastal and inland watching posts' committed to Home Defence.[4] Each of these locations had a telephone link to one of 25 local sub-control centres, which were, in turn, connected to a Central Operations Room, overseen by Ashmore, located at Spring Gardens by Admiralty Arch in London (see map, p.xx).

> This central control consisted essentially of a large squared map fixed on a table, around which sat ten operators (plotters), provided with headphones; each being connected to two or three of the sub-controls...
>
> When aircraft flew over the country, their position was reported every half-minute or so to the sub-control, where the

course was plotted with counters on a large-scale map. These positions were immediately read off by a 'teller' in the sub-control to the plotter in the central control, where the course was again marked out with counters...

I sat overlooking the map from a raised gallery; in effect, I could follow the course of all aircraft flying over the country, as the counters crept across the map. The system worked very rapidly. From the time when an observer at one of the stations in the country saw a machine over him, to the time when the counter representing it appeared on my map, was not, as a rule, more than half a minute.[5]

Alongside Ashmore in the gallery sat Thomas Higgins, now with the rank of brigadier general, commanding the RAF squadrons, and a senior police representative who liaised with the emergency services. It was in essence the core of the system that Britain relied on when German aircraft returned in the summer of 1940.

The RAF wasted no time getting into action, with the first of 84 aircraft rumbling across their airfields at 10.56pm.[6] The skies over London and the south-east soon buzzed like a hornet's nest.

One Gotha had crashed on take-off with two of the crew fatally injured, but the rest created a constant stream of bombers crossing the coast between the Blackwater River in Essex and Dover in Kent, the first passing inland at about 10.40pm. Once inland many crews were turned back by anti-aircraft fire, others with mechanical problems also abandoned their mission, resulting in many bombs dropping over Kent and Essex; about 18 Gothas pushed on to London.

19/20 May 1918, 11.00pm – 1.05am: Kent

The first of 46 bombs in Kent landed west of Herne at about 11.00pm, damaging three cottages. Eight minutes later two Gothas dropped four bombs on the Northdown area of Margate, damaging St Mary's Church, smashing the windows at a pub and more at Northdown House. Two more exploded on Margate beach at 11.29pm. At 11.15pm an army camp at Murston, near Sittingbourne, attracted four bombs, but they caused no damage, and in Thanet, five minutes later, one exploded in a field at Monkton while another smashed windows at Acol. Around 11.25pm three bombs near Detling and five at Stanford and Saltwood, near

Westenhanger, had little effect. About 20 minutes later single bombs at St James on the Isle of Grain and at Higham had a similar result. At 11.55pm three bombs near Rochester broke a few windows at the golf course. Three attacks took place on the Dover area. The first, at 11.40pm, saw two bombs explode in Priory Hill and one in Widred Road, causing widespread chaos and damage to almost 220 houses. About half an hour later bombs fell at Guston near to sheds on the airfield but they inflicted no damage. The final attack, at 1.05am, resulted in six bombs dropped by a departing Gotha exploding harmlessly in fields at St Margaret's. The first success for the defenders, however, had occurred over Kent two hours earlier.

Gotha G.V 960/16, commanded by *Leutnant der Reserve* Rudolf Bartikowski, with *Vizefeldwebel* Fritz Bloch as pilot and *Vizefeldwebel* Heinrich Heilgers as gunner, crossed the coast over Sandwich Bay at about 11.00pm. Encountering anti-aircraft fire from Canterbury and then from Godmersham and Wye, the Gotha changed course towards Faversham.

Major Christopher Joseph Quintin Brand, commanding No. 112 Squadron, took off from Throwley, a few miles south of Faversham, at 11.15pm, to patrol a line from there to Warden Point on the Isle of Sheppey in a Sopwith Camel. Brand had been one of the three pilots who first tested the Camel as a night-fighter back in September 1917.[7] Eight minutes after take-off Brand saw the Gotha over Faversham. It had just dropped a bomb that exploded at the corner of Norman and Saxon roads, damaging a house, injuring three people and smashing many windows. Brand made his move.

> Closed to 50 yards, Enemy Aircraft fired a short burst high and to my left, apparently from forward gun. I then fired about two bursts of 20 rounds each and put Enemy Aircraft's right engine out of action. He then turned sharply and glided nose down North-east.[8]

As the Gotha tried to evade Brand's attack, a bomb fell at Davington, on the north side of Faversham, damaging a door at the parish church, and an incendiary dropped on Graveney Marshes. Brand continued his pursuit.

> Followed Enemy Aircraft down and closed to 25 yards and fired three bursts of about 25 rounds each. Enemy Aircraft burst into flames and fell to pieces. Followed machine down

to 3,000 feet and saw it crash 1½ miles from Harty Landing Ground in the direction of Shellness [Isle of Sheppey] at 11.26. When Enemy Aircraft burst with flames my whole machine was enveloped in the flames and my face and moustache were slightly scorched.

An early success on the night. And there would be more.

19/20 May 1918, 11.10pm – 12.10am: Essex

As bombs whistled down in Kent, other Gothas came inland over the Essex coastline. The police tracked 36 bombs dropped by an estimated seven aircraft, but they inflicted only negligible damage.

The first two fell on Wallasea Island and Potton Island at 11.10pm. At the same time, a Gotha came inland near Wakering and headed towards Southend but turned back when engaged by guns. At 11.20pm the crew released a single bomb at Thorpe Bay, which failed to explode, before dropping four more at Shoeburyness, where three fell on the army ranges. They caused some damage to a caretaker's cottage and broke a few windows. British guns claimed a Gotha shot down as it went out to sea, but that does not tally with German narratives. Another Gotha on its way to London dropped a single bomb at Wennington, between Rainham and South Ockendon, at 11.27pm. At about midnight, when west of Chelmsford, a Gotha released three explosive bombs near the villages of Beauchamp Roding and Berners Roding, but they failed to inflict any damage. Also at midnight, two bombs fell in a field at Bulpham, followed 10 minutes later by one at Stapleford Abbotts; two houses lost their windows in the explosions. Five bombs also damaged crops at Burnham-on-Crouch at 12.05am.

In between the bombs, Gotha G.V 925/16, crewed by *Leutnant* Wilhelm Rist (commander), *Vizefeldwebel* Max Gummelt (pilot) and *Vizefeldwebel* Rudolf Huhnsdorf, approached the Essex coast through thick cloud. The crew, disorientated, believed they were south of the Thames when they emerged from the murk at 2,000ft. Over Bradwell-on-Sea, Rist saw the River Blackwater to the north and turned towards it, thinking it the Thames, but low cloud blinded them again and only after they descended to 600ft did they emerge from the gloom near Clacton. Now the pilot opened the throttles to check the descent but the starboard engine choked. Realising they were about to crash, Rist released his bombs when east of St Osyth and prepared for an emergency landing.

The Gotha clipped a tree before being brought to halt by a hedgerow. Gummelt and Huhnsdorf survived the traumatic experience but *Leutnant* Rist, occupying the nose position of the Gotha, did not.

19 May 1918, 11.30 – 11.40pm: London

The most determined crews held on for London, running the gauntlet of anti-aircraft fire all the way. The first to reach the wider capital area did so between 11.30 and 11.40pm when 24 bombs dropped.[9] In Bexley, six landed in fields, but one at 109 Bexley High Street killed a man and injured four people. In Lower Sydenham, at Delahoy's Dairy on Sydenham Road, a bomb exploded with tragic consequences, killing 18 and injuring 14 more. Among the dead were Mr and Mrs Delahoy and their three daughters, and four of a family at a bakery next door. Across the road at Broadway Parade, men of the Army Service Corps were billeted. Many soldiers were outside watching the progress of the raid when the explosion killed five of them and injured ten. A wounded soldier, P. Leach, home on leave from the Royal Army Medical Corps, had been chatting to a friend, Mr Cross.

> [The bomb] hit near the spot we had left, causing terrible loss of life to Tommies and civilians there... it was like a battlefield afterwards with the dead and dying: and there were civilians lying dead in the gutter... My youngest son and I tore sheets up all night for bandages; for my front room was turned into a dressing station. Mr Cross and I found a Sergeant Oliver with his leg crushed to pulp, and I attended to him first. Others were getting the dead out of the shops. Then I attended to one little mite of a girl who had lost both her feet. While I was doing this, a boy of about 12 came along, with another holding him, and when I looked up I saw that one of his eyes had been destroyed, and his arm was hanging. I said to him, 'I won't be long'. His reply was: 'Alright, sir, I'll be British.' He was the pluckiest boy I have ever met. He never murmured as I did him up as best I could.[10]

The boy's father, John Klingels a naturalised German baker, died in the explosion; another son, home on leave from the army, lost a leg in the blast.

In Catford, bombs damaged 66 houses in Inchmary Road and Sangley Road, leaving a man dead and a woman injured. But other bombs, in Sidcup and Hockendon, only smashed a few windows.

North of the Thames a bomb on an allotment in Lawrence Avenue, Manor Park, injured six, and another in Richards Place, Walthamstow, damaged 100 houses and injured six people. In Poplar there were four bombs, with one that struck 240 St Leonard's Road demolishing 17 houses and injuring seven people, with damage extending to 360 other properties. Another bomb wrecked four houses and damaged 332 in Joshua Street, Barchester Street and Morris Road.

19 May 1918, 11.45 – 11.50pm: London

The capital now reverberated to the sound of Gotha engines and the boom of the guns, while the crump of exploding bombs added to the tumult as the raid developed. In the five minutes between 11.45 and 11.50pm another 11 bombs fell across London. To the north of the Thames, one in Tottenham exploded at the junction of Beaconsfield Road and Grove Park Road, breaking doors, windows and ceilings in 166 houses, and injured a man. In Manor Park bombs struck 14 and 76 Seventh Avenue, damaging 50 houses, leaving four occupants dead and six injured. Three bombs in Bethnal Green proved even more destructive. One, in Corfield Road, wrecked 14 houses, damaged 206 more, killed a man and two women and left 16 others injured. At Latchford's Buildings in the next street, Three Colts Lane, two bombs smashed into the building occupied by Allen & Hanbury Ltd, wholesale chemists and druggists. A ferocious fire took hold that eventually consumed a third of the building. The fire brigade estimated the extent of the damage at £16,760.

About 3 miles to the west, in the exclusive St James district, a bomb exploded amongst the auction houses and antique dealers of King Street, injuring a man and damaging ten of the prestigious buildings. The attacks continued south of the Thames too. Two women in Undercliff Road, Lewisham, were injured in an explosion that damaged 43 houses, and in Bromley, where three bombs dropped, the most harm occurred in Bromley Crescent where a man died, seven people were hurt and 38 houses damaged.

19 May 1918, 11.55pm – Midnight: London

At least 12 more bombs fell in the five-minute period prior to midnight. Three of these were in Kilburn in north-west London, where a 300kg bomb demolished the Carlton Tavern on Carlton Vale, killing the landlord, Arthur Stribling, and his 7-year-old son. One of the rescue team, W.J. Pike, arrived by lorry and quickly got to work.

> The first casualty found in the debris was the landlady, who was in the cellar... and practically unhurt. After two hours' hard work I found a parrot... which said 'Hello!' The landlord was seated in a chair with soil and wreckage up to his knees, and with him was his dog. Both must have been killed instantly.[11]

Of the other two bombs, one in Oxford Road failed to detonate, and one exploded on a railway siding by Canterbury Road where it damaged a few coal trucks.

In the far southern outskirts of London two bombs in Chislehurst smashed windows in six houses. Far more damage occurred around Old Kent Road, when Gotha G.V 979/16 approached over Rotherhithe. The crew, *Leutnant* Joachim Flothow (commander), *Vizefeldwebel* Albrecht Sachtler (pilot) and gunner *Unteroffizier* Hermann Tasche, dropped their first bomb outside a house in Verney Road, followed by another in Rotherhithe New Road. Of ten people injured, nine were in Verney Road where the bomb wrecked five houses and damaged three factories, 25 flats and 69 houses. At 59 Verney Road a mother and her three children had gone downstairs to shelter with the people who lived below them, as one of the children later recalled.

> We had not been down more than five minutes when the place was suddenly plunged into darkness, and everything was chaos. There were five other children downstairs, and five adults. The crash of breaking glass, bricks and mortar falling, and the awful screams of terrified children ring in my ears still; and then my mother's voice frantically calling each of us by name.
>
> How we escaped I do not know. The bomb, though it had come through the roof, had landed outside the street door. The miracle happened and we all got out.[12]

The family found shelter in a local church, where they were provided with clothes, and received food from the Salvation Army until relatives could find them a place to live.

The bomb in Rotherhithe New Road wrecked 12 houses, and damaged 65 others. The residents of neighbouring streets suffered too as the effects of the explosion extended to Barkworth Road and Rolls Road. A third bomb landed on a house in St James's Road but it failed to explode; even so, as it smashed its way down through the building it fatally injured Mary Lynch and killed her 12-year-old son, John. About 300 yards on, two bombs exploded in Avondale Square, off Old Kent Road, at Nos. 9 and 87; the first demolished the building causing other widespread but not serious damage and injured eight; the second also demolished the building it hit, killing a man and a child, injuring seven, and wrecking three other houses. The bombs inflicted lesser damage on 120 more houses in the Square. As the Gotha turned southwards, a bomb fell in the back yard at 469 Old Kent Road, wrecking the house, a stable, a coach-house and shed. The Gotha's final bomb fell nearly three-quarters of a mile to the south-east, on Shard Road, Peckham. It demolished a couple of houses, while others suffered varying degrees of damage, with seven people injured and one man, 49-year-old Thomas French, killed in his home. The Gotha then headed east, making its way back to the coast. But it had not gone unnoticed.

As the Gotha neared Maidstone, Major Frederick Sowrey, commanding No. 143 Squadron, attacked; back in September 1916, as a pilot in No. 39 Squadron, he had shot down Zeppelin L 32.[13] Flying a SE5a, Sowrey had an earlier close encounter with an incoming Gotha at 11.45pm, but now Flothow's Gotha came into view. Sowrey got under it, firing two ammunition drums from his wing-mounted Lewis gun, while the Gotha's gunner, Hermann Tasche, returned fire. The pilot, Sachtler, twisted and turned, then Sowrey's engine stalled, he spun and lost sight of his adversary. But about 5 miles north-east of Sevenoaks, a Bristol Fighter of No. 141 Squadron, crewed by Lieutenant Edward Turner (pilot) and Lieutenant Henry Barwise (observer/rear gunner), spotted the Gotha and attacked. Barwise opened an effective fire, as Turner's report confirms.

> The first burst seemed to hit the Port Engine and R.T.S. [bullets] was seen to burst on it. He immediately put his nose down and appeared to flat turn. A second burst appeared to go into the fuselage and along right wing. H.A. [hostile aircraft] continued to glide and fired short burst from rear gun. My observer fired a third burst but got a stoppage. H.A. fired his front gun vertically into the ground but did not reply with rear gun.

The Gotha appeared to be in trouble, with its crew possibly wounded. With Barwise's gun out of action, Turner prepared to open with the forward-firing Vickers gun, but he had throttled the engine back during the attack and now it would not pick up again, allowing the Gotha to get away. Flares burning at Frinsted ELG, south of Sittingbourne, offered Sachtler a chance to get the damaged Gotha down safely, but he crashed in a field before reaching it. Sachtler died as did Flothow but, nursing a broken arm, the gunner Hermann Tasche staggered clear of the wreckage.

20 May 1918, 12.00 – 12.10am: London

Four bombs fell in the 10 minutes after midnight. One exploded on the railway near Wanstead Station, damaging track and 50 houses, while also injuring a man. But two bombs in Islington exploded with far greater impact. The first, in St Peter Street, gouged a huge crater in the road, while smashing a water main, damaging 134 buildings, including, houses, shops and a pub, and a school in nearby Hanover Street. But the impact of the second bomb haunted local people. It exploded on a house at 110 Packington Street, causing the building to collapse. Six people huddled in the basement were crushed to death: Arthur and Hannah Hearn, Hannah's sister, Esther Cartwright, John and Edith Trathen and Jane Howard. A neighbour, Elizabeth Bell, also died. But not all of those who lived there were killed; on the insistence of a child, one family escaped.

Mrs Chater and her children used to shelter in the basement during raids but this night they changed their routine, as she remembered some 17 years later:

> I said to my boy 'we'll stay here as usual'; but the youngest child who was in bed said: 'Mum, please don't stay in tonight. I'm frightened.' It was a toss-up whether we stayed or not; but I thought it strange the kiddie should have said that, so I snatched him up, just wrapped a coat around him, and we ran to the crypt of St Mary's Church, Upper Street. We stayed until the 'all clear', and on the way home we heard one or two rumours but didn't take much notice. Then, in Packington Street, we saw a large crowd, also fire engines.
>
> A bomb had fallen on our house. Imagine my feeling when I heard that the people in it had all been killed... We had lost

everything. I had no shoes for my little boy; and we walked about all that night. I was dazed and heartbroken. The Salvation Army gave us tea and sandwiches next morning, at 5am.[14]

Rescue workers found the family's pet canary alive in the wreckage of the house. Unable to look after it, Mrs Chater gave it to one of the firemen.

20 May 1918, 12.12 – 12.15am: London

In these three minutes, 11 more bombs exploded across a wide area, with four in Hither Green. At 9 Longhurst Road the blast injured nine people and damaged 35 houses, while one that struck 187 Leahurst Road killed two soldiers and injured six people while damaging 82 houses and shops. Mr and Mrs Brown were at home opposite Hither Green Station, when the sound of the warning maroons woke their four children who rushed to their parents' bedroom in 'sheer terror'; they had a lucky escape as Mrs Brown recalled.

> Then a bomb exploded on the railway line… All the windows were blown in, ceilings collapsed, the side staircase fell in, and the front door was blown several yards along the hall.
>
> Although my bed, on which my children were sheltering, was strewn with broken glass and parts of ceilings, none of us was injured, but had the children been in their own rooms they would certainly have been killed, for their bedrooms were in ruins.[15]

A bomb on the Thames foreshore near Regent's Dock caused extensive damage to a barge, while three landing in Kentish Town in north London met with mixed results. One damaged railway tracks, another wrecked shops and houses in Kentish Town Road, and at 5 Gospel Oak Grove an explosion injured two people and damaged 43 houses. Over Stratford in East London, a Gotha crewed by *Leutnant* Paul Sopkowiak, *Vizefeldwebel* Hans Thiedke (pilot), and *Gefreiter* Wilhelm Schulte (gunner), dropped three bombs. One demolished two houses in Maryland Square, killing Edward and Lizzie White.

> We were working frantically for hours removing the debris, trying to recover two elderly people known to be among it…

> After four hours we found the couple dead, clasping one another.[16]

The explosion also injured seven others and damaged 50 houses.

The other two bombs fell in Leytonstone Road where they damaged houses and business premises. But time for the Gotha had begun to run out. The crew had earlier shrugged off an attack by a Sopwith Camel of No. 78 Squadron, but now they were intercepted near Hainault in Essex by a Bristol Fighter of No. 39 Squadron, piloted by Lieutenant Anthony Arkell with Air Mechanic 1st Class Albert Stagg as observer/gunner. An intense engagement developed, with 19-year-old Arkell zooming in and out as the two-man crew took turns to attack, while the Gotha twisted and turned and returned fire, getting lower all the time. Arkell described the end of the fight.

> Went under his tail again, 1/AM Stagg fired another burst, and right-hand engine or tank burst into flames. He was then at 1,500 feet, did one and a half turns of spin, and hit ground in a clear space at 12.20am, bursting into a sheet of flame.[17]

As the flames took hold, the crew took the dreadful decision to throw themselves to their deaths rather than be burned alive. The blazing Gotha smashed into open ground off Roman Road, East Ham, not far from the embankment of the Northern Outfall Sewer.

20 May 1918, 12.20 – 12.40am: London

At 12.20am, the Gotha that had bombed Kentish Town, passed over Regent's Park and released more bombs. One landed in the Outer Circle of the park, smashing windows and injuring a soldier. Seconds later another dropped in the garden enclosure at Park Crescent, alongside Marylebone Road, where it injured 11 people, most of them soldiers. A third bomb smashed into St Clement's House, a women's hostel and training college in Bolsover Street, destroying part of the building and damaging 50 others; three women and a Canadian army officer were injured in the blast. These bombs were the last to be dropped on London by a Gotha. But there were Giants overhead too. It appears, however, that only one of the three that set out reached the capital.

Approaching over Essex, the Giant released bombs from Barking in the east to the City and out on a north-east course. At King's Road,

Barking, the first damaged 20 houses, then one at Saxon Road, East Ham, damaged 20 more. In Plaistow, a bomb at the junction of Balaam Street and Whitwell Road damaged the West Ham Public Baths and 100 houses, while at West Ham a school in Grange Road bore the brunt of the blast, and at 12 Ladysmith Road, Canning Town, an explosion killed a child and injured three people. In Bow, the next exploded in a garden at 21 Saxon Road, the blast damaging 20 houses. Passing over the City, a bomb caused a huge fire among warehouses in Redcross Street, where estimates put the cost of the damage at £17,340, the most that night by a single bomb. A bomb in Hoxton failed to detonate but the next, in Glebe Road, Kingsland, injured two men and damaged 100 properties, including the Metropolitan Hospital. The final bomb exploded in Hackney at 42 Morning Lane, where it injured 11 people, damaged 131 homes and demolished a stable.

Another Giant appears to have restricted its attention to Essex, keeping close to the coast. It dropped its bombs around midnight at South Fambridge, Canewdon, Burnham-on-Crouch and Foulness with only negligible damage listed. The third Giant, R39, again carried a single 1,000kg bomb, which the crew reported releasing over Chelmsford. The town, however, did not come under attack, and British reports do not note the impact anywhere of a large bomb of this type.

The official report of the raid records 72 bombs on London, 49 on Kent and 36 on Essex, with damage estimated at £130,733 in the capital and an additional £46,584 in Kent and Essex. Casualties amounted to 49 killed (all but one in London) and 177 injured. But for the crews of *Bogohl* 3 the experience was a traumatic one. Of the 38 Gothas that took part, one crashed on take-off, three were brought down by Home Defence pilots and one crash landed after sustaining damage. In addition, another came down in the sea, shot down by the Dover guns and, although two others were claimed by British gunners, evidence appears sketchy; but German reports show at least two Gothas wrecked on landing back in Belgium (perhaps resulting from damage sustained over Britain), with four of the six crew killed. It appears, therefore, that at least eight (21 per cent) of the 38 Gothas were lost – there was no escape from the morale sapping rate of attrition.

Those senior officers concerned with Home Defence were very pleased with the outcome. Yes, bombers had got through to London, but perhaps only 50 per cent of those that set out, and those that did encountered a fierce defence, constantly harassed by aircraft and exposed to a sky alive with bursting shells. As an indication of the dramatic development of Britain's air defences, during London's first

Gotha raid in June 1917 the anti-aircraft guns had fired 360 rounds, but on the night of 19/20 May the LADA guns fired over 30,000.

Delighted by the outcome, Edward Ashmore, commanding LADA, commented:

> For the defences, this night was a success... a typical example of what a hard-hitting defence organisation can accomplish. No scale of defence, however great, can secure complete immunity from bombing; but by suitable arrangements the attacker may be made to suffer such casualties that his efforts will die out.[18]

Despite the losses, Brandenburg and von Bentivegni planned to resume their raids on London, but a requirement to support the latest offensive on the Western Front planned for 27 May took priority. From 21 May, German bombers resumed attacking targets behind the Allied front line, their effectiveness encouraging Germany to continue on this course. In fact, *Bogohl 3* and *Rfa 501* never returned to the skies of Britain and the bomb dropped on Morning Lane, Hackney, by one of the Giants became the last to fall on London in the war. It landed just over a mile from the very first, dropped by Zeppelin LZ 38 on Alkham Road, Stoke Newington, on 31 May 1915.

Of course, the British authorities had every reason to believe the bomber raids were set to continue, and there remained the threat from the indefatigable Peter Strasser and his naval Zeppelins. But for now, those who had experienced this latest raid at close-quarters, like the Reverend Vernon Jones who had been at the Metropolitan Hospital when a bomb exploded nearby in Glebe Road, were just relieved to be alive.

> As I walked up Highgate Hill later there was a beautiful sunrise, and birds began to sing. It was the dawn of a fine spring morning. The horror and danger of a few hours ago seemed incredible.[19]

Chapter 18

'This giant flame of sacrifice'

While the British public remained alert to the Zeppelin threat, the threat itself had much diminished. So far in 1918 there had been just three Zeppelin raids, all aimed at the Midlands and North of England. In Germany too, some realised that despite the great promise offered by these massive airships, their achievements had failed to live up to expectations.

Werner Dietsch, the executive officer on Herbert Ehrlich's L 61, noted that times had changed. Many of Ehrlich's crew had been together since the commissioning of Zeppelin L 5 in July 1915, before serving on L 17, L 35 and, since December 1917, on L 61. But in June 1918 the crew stepped down from front-line service, returning to their old ship, L 35, now a hub of experimentation. The crew were not saddened by the decision, as Dietsch recalled.

> The golden age of airships as weapons of war had passed. It came as no great disappointment to be reassigned, as the second oldest surviving airship crew, to the Trials Unit and our old friend the L 35. Given our long experience we felt we would be in a unique position to assist the future improvement and development of front line airships.[1]

But the clock that marked the hours for the Naval Airship Division had begun to run down, and persistent bad weather in June and July prevented any thought of raiding Britain that summer. In Britain, however, a plan evolved to keep pressure on the Zeppelins by carrying the war to their bases, reminiscent of similar raids in late 1914.[2] The navy had used seaplane carriers previously, transporting aircraft to their deployment area before lowering them over the side prior to take-off.

But HMS *Furious*, modified during construction, had a flight deck fitted in place of the forward gun turret, converting the battlecruiser to an aircraft carrier. On 19 July, supported by a cruiser squadron and a flotilla of destroyers, HMS *Furious*, carrying seven 2F.1 naval variants of the Sopwith Camel, moved to a position about 80 miles north-west of the Zeppelin base at Tondern in Schleswig-Holstein.[3] Shortly after 3.00am the Camels took off, each carrying two 50lb bombs, but one developed engine problems and turned back. Despite encountering thick cloud, the Camels found the target with bombs striking *Toska*,[4] the large double shed, and other buildings. Berthed inside *Toska* were Zeppelins L 54 and L 60.

Kapitänleutnant Treusch Freiherr von Buttlar Brandenfels, the long-serving but exceptionally cautious commander of L 54, lived with his wife 'in the dreary streets of the town of Tondern'. He awoke to the 'whiz and whirr' of a propeller.

> I jumped up and rushed to the window... Suddenly a shadow passed over our house, a few yards above the roof, absurdly low... A British aeroplane!
>
> In a moment the anti-aircraft batteries began to bark... There was more buzzing overhead and... another shadow passed, a second aeroplane! By that time the first was over the shed... My heart was in my mouth. In a terrible straight column, lit up with flames, the smoke rose skyward from the shed. Gruesomely beautiful it was, this giant flame of sacrifice in which our L 54 and L 60 perished.[5]

The flames of burning hydrogen engulfed both Zeppelins in the giant double shed, a captive balloon in another caught fire and, some distance off, a bomb struck an extended munitions store. But the raiders did not all get away. Three of the pilots calculated that increasing wind and low cloud restricted their chances of finding their way back to the ships before their fuel supply ran out, so they crossed into nearby Denmark and landed in the neutral country. Sadly, another pilot, Lieutenant Walter Yeulett, came down in the sea, his body washing ashore on the Danish coast nine days later. The other two pilots, captains William Dickson and Bernard Smart,[6] made it safely back to the fleet, completing the first successful mission launched from an aircraft carrier. Since 3 May, the Naval Airship Division had now lost three operational Zeppelins without any success to report. But Strasser, as always, remained outwardly confident and, on 8 July, 11 days before the Tondern raid, he had received a boost with the arrival at Nordholz of the latest Zeppelin of a new design, L 70.[7]

Although based on the 'v-class', first introduced with L 53, her length had extended by 50ft to 694ft to incorporate an additional gas cell. The new ship offered everything Strasser wanted. With hydrogen capacity increased to over 2 million cubic feet and powered by seven Maybach high-altitude engines, she attained a speed of 81mph in trials and climbed to 23,000ft. However, command of this impressive new Zeppelin did not pass to one of Strasser's long-serving, experienced commanders, instead it went to his 29-year-old adjutant and protégé, *Kapitänleutnant* Johannes von Lossnitzer.

Von Lossnitzer had previously had command of an old 'r-class' Zeppelin, LZ 120, one of those transferred from the army in summer 1917. Von Lossnitzer and LZ 120 operated in the relative backwater of the Baltic where the Russians had offered little aerial threat, and a shortage of hydrogen and troublesome winds limited activity. Later, after a period on the advanced training ship, L 41, Strasser appointed von Lossnitzer as his adjutant. Like Strasser, von Lossnitzer voiced an unshakeable belief in the advantages Zeppelins offered Germany.

> Neither now, nor in the foreseeable future, will our Fleet be able to do so without airships, not only because of our limited number of cruisers, but also because in the Zeppelin airship we have a scouting weapon that the enemy dreads, since he has nothing equivalent to oppose to it. It is our responsibility to develop this weapon to its utmost.[8]

Strasser had found a kindred spirit in this young officer. Another who knew him described von Lossnitzer glowingly: 'A splendid fellow, incomparable in his determination, a rarely capable person and a good comrade, to whom Strasser was particularly attached.'[9] Although relatively inexperienced, on 8 July, Strasser gave von Lossnitzer command of L 70, the largest, most advanced Zeppelin to see service in the war.

On 1 August, von Lossnitzer and two other Zeppelins took part in a routine North Sea patrol; the first active service flight of L 70. Also at sea were the light cruisers and destroyers of the Royal Navy's Harwich Force, intending to launch a coastal motor boat raid. Alerted to their presence by a wireless message, von Lossnitzer steered for their location.

Observing a light cruiser and a group of destroyers through gaps in the clouds he made an attack, dropping four 100kg bombs, but came under a heavy return fire. The navy noted the skilful approach of the Zeppelin, utilising cloud cover before it dropped its bombs and retreated when the guns opened fire. But this injudicious act by von Lossnitzer did not pass unnoticed. 'It seemed that the Zeppelin commanders were losing their sense of caution,' noted the navy, 'and that it would be worthwhile, next time, to take a fighting aeroplane in company.'[10]

On 5 August, 17 days after the Tondern raid, and four days after von Lossnitzer's encounter with the Harwich Force, good weather offered Strasser a rare opportunity to raid Britain. Elsewhere, the German army had lost its momentum, the early successes of the spring offensive had ground to a halt, but Strasser remained focused, determined to continue his attacks despite the losses his command had suffered since January. With the weather and the phase of the moon in his favour, everything seemed aligned for a successful mission. Strasser announced he would accompany the raid onboard L 70, to observe his majestic new ship in action – and he had not entirely given up on London as his orders make clear: 'Attack on south or middle (London only at order of Leader of Airships)... Participants: L 53, L 56, L 63, L 65, L 70... Preserve careful wireless discipline.'[11]

At 8.10pm (British time) three Zeppelins – L 53, L 65 and L 70 – were observed in the distance from the Leman Tail lightship, anchored about 30 miles from the Norfolk coast. They remained in sight for over an hour and then from the Happisburgh lightship too. The British report on the raid makes an important observation: 'No previous airship raid had been attempted with so low a barometer, which had its effect on the rising power of the airships.'[12] This low air pressure over the North Sea prevented the Zeppelins climbing beyond the reach of British aircraft.

The crews on the lightships telephoned news of the sighting ashore. At 9.00pm Strasser sent a wireless message authorising the raid to commence. The other pair of Zeppelins, L 56 and L63, were about 30 miles to the south of Strasser's group of three.

A message recalling him to RNAS Yarmouth air station found Major Egbert Cadbury at a concert in the town. Making all speed, he focused on securing a DH4, the best aeroplane on the base for the task in hand.

> I roared down to the station in an ever-ready Ford, seized a scarf, goggles and helmet, tore off my streamline coat, and, semi-clothed, with a disreputable jacket under my arm,

> sprinted as hard as ever Nature would let me, and took a running jump into the pilot's seat. I beat my most strenuous competitor [Captain C.B. Sproat] by one-fifth of a second....
>
> I saw [the Zeppelins] as I left the aerodrome, and gave immediate chase... I had as my observer 'Bob' Leckie, D.S.O., D.S.C., who has had a good many scraps with Zeppelins and has destroyed one... Thus I had an expert in the back seat.[13]

Cadbury failed to mention that he too had shot down a Zeppelin back in November 1916. Fully focused on the three Zeppelins about 40 miles away, Cadbury failed to notice L 56 and L 63 closer at hand. A DH9, also from Yarmouth, flown by Captain C.S. Iron with Lieutenant H.G. Owen as observer/gunner, joined the chase, as Iron later recalled.

> Curbing our impatience we continued to climb, with painful slowness, up through the thousand-foot gap which separated us from our target, when, suddenly a startling metamorphosis took place before our astonished gaze. A small ball of fire had appeared at the after end of our Zeppelin; with amazing rapidity this grew into a blaze; a few seconds later we could see that the whole of the Zeppelin's tail was well alight.[14]

L 70, the ultimate Zeppelin, Strasser's pride, was now on fire.

Just 3,000 metres away, *Kapitänleutnant* Walter Dose looked out from the command gondola of L 65.

> Suddenly we saw a small light on the otherwise quite dark ship which rapidly spread, and shortly afterwards the whole ship was in flames. She started to fall with running engines, then faster and faster, and was broken to pieces shortly before she entered the... cloud screen.[15]

Major Cadbury had made the attack, finding L 70 flying at 17,000ft.

> At 22.20 we had climbed to 16,400 feet and I attacked the Zeppelin ahead slightly to port... My observer trained his gun on the bow of the airship and the fire was seen to concentrate on a [spot]... under the Zeppelin, three-quarters way aft.

> The 'Z.P.T.' [Pomeroy explosive bullet] was seen to blow a great hole in the fabric and a fire started which quickly ran along the length of the Zeppelin. The Zeppelin raised her bows as if in an effort to escape, then plunged seaward, a blazing mass. The airship was completely consumed in about three-quarters of a minute.[16]

Zeppelin L 70 plummeted into the sea about 8 miles north of Wells-next-the-Sea on the Norfolk coast. There were no survivors – *Fregattenkapitän* Peter Strasser, *Führer der Luftschiffe*, the father of the Naval Airship Division was dead.

The other two Zeppelins that had accompanied L 70 immediately turned away but Cadbury pursued one of them, L 65.

> I again attacked bow on and my observer opened fire, when within 500 feet of airship. Fire immediately broke out in the midships gondola. At this point my observer's gun jammed... which in the darkness could not be cleared. The fire on the Zeppelin became extinguished. I maintained contact with Zeppelin for approximately five minutes while my observer attempted to clear jam, but without success. I was unable to use my front gun as I had reached my ceiling.[17]

Cadbury failed to mention in his report that his observer, Bob Leckie, had forgotten his gloves in the mad scramble to get airborne and now had frost-bite in two of his fingers making it impossible to clear the stoppage. Cadbury also made an error when reporting a fire in the gondola. Walter Dose, commander of L 65, later explained that an engineer had briefly pulled a black curtain aside, revealing the lighted interior of an engine gondola. 'This event,' Dose explained, 'has probably induced Major Cadbury to believe that he set fire to the gondola.'[18]

L 65 got back in one piece – just – having also survived an attack by a second British aeroplane, which peppered the gas cells with over 300 holes. Throughout the raid, wireless bearings relayed to the Zeppelins were inaccurate and, with low cloud blocking out the ground, the returning commanders reported bombing King's Lynn, Boston, the Humber defences and Norwich, but all bombs dropped some distance out to sea. Only one Zeppelin, L 56, briefly came inland, her commander unaware he had passed over Lowestoft.

A determined effort to locate the wreckage of L 70 proved successful when two days later searchers found it resting on a sandbank at a depth of 48ft. Admiralty trawlers dragged the area for around three weeks, bringing up most of the wreckage as well as five bodies. Among the recovered bodies they found that of Peter Strasser, 'completely untouched' and adding that 'his death was due either to drowning or to the shock of the impact with the water... he showed no disfigurement or burns or injuries of any kind'.[19] After a careful search for papers the bodies were buried at sea. Others washed ashore on the Lincolnshire coast but, when people objected to their burial in the local churchyard, they too were taken out again and committed to the sea. The salvage operation recovered the gondolas, engines and framework of this very latest Zeppelin design, while valuable documents revealed much more. Just a month after L 70 joined the Naval Airship Division, the British knew its secrets.

Inevitably in Germany they felt Peter Strasser's loss deeply. Ernst Lehmann, himself an experienced Zeppelin commander, highlighted the respect many felt for him.

> The death of Captain Strasser was a severe blow to the naval air service. He had been its guiding genius. Throughout Germany officials and civilians alike mourned the loss of the leader who had courageously declined to send ships or subordinates on any mission that he himself dared not undertake.[20]

Admiral Scheer, commander-in-chief of the High Seas Fleet, and about to become Chief of Naval Staff, had been a great supporter of Strasser. Following the confirmation of his death, he telegraphed the Naval Airship Division.

> The airship, which was created by the inventive genius and stubborn perseverance of Count Zeppelin, was developed by Peter Strasser, as Leader of Airships, with untiring zeal, and in spite of every obstacle, into a formidable weapon of attack. The spirit with which he succeeded in inspiring his particular arm on many an air raid he has crowned by his heroic death over England. As Count Zeppelin will live forever in the grateful memory of the German people, so will Captain Strasser.[21]

But Strasser, normally so meticulous in his planning, made basic errors in his final raid. He had arrived off the coast of Britain before darkness set in, and remained there within range of British aircraft without being able to climb beyond their ceiling. For these mistakes he paid the ultimate price.

The final word goes to *Kapitänleutnant* von Buttlar. He had served under Strasser since he flew as executive officer on L 3 in May 1914, and had operated under his orders longer than any other commander. Unsurprisingly he felt the loss greatly.

> We were overcome with grief. There was not one among us, whether he was an officer, a petty officer, or an able seaman, who did not feel that Strasser's death left a yawning gulf that nothing could fill. We no longer took the same interest in flying; for the spark which Peter had kindled in our breasts had been extinguished.[22]

The man given the unenviable task of replacing Strasser, *Korvettenkapitän* Paul Werther, at the time commanded airship-handling ground troops and the airship school. No reconnaissance patrols took place for four days before they resumed on 10 August. The following day Eduard Prölss and L 53 were ordered out to perform the scouting role. His deployment coincided with the appearance of a another new development in Britain's anti-Zeppelin arsenal.

After von Lossnitzer's rather reckless attack on ships of the Harwich Force on 1 August, the Navy decided that they would take a 'fighting aeroplane' out with them on the next patrol. Experiments launching a Sopwith Camel from a lighter towed into the wind by a destroyer had ultimately proved successful when Lieutenant Stuart Culley successfully got airborne on 31 July. On 10 August, HMS *Redoubt* towed Culley's Camel on the lighter out with the Harwich Force towards the island of Terschelling, as part of a plan to launch another coastal motor boat attack. The following day observers spotted a Zeppelin – L 53 – at great height. The Harwich Force began making smoke, hoping to lure the Zeppelin into following them. Prölss obliged.

Culley took off from the lighter at 8.58am, climbing rapidly and keeping the sun behind him, ensuring his tiny Sopwith Camel 2F.1 remained unseen in the vast open sky. About 30 minutes later Culley reached 18,000ft, about 1,000ft below L 53. By 9.58am he had pushed his aircraft to its limits but it plateaued still 200ft below the Zeppelin. Heading straight for the bow, the pilot pulled the control stick back hard, pushing his nose up and, as the engine stalled, he opened fire with the twin Lewis guns fixed on the Camel's upper wing. He wrote a report, brief and to the point: 'Fired 7 rounds from No. 1 gun, which jammed, and a double charge from No. 2. Zeppelin burst into flames and was destroyed.'[23] A 'double charge' signified a 97-round ammunition drum.

As Culley dived away, his engine picked up and he snatched a quick glance over his shoulder. He saw exactly what he hoped for; flickers of flame were taking hold. Moments later those flickers transformed into a furious fire as the hydrogen gas cells inside L 53 ignited one after the other until fire consumed the Zeppelin and it rushed down towards the sea. Culley looked on, transfixed by the spectacle as a man with his clothes on fire threw himself overboard. Zeppelin L 53 broke up as it fell and had burnt out before the wreckage hit the sea, the smoke trail assuming the shape of a huge question mark. After a somewhat desperate search, Culley relocated the Harwich Force and put down in the sea alongside HMS *Redoubt*; both he and his aircraft were safely hoisted aboard.[24]

Although L 70's sister ship, L 71, joined the Naval Airship Division on 10 August she never saw active service; the death of Strasser and the loss of two Zeppelins in the space of six days brought the final curtain down on the already waning Zeppelin campaign against Britain. The Zeppelin menace, significantly enervated since the autumn of 1916, had come to an end.

And what of the Gothas and the Giants?

After the attack on London on the night of 19/20 May, the crews of *Bogohl 3* and *Rfa 501* resumed bombing raids behind the Allied lines on the Western Front. Although Brandenburg and von Bentivegni hoped to return to England in July, both attempts were cancelled by Army High Command before they got underway. But behind the scenes Germany had developed a new weapon, the B-1E (*Brandbombe 1kg Elektron*), the Elektron incendiary bomb. Disappointed by the performance of previous incendiary bombs, German scientists had created a small, lightweight bomb that threatened to create the devastating firestorms in London and Paris that Germany had long intended. These bombs, weighing just 1kg, had a magnesium alloy casing, which itself would ignite when the thermite contents began to burn at extraordinary high temperatures, between 2,000 and 3,000 degrees Celsius. And water could not extinguish them, the burning magnesium of the casing converting the oxygen in the water into fuel, thus spreading the fire even further. They were similar to those dropped on Britain by the *Luftwaffe* during the Second World War and, due to their weight, could be carried in great numbers; at full strength *Bogohl 3* could unload over 14,000 of these bombs in a single raid. Now Germany had a genuine chance to unleash an overwhelming firestorm in London. The bombs were stockpiled during August, but two dates earmarked for the raid, in August and early September, were reached and passed without the order forthcoming. Not until 23 September, when a near full moon coincided with a predicted period of settled weather, were orders finally issued authorising the raid and final briefings took place. *Bogohl 3 – Der Englandgeschwader* – and *Rfa 501* would target London, while other squadrons would deliver the firestorm to Paris. All crews knew they were about to embark on a testing mission, the air defences of both cities regularly turned the bombers back before they could reach their target, and fighter aircraft always lay in wait for a chance to pounce. And this time, to capitalise on the good weather, as soon as the crews returned to base, their aircraft were to be refuelled, re-armed and sent back with another load. It became clear to the men that many of them would not survive.

But even as final details were being checked, senior figures, both military and political, doubted the wisdom of the enterprise. On 8 August the Allies launched a major offensive on the Western Front. By early September the German line had been pushed back to a position not far from where it had launched its own offensive six months earlier. Allied strength now built up in preparation for a push of its own in late September. The morale of the German Army was failing, that of the civilian population too; it appeared unlikely that air raids on London and Paris could now change the course of the war. And all the time Allied aircraft were dropping bombs on Germany.

Even so, the Elektron bomb raids on London and Paris were to go ahead. The Gothas ordered to bomb Paris were loaded and on the runway, *Bogohl 3's* raid due to follow an hour later. As the Paris bombers awaited the order to depart, a car sped onto the airfield while another headed to the headquarters of *Bogohl 3*. Staff officers stepped from the cars and handed over new orders; there would be no firestorm raid. *Erster Generalquartiermeister* Erich Ludendorff explained his thinking.

> Our position was now so serious that General Headquarters could not hope that air-raids on London and Paris would force the enemy to make peace. Permission was therefore refused for the use of a particularly effective incendiary bomb, expressly

designed for attacks on the two capitals... The great amount of damage that they were expected to cause would no longer have affected the course of the war, and sheer destructiveness had never been permitted. [German Chancellor] Count von Hertling, had requested General Headquarters not to use these new incendiary bombs on account of the reprisals on our own towns that would follow. My views of the general military situation, however, were the real ground for the decision.[25]

Germany knew it could no longer win the war; persevering with air raids failed to serve any useful purpose, and the act of dropping more bombs left Germany open to devastating reprisals. Germany's threat to Britain from the air was at an end.

***

What did the raids achieve?

The raids of 1917 and 1918 continued the course that began way back at Christmas 1914. But whereas most raids in 1915 and 1916 were made by airships, supported by floatplanes making coastal attacks, from 1917 to the end of the war airships took on a secondary role, the main threat now coming from the Gotha, augmented by the R-type bombers – the Giants – of *Rfa 501*.

As far back as 1914, before any nation had ever undertaken a sustained, strategic bombing campaign against an enemy country, Germany could only estimate the effect it would have. Yet a belief that an aerial assault on a city like London had the potential to break the morale of its civilian population prove attractive as Germany contemplated total war, that belief given voice in August 1914 by *Konteradmiral* Paul Behncke, Deputy Chief of the Naval Staff. He recognised the importance of bombing the capital, its docks and, as a naval man, the Admiralty building in Whitehall. He expected these attacks, 'whether they involve London or the neighbourhood of London, to cause panic in the population which may possibly render it doubtful that the war can be continued'.[26] Behncke also highlighted the importance of striking against the Dover and Portsmouth naval bases and included among suggested targets the Humber and Tyne as well as Plymouth, Glasgow and the Firth of Forth. 'Air attacks ... particularly with airships,' he concluded, 'promise considerable material and moral results.' Of these places, London and its docks were targeted, as were Dover, the rivers Humber, Tyne and the Firth of Forth, and Portsmouth, just once. Plymouth and Glasgow, however, were never troubled. But any idea that a Zeppelin could identify a single building in a city, such as the Admiralty, while assaulted by searchlights, anti-aircraft guns and fighter aircraft, demonstrated a certain naivety on Behncke's part. But that is understandable when contemplating something completely new and untried. Perhaps it would have been possible in 1914 when London's air defences were negligible, but by 1915, when the raids began, the defensive situation had improved.

The Zeppelin raids that followed, on London and across Britain, from Portsmouth in the south to the Highlands of Scotland in the north, never led to widespread panic. The reaction of ordinary people to this threat from the sky is interesting. Although raids were often undertaken by large numbers of airships, due to the vagaries of the wind and weather, rarely did more than one appear over a target at a time. This made an attack by a Zeppelin a rare and thrilling sight for many of the population who often left their beds in the hours of darkness to catch a glimpse of one of these futuristic aerial raiders, and some felt cheated if they never saw one! Of course, for those who found themselves directly in the path of a Zeppelin attack, as bombs whistled down, edging ever nearer, to explode near you or destroy your home, the experience became a very different one. The horror of indiscriminate bombing devastated families and communities as they tried to come to terms with this previously unthinkable way of making war.

The reaction of the population to the Gotha raids differed. A Zeppelin could be seen and followed in the sky, particularly if lit by searchlights. At a height of 2 or 3 miles, a Zeppelin flying at up to 60mph appeared from the ground to be moving very slowly and it became abundantly clear if you were in the path of danger or not. Unlike the Zeppelins, which only attacked at night, the Gothas initially carried out their raids in daylight, arriving as a squadron and sweeping across the sky, leaving no one feeling safe from attack. When a switch to night bombing followed in September 1917, although heard from the ground, the bombers were extremely difficult to see unless a searchlight managed to hold one in its beam. An unseen danger in the dark did lead to a nervousness in London in particular, resulting at times to panics in the rush for shelter.

The great belief held by the German people in the technical ability of airships to effectively take the war to Britain held firm, constantly fuelled by inaccurate and optimistic press releases describing effective raids on Britain. But the need for Zeppelins to operate at ever greater heights, after losses sustained in the autumn of 1916, meant it became increasingly difficult to locate targets and bomb them with any pretence of accuracy. The six Zeppelin raids in 1917, inflicted total damage estimated at £87,749 (one raid, 19/20 October, accounting for 62 per cent of the total), while the three raids in 1918 inflicted damage estimated at £29,427.[27] Across 1917-1918, these Zeppelin raids claimed 56 lives and injured 134.[28] During this same period, Germany lost 23 Zeppelins, shot down, destroyed in accidents, or wrecked in difficult landings. It has been estimated that the later Zeppelin types each cost in the region of £150,000 to build.[29] The total damage inflicted by Zeppelins in 1917-1918 equated to less than the cost of constructing a single airship. From a financial perspective, the cost of the Zeppelin campaign to Germany far exceeded the value of the damage it wrought in Britain. Yet the fanciful reporting of apparently successful raids by individual Zeppelin commanders fuelled the belief in Germany that they were having a significant impact, which in turn allowed Peter Strasser to demand and receive continuing support for the campaign.

The main threat in the last two years of the war, however, came from aeroplanes, with the arrival of the G-type bombers – the Gothas – in May 1917, which changed the nature of the air raids, later further enhanced by the R-type Giants. At full strength, *Bogohl 3* fielded 36 aircraft while *Rfa 501* mustered six Giants, yet *Bogohl 3* only managed to despatch a full-strength squadron on one occasion (19/20 May 1918). Likewise, *Rfa 501* only once managed to attack with all six Giants (7/8 March 1918).

German aeroplanes appeared over London and south-east England on 32 occasions between January 1917 and May 1918, inflicting damage estimated at £1,423,019, claiming the lives of 837 people and injuring another 1,991. The total achievements of the Zeppelin campaign across 1917 and 1918 were surpassed by the first daylight Gotha raid on London in June 1917 when, taking the population completely by surprise, the Gothas caused damage estimated £129,498, with 162 killed and 432 injured.[30] But the Gothas also suffered significant losses during the war, with at least 19 brought down by Britain's defences, and around 38 crashing when returning from raids. Clearly *Bogohl 3* needed a constant stream of replacement aircraft to remain viable. The Giants lost no aircraft at the hands of Britain's defences, but at least six were wrecked or seriously damaged when landing; *Rfa 501* could only muster three for the final raid in May 1918.

Those infrequent Zeppelin raids, however, did have an impact on Britain's defence resources, and at the end of the war five RAF squadrons[31] remained in Scotland, the North of England and the Midlands. Other than No. 36 Squadron, however, who were flying Bristol Fighters, the rest had second rate aircraft, mainly the Avro 504K. Even so, the specialist manpower allocated to these squadrons would have been extremely useful at the Front. This also applies to the anti-aircraft guns, searchlights and those manning them in these rarely-troubled regions. A snapshot of the Northern air defences in June 1918 shows 173 anti-aircraft guns and 259 searchlights in position. At the same time LADA manned 278 guns and 355 searchlights.[32]

The air raids on Britain also affected the production of war materiel. When air raids threatened, many munitions workers sought shelter, often leaving the work place and not returning after the raid's conclusion. Figures are available for small arms ammunition production at Woolwich Arsenal for the first two nights of the Harvest Moon Offensive in September 1917. Winston Churchill, then Minister of Munitions, stated that the figures were 'typical of what was taking place over a wide area'.[33]

On 24 September, the first night of this offensive, guns around Woolwich were in action shortly after 8.00pm. Only 27 per cent of night-shift workers producing .303-inch rifle ammunition remained at their posts, with normal shift production dropping from 850,000 bullets to 140,000. Although no aerial attack threatened during the following day-shift, output still dropped to 75 per cent of normal delivery.

Gothas returned to London the following night and bombs again fell in south-east London. Although 64 per cent of the .303-inch ammunition workforce continued through the raid, production reached only 33 per cent of normal output. The raids clearly had an impact on war production, but they were not frequent enough for this to have a significant effect overall.

By the end of the war, Britain had been under the real threat of air attack from December 1914 to May 1918, a period of 1,244 days. But German aircraft, both airships and aeroplanes, raided on just 101 of those days. In this earliest of sustained aerial campaigns, the unreliability of aero engines and the impossibility for Germany's meteorologists to predict adverse weather patterns approaching the British Isles from the Atlantic Ocean, both key factors in the campaign, restricted the raiders' options. While engine development did make significant advancements during the war, the ability to forecast approaching weather systems did not. Although at the beginning of the war Germany anticipated its airships regularly threatening London, these problems, combined with an increasing effective aerial defence system, resulted in just 12.5 per cent of total bomb tonnage dropped by airships landing in the wider

London area. Aeroplanes attained a much higher figure, 42.8 per cent, the capital being the extent of the Gothas' range and the enduring target of their missions.

Of the total weight of bombs dropped on Britain, airships were responsible for about 73 per cent, but these inflicted only about 51 per cent of the recorded damage. This being in part due to the increasing height airships operated at as the war progressed. It meant accurate navigation over areas of the country where most towns eventually had an effective black-out in operation proved extremely difficult. This resulted in many bombs falling wastefully in the open rural landscape where lights were often still showing, many in these regions feeling less need to adopt the black-out, considering they had nothing there of value to the war effort worth bombing – unaware of the navigation and observation difficulties the raiders faced.

Britain's defence system had grown considerably since the beginning of the war, when the country had just a handful of effective guns in an anti-aircraft role and an eclectic mix of naval aeroplanes as the Admiralty took on the aerial defence role as a temporary measure. Improvements were slow initially, but a more organised approach followed the eventual transfer of responsibility to the War Office in February 1916. By June 1918, shortly after the final German air raid, there were 451 anti-aircraft guns positioned across the country and 16 RAF squadrons, combining to form a defensive barrier the length of Britain. The War Office had also recognised the need for an efficient warning system, and by May 1916 had divided Britain into 54 numbered districts linked to eight Warning Control centres, using the telephone network to advise when raids threatened specific areas. Later, in the LADA area, under the watchful eye of Edward Ashmore, the monitoring system tracked incoming bombers from the coast all the way to the capital. Forged in adversity, this effective and ground-breaking system utilised techniques and equipment that would be resurrected when German bombers returned in the summer of 1940.

The rapidly changing nature of the war in Europe in the autumn of 1918 brought an end to this first sustained, strategic bombing campaign in history. First airships – both Zeppelin and Schütte-Lanz – and then G-type and R-type bombers, attempted to destabilise the population's morale, debilitate its industrial output and disrupt the supply system, but they failed to make a significant impact. Yet this campaign marked a change in the way future wars would be fought; air power, largely unheard of before the war, would have a vital part to play in all future wars. Dwarfed by the enormity of air wars yet to come, this first Blitz has become largely forgotten. But those who took part, those who fought these first aerial duels, those whose lives were taken as their homes were reduced to dust and rubble around them, those who continued to fly when technical advances made their journeys almost suicide missions, they all deserve to be remembered. It should not be the Forgotten Blitz.

***

Peace

The end for the men of *Bogohl 3* came quickly. As the Allied advance drew closer to Ghent, in October 1918 the squadron relocated about 30 miles to the south-east, to the former Zeppelin base at Evere, near Brussels. The Elektron bombs were dumped in the River Scheldt. The signing of the Armistice required *Bogohl 3*, like other bomber squadrons, to surrender their aircraft within 48 hours; this they did, handing them over to a commission of British officers. Brandenburg and the men of *Der Englandgeschwader* clambered aboard lorries and left Evere, to make a dispiriting eight-day journey back through a defeated Germany, ravaged by food shortages and with revolution in the air. *Bogohl 3* demobilised at the end of November.

For the German Navy the war ended in serious unrest. A plan for one last, inevitably futile attempt to engage the Royal Navy, was thwarted by a sailors' mutiny at the end of October, leading to a revolution which spread rapidly across the country. During this period of turmoil, however, many of the Zeppelin flight crews remained loyal to their organisation. On 9 November, *Kaiser* Wilhelm II abdicated. On that same day the crews demobilised the Zeppelin fleet. They deflated the hydrogen gas bags and hung the Zeppelins' empty carcasses in their sheds, supported on trestles. And there they remained while the Allies considered how best to distribute these prizes. The navy's ships were in a similar situation.

After November 1918, 74 ships of Germany's High Seas Fleet lay at Scapa Flow, the Royal Navy's base in the Orkney Islands, pending a decision on their future. Discussions dragged on and, on 21 June 1919, after seven months of waiting, their skeleton crews took matters into their own hands and succeeded in scuttling 52 ships, preventing them being handed over to the Allies.

Two days later the loyal Zeppelin crews followed this defiant action, entering the sheds at Nordholz, Wittmundhafen and Ahlhorn planning to destroy those Zeppelins inside. At Ahlhorn the plan failed, but at Nordholz and Wittmundhafen the conspirators were unchallenged and, having removed supporting cables and trestles, seven dormant Zeppelins crashed to the ground, crushing themselves under their own weight. Having carried death and destruction to the population of Britain, all that remained of these once majestic airships were chaotic piles of twisted metal scrap.[34]

Appendix I

Air Raids 1917–1918

Airship Raids 1917-1918

Date	Airships over Britain	Material Damage (£)	Casualties	
			Killed	Injured
1917				
16/17 March	L 35, L 39, L 40, L 41	163	0	0
23/24 May	L 40, L 42, L 43, L 45	599	1	0
16/17 June	L 42, L 48	28,159	3	16
21/22 August	L 41	2,272	0	1
24/25 September	L 35, L 41, L 46, L 53, L 55	2,210	0	3
19/20 October	L 41, L 44, L 45, L 46, L 47, L 49, L 50, L 52, L 53, L 54, L 55	54,346	36*	55
1918				
12/13 March	L 61, L 62, L 63	3,474	1	0
13/14 March	L 42	14,280	8	39
12/13 April	L 60, L 61, L 62, L 63, L 64	11,673	7	20
	TOTALS	117,176	56	134

*Casualty totals are from official records, but I can only find evidence of 35 people killed in this raid.

Aeroplane Raids 1917-1918

Date	Bombers over Britain**	Material Damage (£)	Casualties Killed	Injured
1917				
1 March	1xFP	700	0	6
16 March	1xFP	45	0	0
5 April	1xFP	4	0	0
6/7 May	1xC-type	510	1	2
25 May	21xG-type	19,405	95	195
5 June	22xG-type	5,003	13	34
13 June	18xG-type	129,498	162	432
4 July	18xG-type	2,065	17	30
7 July	22xG-type	205,622	57	193
22 July	16xG-type	2,780	13	26
12 August	10xG-type	9,600	32	46
22 August	9xG-type	17,145	12	27
2 September	2xG-type	3,486	1	10
3/4 September	4xG-type	3,993	132	96
4/5 September	9xG-type	46,047	19	71
24 September	13xG-type	30,818	21	70
25 September	14xG-type	16,394	9	23
28 September	3xG-type, 1xR-type	129	0	0
29/30 September	4xG-type, 3xR-type	23,154	14	87
30 September	10xG-type, 1xC-type	21,482	14	38
1 October	11xG-type, 1xR-type	45,570	11	42
29 October	1xG-type	0	0	0
31 October	2xUnknown	2	0	0
31 Oct/1 Nov	22xG-type	22,822	10	22
6 December	16xG-type, 2xR-type	103,408	8	28
18 December	13xG-type, 1xR-type	238,861	14	83

Date	Bombers over Britain**	Material Damage (£)	Casualties	
			Killed	Injured
1918				
28/29 January	7xG-type, 1xR-type	187,350	67	166
29/30 January	3xR-type	8,968	10	10
16 February	5xR-type	19,264	12	6
17 February	1xR-type	38,922	21	32
7/8 March	5xR-type	42,655	23	39
19/20 May	31xG-type, 2xR-type, 2xC-type	177,317	49	177
	TOTAL	1,423,019	837	1,991

**
FP = Floatplane
C-type = Two-seater
G-type = Gotha
R-type = Riesenflugzeug (Giant)

Appendix II

Summary of Air Raid Statistics 1914–1918

AIRSHIPS

	Bomb Total (UK tons)	(London MPD*) (UK tons)	Bomb Total (kg)	(London MPD*) (kg)	Estimated Damage £	Total Killed	Injured
						Figures in ( ) are for London	
1914	0	(0)	0	(0)	0	0	0
1915	34.9	(7.8)	35,460	(7,925)	815,866	208 *(104)*	532 *(310)*
1916	119.5	(15.8)	121,418	(16,053)	594,543	293 *(46)*	692 *(156)*
1917	28.5	(1.1)	28,957	(1,118)	87,749	40 *(33)*	75 *(50)*
1918	13.5	(0)	13,717	(0)	29,427	16 *(0)*	59 *(0)*
Total	196.4	(24.7)	199,552	(25,096)	1,527,585	557 *(183)*	1,358 *(516)*

AEROPLANES

	Bomb Total (UK tons)	(London MPD*) (UK tons)	Bomb Total (kg)	(London MPD*) (kg)	Estimated Damage £	Killed	Injured
						Figures in ( ) are for London	
1914	0.03	(0)	30.5	(0)	40	0	0
1915	0.20	(0)	203.2	(0)	530	2 *(0)*	6 *(0)*
1916	2.00	(0.06)	2,032	(60)	10,937	18 *(0)*	61 *(10)*
1917	48.75	(17.87)	49,532.3	(18,156)	948,543	655 *(308)*	1,561 *(1,016)*
1918	22.60	(13.61)	22,963	(13,826)	474,476	182 *(179)*	430 *(418)*
Total	73.58	(31.54)	74,761	(32,042)	1,434,526	857 *(487)*	2,058 *(1,444)*

TOTAL (Airships and Aeroplanes Combined)							
	Bomb Total (UK tons)	(London MPD*) (UK tons)	Bomb Total (kg)	(London MPD*) (kg)	Estimated Damage £	Killed	Injured
						(Figures in ( ) are for London)	
1914	0.03	(0)	30.5	(0)	40	0	0
1915	35.10	(7.80)	35,663.2	(7,925)	816,396	210 *(104)*	538 *(310)*
1916	121.50	(15.86)	123,450	(16,113)	605,480	311 *(46)*	753 *(166)*
1917	77.25	(18.97)	78,489.3	(19,274)	1,036,292	695 *(341)*	1,636 *(1,066)*
1918	36.10	(13.61)	36,680	(13,826)	503,903	198 *(179)*	489 *(418)*
Total	269.98	(56.24)	274,313	(57,138)	2,962,111	1,414 *(670)*	3,416 *(1,960)*

* Figures are compiled from Jones, H.A.: *The War in the Air,* Vol. III (App. III and App. IIIb), and Vol. V (App. I (Table A and B)).

While these sources break down the bomb tonnage and casualties for London based on the Metropolitan Police District (MPD), the available London monetary damage figures are based on the County of London, which is a smaller area. As they are not comparable, I have not given a separate figure for monetary damage sustained in London.

Appendix III

Individuals Killed in Air Raids 1917–1918

The list of the names of those killed in air raids, which I commenced in *Zeppelin Onslaught* and continued in *Zeppelin Inferno*, concludes in this final book of the Forgotten Blitz trilogy. Right from the start of this project I was determined to bring as many of these names out from the shadows as I could, for the government of the time never thought to create an official list. These men, women and children were victims of the war too, like the soldiers in the trenches and sailors at sea, and deserve to be remembered. The beginning of the Gotha raids created a dramatic increase in casualties and, in some cases, this appears to have overwhelmed the public reporting of coroner's inquests, leaving significant gaps yet to be filled. It has certainly proved harder to complete the lists for 1917 and 1918 than for those of previous years of the war. The official total of air raid deaths for 1917/1918 stands at 893. In the list below I have been able to include the names of 797 of the victims.

In the lists I have indicated where names are still missing; perhaps, in time some of these gaps can be filled. If you know of any names I have missed, I would be delighted to hear from you.

Ian Castle
www.IanCastleZeppelin.co.uk

Abbreviations used below:

AS	Able Seaman
Act. AM1	Acting Air Mechanic 1st Class
AM	Air Mechanic
AM1	Air Mechanic 1st Class
AM2	Air Mechanic 2nd Class
Cpt. of Inv.	Captain of Invalids
CPO	Chief Petty Officer
Coy. QMS.	Company Quartermaster Sergeant
Cpl.	Corporal
Dvr.	Driver
F'man	Fireman
Gnr.	Gunner
JP	Justice of the Peace
L/Cpl.	Lance Corporal
LM	Leading Mechanic
LStr.	Leading Stoker
Lt.	Lieutenant
Lt. Col.	Lieutenant Colonel
Off. Stew.	Officer's Steward
PC	Police Constable
Pte.	Private
Rfm.	Rifleman
Spr.	Sapper
2nd Lt.	Second Lieutenant
Sgt.	Sergeant
Sgt. Maj.	Sergeant Major
Trm.	Trimmer

In the lists below, *shows that the victim is known to have been killed by a falling AA shell.
(L) – Indicates an area of London.

Individuals Killed in Air Raids 1917–1918

Deaths during Zeppelin Raids 1917/1918

Date	Name	Age	Place
23/24 May 1917	Frederick Pile	45	Wellingham
16/17 June 1917	Eliza Hamlin	57	Ramsgate
	Jonathan Hamlin	61	Ramsgate
	Benjamin Thouless	67	Ramsgate
19/20 October 1917	Mabel Barrington *(see page 154)*	25	Piccadilly Circus (L)
	James Canavan	18	Piccadilly Circus (L)
	No.1 Depot, Royal Garrison Artillery		
	Gnr. Walter Dennis Dudley	34	Piccadilly Circus (L)
	1st Regiment, South African Infantry		
	Lt. Harold Edward Prew	29	Piccadilly Circus (L)
	Duke of Wellington's (West Riding Regt.)		
	2nd Lt. Arthur Thornton Phripp	23	Piccadilly Circus (L)
	Kate Phripp	56	Piccadilly Circus (L)
	Christopher George Wildman	23	Piccadilly Circus (L)
	Edwin Thomas Balls	3	Camberwell (L)
	Reginald Edward Balls	6	Camberwell (L)
	Ivy Brame	19	Camberwell (L)
	Royal Navy, HMS P.14		
	Off. Stew. Alfred L. Fowler	25	Camberwell (L)
	Alice M. Glass	21	Camberwell (L)
	Emily L. Glass	8	Camberwell (L)

Date	Name	Age	Place
	Emma M. Glass	53	Camberwell (L)
	Royal Navy, HMS P.14		
	AS Stephen J. Glass	20	Camberwell (L)
	Jessie Martin	22	Camberwell (L)
	Stephen Skelton	15	Camberwell (L)
	Emma Dorey	72	Hither Green (L)
	Frances Grant	32	Hither Green (L)
	Edith Jenner	8	Hither Green (L)
	Annie A. Kingston	18	Hither Green (L)
	Bridget M. Kingston	16	Hither Green (L)
	Edith E. Kingston	3	Hither Green (L)
	Kathleen V. Kingston	10	Hither Green (L)
	Mary E. Kingston	11	Hither Green (L)
	Richard Kingston	8	Hither Green (L)
	Thomas J. Kingston	6	Hither Green (L)
	Edith Milgate	18	Hither Green (L)
	Elsie Milgate	13	Hither Green (L)
	Leonard Milgate	8	Hither Green (L)
	Samuel Milgate	53	Hither Green (L)
	William J. Turner	13	Hither Green (L)
	Eliza Gammons	51	Northampton
	Gladys Gammons	13	Northampton
	Lily Gammons	13	Northampton
12/13 March 1918	Sarah Masterman	58	Hull
13/14 March 1918	John Robinson Bamlett	40	W.Hartlepool
	Jane Ann Fordham	67	W.Hartlepool
	Henry M. Harrison	64	W.Hartlepool
	Louisa Harrison	68	W.Hartlepool
	Harry W. Kershaw	8	W.Hartlepool
	Joseph Middleton	11	W.Hartlepool

Individuals Killed in Air Raids 1917–1918

Date	Name	Age	Place
	Helen Readman	4	W.Hartlepool
	Mary Readman	1	W.Hartlepool
12/13 April 1918	Margaret Ashurst	34	Wigan
	Mary Cumberbirch	22	Wigan
	Alfred Harris	5 months	Wigan
	Walter Harris	31	Wigan
	Jane Tomlinson	58	Wigan
	Samuel Tomlinson	49	Wigan
	Unknown Woman	47	'Midlands village'

Deaths during Aeroplane Raids 1917/1918

Date	Name	Age	Place
6/7 May 1917	Frederick Dawson	45	Highbury (L)
25 May 1917	Gladys Alice Sparkes	18	Ashford
	Dorothy Lilian Burgin	16	Cheriton
	Francis Henry Considine	5	Cheriton
	Alfred Durrett Down	54	Cheriton
	May Alexandra Arnold	21	Folkestone
	Harold Hayward Banks	25	Folkestone
	Eliza Mary Barker	33	Folkestone
	Maggie Gray Bartleet	24	Folkestone
	Annie Beer	28	Folkestone
	Annie Beer	2	Folkestone
	Arthur Stephen Beer	11	Folkestone
	William James Beer	9	Folkestone

Date	Name	Age	Place
	5th Labour Battalion, Labour Corps		
	Pte. George H. Bloodworth	19	Folkestone
	Gertrude Elizabeth Bowbrick	12	Folkestone
	Mabel Esther Bowbrick	9	Folkestone
	Sydney Brockway	63	Folkestone
	David John Burke	42	Folkestone
	Hilda Elizabeth Burvill	20	Folkestone
	George Edward Butcher	44	Folkestone
	Annie Elizabeth Cason	46	Folkestone
	Albert Edward Castle	41	Folkestone
	Kathleen Chapman	16	Folkestone
	William Clark	12	Folkestone
	Phyllis Aimes Cooper	9	Folkestone
	Albert Dennis Daniels	12	Folkestone
	Frederick Charles Day	47	Folkestone
	Edith Agnes Dicker	12	Folkestone
	Sarah Jane Dicker	41	Folkestone
	Florence Edith Dukes	18	Folkestone
	Florence Elizabeth Dukes	51	Folkestone
	Edith May Eales	17	Folkestone
	Nellie Feist	50	Folkestone
	Stanley Albert Feist	5	Folkestone
	Florence Francis	33	Folkestone
	Edward Stephen Gould	39	Folkestone

Individuals Killed in Air Raids 1917–1918

Date	Name	Age	Place
	Richard Ashby Graves	40	Folkestone
	Edith Mary Grimes	24	Folkestone
	William Henry Hall	64	Folkestone
	Johanna Mary Hambly	67	Folkestone
	Ethel L. Hambrook	12	Folkestone
	Caroline Harris	35	Folkestone
	Fanny Harrison	39	Folkestone
	Dennis William Hayes	2	Folkestone
	Martha Godden Hayes	30	Folkestone
	Louisa Alice Hayward	37	Folkestone
	Arthur David Hickman	5	Folkestone
	Mary Philomena Holloway	9	Folkestone
	Veronica Mary Holloway	16 months	Folkestone
	Edward James Horn	45	Folkestone
	13ᵉ *Régiment de ligne, Belgian Army*		
	Soldat Constant Houdart	33	Folkestone
	Rosina Caroline Hughes	34	Folkestone
	Dorothy Bertha Jackman	14	Folkestone
	Katherine Euphemia Laxton	72	Folkestone
	William Lee	46	Folkestone
	Agnes Curran McDonald	22	Folkestone
	Albert Edward McDonald	12	Folkestone
	Jane Marshment	50	Folkestone
	Elizabeth Maxted	31	Folkestone

Date	Name	Age	Place
	Ernest Henry McGuire	6	Folkestone
	Jane Charlotte May Moss	20	Folkestone
	Walter George Moss	2	Folkestone
	Florence Kathleen Norris	2	Folkestone
	Florence Louise Norris	24	Folkestone
	William Alfred Norris	10 months	Folkestone
	Mabel Reed	12	Folkestone
	John Walter Francis Robinson	5	Folkestone
	Florence Rumsey	17	Folkestone
	Marie Snauwaert	43	Folkestone
	Arthur Ernest Stokes	14	Folkestone
	William Henry Stokes	46	Folkestone
	Edith Gwendoline Terry	13	Folkestone
	Alfred Vane	35	Folkestone
	Militaire Censuur, Belgian Army		
	Soldat Hippolyte Verschueren	41	Folkestone
	Doris Eileen Spencer Walton	16	Folkestone
	Elizabeth Charlotte Waugh	48	Folkestone
	Isabel Wilson	80	Folkestone
	Daniel Stringer Lyth	54	Hythe
	Amy Gertrude Parker	42	Hythe
	2/4th Battalion, South Lancashire Regiment		
	Pte. John Miller	41	Shorncliffe

Individuals Killed in Air Raids 1917–1918

Date	Name	Age	Place
	Reserve Brigade, Canadian Field Artillery		
	Gnr. Bert Arbuckle	38	Shorncliffe
	Gnr. William Brown	21	Shorncliffe
	Gnr. James Alexander Bruce	21	Shorncliffe
	Gnr. Jules B.A. Desaleux	29	Shorncliffe
	Gnr. James D. McNulty	25	Shorncliffe
	Reserve Cavalry Regiment, Canadian Army		
	Pte. Lloyd G. Yeo	18	Shorncliffe
	3rd (Reserve) Battalion, Canadian Infantry		
	Coy. QMS. Oron Alfred Jenner	26	Shorncliffe
	184th Battalion, Canadian Infantry		
	Pte. Charles Marshall	23	Shorncliffe
	Pte. A.W. Merchant	34	Shorncliffe
	200th Battalion, Canadian Infantry		
	L/Cpl. Arthur Doig	24	Shorncliffe
	Pte. James McArthur	21	Shorncliffe
	Pte. Robert MacDonald	19	Shorncliffe
	Pte. Hugh McNair	20	Shorncliffe
	Pte. Frank Padley	24	Shorncliffe
	Pte. Ralph Pelluet	25	Shorncliffe
	Pte. Jack Sutherland	31	Shorncliffe
	Pte. Ernest Tennyson	36	Shorncliffe

Date	Name	Age	Place
5 June 1917	George James Frier	50	Sheerness
	Herbert Lucas	31	Sheerness
	Edward Perry	27	Sheerness
	HMS Actaeon, Royal Navy		
	CPO Samuel Hawes	41	Sheerness
	HMS Dominion, Royal Navy		
	Off. Stew. Joseph Davies	22	Sheerness
	HM Torpedo Boat No.7, Royal Navy		
	Gnr. Herbert H. Gandy	26	Sheerness
	5th Battalion, King's Royal Rifle Corps		
	Rfm. William Amos	35	Sheerness
	Rfm. Arthur Galley	18	Sheerness
	Rfm. William J. Tapper	18	Sheerness
	2nd Garrison Battalion, Northamptonshire Regiment		
	Pte. Benjamin Corby	29	Sheerness
	5th Company, Labour Corps		
	Pte. Frank Smith	27	Sheerness
	Royal Field Artillery		
	Gnr. William Staines	18	Shoeburyness
	Dvr. Thomas Toone	19	Shoeburyness

Individuals Killed in Air Raids 1917–1918

Date	Name	Age	Place
13 June 1917	George William Larkins	49	Albert Docks (L)
	Henry Alexander Peck	39	Albert Docks (L)
	Arthur Ernest Simmonds	48	Albert Docks (L)
	George Frank Coleman	25	Barbican (L)
	Eric T. Cowley	26	Barbican (L)
	Thomas Edwin Lucas	24	Barbican (L)
	Arthur Miller	15	Barbican (L)
	Howard Eagle Nash	28	Barbican (L)
	William Nicoud	18	Barbican (L)
	Alfred Reeves	40	Barbican (L)
	Walter Maurice Golder	55	Bermondsey (L)
	Thomas Parfitt	42	Bermondsey (L)
	Bessie Moss	9 months	Bethnal Green (L)
	Cissie Moss	9 months	Bethnal Green (L)
	Esther Moss	5	Bethnal Green (L)
	Hettie Moss	11	Bethnal Green (L)
	Rebecca Moss	35	Bethnal Green (L)
	Annie Stanford	3	Bethnal Green (L)
	Ivy Victoria Stanford	9 months	Bethnal Green (L)
	Charles Frederick Ware	21	Bethnal Green (L)
	Sidney Arnold	34	City (L)
	Sydney Chaplin	50	City (L)
	Thomas Howard Eastwood	42	City (L)
	Thomas Howard	26	City (L)
	John Kelly	14	City (L)
	3rd *(Reserve) Battalion, Bedfordshire Regiment*		
	Cpl. Harry Kitchener	19	City (L)

Date	Name	Age	Place
	Edward George Moyle	35	City (L)
	Albert Henry Rudd	28	City (L)
	Marcel Veyrieras	50	City (L)
	Mary Ann Cordell	68	Dalston (L)
	Hilda Beatrice Reynolds	9	Dalston (L)
	Ivy Maud Reynolds	13	Dalston (L)
	Lilian Rose Reynolds	1	Dalston (L)
	Robert James Reynolds	4	Dalston (L)
	Elizabeth Botham	46	East Ham (L)
	Christina Mary Clarke	38	East Ham (L)
	George Albert Victor Clarke	4	East Ham (L)
	Elizabeth Emily Mastin	52	East Ham (L)
	William Bennett	55	Fenchurch St (L)
	George Leopold Devallée	52	Fenchurch St (L)
	Lucy Linden	23	Fenchurch St (L)
	Lilian Rebecca Roberts	37	Fenchurch St (L)
	Richard F. Roberts	67	Fenchurch St (L)
	Violet Mary Tripp	42	Fenchurch St (L)
	Andrew Wahlberg	46	Fenchurch St (L)
	George Wherland	46	Fenchurch St (L)
	Israel Benjamin	42	Finsbury (L)
	Elizabeth Jane Cain	80	Finsbury (L)
	Jane Agnes Child	47	Finsbury (L)
	George Potts	43	Finsbury (L)
	Metropolitan Police		
	PC Alfred Smith	37	Finsbury (L)
	Alfred Charles Terry	45	Finsbury (L)

Individuals Killed in Air Raids 1917–1918

Date	Name	Age	Place
	Caroline White	57	Finsbury (L)
	Florence Phillips	39	Limehouse (L)
	William Jones	?	Limehouse (L)
	William Argyle	40	Liverpool St.Stn.(L)
	Robert Lesley Cherry	16	Liverpool St.Stn.(L)
	Herbert Henry Daniel	28	Liverpool St.Stn.(L)
	Thomas Ivor Moore JP	58	Liverpool St.Stn.(L)
	Herbert T. King	53	Liverpool St.Stn.(L)
	25th Battalion, King's (Liverpool Regiment)		
	Coy. QMS Tom Midgley	27	Liverpool St.Stn.(L)
	Francis William Reeves	27	Liverpool St.Stn.(L)
	Albert Ruscoe	27	Liverpool St.Stn.(L)
	3rd Dragoon Guards		
	Sgt. Maj. Charles Stone	58	Liverpool St.Stn.(L)
	Essex Regiment		
	Pte. William Wiseman	27	Liverpool St.Stn (L)
	Louise Annie Acampora	5	Poplar (L)
	Alfred Earnest Batt	5	Poplar (L)
	Leonard Charles Bareford	5	Poplar (L)
	John Percy Brennen	5	Poplar (L)
	William Thomas Henry Challen	5	Poplar (L)
	Vera Margaret Clayson	4	Poplar (L)
	Alice Maud Cross	5	Poplar (L)

Date	Name	Age	Place
	William Hollis	5	Poplar (L)
	George Albert Hyde	5	Poplar (L)
	Grace Jones	5	Poplar (L)
	Rose Martin	11	Poplar (L)
	George Morris	6	Poplar (L)
	James Henry Nash	20	Poplar (L)
	Charles O'Brien	29	Poplar (L)
	Lily Eileen O'Brien	1	Poplar (L)
	Edwin Cecil William Powell	12	Poplar (L)
	Robert Stimson	5	Poplar (L)
	Elizabeth Taylor	5	Poplar (L)
	Rose Tuffin	5	Poplar (L)
	Frank Winfield	5	Poplar (L)
	Florence Lillian Wood	5	Poplar (L)
	Howard M. Avery	26	Royal Mint (L)
	William Beadle	17	Royal Mint (L)
	Albert H. Crabb	16	Royal Mint (L)
	George F. Cavell	43	Royal Mint (L)
	John Thomas Douglass	75	Shoreditch (L)
	William Hawkes	45	Shoreditch (L)
	Sarah Ann Jones	66	Shoreditch (L)
	Phyllis H. Barker	15	Southwark (L)
	Winifred Churchill	14	Southwark (L)
	Florence Mitchell	2	Stepney (L)
	Mary A. Mitchell	49	Stepney (L)
	Nathan Cohen	15	Whitechapel (L)
	David Marks	16	Whitechapel (L)
	John Maguire	27	Whitechapel (L)
	William George Sherringham	69	Whitechapel (L)
	Henry Conrad Stracker	14	Whitechapel (L)

Individuals Killed in Air Raids 1917–1918

Date	Name	Age	Place
	London Fire Brigade		
	F'man Alfred H. Vidler	24	Whitechapel (L)
	Herbert Leonard Caste	17	London
	Beatrice Maud Cuthbert	15	London
	Frank Charles F. Dawson	38	London
	Arthur George Dew	16	London
	Robert John Dore	35	London
	Leonard Gordon	15	London
	Eliza Larkman	70	London
	Carl Ludwig Theodore Pantel	61	London
	Charles Robinson	42	London
	James Shine	8	London
	49 victims currently unidentified		London
4 July 1917	*3rd (Reserve) Battalion, Suffolk Regiment*		
	Sgt. Henry Archer	41	Felixstowe
	L/cpl. William E. Rump	20	Felixstowe
	Pte. Amos Savidge	34	Felixstowe
	Pte. George Short	24	Felixstowe
	Pte. George Simmons	23	Felixstowe
	RNAS Felixstowe		
	AM1 Andrew Austins	31	Felixstowe
	AM2 James Cordell	21	Felixstowe

Date	Name	Age	Place
	Thomas Horne (Civilian)	49	Felixstowe
	George Hubbard (Civilian)	54	Felixstowe
	AM1 Alfred J. Huggett	28	Felixstowe
	LM James Gilmour	28	Felixstowe
	Charles Newman (Civilian)	46	Felixstowe
	AM1 Ernest Sanders	23	Felixstowe
	AM James Stevens	27	Felixstowe
	RNAS Balloon Section		
	AM1 Frederick Grimes	26	Shotley
	Act. AM1 David E. Pigg	23	Shotley
	AM1 Herbert Whitehouse	21	Shotley
7 July 1917	Frederick George Ambrose	57	London
	Henry Stanley Bennett	33	London
	Frederick Tovey Billington	44	London
	Ebenezer Bird	67	London
	William I. Blackbrough	45	London
	William J. Blackbrough	11	London
	James Alfred Blackburn	62	London
	Bertram Francis Browning	52	London
	James Casley	15	London
	Stanley Ernest Cobb	17	London

Individuals Killed in Air Raids 1917–1918

Date	Name	Age	Place
	John Joseph Cummins	9	London
	Ellen Frances Harriet Davies*	54	London
	Julia Caroline Dunbar	4	London
	William Dunbar	51	London
	Royal Army Medical Corps		
	Pte. David Thomas Evans	19	London
	Elizabeth Frantzmann	19	London
	Phillip Frantzmann	60	London
	Edward Jarrett	16	London
	James Charles Hall	75	London
	Henry Harry Haycock	52	London
	Samuel Hillier	59	London
	Henry John Hoppe	65	London
	James Lewis	31	London
	Walter Lewis	4	London
	James Livingstone	33	London
	Thomas Henry Lovejoy	52	London
	Leonard Charles Matthews	2	London
	Ada Mary Moody	17	London
	David Murdock	29	London
	William Murray	64	London
	Simon Percival Noad*	32	London
	Alice Peel	35	London
	5th Battalion, North Staffordshire Regt.		
	Pte. William Henry Pope	19	London

287

Date	Name	Age	Place
	RNAS, HMS President II		
	AM2 Evan R. Roberts	31	London
	George Ruffles	11	London
	Amelia E. Rumble	42	London
	William Poole Saunders	66	London
	Edwin Thomas Scuse	52	London
	Albert Henry Slade	17	London
	Florence Smalpage	44	London
	James Gladwin Smith	18	London
	Phineas Stone*	75	London
	Charles Joseph Summers	12	London
	103rd Protection Company, Royal Defence Corps		
	Pte. John Taylor	53	London
	Frederick Wade	51	London
	Leonard Charles Wheatley	15	London
	William Bennett Wigzell	51	London
	Henry Litchfield Woods	37	London
	William Woolford	43	London
	5 casualties currently unidentified		*London*
	Agnes Mary Cooper	50	Margate
	James Alexander Marks	69	Margate
	Jane Ann Marks	69	Margate
22 July 1917	Edgar Ludbrook	17	Felixstowe
	3rd (Reserve) Battalion, Bedfordshire Regiment		
	Pte. Alfred John Alder	40	Felixstowe

Individuals Killed in Air Raids 1917–1918

Date	Name	Age	Place
	2nd Lt. Frederick Amess	29	Felixstowe
	Pte. George Garrod	23	Felixstowe
	Pte. Charles Masson	21	Felixstowe
	Pte. Herbert Phipps	29	Felixstowe
	Pte. James H. Pratt	23	Felixstowe
	Pte. Geoge Smith	20	Felixstowe
	Pte. Albert Wilton	30	Felixstowe
	3rd (Reserve) Battalion, Suffolk Regiment		
	Pte. Charles Nash	22	Felixstowe
	Sgt. George Taylor	32	Felixstowe
	239th Horse Transport Coy., Army Service Corps		
	Dvr. Herbert G. Broyd	38	Felixstowe
	Royal Naval Air Service		
	AM1 William Allen	25	Felixstowe
12 August 1917	Edith Batty	32	Southend-on-Sea
	Walter Henry Batty	42	Southend-on-Sea
	Ada Childs	32	Southend-on-Sea
	John Cohen	53	Southend-on-Sea
	Leah Cohen	52	Southend-on-Sea
	Annie Collier	27	Southend-on-Sea
	Emily Gladys Cornish	13	Southend-on-Sea
	Thomas Henry Cornish	52	Southend-on-Sea
	George Henry Crees	70	Southend-on-Sea
	Mary Ann Donaldson	44	Southend-on-Sea
	Clara Gavell	29	Southend-on-Sea
	Jessie Camilla Galloway	17	Southend-on-Sea
	Lena Gooding	7	Southend-on-Sea

Gotha Terror

Date	Name	Age	Place
	James Grant	10	Southend-on-Sea
	Frederic Hawes	14	Southend-on-Sea
	William Hill	42	Southend-on-Sea
	Arthur Hills	39	Southend-on-Sea
	Charles Humphries	59	Southend-on-Sea
	Ellen May Jess	5	Southend-on-Sea
	Alfred Lewis	74	Southend-on-Sea
	Violet Elizabeth Mann	36	Southend-on-Sea
	Florence Mason	14	Southend-on-Sea
	Jessie Orton	28	Southend-on-Sea
	Jessie Orton	5	Southend-on-Sea
	Dorothy Evelyn Rice	12	Southend-on-Sea
	Harry Russell	53	Southend-on-Sea
	Victor William Sullivan	10	Southend-on-Sea
	Beatrice Watson	27	Southend-on-Sea
	Oliver Watson	32	Southend-on-Sea
	Elizabeth Mary West	55	Southend-on-Sea
	Gladys West	13	Southend-on-Sea
	Emelia Whittlesey	48	Southend-on-Sea
22 August 1917	Lucy Wall	17	Dover
	32nd Training Reserve Battalion		
	Pte. William Cobell	18	Dover
	Pte. Charles Ward	18	Dover
	George Baker	71	Ramsgate
	Alfred John Coomber	56	Ramsgate
	John Debling	47	Ramsgate
	Nellie Alice Attrail Fox	5	Ramsgate

Individuals Killed in Air Raids 1917–1918

Date	Name	Age	Place
	Walter Charles Melhuish	45	Ramsgate
	Henry Hope Minter	63	Ramsgate
	Walter Clarence Spain	57	Ramsgate
	Medical Corps, Canadian Army		
	Pte. David Crighton	28	Ramsgate
	5th Brigade, Canadian Field Artillery		
	Gnr. John Paul	20	Ramsgate
2 September 1917	*6th (Reserve) Battalion, Royal Fusiliers*		
	2nd Lt. Henry Larcombe	19	Dover
3 September 1917	Mary Longley	58	Chatham
	Royal Navy		
	Claude McIntyre	22	Chatham
	John Abrey	54	Chatham Drill Hall (CDH)
	Robert Anderson	27	CDH
	Alfred Andrews	20	CDH
	Harry Barker	22	CDH
	Harry L. Barker	28	CDH
	Joseph Beha	26	CDH
	Frederick Benmore	21	CDH
	William Berwick	21	CDH
	Walter Beverley	23	CDH
	Henry Bird	19	CDH
	George Boyd	27	CDH
	Joseph Brightwell	22	CDH
	Michael Brown	24	CDH
	William Bullock	32	CDH

Date	Name	Age	Place
	George Butler	18	CDH
	Frederick Cable	26	CDH
	George Cain	20	CDH
	Albert Cairns	23	CDH
	Charles Cash	23	CDH
	Arthur Charlton	25	CDH
	Reginald Clark	21	CDH
	Robert Collett	24	CDH
	Benjamin Corker	27	CDH
	William Curd	25	CDH
	John Diaper	19	CDH
	Frederick Diver	29	CDH
	Victor Duckett	30	CDH
	Robert Ferrett	27	CDH
	Alfred Finlay	24	CDH
	Leonard Fish	23	CDH
	Alfred Gibbs	23	CDH
	George Gilbert	51	CDH
	William Gillett	26	CDH
	Albert Goddard	26	CDH
	Horace Godden	28	CDH
	Charles Goodsell	20	CDH
	John Green	20	CDH
	John Hammond	18	CDH
	Stephen Hare	20	CDH
	Frederick Hartnall	25	CDH
	Thomas Haville	20	CDH
	Arthur Haxell	19	CDH
	Archibald Hay	18	CDH
	Henry Hill	25	CDH
	Ernest Hoskins	28	CDH

Individuals Killed in Air Raids 1917–1918

Date	Name	Age	Place
	Arthur Humphrey	36	CDH
	Joseph Jackson	32	CDH
	Sydney Jackson	31	CDH
	Henry Jones	37	CDH
	Archibald Langridge	28	CDH
	Charles Lemmon	25	CDH
	John Loose	25	CDH
	Frederick Lutitt	30	CDH
	Sidney Macey	19	CDH
	William Magog	19	CDH
	Roland Mayes	21	CDH
	John McGregor	19	CDH
	Alexander McLean	24	CDH
	Percy Moore	28	CDH
	Alfred Moss	32	CDH
	Percy Nicholls	19	CDH
	William Nolan	24	CDH
	John Oakes	24	CDH
	William Osborne	25	CDH
	Frederick Parker	27	CDH
	William Payne	20	CDH
	Bertie Pegram	24	CDH
	Alfred Purton	22	CDH
	Frederick Reyner	33	CDH
	James Richards	25	CDH
	Sydney Rigden	20	CDH
	Jesse Sandy	22	CDH
	Sidney Seymour	22	CDH
	Horace Sharp	23	CDH
	William Shirley	21	CDH
	George Shuttle	18	CDH

Date	Name	Age	Place
	Robert Smith	28	CDH
	William Smith	31	CDH
	William Steed	20	CDH
	Arthur Voice	22	CDH
	William Wakeford	32	CDH
	Edmund Walsh	32	CDH
	William Walton	51	CDH
	James Warne	33	CDH
	Henry Wate	20	CDH
	Alfred Watts	20	CDH
	Arthur Webb	18	CDH
	Alexander Westgarth	32	CDH
	George Wooton	18	CDH
	Royal Naval Reserve		
	James Anderson	25	CDH
	George Bell	28	CDH
	John Benson	25	CDH
	Thomas Carmichael	28	CDH
	William Clark	33	CDH
	Charles Clarke	29	CDH
	Herbert Cooney	27	CDH
	Thomas Cropley	34	CDH
	John Foreman	39	CDH
	Alfred Gladwell	31	CDH
	George Gunn	25	CDH
	Samuel Hadley	25	CDH
	John Henderson	?	CDH
	Alexander Kennedy	21	CDH
	William Littlewood	31	CDH
	Alexander MacGregor	26	CDH

Individuals Killed in Air Raids 1917–1918

Date	Name	Age	Place
	Neil Mackay	33	CDH
	Gilbert McLoughlin	20	CDH
	Neil Moore	35	CDH
	James Pye	28	CDH
	George Rae	33	CDH
	John Raven	42	CDH
	George Simpson	42	CDH
	James Stables	48	CDH
	Alexander Sutherland	18	CDH
	John Venney	27	CDH
	Royal Naval Volunteer Reserve		
	John Clements	25	CDH
	Raymond Ellis	18	CDH
	Robert Franklin	22	CDH
	William Godwin	20	CDH
	John McNish	20	CDH
	Jack Nicholson	20	CDH
	Robert Peters	24	CDH
	William Sullivan	18	CDH
	Frederick Upson	20	CDH
	George Watson	22	CDH
	Newfoundland Royal Naval Reserve		
	Albert Cluett	21	CDH
	Francis Crocker	20	CDH
	Thomas Ginn	22	CDH
	Nathaniel Gooby	19	CDH
	Royal Naval Canadian Volunteer Reserve		
	Knight Cooke	24	CDH

Date	Name	Age	Place
4/5 September 1917	Edward Little	73	Dover
	Henry Long	29	Dover
	Minnie Rhoda Smith	40	Dover
	3rd Battalion, Canadian Infantry		
	Pte. Albert Henry Bond	20	Charing Cross (L)
	George Brabham	53	Charing Cross (L)
	Eileen Dunleary	35	Charing Cross (L)
	2nd Battalion, Canadian Infantry		
	Sgt. Bartley Lumley	27	Charing Cross (L)
	Alfred Buckle	32	Vic. Embankment (L)
	Amy Eleanor Cuthbert	28	Vic. Embankment (L)
	Richard Daniel McCaughlin	44	Vic. Embankment (L)
	Rosa Sophia Hannell	64	Greenwich (L)
	Elsie Amelia Allen	5	Kentish Town (L)
	Mary Jane Allen	45	Kentish Town (L)
	14th Heavy Battery, Royal Garrison Artillery		
	Gnr. William Calow	24	Kentish Town (L)
	Thirza Darwood	35	Kentish Town (L)
	Maria Sarah Verity	46	Kentish Town (L)
	Mary Hayes	66	Paddington (L)
	Henry Over Parsons	33	Paddington (L)
	William Gibson	37	West Ham (L)
24 September 1917	Annie Keates	52	Dover
	Annie Evelyn Keates	12	Dover
	Edwin Kenward	77	Dover
	Ellen Kenward	55	Dover
	Dorothy Eleanor Wood	17	Dover

Individuals Killed in Air Raids 1917–1918

Date	Name	Age	Place
	2/1st Lincolnshire Yeomanry		
	Cpl. Alfred Millner	28	Leybourne
	Pte. James Shaw	18	Leybourne
	Elsie Clarke	19	Bloomsbury (L)
	2nd Field Company, Australian Engineers		
	Spr. John Ferns	33	Bloomsbury (L)
	John Harris	20	Bloomsbury (L)
	Joseph Hillier	16	Bloomsbury (L)
	Patrick Kennedy	23	Bloomsbury (L)
	Claude Helton Lennon	22	Bloomsbury (L)
	George Martin	21	Bloomsbury (L)
	Peter Ryan	29	Bloomsbury (L)
	William Sadler	51	Bloomsbury (L)
	Frederick Seiler	30	Bloomsbury (L)
	George J. Stevens	48	Bloomsbury (L)
	George Alexander Watson	27	Bloomsbury (L)
	1 man currently unidentified	?	Bloomsbury (L)
	James Frederick Sharpe	15	Kings Cross (L)
25 September 1917	*282nd Army Brigade, Royal Field Artillery*		
	Dvr. Andrew Gebbett	27	Bermondsey (L)
	Sarah Alice Gill	30	Bermondsey (L)
	William Phillip Probert	50	Bermondsey (L)
	William Thomas Sanger	67	Bermondsey (L)

Date	Name	Age	Place
	Martha Avery	27	Camberwell (L)
	John Martin Stripple	36	Camberwell (L)
	Merchant Navy, SS Stockwell		
	Joaquin Fernandes*	28	R. Albert Dock (L)
	Karimullah Nizamuddin*	?	R. Albert Dock (L)
	Jonas Pires*	?	R. Albert Dock (L)
29 September 1917	Edith Owers	51	Deal
	Elizabeth Clara Lyell	41	Barnes (L)
	George Temple Lyell	47	Barnes (L)
	Mabel Hall	32	Dalston (L)
	Percy Hall	6	Dalston (L)
	Ethel Winifred Lee	6	Dalston (L)
	William Joseph Edward Lee	11	Dalston (L)
	1 man currently unidentified	?	Haggerston (L)
	Janet Rebecca Crouch	28	Holloway (L)
	William Kyte	48	Holloway (L)
	Kathleen O'Hara	10	Holloway (L)
	Ellen Rose	68	Holloway (L)
	342nd (Home Service) Labour Company		
	Pte. Henry Thomas Slark	23	Holloway (L)
	Thomas Weight*	59	Shepherd's Bush (L)
30 September 1917	William Simmons	79	Bow (L)
	Walter Stanley Douch*	38	Southwark (L)
	Thomas Edward Ransom*	46	Stratford (L)

Individuals Killed in Air Raids 1917–1918

Date	Name	Age	Place
	Alice Coleman	37	Margate
	Annie Emptage	77	Margate
	Eliza Emptage	43	Margate
	Ellen 'Jane' Lee	43	Margate
	Thomas Parker	60	Margate
	William Lewis Walker	47	Margate
	834th Horse Transport Company, Army Service Corps		
	Dvr. William Leonard Hollins	29	Margate
	18th Battalion, Yorkshire Regiment		
	Pte. Benjamin Farnhill	41	Margate
	Inland Waterways and Docks, Royal Engineers		
	Spr. Thomas Armstrong	31	Margate
	Spr. John McGratty	33	Margate
	Spr. Frank Williams	38	Margate
1 October 1917	Ada Parker*	43	Dulwich (L)
	1 woman currently unidentified	?	Finsbury Park (L)
	Emily Harper	48	Haggerston (L)
	Charles Edward Hollington	66	Haggerston (L)
	Amelia Singleton	56	Haggerston (L)
	William Henry Singleton	56	Haggerston (L)
	Harriet Sears	78	Highbury (L)

Date	Name	Age	Place
	Frederick Charles Hanton	17	Pimlico (L)
	George Ernest Fennemore	17	Pimlico (L)
	Leo Joseph Fitzgerald	18	Pimlico (L)
	Henry James Greenway	17	Pimlico (L)
31 October/1 November 1917	*Royal Naval Reserve, HMS Attentive III*		
	Trm. Walter Gibbs	45	Dover
	George Robert Jarvis	65	Erith (L)
	Caroline Sutton	87	Erith (L)
	Anna Silcocks*	62	Hammersmith (L)
	Harold Crother Greenwood	49	Tooting (L)
	Frank Herbert Marwood	39	Tooting (L)
	Alfred John Page	42	Tooting (L)
	Alfred Thomas Page	13	Tooting (L)
	Sarah Statt	50	Tooting (L)
	East Lancashire Regiment		
	2nd Lt. David T. Douglas	22	Tooting (L)
6 December 1917	Edith Elizabeth Callaway	12	Dulwich (L)
	Edith Esther Howie	46	Dulwich (L)
	*1 woman currently unidentified**	?	Wanstead (L)
	Amelia Roberts	68	Margate
	Laura J. Cox	37	Sheerness
	Mary A. Hubbard	55	Sheerness

Individuals Killed in Air Raids 1917–1918

Date	Name	Age	Place
	James F. Hubbard	31	Sheerness
	Horace H. Mouatt	27	Sheerness
18 December 1917	Mary Ann Johnson	28	Bermondsey (L)
	Ellen Elizabeth Tullemach	5	Bermondsey (L)
	Daniel Pulham	76	Clerkenwell (L)
	Beatrice Bowen	24	Vic. Embankment (L)
	Minnie Mary Constantine	32	Vic. Embankment (L)
	Henry Willis Shields King	38	Vic. Embankment (L)
	Edith Maubon	26	Vic. Embankment (L)
	Thomas George Crawley	59	Farringdon (L)
	Herbert De Voy Mainwaring	42	Farringdon (L)
	Lilian Hope*	3	Hackney (L)
	Violet Edith Russell	3	King's Cross (L)
	John Joseph Whelan	15	King's Cross (L)
	George Parker*	60	Tottenham (L)
	Madeline Elsie Bates	34	Shenfield
28/29 January 1918	Edward Charles Ewington	45	Bethnal Green (L)
	George Page Marchant	50	Kilburn (L)
	Caroline Cox Thorpe	80	Kilburn (L)
	William Edgar Seager	15	Limehouse (L)
	Charles Robert Smith	17	Limehouse (L)
	John Wall	65	Limehouse (L)
	Sarah Allen	54	Long Acre (L)
	Jane Allport	22	Long Acre (L)
	Sidney Beckett	43	Long Acre (L)
	Annie Charteris	49	Long Acre (L)

301

Date	Name	Age	Place
	Thomas Charteris	63	Long Acre (L)
	Winifred Cousins	5	Long Acre (L)
	David Sidney Cox	13	Long Acre (L)
	Elizabeth G. Finch	25	Long Acre (L)
	Florence L. Finch	18	Long Acre (L)
	Sarah Goertz	48	Long Acre (L)
	Julia Hannaford	66	Long Acre (L)
	Rosina Holland	41	Long Acre (L)
	Robert William Holmes	33	Long Acre (L)
	Maria Jones	54	Long Acre (L)
	Florence Lindop	25	Long Acre (L)
	Jane Martin	?	Long Acre (L)
	Ellen D. McClaskey	2	Long Acre (L)
	Dorothy Moore	8	Long Acre (L)
	Lilian Moore	7	Long Acre (L)
	Marie Moore	10 months	Long Acre (L)
	Rev. Edward Henry Mosse	61	Long Acre (L)
	Minnie M. Noyce	46	Long Acre (L)
	Philip F. Ordway	2	Long Acre (L)
	Alfred Pinnock	61	Long Acre (L)
	Alice Plumpton	53	Long Acre (L)
	Ernest Plumpton	52	Long Acre (L)
	Joseph A Pretty	6	Long Acre (L)
	Catherine Scola	35	Long Acre (L)
	9 victims currently unidentified		Long Acre (L)
	Frederick Charles Myhill	54	Poplar (L)
	John Albert Newman	55	Poplar (L)
	James Day	64	Stepney (L)
	Isaac Kamanovitz	56	Stepney (L)

Individuals Killed in Air Raids 1917–1918

Date	Name	Age	Place
	Frederick Gower	47	Vauxhall (L)
	Matthew Walker	48	Vauxhall (L)
	George Witten	55	Vauxhall (L)
	Bishopsgate LNER Goods Depot		
	Woolf Biber	58	Shoreditch (L)
	Cissie Bodie	5	Shoreditch (L)
	Fanny Bodie	28	Shoreditch (L)
	Hetti Bodie	1	Shoreditch (L)
	Millie Cohen	45	Shoreditch (L)
	Marks Green	8	Shoreditch (L)
	Rosie Green	14	Shoreditch (L)
	Kate Greenland	40	Shoreditch (L)
	Abraham Hankin	6 months	Shoreditch (L)
	Esther Harris	68	Shoreditch (L)
	Rachel Jacobs	30	Shoreditch (L)
	Rachel Sachs	48	Shoreditch (L)
	Isadore Schagrin	7	Shoreditch (L)
	Louis Selitsky	5	Shoreditch (L)
	Commercial Road Midland Railway Goods Depot		
	Jane Rosa Ferminsky	60	Whitechapel (L)
	HM Torpedo Boat No.19, Royal Navy		
	LStr. Charles W. Hibbins	30	Sheerness
	HMS Wildfire, Royal Navy		
	AS Albert Winmill	48	Sheerness
29/30 January 1918	George Bentley	40	Brentford (L)
	Catherine Berrows	70	Brentford (L)
	Frederick William Finch	43	Brentford (L)

Date	Name	Age	Place
	Daisy Maud Kerley	3	Brentford (L)
	Ellen Louisa Kerley	3 months	Brentford (L)
	Florence A.M. Kerley	12	Brentford (L)
	Henry Ralph Kerley	8	Brentford (L)
	Hilda Winifred Kerley	22	Brentford (L)
	Lilian Doris Kerley	5	Brentford (L)
	May Kerley	38	Brentford (L)
16 February 1918	Alice Copley	29	Chelsea (L)
	Bernard Ludlow	4	Chelsea (L)
	Ernest Ludlow	10	Chelsea (L)
	Cpt. of Inv. Ernest Ludlow	41	Chelsea (L)
	Jessie Ludlow	37	Chelsea (L)
	Alice M. Cull	31	Woolwich (L)
	Henry J. Cull	2	Woolwich (L)
	8th Battery, 5th Reserve Brigade, Royal Field Artillery		
	Dvr. John Nish Ferguson	26	Woolwich (L)
	Alice F. Gregory	55	Woolwich (L)
	John A. Gregory	29	Woolwich (L)
	Gertrude L. Keyworth	28	Woolwich (L)
	2nd Brigade, Australian Field Artillery		
	Gnr. Eric Munro	24	Woolwich (L)
17 February 1918	Ada Close	34	St.Pancras (L)
	Edward Close	48	St.Pancras (L)
	Winifred Doris Coates	20	St.Pancras (L)
	Royal Flying Corps		
	Sgt. Fred Darlington	20	St.Pancras (L)

Individuals Killed in Air Raids 1917–1918

Date	Name	Age	Place
	Albert J. Harriman	27	St.Pancras (L)
	Charles W. Harriman	30	St.Pancras (L)
	Herbert Robinson	18	St.Pancras (L)
	Maud Sugars	21	St.Pancras (L)
	11 men and 1 woman currently unidentified		St.Pancras (L)
	John Thomas Bannister	23	Southwark (L)
7/8 March 1918	*1 man currently unidentified*	?	Eltham (L)
	1 woman currently unidentified	?	Leyton (L)
	Mary Kate Daly	26	Maida Vale (L)
	Lena Guilbert Ford	47	Maida Vale (L)
	Walter Ford	26	Maida Vale (L)
	Alice Maud Hannah Gardam	55	Maida Vale (L)
	Magnus Goldring	50	Maida Vale (L)
	Fanny Sophia Lindo	82	Maida Vale (L)
	Henry Middlemass	47	Maida Vale (L)
	Benita Georgia Pyke	56	Maida Vale (L)
	Austin Thomas	30	Maida Vale (L)
	George Thomas	39	Maida Vale (L)
	Margaret Thomas	30	Maida Vale (L)
	Nigel Thomas	1	Maida Vale (L)
	Edith Frances Chick	26	St.John's Wood (L)
	Frederick William Chick	34	St.John's Wood (L)
	Marjorie Chick	8	St.John's Wood (L)
	Clifford Hulse	11	St.John's Wood (L)
	Harry Hulse	40	St.John's Wood (L)
	Lilian Hulse	39	St.John's Wood (L)

Date	Name	Age	Place
	'K' Bty., 13th Reserve Brig. Royal Field Artillery		
	Dvr. Sidney Reeves	30	St.John's Wood (L)
	4th Battalion, Rifle Brigade, attached to 1/5th Suffolk Regiment		
	Lt. Col. Frederick Wollaston	39	St.John's Wood (L)
	1 man currently unidentified	?	Whetstone (L)
19/20 May 1918	Thomas Austen*	35	Canterbury
	Elizabeth Gorman	69	Bethnal Green (L)
	Leo Grogan	7	Canning Town (L)
	Elizabeth Bell	73	Islington (L)
	Esther Cartwright	63	Islington (L)
	Arthur Hearn	75	Islington (L)
	Hannah Hearn	64	Islington (L)
	Jane Howard	65	Islington (L)
	Edith Trathen	37	Islington (L)
	John Trathen	45	Islington (L)
	Army Service Corps		
	Pte. James Oswald	32	Lewisham (L)
	Arthur Stribling	46	Maida Vale (L)
	Arthur G. Stribling	7	Maida Vale (L)
	Thomas Henry French	49	Peckham (L)
	John Lynch	12	Rotherhithe (L)
	Mary Lynch	38	Rotherhithe (L)
	Edward White	47	Stratford (L)
	Lizzie White	49	Stratford (L)
	Emma E. Cook	23	Sydenham (L)
	Beatrice F. Delahoy	17	Sydenham (L)
	Eliza Delahoy	57	Sydenham (L)

Individuals Killed in Air Raids 1917–1918

Date	Name	Age	Place
	Isaac W. Delahoy	57	Sydenham (L)
	Laura Delahoy	20	Sydenham (L)
	Mary V. Delahoy	14	Sydenham (L)
	Elizabeth Hambrook	57	Sydenham (L)
	John Klingels	58	Sydenham (L)
	William A. Phillips	72	Sydenham (L)
	Emma Pout	48	Sydenham (L)
	Rosina G. Smith	24	Sydenham (L)
	Redvers B. Westley	17	Sydenham (L)
	Rosalind M. Westley	47	Sydenham (L)
	Army Service Corps		
	Pte. John McLachlan	39	Sydenham (L)
	Pte. John William White	40	Sydenham (L)
	Pte. Trevor Williams	23	Sydenham (L)
	Pte. Francis Smith	31	Sydenham (L)
	Pte. John O'Grady	24	Sydenham (L)
	13 currently unidentified		London

Bibliography

Ashmore, Maj Gen E.B.: *Air Defence*, (London 1929)
Austen, Chas, A.F.: *Ramsgate Raid Records 1915-1918*, (originally published around 1919, reprint Ramsgate 2006)
Beesly, Patrick, *Room 40 – British Naval Intelligence 1914-18*, (London 1982)
Boyle, Andrew: *Trenchard – Man of Vision*, (London 1962)
Brittain, Vera: *Testament of Youth*, (1933, rept. London 1978)
Buttlar Brandenfels, Freiherr Treusch von: *Zeppelins Over England*, (London 1931)
Castle, H.G.: *Fire Over England – The German Air Raids in World War 1*, (London 1982)
Castle, Ian: *The First Blitz – Bombing London in the First World War*, (Oxford 2015)
Castle, Ian: *The First Blitz in 100 Objects*, (Barnsley 2019)
Castle, Ian: *Zeppelin Inferno – The Forgotten Blitz 1916*, (Barnsley 2022)
Castle, Ian: *Zeppelin Onslaught – The Forgotten Blitz 1914-1915*, (Barnsley 2018)
Charlton, L.E.O.: *War Over England*, (London 1936)
Cockburn, Ernest: *Cockburn's Diary – Ramsgate Life in the First World War*, (Ramsgate 2006)
Cole, Christopher, & Cheesman, E.F.: *The Air Defence of Britain 1914-1918*, (London 1984)
Credland, Arthur G.: *The Hull Zeppelin Raids 1915-1918*, (Stroud 2014)
Dover Express: *Dover and the European War 1914-18*, (Dover 1919)
Easdown, Martin, with Genth, Thomas: *A Glint in the Sky*, (Barnsley 2004)
Fegan, Thomas: *The 'Baby Killers' – German Air Raids on Britain in the First World War*, (Barnsley 2002)
Fredette, Major Raymond, *The First Battle of Britain 1917-1918*, (London 1966)
Grayzel, Susan R.: *At Home and Under Fire – Air Raids and Culture in Britain from the Great War to the Blitz*, (Cambridge 2012)
Griel, Manfred, & Dressel, Joachim: *Zeppelin! The German Airship Story*, (London 1990)
Grosz, Peter M.: *Gotha!*, (Berkhamsted 1994)

Haddow, G.W., & Grosz, Peter M.: *The German Giants - The Story of the R-planes 1914-1919*, (London 1962)

Hall, Ian: *Zeppelins Over the North East*, (Alnwick 2014)

Hanson, Neil: *First Blitz*, (London 2008)

Hoeppner, General Ernest von, *Germany's War in the Air*, (English translation, Nashvlle 1994)

Hyde, Andrew P.: *The First Blitz*, (Barnsley 2002)

Jones, H.A.: *The War in the Air – Being the Story of the part played in the Great War by the Royal Air Force*, Vol. III, (Oxford 1931), Vol. V (Oxford 1935), Vol. VI (Oxford 1937) and Appendices (Oxford 1937)

Kollman, Franz: *Das Zeppelinluftschiff – seine Entwicklung, Tätigkeit und Leistungen*, (Berlin 1924)

Lehmann, Ernst: *Zeppelin - The story of lighter-than-air craft*, (1937, rept. 2015)

Lehmann, Capt. E.A., & Mingos, H.: *The Zeppelins*, (London 1927)

Lewis, Cecil: *Sagittarius Rising*, (Orig. London 1936, rept. London 2000)

Ludendorff, Erich von: *Ludendorff's Own Story – August 1914-November 1918*, Vol. II (London & New York 1919)

MacDonagh, Michael: *In London During the Great War – The Diary of a Journalist*, (London 1935)

Marben, Rolf: *Zeppelin Adventures*, (London 1931)

Marks, David: *Let The Zeppelins Come*, (Stroud 2017)

Marks, David: *The Zeppelin Offensive – A German perspective in Pictures & Postcards*, (Barnsley 2019)

Metzmacher, Andreas, *Gotha Aircraft*, (Stroud 2021)

Monson, Major E.C.P., and Marsland, Ellis: *Air Raid Damage in London*, London 1923

Morison, Frank: *War on Great Cities – A Study of the Facts*, (London 1937)

Morris, Joseph: *German Air Raids on Britain 1914-1918*, (1925, rept. Dallington 1993)

Mückler, Jörg: *Deutsche Bomber Im Ersten Weltkreig*, (Stuttgart 2017)

Munsun, J. (ed.), *Echoes of the Great War – The Diary of the Reverend Andrew Clark, 1914-1919*, (Oxford 1985)

Neumann, Major Georg Paul (trans. Gurdon, J.E.): *The German Air Force in the Great War*, (1921, rept. Bath 1969)

Oak-Rhind, Edwin Scoby: *The North Foreland Lookout Post in the Great War 1915-1917*, (Ramsgate 2005)

Poolman, Kenneth: *Zeppelins Over England*, (London 1960)

Rawlinson, A.: *The Defence of London 1915-1918*, (London 1923)

Rimell, Raymond L.: *Zeppelin! A Battle for Air Supremacy in World War I*, (London 1984)

Rimell, R.L.: *The Last Flight of the L48*, (Berkhamsted 2006)

Robinson, Douglas H.: *The Zeppelin In Combat – A History of the German Naval Airship Division, 1912-1918*, (Atglen, PA 1994)

Sassoon, Siegfried: *Memoirs of an Infantry Officer*, (London 1930, rept. 1931)
Scheer, Admiral Reinhardt: *Germany's High Sea Fleet in the World War*, (English translation, London 1920)
Simpson, Alan: *Air Raids on South-West Essex in the Great War*, (Barnsley 2015)
Smith, Peter J.C.: *Zeppelins Over Lancashire*, (Radcliffe 1991)
Snowden Gamble, C.F.: *The Story of a North Sea Air Station*, (Original 1928, Reprint, London 1967)
Strahlmann, Dr. Fritz (ed.): *Zwei deutsche Luftschiffhäfen des Weltkrieges, Ahlhorn und Wildeshausen*, 1926 (English translation by Alex Reid retitled, *Memories of Ahlhorn*, (privately published 2016)
Thanet Advertiser: *Thanet's Raid History*, (Ramsgate 1919, rept. 2006)
Van Emden, Richard, and Humphries, Steve: *All Quiet on the Home Front – An Oral History of Life in Britain during the First World War*, (London 2003)
White, C.M.: *The Gotha Summer*, (London 1986)

Journal

Krusenstiern, Alfred von (Translator): *Bombing Missions on Two Fronts – The wartime letters of Ltn. D. Res. Immanuel Braun, KAGOHL 1 and BOGOHL 3*, Cross & Cockade Journal, Vol. 23, No. 1, Spring 1982

Archive material

The National Archives, Kew, London

Air Ministry: Air Historical Branch: Papers (Series I)
AIR1/587/16/15/190-195
AIR1/588/16/15/196-198
AIR1/589/16/15/199-200
AIR1/590/16/15/201-203
AIR1/591/16/15/204-207
AIR1/592/16/15/208-209
AIR1/593/16/15/210-212
AIR1/594/16/15/213-214
AIR1/595/16/15/215-216
AIR1/596/16/15/217
AIR1/597/16/15/218-220
AIR1/598/16/15/221-222
AIR1/599/16/15/223-225
AIR1/600/16/15/226-228
AIR1/601/16/15/229-231
AIR1/602/16/15/232
AIR1/603/16/15/233-234

AIR1/2417/303/42

Metropolitan Police: Office of the Commissioner: Correspondence and Papers
MEPO2/1735

War Office: Military Headquarters: Correspondence and Papers, First World War
WO158/947-959
WO158/976-979

Online resources

British Newspaper Archive. www.britishnewspaperarchive.co.uk
Great War Forum. www.greatwarforum.org
Kagohl 3 War Diary. http://www.airhistory.org.uk/rfc/Kagohl3-diary.html
Old Maps Online. www.oldmapsonline.org
The Times Digital Archive
Willoughby, Roger: *For God and the Empire: The Medal of the Order of the British Empire.* www.academia.edu/34552514/For_God_and_the_Empire_The_Medal_of_the_Order_of_the_British_Empire_1917_1922

Notes

Chapter 1: 1917 – They Think it's all over

1. *The Times* Digital Archive (TDA): *The Times*, 29 Nov 1916, p.9
2. Cole & Cheesman, *Air Defence of Britain*, p.190
3. Jones, H.A.: *War in the Air*, Vol. V, p.8
4. British Newspaper Archive (BNA): *Thanet Advertiser*, 3 Mar 1917, p.5
5. Robinson: *Zeppelin in Combat*, p.225
6. On the raid of 23/24 September 1916, the standard 'r-class' Zeppelin, L 31, carried bombs weighing 4,195kg (about 4.1 tons).
7. Robinson, *op.cit.*, p.229
8. Account of raid compiled from TNA: AIR1/587/16/15/192 and WO158/947
9. BNA: *Aberdeen Daily Journal*, 19 Mar 1917, p.3
10. TNA: WO158/947, p.6
11. Great War Forum (GWF): https://www.greatwarforum.org/topic/63379-2nd-lt-david-dennys-fowler-rfc/ (accessed 17 Jul 2022), and Cole & Cheesman, *op.cit.*, pp.198-199

Chapter 2: 'The scene was too awful'

1. Von Hoeppner, *Germany's War in the Air*, p.78
2. *Ibid*, p.90
3. The name Gotha taken from the manufacturer, the Gothaer Waggonfabrik AG, originally specialist builders of railway trucks and carriages.
4. Castle, *The First Blitz*, p.102
5. *Ibid*, p.104
6. Jones, *op. cit.*, pp.11-12
7. BNA: *Daily News*, 7 Apr 1917, p.1
8. Castle, *Zeppelin Inferno*, pp.307-310
9. BNA: *Daily Mirror*, 8 May 1917, p.2
10. BNA: *Pall Mall Gazette*, 9 May 1917, p.5
11. *Ibid*
12. Originally Zeppelins had sent departure signals when leaving their bases, but once Germany realised British listening stations were intercepting these, they ceased, although they were still sent by Zeppelins on scouting missions.

13. Snowden Gamble, *Story of a North Sea Air Station*, pp.237-238
14. Scheer, *Germany's High Seas Fleet*, pp.283-284
15. Snowden Gamble, *op. cit.*, p.242
16. Snowden Gamble, *op. cit.*, p.241
17. Details of raid drawn from TNA: WO158/976 and AIR1/588/16/15/197
18. Easdown, *A Glint in the Sky*, p.103
19. BNA: *Dover Chronicle*, 2 Jun 1917, p.3
20. TNA: AIR1/2417/303/42, *London Evening News*, 6 Mar 1935
21. Emden & Humphries, *All Quiet on the Home Front*, pp. 176-177
22. Information by email from Richard Willcocks, Ernest McGuire's nephew.

Chapter 3: Gothas Over London

1. White, *The Gotha Summer*, p.96
2. Jones, *op. cit.*, p.23
3. *Ibid*, p.24-25
4. BNA: *Westerham Herald*, 9 Jun 1917, p.8
5. Information from the logbook of HMMS *London Belle* provided by John Henderson, whose great uncle served onboard.
6. BNA: *East Kent Gazette*, 9 Jun 1917, p.6
7. BNA: *Westerham Herald*, 9 Jun 1917, p.8
8. TDA: *The Times*, 4 Jul 1917, p.5
9. Cole & Cheesman, *op.cit.*, p.244
10. TDA: *The Times*, 4 Jul 1917, p.5
11. Munsun, J. (ed.), *Echoes of the Great War*, p.196
12. TDA: *The Times*, 4 July 1917, p.5
13. TNA: AIR1/2417/303/42, *London Evening News*, 1 Mar 1935
14. Von Hoeppner, *op.cit.*, p.106
15. TDA: *The Times*, 4 Jul 1917, p.5
16. Brittain, *Testament of Youth*, p.365
17. Castle, *The First Blitz*, p.121
18. BNA: *The Globe*, 15 Jun 1917, p.2
19. Sassoon, *Memoirs of an Infantry Officer*, p.277
20. TNA: AIR1/2417/303/42, *London Evening News*, 4 Mar 1935
21. BNA: *Pall Mall Gazette*, 15 Jun 1917, p.5
22. TNA: AIR1/2417/303/42, *London Evening News*, 14 Feb 1935
23. Hyde, *The First Blitz*, p.125
24. Morison, *War on Great Cities*, p.126
25. TNA: AIR1/2417/303/42, *London Evening News*, 21 Feb 1935
26. BNA: *Pall Mall Gazette*, 16 Jun 1917, p.2
27. BNA: *Dublin Daily Express*, 19 Jun 1917, p.7
28. TDA: *The Times*, 21 Jun 1917, p.3. London continued to remember the child victims and in 2017 Queen Elizabeth II attended a memorial service in Poplar to mark the centenary of the incident.
29. Cole-Hamilton died 19 days later in a flying accident.
30. http://www.airhistory.org.uk/rfc/Kagohl3-diary.html (accessed 20 Aug 2022)

Chapter 4: 'The lights of death'

1. BNA: *Pall Mall Gazette*, 15 Jun 1917, p.5
2. Jones, *op. cit.*, p.31
3. Lewis, *Sagittarius Rising*, p.184
4. Jones, *op. cit.*, p.44
5. Robinson, *op. cit.*, p.259
6. *Ibid*, pp.259-261
7. *Ibid*, p.246
8. Thanet Advertiser, *Thanet's Raid History*, p.19
9. A shallow-draught naval vessel designed for inshore bombardment.
10. Cockburn, Diary entry for 17 Jun 1917
11. Robinson, *op. cit.*, p.247
12. Willoughby, *For God and the Empire: The Medal of the Order of the British Empire*
13. Austen, *Ramsgate Raid Records*, p.23
14. BNA: *Thanet Advertiser*, 23 Jun 1917, p.5
15. *Ibid*
16. On 28 June the Borough Surveyor gave an official figure of £25,500, but Ramsgate's chief constable added, 'the estimate... is quite the minimum as it is feared that when repairs are commenced internal structural damage to a much greater extent... will be revealed'. TNA: AIR1/589/16/15/200.
17. Thanet Advertiser, *Thanet's Raid History*, p.21
18. BNA: *Bury Free Press*, 23 Jun 1917, p.3
19. TNA: AIR1/589/16/15/200
20. *Ibid*
21. *Ibid*
22. Cole & Cheesman, *op. cit.*, p.254
23. BNA: *Bury Free Press*, 23 Jun 1917, p.3
24. BNA: *Halesworth Times*, 19 Jun 1917, p.4
25. BNA: *Suffolk and Essex Free Press*, 20 Jun 1917, p.7
26. Robinson, *op. cit.*, p.251
27. Marben, *Zeppelin Adventures*, pp.55-59
28. Rimell, *The Last Flight of the L48*, p.17
29. *Ibid*, p.16
30. Robinson, *op. cit.*, p.253
31. BNA: *Essex Newsman*, 7 July 1917, p.3
32. TNA: AIR1/2417/303/42, *London Evening News*, 2 Mar 1935
33. Lewis, *op. cit.*, p.187

Chapter 5: 'The damned impudence'

1. White, *op. cit.*, p.137
2. *Ibid*, p.143
3. TNA: AIR1/2417/303/42, *London Evening News*, 11 Feb 1935
4. *Ibid*, 9 Mar 1935
5. TNA: AIR1/590/16/15/202 Part II, *Daily Chronicle*, 9 Jul 1917

Notes

6. TNA: AIR1/2417/303/42, *London Evening News*, 23 Feb 1935
7. TNA: *Ibid*, 26 Feb 1935
8. Bartholomew Close had suffered previous damage during a Zeppelin raid on 8 September 1915 (see Castle, *Zeppelin Onslaught*, pp.222-224).
9. MacDonagh, *In London During the Great War*, p.201
10. TNA: AIR1/2417/303/42, *London Evening News*, 2 Mar 1935
11. *Ibid*, 25 Feb 1935
12. *Ibid*, 28 Feb 1935
13. *Ibid*, 13 Feb 1935
14. TNA: AIR1/590/16/15/202
15. TNA: AIR1/2417/303/42, *London Evening News*, 11 Feb 1935
16. TNA: AIR1/590/16/15/202
17. MacDonagh, *op. cit.*, p.200
18. *Ibid*, p.202
19. Jones: *op. cit.*, pp.39-40
20. *Ibid*, pp.38-39
21. *Ibid*, pp.487-491. Smuts report on 'Home Defence'.
22. *Ibid*
23. No. 44 began to form (from elements of No. 39 Squadron) at Hainault Farm, Essex, on 24 July; No. 112 (from elements of No. 50 Squadron) at Throwley, Kent, on 30 July; No. 61 (from elements of No. 37 Squadron) at Rochford, Essex, on 2 August.
24. TNA: *The Times*, 18 Jul 1917, p.6
25. Jones, *op. cit.*, pp.45-51
26. In the 1930s Bawdsey Manor became an important radar research centre and the setting for one of the earliest Chain Home radar stations which detected incoming German bombers in the Second World War.
27. Details of raid from TNA: AIR1/590/16/15/203 and WO158/977
28. BNA: *Daily News*, 23 Jul 1917, p.1
29. *Ibid*
30. *Ibid*
31. BNA: *Daily Mirror*, 23 Jul 1917, p.3

Chapter 6: 'A senior officer of first-rate ability'

1. Ashmore, *Air Defence*, p.40
2. *Ibid*, pp.41-42
3. *Ibid*, p.39
4. *Ibid*, p.42
5. *Ibid*, p.43
6. *Ibid*
7. *Ibid*, pp.43-44
8. TNA: AIR1/591/16/15/204, *Daily Telegraph*, 14 Aug 1917
9. *Ibid*
10. *Ibid*, *Daily Express*, date unknown
11. TDA: *The Times*, 14 Aug 1917, p.6

12. TNA: AIR1/591/16/15/204
13. Cole & Cheesman, *op. cit.*, pp.280-281
14. *Ibid*
15. During the Second World War, Kerby rose to the rank of Air Vice Marshal.
16. TNA: WO158/978
17. Robinson, *op. sit.*, pp.283-284
18. Tondern is now Tønder in Denmark.
19. Rimell, *Zeppelin!*, p.196
20. Robinson, *op. sit.*, p.262
21. *Ibid*, pp.284-285
22. This account of raid is based largely on documents in TNA: AIR1/591/16/15/205 and WO158/948
23. BNA: *Yorkshire Post*, 23 Aug 1917, p.5
24. *Ibid*
25. *Ibid*
26. TNA: AIR1/591/16/15/205
27. TNA: This account of the raid is based on papers held in WO158/978 and AIR1/591/16/15/206
28. BNA: *Dover Chronicle*, 25 Aug 1917, p.6
29. TNA: AIR1/591/16/15/206, *Daily News*, 23 Aug 1917
30. BNA: *Thanet Advertiser*, 4 Jan 1919, p.5
31. *Ibid*
32. *Ibid*
33. BNA: *South Eastern Gazette*, 28 Aug 1917, p.8
34. Cockburn, *op. cit.*, entry for 22 Aug 1917
35. BNA: *Dover Chronicle*, 25 Aug 1917, p.6

Chapter 7: 'I shall never forget that night'

1. Jones, *War in the Air*, Appendices volume, p.10
2. *Ibid*, p.13
3. *Ibid*
4. Boyle, *Trenchard*, pp.232-233
5. TNA: AIR1/591/16/15/207
6. Dover Express, *Dover and the European War*, pp.32-33
7. Ashmore, *op. cit.*, pp.48-49
8. *Ibid*, pp.49-52
9. BNA: *The Globe*, 4 Sep 1917, p.1
10. TNA: AIR1/2417/303/42, *London Evening News*, 15 Feb 1935
11. Fegan, *The Baby-Killers*, pp.57-58
12. The list of those killed now displayed in the Drill Hall Library gives 131 names, however, one of them, Engine Room Artificer Claude McIntyre, was killed by a bomb elsewhere in Chatham. In a similar vein 87 men are recorded as injured, but one of these, was with McIntyre at the time.
13. BNA: *Daily News*, 7 Sep 1917, p.6
14. BNA: *Kent Messenger*, 8 Sep 1917, p.1
15. Lewis, *op. cit.*, p.203

16. Ashmore, *op. cit.*, p.53
17. *Ibid*
18. TNA: AIR1/592/16/15/209
19. *Ibid*
20. *Ibid*
21. BNA: *Sydenham, Forest Hill and Penge Gazette*, 7 Sep 1917, p.5

Chapter 8: 'Am I dead or alive?'

1. BNA: *Leicester Daily Post*, 6 Sep 1917, p.1
2. *Ibid*
3. TNA: AIR1/2417/303/42, *London Evening News*, 4 Feb 1935
4. BNA: *Evening Mail*, 7 Sep 1917, P.8
5. TNA: AIR1/2417/303/42, *London Evening News*, 14 Feb 1935
6. BNA: *Pall Mall Gazette*, 5 Sep 1917, p.2
7. TNA: AIR1/2417/303/42, *London Evening News*, 1 Mar 1935
8. BNA: *Evening Mail*, 7 Sep 1917, p.8
9. This damage is still visible today.
10. BNA: *Westminster Gazette*, 7 Sep 1917, p.7
11. BNA: *The Globe*, 7 Sep 1917, p.1
12. BNA: *Scotsman*, 12 Sep 1917, p.8
13. TNA: AIR1/2417/303/42, *London Evening News*, 20 Feb 1935
14. Titchborne Street no longer exists.
15. BNA: *Daily News*, 8 Sep 1917, p.3
16. Jones, *The War in the Air*, Vol. V, pp.491-492
17. *Ibid*, p.493
18. Ashmore, *op. cit.*, p.54
19. *Ibid*
20. Jones, *op. cit.*, pp.76-77
21. Lewis, *op. cit.*, pp.212-214
22. TNA: AIR1/593/16/15/210
23. TDA: *The Times*, 26 Sep 1917, p.7
24. *Ibid*
25. BNA: *Pall Mall Gazette*, 29 Sep 1917, p.5
26. TNA: AIR1/2417/303/42, *London Evening News*, 25 Feb 1935

Chapter 9: 'If only we had had a warning'

1. BNA: *Evening Mail*, 8 Oct 1917, p.8
2. TNA: AIR1/593/16/15/212 *Daily Express* report
3. TNA: AIR1/2417/303/42, *London Evening News*, 21 Feb 1935
4. TNA: AIR1/593/16/15/212, *Pall Mall Gazette*, 26 Sep 1917
5. *Ibid*, *Guardian* report (undated)
6. BNA: *The Globe*, 28 Sep 1917, p.1
7. BNA: *Westminster Gazette*, 28 Sep 1917, p.7
8. BNA: *The Globe*, 28 Sep 1917, p.1
9. BNA: *Pall Mall Gazette*, 26 Sep 1917, p.2

10. BNA: *Ibid*, 29 Sep 1917, p.1
11. Fredette, *First Battle of Britain*, p.140
12. *Ibid*, pp.140-141
13. *Ibid*, p.141
14. TNA: AIR1/594/16/15/213
15. *Ibid*
16. TNA: AIR1/594/16/15/215 Part II
17. BNA: *South Western Star*, 5 Oct 1917, p.8
18. BNA: *The Globe*, 3 Oct 1917, p.5
19. BNA: *Dundee Evening Telegraph*, 2 Oct 1917, p.1
20. Now the site of Arsenal Football Club's Emirates Stadium.
21. TNA: AIR1/2417/303/42, *London Evening News*, 26 Feb 1935
22. *Ibid*, 19 Feb 1935
23. TNA: HO 45/11071/380323
24. TNA: AIR1/2417/303/42, *London Evening News*, 12 Feb 1935
25. *Ibid*, 1 Feb 1935

Chapter 10: 'A growing confidence'

1. This figure is at least twice as many that sheltered on the Underground during the Blitz of the Second World War.
2. Jones, *op. cit.*, p.90
3. TNA: MEPO2/1735
4. BNA: *Thanet Advertiser*, 6 Oct 1917, p.3
5. BNA: *East Kent Times*, 3 Oct 1917, p.2
6. Cross & Cockade Journal, Vol. 23, No. 1, Spring 1982, p.50
7. Dover Express, *Dover and the European War*, p.35
8. TNA: AIR1/595/16/15/215. Unidentified newspaper report, date 2 Oct 1917
9. Account of raid based on reports in TNA: AIR1/595/16/15/215 and WO158/950
10. TNA: AIR1/595/16/15/215
11. *Ibid*
12. TNA: AIR1/595/16/15/216
13. Account of raid based on reports in TNA: AIR1/595/16/15/216 and WO158/950
14. BNA: *Leicester Daily Post*, 3 Oct 1917, p.1
15. *Ibid*
16. BNA: *Birmingham Daily Mail*, 3 Oct 1917, p.3
17. TNA: AIR1/595/16/15/216
18. BNA: The Freeman's Journal, 3 Oct 1917, p.5
19. The official report states 16 bombs were dropped by two Gothas but this seems unlikely; all bombs fell within 2 minutes and Gothas did not operate in tandem. In addition, there appears to be 19, all weighing 50kg, beyond the bombload of two Gothas. British reports state no Giants took part but Germany reported that one bombed London. It seems likely that this attack was made by a Giant.
20. This area has seen major redevelopment over the years and many of the roads have disappeared, others have changed names.
21. BNA: *Westminster Gazette*, 5 Oct 1917, p.6
22. Rawlinson, *Defence of London*, p.209

23. Jones, *op. cit.*, pp.86 & 89
24. TNA: AIR1/595/16/15/216
25. Jones, *op. cit.*, p.87

Chapter 11: The Silent Raid

1. Air cooled to extreme low temperatures until it condenses into a liquid, which returns to its natural form when re-heated.
2. Robinson, *op. cit.*, p.288
3. Von Buttlar Brandenfels, *Zeppelins Over England*, pp.116-117
4. The official report (WO158/951) appears to confuse the movement of L 44 and L 53. Historian Douglas Johnson identified this error in the 1960s in his book, *The Zeppelin in Combat*.
5. For this story see, Castle, *Zeppelin Inferno*, pp.150-153
6. The movements of L 49 and L 50 are based on the official War Office report (WO158/951), but it is possible that it may have confused the paths of the two Zeppelins; they were operating within 18 miles of each other. It is worth noting that Gayer (L 49) did claim to have bombed an airfield, while Schwonder (L 50) does not.
7. TNA: WO158/951
8. Robinson, *op. cit.*, p.299
9. BNA: *Northampton Daily Echo*, 20 Oct 1917, p.3
10. Robinson, *op. cit.*, p.299
11. *Ibid*
12. TNA: AIR1/2417/303/42, *London Evening News*, 8 Feb 1935
13. Mabel Barrington does not appear to be the victim's real name; she does not appear on the GRO Death Index. Her maid identified the body from the jewellery but added 'that she had no idea who her mistress was or where she came from, although she had been with her for six months'.
14. TNA: AIR1/2417/303/42, *London Evening News*, 2 Mar 1935
15. On the centenary of the raid, I gave a talk in Camberwell and was honoured by the presence of Greta, at the grand age of 101, along with members of her family.
16. BNA: *Pall Mall Gazette*, 25 Oct 1917, p.5
17. Later renamed Nightingale Grove.
18. BNA: *Sydenham, Forest Hill & Penge Gazette*, 26 Oct 1917, p.6
19. Cole & Cheesman, *op. cit.*, p.451
20. Jones, *op. cit.*, p.102

Chapter 12: 'Got it!'

1. 181 incendiary bombs and 93 explosive.
2. Details of bombs extracted from TNA: AIR1/597/16/15/220 Part 1
3. Thanet Advertiser, *Thanet's Raid History*, pp.27-28
4. BNA: *The Globe*, 1 Nov 1917, p.1
5. *Ibid*
6. TNA: AIR1/2417/303/42, *London Evening News*, 7 Feb 1935
7. BNA: *Leicester Daily Post*, 3 Nov 1917, p.1

8. TNA: AIR1/2417/303/42, *London Evening News*, 13 Feb 1935
9. TNA: AIR1/597/16/15/220 Part 1. Metropolitan Police reports states '100 houses' damaged.
10. TDA: *The Times*, 3 Nov 1917, p.8
11. *Ibid*
12. Of the 420 bombs plotted on land, all but 28 were incendiaries.
13. Bateson's letter shown to me by his grandson, David Jones.
14. TNA: AIR1/598/16/15/221 Part 1. Another report states: 'I understand that one of the German Officers told one of our men that they had 48 bombs on board. I cannot vouch for the accuracy of this, but I myself saw a very large number of bombs and 4 aerial torpedoes.'
15. Lewis, *op. cit.*, p.230
16. *Ibid*, pp.230-231
17. TDA: *The Times*, 7 Dec 1917, p.9
18. BNA: *Birmingham Daily Mail*, 11 Dec 1917, p.3
19. TDA: *The Times*, 7 Dec 1917, p.10
20. http://www.airhistory.org.uk/rfc/Kagohl3-diary.html (accessed 20 Feb 2023)
21. Jones, *op. cit.*, pp.104-105. Quoted from *Die Luftwacht*, Jun 1927
22. Fredette, *op. cit.*, pp.175-176
23. TNA: WO158/952, p.3

Chapter 13: 'I'll shoot the first man to light a match'

1. BNA: *Essex County Chronicle*, 28 Dec 1917, p.2
2. BNA: *Evening Mail*, 19 Dec 1917, p.4
3. BNA: *Birmingham Daily Mail*, 21 Dec 1917, p.3
4. TNA: AIR1/2417/303/42, *London Evening News*, 8 Mar 1935
5. BNA: *Yorkshire Evening Post*, 21 Dec 1917, p.6
6. BNA: *Pall Mall Gazette*, 22 Dec 1917, p.5
7. *Ibid*
8. *Ibid*, 21 Dec 1917, p.5
9. *Ibid*
10. BNA: *Reynolds's Newspaper*, 23 Dec 1917, p.3
11. BNA: *Birmingham Daily Mail*, 21 Dec 1917, p.3
12. TNA: AIR1/598/16/15/222
13. There is an error in the official report of the raid (TNA: WO158/952 – page 35), where the figure of £317,661 is given. However, this reflects the total of damage in London for December 1917 (6 Dec and 18 Dec raids combined).
14. Details from TNA: AIR1/599/16/15/223 and http://www.airhistory.org.uk/rfc/Kagohl3-diary.html (accessed 8 Mar 2023)
15. Jones, *op. cit.*, p.108
16. Cole & Cheesman, *op. cit.*, p.377
17. TNA: AIR1/2398/267/19
18. Strahlmann, (ed.), *Memories of Ahlhorn* (translation of *Zwei deutsche Luftschiffhäfen*), pp.181-183
19. *Ibid*, 190-193
20. Robinson, *op. cit.*, p.326

Chapter 14: 'A desperate struggle for life'

1. BNA: *Thanet Advertiser*, 11 Jan 1919, p.5
2. *Ibid*
3. *Ibid*
4. TNA: AIR1/599/16/15/224
5. *Ibid*
6. Jones, *op. cit.*, pp.109-110
7. Details of the raid from TNA: AIR1/599/16/15/224
8. BNA: *Daily News*, 30 Jan 1918, p.1
9. *Ibid*
10. TNA: AIR1/2417/303/42, *London Evening News*, 16 Feb 1935
11. London, Tilbury and Southend Railway, acquired by Midland in 1912.
12. A newspaper report gives the name as Serminsky, but it is Ferminsky on her death certificate.
13. BNA: *Pall Mall Gazette*, 31 Jan 1918, p.8
14. These two Gothas were over London at the same time and official reports cannot with certainty say which Gotha dropped which bombs. However, I have plotted all the bombs on a map and created flight lines between them which has resulted in the conclusions I have drawn.
15. BNA: *Evening Mail*, 1 Feb 1918, p.8
16. Van Emden, & Humphries, *op. cit.*, pp.184-186
17. TNA: AIR1/599/16/15/224
18. TNA: WO158/955
19. BNA: *Gloucestershire Echo*, 30 Jan 1918, p.4
20. BNA: *Yarmouth Independent*, 2 Feb 1918, p.3
21. *Ibid*
22. The GHQ, Home Forces report incorrectly gave the name as Frunds Farm, and this has subsequently been repeated, but it is Friern's Farm on contemporary maps.
23. BNA: *Gloucestershire Echo*, 30 Jan 1918, p.4
24. Monson, *Air Raid Damage in London*, p.17
25. TNA: AIR1/2417/303/42, *London Evening News*, 4 Mar 1935
26. *Ibid*, 9 Mar 1935
27. Locations of bombs from TNA: AIR1/599/16/15/225
28. TNA: AIR1/2417/303/42, *London Evening News*, 5 Feb 1935
29. A different George Bentley to the one who witnessed the Whitestile Road bomb.
30. Willoughby, *op. cit.*, p.133
31. TNA: WO158/955
32. Cole & Cheesman, *op. cit.*, pp.394-395

Chapter 15: Giants in the Sky

1. All pilot reports from TNA: AIR1/599/16/15/225
2. Cross & Cockade Journal, *op. cit.*, p.53
3. Cole & Cheesman, *op. cit.*, pp.398-399, and Haddow & Grosz, *The German Giants*, p.7
4. Unidentified personal diary in Royal Hospital Chelsea archive.

5. Another Captain of Invalids, Geoffrey Bailey, survived the explosion. Rebuilt in 1921, the wing was destroyed again in January 1945 by a V2 rocket. Bailey, still serving as Captain of Invalids, was in the building but this time he did not survive.
6. Helen Banon's diary is in the Royal Hospital Chelsea archive.
7. Haddow & Grosz, *op. cit.*, p.32
8. BNA: *Western Morning News*, 21 Feb 1918, p.6
9. TNA: AIR1/2417/303/42, *London Evening News*, 27 Feb 1935
10. BNA: *Sheffield Independent*, 19 Feb 1918, p.1
11. BNA: *Daily News*, 22 Feb 1918, p.4
12. *Ibid*
13. TNA: AIR1/2417/303/42, *London Evening News*, 7 Mar 1935
14. BNA: *The Scotsman*, 19 Feb 1918, p.5
15. TNA: AIR1/2417/303/42, *London Evening News*, 31 Jan 1935
16. TNA: *Ibid*, 27 Feb 1935
17. TNA: AIR1/600/16/15/227. It has been stated in books published in Britain that the man responsible was *Leutnant* Max Borchers, however, from communications with a German historian it appears credit should go to Hans-Wolff Fleischhauer.
18. *Ibid*
19. TNA: AIR1/600/16/15/227
20. Haddow & Grosz, *op. cit.*, p.33
21. TNA: WO158/955
22. Haddow & Grosz, *op. cit.*, pp.34-35
23. TNA: AIR1/2417/303/42, *London Evening News*, 4 Feb 1935
24. TNA: AIR1/601/16/15/229 Cutting from *Daily Express*, 9 Mar 1918
25. BNA: *Daily News*, 12 Mar 1918, p.3
26. TNA: AIR1/2417/303/42, *London Evening News*, 6 Mar 1935
27. TNA: AIR1/601/16/15/229 Cutting from *Daily Telegraph*, 9 Mar 1918
28. Haddow & Grosz, *op. cit.*, p.35

Chapter 16: The Zeppelins Return

1. L 42, L 52, L 53, L 54, L 56, L 61, L 62, L 63
2. Von Buttlar Brandenfels, *op. cit.*, p.158
3. *Ibid*, p.162
4. Robinson, *op. cit.*, pp.327-329
5. TNA: AIR1/601/16/15/230 Part 2
6. *Ibid*
7. Marben, *op. cit.*, pp.30-32
8. This account of the raid is built from TNA:WO158/956 and AIR1/601/16/15/231
9. BNA: *Fife Free Press*, 16 Mar 1918, p.2
10. Two died in Frederick Street and one in Burbank Street, but it is not clear who died where.
11. BNA: *Daily News*, 15 Mar 1918, p.1
12. Marben, *op. cit.*, pp.33-34
13. Cole & Cheesman, *op. cit.*, p.413
14. TNA: AIR1/602/16/15/232 Part 2

15. Jones, *op. cit.*, p.126
16. The damaged milestone can now be seen displayed in Victoria Park, Widnes.
17. www.suttonbeauty.org.uk/suttonhistory/suttonwar1 *Zeppelin Attack at Bold* (accessed 16 May 2023)
18. Robinson, *op. cit.*, p.332
19. TNA: AIR1 602/16/15/232 and WO158/957. Details of the raid extracted from these files.
20. Willoughby, *op. cit.*, pp.49-50
21. Smith, *Zeppelins Over Lancashire*, p.27
22. BNA: *Liverpool Echo*, 22 Apr 1918, p.4
23. BNA: *Westminster Gazette*, 16 Apr 1918, p.6
24. Cole & Cheesman, *op. cit.*, p.412
25. See Chapter 7, p.88

Chapter 17: 'Dawn of a fine spring morning'

1. Robinson, *op, cit.*, p.338. The uncertainty behind the cause of the explosion is explored here.
2. Fredette, *op. cit.*, pp.195-196, and http://www.airhistory.org.uk/rfc/Kagohl3-diary.html (accessed 20 Jun 2023)
3. This and the report of the Fan Bay mirror in action during the Gotha raid of 1/2 October 1917, are the only documented instances of the use of sound mirrors during the war that I am aware of.
4. Ashmore, *op. cit.*, pp.92-93
5. *Ibid*
6. Mainly first-class types: 31 Sopwith Camels, 28 SE5as, 14 Bristol Fighters, with the addition of 3 BE12bs.
7. See Chapter 7, p.96.
8. TNA: AIR1/603/16/15/233
9. *Ibid*. For timings I have used those shown in the Metropolitan Police reports.
10. TNA: AIR1/2417/303/42, *London Evening News*, 13 Feb 1935
11. *Ibid*, 8 Mar 1935
12. *Ibid*, 26 Feb 1935
13. Castle, *Zeppelin Inferno*, pp.254-257
14. TNA: AIR1/2417/303/42, *London Evening News*, 11 Mar 1935
15. *Ibid*, 6 Mar 1935
16. *Ibid*, 26 Feb 1935
17. TNA: AIR1/603/16/15/233
18. Ashmore, *op. cit.*, p.89
19. TNA: AIR1/2417/303/42, *London Evening News*, 5 Feb 1935

Chapter 18: 'This giant flame of sacrifice'

1. Strahlmann (ed.), *op, cit.*, p.75.
2. See Castle, *Zeppelin Onslaught*, pp.16-30, 40-43
3. Now Tønder in Denmark.

4. Using the letters TO from Tondern as the base, the three sheds were named *Toska, Toni* and *Tobias*.
5. Von Buttlar Brandenfels, *op. cit.*, p.207
6. Smart had previously shot down Zeppelin L 23 over the North Sea in August 1917, flying a Sopwith Pup from HMS *Yarmouth*. See Chapter 6, pp.78-79
7. As the L 70 marked a class – the 'x-class' – the numbering system jumped from L 65 to L 70; there was no L 66 to L 69.
8. Robinson, *op. cit.*, pp.281-282
9. *Ibid*, p.342
10. Jones, *op. cit.*, Vol. VI, p.370
11. Robinson, *op. cit.*, p.353
12. TNA: WO158/959
13. Snowden Gamble, *op. cit.*, pp.408-409
14. Robinson, *op. cit.*, p.354
15. Snowden Gamble, *op. cit.*, p.411
16. *Ibid*, p.409
17. *Ibid*, p.410
18. *Ibid*, p.411
19. Robinson, *op. cit.*, pp.358-359
20. Lehmann, *The Zeppelins*, p.287
21. *Ibid*, p.360
22. Von Buttlar Brandenfels, *op. cit.*, p.15
23. Snowden Gamble, *op. cit.*, p.417
24. Culley's Sopwith Camel is in the possession of the Imperial War Museum.
25. Ludendorff, *Ludendorff's Own Story*, Vol. 2, pp.351-352
26. Robinson, *op. cit.*, p.78
27. For a detailed breakdown of raid statistics, see Appendices I and II.
28. See Appendix I
29. Cole & Cheesman, *op. cit.*, p.451. In contrast, the BE2c, successful against the airships in autumn 1916, cost in the region of £1,600 to build. Jones, *op. cit.*, Appendices, pp.155 and 157.
30. Jones, Vol. V, *op. cit.*, p.479
31. Squadron Nos. 36, 76 and 77 (46th Wing) and Nos. 33 and 90 (48th Wing)
32. Jones, Appendices Volume, *op. cit.*, pp.165-167, 169
33. Jones, *op. cit.*, Vol. V, pp.86-87
34. The Allies seized the three surviving front-line Zeppelins – L 61, L 64 and L 71 – as well as the obsolete L 30, L 37, LZ 113 and LZ 120. L 72 was nearing completion. As part of war reparations, France received L 72 (renamed *Dixmude*), LZ 113 and a smaller commercial airship, *Nordstern*, which they renamed *Méditerranée*. Zeppelins L 64 and L 71 went to Britain and Italy received L 61, LZ 120, along with another commercial ship, *Bodensee* (renamed *Esperia*). L 30 went to Belgium and L 37 to Japan, but as neither country had anywhere to house them, they were broken up and only selected parts removed. None were allocated to America but, after lengthy discussions, Germany built a new L 70-type airship for the US. In October 1924, the LZ 126 transferred across the Atlantic as the *Los Angeles*.

Index

Admiralty 2, 16, 25, 30, 88, 104, 116, 142, 259-60, 263
Aeroplanes, British
  Armstrong Whitworth FK8 62, 181
  Avro 504K 262
  BE2c 18, 116, 325 (n.29)
  BE2e 8, 10, 115, 181, 204
  BE12/12a/12b xv, 18, 45, 81, 87, 112, 181, 201
  Bristol F.2B Fighter 38, 181, 197, 243, 246, 262, 324 (n.6)
  Bristol Scout 27, 30
  DH2 xv, 46-47
  DH4 52, 55, 61, 252
  DH9 253
  FE2b xv, 45-6, 226, 229
  FE2d 115, 226
  H-12 'Large America' flying boat 15-17, 41-2, 53
  SE5/SE5a 40, 181, 213, 243, 324 (n.6)
  Sopwith 1½Strutter 27, 62, 181
  Sopwith Baby 31
  Sopwith Camel 24, 54, 76, 86, 96, 104-105, 107, 112, 181, 182, 196, 202, 203, 204-205, 238, 246, 256, 257, 324 (n.6)
  Sopwith Camel 2F.1 250, 256, 325 (n.24)
  Sopwith Pup 24, 27, 30, 40, 54, 55, 61, 68, 69, 76, 78-9, 325 (n.6)
  Sopwith Triplane 24, 29, 30, 76
Aeroplanes, German
  G-type, *Grosskampfflugzeug*, Gotha bomber 12, 19, 29, 30, 61, 62, 66, 77, 83, 89, 99, 105, 108, 122, 169-70, 173, 182, 183, 184, 195-6, 205, 238, 239, 242-3, 245-6, 259
  R-type, *Riesenflugzeug*, Giant bomber 12, 108, 204-205, 219, 235
  R12 108, 123, 176, 181, 183, 197, 198, 200, 206, 207-208
  R13 108
  R25 124, 200, 202-203, 204-205, 206, 209-12
  R26 124, 200, 202, 235
  R27 214, 218-19
  R29 235
  R32 235
  R33 206
  R34 235
  R36 206
  R39 124, 200-202, 206, 214-16, 235, 247
  Albatros C VII 14
  Albatros (two-seater) 39
  Rumpler C.IV 166
  Rumplar C.VII 236
Air Board 88, 198
Aircrew, British
  Arkell, Lieutenant (Lt) Anthony, RFC 246
  Ashby, Sergeant (Sgt) Sydney, RFC 46
  Banks, Second Lieutenant (2nd Lt) Charles, RFC 96, 107, 112, 196-7
  Barwise, Lt Henry, RFC 243-4
  Blake, Flight sub-Lieutenant (Flt sub-Lt) Edward, RNAS 86
  Brand, Captain (Capt) (later Major (Maj)) Christopher Joseph Quintin, RFC 96, 238

325

Brown, Lt William, RFC 230
Butler, Squadron Commander Charles, RNAS 29
Cadbury, Flight Lieutenant (Flt Lt) (later Major (Maj)) Egbert, RNAS 18, 252-4
Chandler, 2nd Lt Noel, RFC 212
Cole-Hamilton, Capt Con, RFC 38, 314 (n.29)
Cook, 2nd Lt William, RFC 115
Culley, Lt Stuart, RNAS 256-7, 325 (n.24)
Dennis, Capt Arthur, RFC 201
Dickson, Capt William, RNAS 250
Edwardes, 2nd Lt Henry, RFC 204-205
Fowler, 2nd Lt David, RFC 10, 312 (n.11)
Galpin, Flt Lt Christopher, RNAS 16
Goodyear, Lt John, RFC 197
Grace, 2nd Lt Frederick, RFC 62
Hackwill, Capt George, RFC 196-7
Hall, 2nd Lt R.N., RFC 204
Holder, Lt Frank, RFC 45-6
Iron, Capt C.S., RNAS 253
James, Air Mechanic (AM) F., RFC 61
Jessop, AM, RFC 52, 61
Joyce, Sgt Arthur, RFC 226
Keevil, Capt Cecil, RFC 38
Kerby, Flt Lt Harold, RFC 76-7, 316 (n.15)
Kynoch, Capt Alexander, RFC 219
Laycock, AM John, RNAS 16
Leckie, Flt sub-Lt Robert, RNAS 16, 253-4
Lewis, Lt (later Capt) Cecil, RFC 41, 54, 96, 107, 169, 213
Lewis, 2nd Lt Leonard, RFC 87
Luxmore, Capt Francis, RFC 202
Merchant, AM Walter, RFC 197
Murlis Green, Capt (later Maj) Gilbert, RFC 96, 107, 181-2, 204-205
Murray, 2nd Lt George, RFC 62
Noble-Campbell, Lt Cecil, RFC 229-30
O'Neill, 2nd Lt T.M., RFC 204-205
Owen, Lt H.G., RNAS 253
Palethorpe, Capt John, RFC 52, 61
Pritchard 2nd Lt Thomas, RFC 158
Ridley, Capt Claude, RFC 68-9
Salmon, 2nd Lt Wilfred, RFC 61
Saundby, Capt Robert, RFC 46-7
Smart, Flt sub-Lt (later Capt) Bernard, RNAS 78-9, 250, 325 (n.6)
Smith, Flt sub-Lt Harold, RNAS 18
Sowrey, Maj Frederick, RFC 243
Stagg, AM1 Albert, RFC 246
Stroud, Capt Henry, RFC 219
Taylor, AM Cyril, RFC 62
Turner, Lt Edward, RFC 243-4
Watkins, Lt Loudon, RFC 45-7
Whatling, Chief Petty Officer Vernon, RNAS 16
Yeulett, Lt Walter, RNAS 250
Young, 2nd Lt John, RFC 62

Aircrew, German
Barnard *Leutnant (Lt)* P. 173
Bartikowski, *Leutnant der Reserve (Lt d R)* Rudolf 238
Bloch, *Vizefeldwebel (Vfw)* Fritz 238
Braun, *Lt d R* Immanuel 134
Döbrick, *Lt* W. 183
Eichelkamp, *Vfw* Ernst 83
Egener, *Gefreiter (Gef)* Friedrich 130
Elsner, *Lt d R* Max 62
Emmler, *L d R* Martin 124
Flothow, *Lt* Joachim 242-4
Francke, *Lt d R* Hans 29
Fries, *Unteroffizier (Uffz)* Theodor 99
Fulda, *Oberleutnant (Oblt)* Echart 83
Gaede, *Vfw* Kurt 61
Genth, *Lt* Adolf 61
Götte, *Lt* 207
Gummelt, *Vfw* Max 239-40
Hansen-Beck, *Vfw* Hans 99
Heiden, *Uffz* Walther 195, 197
Heilgers, *Vfw* Heinrich 238
Herzberg, *Lt d R* Alfred 122
Hoffman, *Uffz* G. 183
Hölger, *Vfw* Franz 62
Huhnsdorf, *Vfw* Rudolf 239-40
Jakobs, *Vfw* O. 169
Joschkowetz, *Lt* Werner 83
Ketelsen, *Lt* Friedrich 182
Klaus, *Vfw* H. 183
Klimke, *Offizierstellvertreter (OStv)* Rudolf 14-15

Index

Kluck, *Vfw* Erich 29
Latowski, *Lt* Walter 83
Leon, *Oblt* Walter 14-15
Lorenz, *Oblt* Fritz 122-3
Mickel, *Uffz* Georg 62
Radke, *Lt* G. 61
Rahning, *Lt d R* Franz 122
Rist, *Lt* Wilhelm 239-40
Rolin, *Lt d R* Hans 77
Röselmüller, *Lt d R* Max 63
Rosinsky, *Uffz* Otto 77
Rzechtalski, *Gemeiner* J. 169
Sachtler, *Vfw* Albrecht 242-4
Schildt, *Uffz* Heinrich 83
Schneider, *Uffz* Bruno 83
Schoeller, *Hauptmann* Arthur 214, 218, 219
Schulte, *Lt* Franz 173
Schulte, *Gef* Wilhelm 245
Schumacher, *Uffz* Georg 29
Senf, *Vfz* B. 173
v. Seydlitz-Gerstenberg, *Oblt* Hans-Joachim 207
Siegfried, *Oblt*, Wilhem, *Graf Adelmann von und zu Adelmannfelden* 205
Sopkowiak, *Lt* Paul 245
v. Stachelsky, *Oblt* Gerhard 182
Stolle, *Uffz* Rudi 77
Tasche, *Uffz* Hermann 242-3
Thiedke, *Vfw* Hans 245
v. Thomsen, *Lt* Friedrich 195, 197
v. Trotha, *Oblt* Hans-Ulrich 39
Walter, *Oblt* Richard (temp. commander *Kagohl 3*) 73-4, 82, 175
Weissmann, *Gef* A. 182
Wessels, *Lt* R. 169
Wienecke, *Vfw* Wilhelm 122
van Zanthier, *Oblt* Helmuth 99
Ziegler, *Uffz* Karl 195, 197
Airfields (RFC) (for RNAS see Air stations)
  Bekesbourne xvi, 8, 40, 54, 176
  Biggin Hill xvi, 112
  Cuxwold (Emergency Landing Ground – ELG) 113
  Detling xvi, 147
  East Guldeford (ELG) 10
  Frinsted (ELG) 244
  Goldhanger xv, xvi, 27, 45, 109
  Gosberton Fen (ELG) 113
  Hadleigh 145
  Hainault Farm xvi, 96, 107, 181, 315 (n.23)
  Lympne xvi, 21
  Martlesham Heath xvi, 52, 61, 123-4
  Orfordness xv, xvi, 45, 97
  Rochford xvi, 27, 40, 62, 74, 169, 315 (n.23)
  Ruskington Fen (ELG) 113
  Scampton 81
  Snarehill (ELG) 149
  Stow Maries xvi, 18, 27, 54
  Sutton's Farm xvi, 64, 68
  Swingate Down 160
  Swingfield (ELG) 9
  Telscombe Cliffs xvi, 10
  Throwley xvi, 129, 238, 315 (n.23)
  Tydd St Mary 229
  Waddington 228
  Wittering 145
Airfields, German
  Evere 264
  Gontrode (Ghent) xiii, xiv, 12, 30, 39, 51, 112
  Mariakerke (Ghent) xiii, xiv, 12
  Nieuwmunster xiii, 19, 20
  Scheldewindeke (Ghent) xiii, xiv, 214, 235
  Sint-Denijs-Westrem (Ghent) xiii, xiv, 12, 30, 51, 108
Air Ministry 88, 198
Air raid shelters 84, 127, 131, 164, 178-179, 189-90, 191-2, 193, 198-9, 209, 210, 244, 262
Air raid warnings 40-1, 66, 69, 91, 93, 98, 108, 110, 114, 117, 122, 127, 128, 131, 134, 138, 147, 153, 155, 163, 164, 165, 166, 193, 210, 228, 231, 245
Air raid warning system 41, 65, 66, 70, 91-92, 98, 116, 176, 183-4, 236-7, 263
Air stations (RNAS)
  Covehithe 54
  Eastchurch xvi, 76, 87
  East Cliffe 161
  Felixstowe xvi, 15, 42, 53, 68
  Great Yarmouth 15, 252, 253
  Holt 18
  Howden (airships) 223

Manston xvi, 20, 27, 29, 30, 44, 68, 76, 86, 87, 116, 168
Shotley (kite balloons) 53
Walmer xvi, 76, 87
Westgate xvi, 20, 31
Anti-aircraft commanders 3, 30, 67, 141
Anti-aircraft guns (also see Barrage fire) 1, 2-4, 10, 24, 25, 30, 41, 65, 71, 72, 91, 106, 142, 236, 248, 262, 263
Ashmore, Major General Edward Bailey (LADA) 71-2, 73, 74, 86, 90-1, 96, 106, 107, 236, 248, 263

Balloon apron xix, 105, 184, 203, 207-208, 236
Barrage fire 65, 106, 109-10, 112, 117-18, 121, 124-5, 129, 134, 137, 138, 141, 162, 163, 165, 169, 170, 172, 195
Bawdsey Manor 67, 315 (n.26)
Behncke, *Konteradmiral* Paul, (Deputy Chief of the German Naval Staff) 259-60
v. Bentivegni, *Hptm* Richard, (commander *Rfa 501*) 108, 200-202, 206, 209, 213, 214-15, 235, 236, 248, 257
Bombed, counties
  Bedfordshire: *19 Oct. 1917*, 146-147; *8 Mar. 1918*, 218
  Cambridgeshire: *19 Oct. 1917*, 148
  County Durham: *13 Mar. 1918*, 224-246
  Essex: *5 Jun. 1917*, 27-8; *4 Jul. 1917*, 53; *22 Jul. 1917*, 68-9; *12 Aug. 1917*, 74-6; *4 Sep. 1917*, 97; *28 Sep.1917*, 123; *30 Sep. 1917*, 134; *1 Oct. 1917*, 141; *19 Oct. 1917*, 145, 147, 148; *29 Oct. 1917*, 160; *1 Nov. 1917*, 162; *6 Dec. 1917*, 169; *18 Dec. 1917*, 176; *29 Jan. 1918*, 196-7; *8 Mar. 1918*, 218; *19-20 May 1918*, 239, 246-7
  Hertfordshire: *19 Oct. 1917*, 147, 148; *8 Mar. 1918*, 218-19
  Huntingdonshire: *19 Oct. 1917*, 145
  Kent: *1 Mar. 1917*, 4-5; *16 Mar. 1917*, 5-6, 8-9; *5 Apr. 1917*, 13-14; *25 May 1917*, 20-4; *5 Jun. 1917*, 28-9; *13 Jun. 1917*; *30-1*, *17 Jun. 1917*, 43-5; *7 Jul. 1917*, 56; 12 Aug 1917, 76; *22 Aug. 1917*, 83-6; *2 Sep. 1917*, 89-90; *3 Sep.* *1917*, 92-6; *4 Sep. 1917*, 97-8; *24 Sep. 1917*, 108-109; *25 Sep. 1917*, 116-17; *28 Sep. 1917*, 123; *29 Sep. 1917*, 124, 129-30; *30 Sep. 1917*, 132-4; *1 Oct. 1917*, 137-8; *19 Oct 1917*, 147, 148; 31 Oct. 1917, 161-2; *6 Dec. 1917*, 166-8; *18 Dec. 1917*, 176-7; *28 Jan. 1918*, 189-91; *16 Feb. 1918*, 206; *8 Mar. 1918*, 219; *19-20 May 1918*, 237-9
  Lancashire: *12 Apr 1918*, 230-3
  Lincolnshire: *25 Sep. 1917*, 113; *19 Oct. 1917*, 145, 147; *12 Apr. 1918*, 227, 228
  London: *7 May 1917*, 14-15; *13 Jun. 1917*, 32-8; *7 Jul. 1917*, 56-61; *4 Sep. 1917*, 99-104; *24 Sep. 1917*, 109-12; 25 Sep. 1917, 117-22; *29 Sep. 1917*, 125-9; *30 Sep. 1917*, 134-7; *1 Oct. 1917*, 138-41; *19 Oct. 1917*, 153-8; *31 Oct.-1 Nov. 1917*, 162-6; *6 Dec. 1917*, 170-2; *18 Dec. 1917*, 177-81; *28-29 Jan. 1918*, 191-200; *29-30 Jan. 1918*, 201-202; *16 Feb. 1918*, 206-208; *17 Feb. 1918*, 209-12; *7-8 Mar. 1918*, 215-18; *19-20 May 1918*, 240-7
  Norfolk: *19 Oct. 1917*, 146, 148, 149; *12 Apr. 1918*, 229
  Northamptonshire: *19 Oct 1917*, 146, 151-2; *12 Apr. 1918*, 229
  Staffordshire: *19 Oct. 1917*, 146
  Suffolk: *4 Jul. 1917*, 52-3; *22 Jul. 1917*, 67-8; *4 Sep. 1917*, 97; *28 Sep. 1917*, 123-4; *19 Oct. 1917*, 145
  Sussex: *16 Mar. 1917*, 10
  Warwickshire: *19 Oct. 1917*, 146; *12 Apr. 1918*, 229
  Worcestershire: *19 Oct. 1917*, 146
  Yorkshire: *22 Aug. 1917*, 79-81; *25 Sep. 1917*, 113-14; *12 Mar. 1918*, 222-3
Boy Scouts 164, 216
Brandenburg, *Hptm* Ernst, (commander *Kagohl 3*) 12, 15, 19-20, 26-7, 29, 32, 38, 39, 51, 174, 175, 213, 235, 236, 248, 257, 264
British Army
  Bedfordshire Regiment 68, 288
  King's Royal Rifle Regiment 28-9, 280
  Royal Fusiliers 89-90, 291

Index

Suffolk Regiment 52, 67
Royal Defence Corps 59, 71, 85, 184
Royal Engineers 14, 133, 215-16
British Empire Medal 44, 128, 202, 216, 232
Bullets
  Buckingham 185
  Pomoroy 47, 254
  R.T.S. 184, 205
  'Tracer' 47, 182, 202
v. Bülow, *Major* Freiherr (historian) 173-4

Calais 9, 12, 40, 54, 160, 235
Cave, George (Home Secretary) 41
Churchill, Winston S. (Minister of Munitions) 112, 142, 262
Cloessner, *Leutnant* (weather officer, *Kagohl 3*) 26, 30, 51

Distinguished Service Order 79
Dunkirk 27, 29, 51, 54, 69, 77, 122, 150, 173, 235

Elektron incendiary bomb 257-8, 264
Ellerkamm, Heinrich (Zeppelin crewman) 48
Engines
  Maybach 185, 206, 251
  Mercedes 19, 51, 206
Escadrille N.152 (French squadron) 149

Ford, Lena Guilbert (lyricist) 216
French, Field Marshal Lord John, (Commander-in-Chief, Home Forces) 3, 13, 25-6, 55-6, 66, 72, 184

GHQ, Home Forces 27, 30, 31, 65, 322 (n.22)
George V, King 66
Georgii, *Leutnant* Walter (weather officer, *Kagohl 3*) 51, 67, 73, 82, 122

Haig, Field Marshal Sir Douglas (commander British Army, Western Front) 40, 64
Harvest Moon Offensive 108, 130, 131, 141, 142-3, 160
Harwich Force (Royal Navy) 251, 252, 256-7

Henderson, Sir David, (Director-General of Military Aeronautics) 3, 25, 65, 87, 88
Higgins, Colonel Thomas C.R., (commanding Home Defence Group, RFC) 26, 230, 234, 237
v. Hoeppner, General Ernst, (*Kogenluft*) 11-12, 15, 38, 40, 51, 174, 175, 213

Ingram system 72

Kingscote, Captain A.R.F., Royal Garrison Artillery 106
Kleine, *Hptm* Rudolf (commander *Kagohl 3*) 51, 56-7, 66-7, 73, 78, 81-3, 86, 89, 92, 96-7, 108, 116, 122, 124, 131, 132, 137, 160-161, 166, 173-5, 176; Awarded PLM, 143; British opinion of, 77, 174

Lehmann, Ernst 255
Lightships 20, 25, 27, 52, 56, 82, 166, 252
Lloyd, Lieutenant General Sir Francis, (Officer Commanding, London District) 3
Lloyd George, David, (prime minister) 41, 65
London Air Defence Area (LADA) xix, xx, 71-2, 86, 90-2, 98, 106, 107, 112, 115, 125, 137, 166, 236, 248, 262-3
London Underground 70, 98, 110, 122, 131, 177, 318 (n.1)
Ludendorff, Erich, *Erster Generalquartiermeister* 78, 258
Luftstreitkräfte (German army air service) 11, 174, 175
  Bombengeschwader 3 der Obersten Heeresleitung (Bogohl 3) 175, 176-83, 189-97, 200, 205, 206, 213, 220, 235-6, 247, 248, 257-8, 261, 264
  Kampfgeschwader 1 der Obersten Heeresleitung (Kagohl 1) 12, 51
  Kagohl 3 12-13, 15, 19, 39, 51, 69, 81, 89, 90, 108, 143, 174, 175, 205; Raids 20-4, 27-9, 30-8, 51-4, 56-63, 67-8, 74-7, 82-6, 92, 108-12, 116-22, 122-9, 132-7, 141, 161-6, 166-73
  Kagohl 4 89-90, 97

329

Riesenflugzeug Abteilung (Rfa) 501 (Giants) 12, 108, 204–205, 206, 235, 257-8, 259, 261, *Raids,* 122-3, 166-7, 189, 197-200, 200-203, 206-208, 208-13, 213-19, 246-7, 248

MacDonagh, Michael, (journalist) 58-9, 63
Merchant Navy
  SS *Stockwell* (freighter) 121
Military Cross 52, 197

Naval Airship Division (German) 6, 18, 42, 78, 81, 143, 158, 185, 187, 220, 221, 249, 250, 254, 255, 257
Neame gunsight 184, 205
Netherlands 16, 17, 42, 82, 124, 145, 146, 149

Observers (ground) 46, 65, 86, 98, 124, 129, 184, 206, 216, 230, 236
Ostend 12, 14, 63, 76, 77, 145

Police 1, 34, 59, 60, 98, 101, 111, 163, 169, 180, 184, 192, 194, 195, 237, 270; Attending bombs, 15, 35, 44, 95, 100, 125, 154, 155, 157, 212, 215, 216; Issuing warnings, 66, 91, 98, 110, 117, 134, 154, 184, 192, 225; Reports, 6, 109, 123, 137, 148, 181, 183, 209, 218, 228, 230, 239; Special constables, 53, 98, 128, 173, 178, 192
Pour le Mérite 39, 143, 221
Prüfanstalt und Werft der Fliegertruppen (PuW) 19

Rawlinson, Lieutenant Colonel Alfred (AA commander, West London) 141
Restricted Coast Area 3-4
Robertson, William, (Chief of the Imperial General Staff) 3, 55, 63
Royal Air Force (RAF) 88, 234, 236-7, 261, 263
Royal Flying Corps (RFC) 3, 4, 13, 24, 26, 40, 47, 56, 65-6, 71, 87, 88, 115, 169, 181, 234
  No. 1 Squadron 174
  No. 33 Squadron 81, 115, 223

  No. 35 (Training) Squadron 38
  No. 36 Squadron 115, 223, 226, 262
  No. 37 Squadron 18, 20, 27, 45, 47, 54, 56, 62, 68, 71, 73, 96, 109, 201, 204, 219, 315 (n.23)
  No. 38 Squadron 229
  No. 39 Squadron 112, 158, 197, 243, 246, 315 (n.23)
  No. 44 Squadron 96, 104, 105, 107, 112, 181, 196, 204
  No. 46 Squadron 66, 68, 74
  No. 48 Squadron 69
  No. 50 Squadron 62, 73, 87, 315 (n.23)
  No. 51 Squadron 229
  No. 56 Squadron 40-1, 54
  No. 61 Squadron 74, 76, 169, 213
  No. 63 (Training) Squadron 61
  No. 66 Squadron 44, 55
  No. 75 Squadron 145
  No. 76 Squadron 81, 115, 223
  No. 78 Squadron 10, 202, 212, 246
  No. 112 Squadron 238
  No. 141 Squadron 243
  No. 143 Squadron 243
  Martlesham Heath Testing Squadron xvi, 52, 61, 123
Royal Navy
  HM Minesweeper *London Belle* 28, 313 (n.5)
  HM Minesweeper *Touchstone* 68
  HM *Torpedo Boat No.7* 28
  HM *Torpedo Boat No. 19* 191
  HMS *Canterbury* (light cruiser) 53
  HMS *Concord* (light cruiser) 53
  HMS *Conquest* (light cruiser) 53
  HMS *Dominion* (battleship) 28
  HMS *Furious* (aircraft carrier) 250
  HMS *Ganges* (shore establishment) 53
  HMS *General Wolfe* (monitor) 62
  HMS *Kestrel* (destroyer) 83
  HMS *Marshal Ney* (monitor) 44
  HMS *Nith* (destroyer) 81
  HMS *Patrol* (scout cruiser) 81
  HMS *Redoubt* (destroyer) 256, 257
  HMS *Actaeon* (shore establishment) 29
  HMS *Violet* (destroyer) 191
  HMS *Yarmouth* (cruiser) 78, 325 (n.6)

Index

Royal Naval Air Service 4, 5, 6, 14, 15-16, 24, 27, 53, 65, 88, 104, 165, 223, 234
  No. 4 (Naval) Squadron 24, 27, 54
  Covehithe 54
  Dover 87, 161
  Eastchurch 76, 87
  Felixstowe 15, 68
  Holt 18
  Manston 20, 27, 29, 30, 44, 68, 76, 86, 87, 116
  Walmer 76, 87
  Westgate 20, 31
  Yarmouth 15, 252

Scapa Flow 264
Scheer, Admiral Reinhard (commander German High Seas Fleet) 50, 78, 255
Schütte-Lanz airships 11, 263
  SL 3 8
  SL 20 185-6, 187
Searchlight defences 3, 7, 43, 71-2, 80-1, 86, 89, 91, 93, 97, 99, 102, 105, 106, 114, 116, 118, 125, 141, 152, 161, 165, 182, 183, 196, 201, 203, 224, 229, 236, 260, 262
Siegert, Major Wilhelm 12
Simon, Lieutenant Colonel Maximilian St Leger, (AA Defence Commander, London) 3-4, 30, 41, 72, 106, 125
Smuts, Lieutenant General Jan Christian (War Cabinet) 65-6, 71, 87-9, 105, 184
Sound (Acoustic) Mirrors 142, 236, 324 (n.3)
Strasser, *Fregattenkapitän* Peter, *Führer der Luftschiffe* 6-7, 9-10, 11, 15, 16, 41, 42, 48, 50-1, 78, 113, 143, 144, 159, 185, 186-8, 213, 220, 223, 226, 227, 231, 235, 248, 251-7, 261; On missions, 8, 16, 18, 79, 81, 113, 220, 222, 252

Terschelling 17, 42, 256
Trenchard, Major General Hugh (commander RFC, Western Front) 40, 88
Tube (see London Underground)

Unger, Wilhelm (Zeppelin crewman) 50

Vlieland 42
Voluntary Aid Detachment (VAD) 33, 44, 90, 98, 208

War Cabinet 40, 41, 64, 65, 105
War Office 26, 30, 34, 47, 55, 63, 263
Weather forecasts 8, 19, 20, 26, 30, 42, 51, 56, 67, 73, 79, 82, 107, 113, 143, 144, 160, 166, 175, 185, 187, 209, 220, 227, 236, 249, 252, 258, 262
Werther, *Korvettenkapitän* Paul (commander German Naval Airship Division) 256
Wilhelm II, *Kaiser* 39, 143, 221, 264
Wireless Telegraphy 8, 16, 24, 25, 45, 73, 78, 87, 145, 148, 149, 159, 166, 214, 221, 224, 251, 252, 254
Wollaston, Lieutenant Colonel Frederick, Rifle Brigade 217
Woolwich Arsenal 142, 262

Zeebrugge 5, 13, 82
v. Zeppelin, *Graf* (Count) Ferdinand 7
Zeppelin airships 6, 7, 11, 227, 251, 260, 312 (n.6), 325 (n.7)
  L 5 230, 249
  L 11 42
  L 14 228
  L 17 230, 249
  L 20 148
  L 22 16, 17
  L 23 78-9, 325 (n.6)
  L 24 8
  L 30 6, 326 (n.34)
  L 32 243
  L 35 7, 8, 9, 79, 114, 230, 249
  L 36 7, 42
  L 37 326 (n.34)
  L 39 7, 8-9
  L 40 7, 8, 9-10, 16-17, 41, 42
  L 41 7, 8, 10, 79-81, 114-15, 146, 228, 251
  L 42 7-8, 16, 17, 42, 43-4, 50, 79, 144, 223, 224-226
  L 43 16, 17-18, 42
  L 44 16, 18, 42, 79, 113, 148, 149, 150, 319 (n.4)
  L 45 16, 17, 42, 79, 144, 150-8
  L 46 42, 79, 81, 113, 146, 185-6, 187

L 47 16, 42, 79, 145, 146, 185-6, 222
L 48 42, 45-50, 79
L 49 148-50, 320 (n.6)
L 50 148, 149, 150, 320 (n.6)
L 51 79, 144, 185-6, 187
L 52 147, 223, 224, 227, 323 (n.1)
L 53 113, 146-7, 220, 221-2, 227, 251, 252, 256-7, 319 (n.4)
L 54 145, 220, 221, 250, 323 (n.1)
L 55 113-14, 115, 147-8
L 56 223, 224, 252, 253, 254, 323 (n.1)
L 58 185-6, 220
L 59 185, 220, 227
L 60 185, 227, 250
L 61 185, 220, 223, 227, 230-3, 249, 323 (n.1), 326 (n.34)
L 62 220, 222-3, 227, 228-30, 234, 235, 323 (n.1)
L 63 220, 222, 227, 228, 252, 253, 323 (n.1)
L 64 227, 228, 326 (n.34)
L 65 235, 252, 253, 254, 325 (n.7)
L 70 251, 252, 253-5, 257, 325 (n.7), 326 (n.34)
L 71 257, 326 (n.34)
L 72 326 (n.34)
LZ 113 326 (n.34)
LZ 120 326 (n.34)
LZ 126 326 (n.34)
Zeppelin bases
　Ahlhorn 9, 10, 42, 144, 146, 147, 148, 185-8, 220, 222, 265
　Dresden 9
　Evere 264
　Nordholz 7, 42, 50, 144, 147, 185, 188, 226, 251, 265
　Tondern 78, 144, 221, 250-1, 252, 316 (n.18), 325 (n.4)
　Wittmundhafen 16, 144, 147, 265

Zeppelin officers
　v. Buttlar-Brandenfels, *Kapitänleutnant (Kptlt)* Horst Julius Ludwig Otto, *Freiherr* Treusch 145, 221, 250, 256
　Dietrich, *Kptlt* Martin 7-8, 17, 43-4, 50, 224-6
　Dinter, *Oberleutnant-zur-See (Oblt-s-Z)* Bernhard 78-9
　Dose, *Kptlt* Walter 253, 254
　Ehrlich, *Kptlt* Herbert 9, 114, 223, 230-3, 249
　Eichler, *Kapitänleutnant der Reserve (Kptlt-d-R)* Franz 45, 48
　Flemming, *Kptlt* Hans Kurt 113-14, 147-8, 227
　v. Freudenreich, *Kptlt* Michael 145, 222, 227-8
　Friemel, *Oblt-s-Z* Kurt 147
　Gayer, *Kptlt* Hans-Karl 149, 320 (n.6)
　Hollender, *Kptlt* Heinrich 42, 113, 146, 187
　Koch, *Kptlt* Robert 8-9
　Kölle, *Kptlt* Waldemar 17, 144, 150-2, 158
　Kraushaar, *Kptlt* Hermann 17, 42
　v. Lossnitzer, *Kptlt* Johannes 226, 251-2
　Manger, *Hauptmann* Kuno 10, 80-1, 114, 146, 222-3, 228-9, 235
　Mieth, *Leutnant-zur-See* Otto 50
　Prölss, *Kptlt* Eduard 113, 146-7, 221-2, 256
　Schütze, *Korvettenkapitän (KKpt)* Arnold 186, 228
　Schütze, *KKpt* Viktor 42, 45, 48, 51, 79
　Schwonder, *Kptlt* Roderich 149, 150, 320 (n.6)
　Sommerfeldt, *Kptlt* Erich 9-10, 16-17, 42
　Stabbert, *Kptlt* Franz 148